Diagnostic and Remedial Reading

for Classroom and Clinic

Fourth Edition

Robert M. Wilson
University of Maryland

90-201

CHARLES E. MERRILL PUBLISHING COMPANY
A Bell & Howell Company
Columbus   Toronto   London   Sydney

Photos

Photo courtesy of the Keystone View Company: page 71.
Photo by Jerry Harvey: page 80.
Photo by Jean-Claude Lejeune: page 194.
Photo by David S. Strickler: page 200.
Photo by Jan Smyth: page 205.
Photo by Celia Drake: page 350.
Photos for remainder of text by Irma D. McNelia.

Credits

Page 58	Reproduced from the *Wechsler Intelligence Scale for Children-Revised*, cover page of Record Form, copyright©1971, 1974 by The Psychological Corporation. All rights reserved.
Page 72	*Keystone School Vision Screening*, copyright©1972 by Keystone View Company, 2212 East 12th Street, Davenport, Iowa 52803. Reprinted by permission.
Page 80	From William L. Heward and Michael D. Orlansky, *Exceptional Children*, p. 183 (Columbus, Ohio: Charles E. Merrill Publishing Company, 1980). Reprinted by permission.
Page 106	*Botel Reading Inventory, Word Opposites Test*, by Morton Botel. Copyright©1978 by Follett Publishing Company. Used by permission.
Page 156	Reprinted by permission of the publisher, *Diagnostic Reading Scales*, List 1, p. 3, CTB/McGraw-Hill, Del Monte Research Park, Monterey, CA 93940. Copyright©1963 by McGraw-Hill, Inc. All rights reserved. Printed in the U.S.A.
Pages 164-165	From Arthur I. Gates and Anne S. McKillop, *Gates-McKillop Reading Diagnostic Tests*, Pupil Record Booklet, Form 1, p. 1 and I. Oral Reading, p. 2 (New York: Teachers College Press, 1962). Reprinted by permission of the publisher. All rights reserved.
Page 184	From the *Survey of Study Habits and Attitudes*, Manual, p. 17, Brown-Hotteman, copyright©1953, 1964, 1967 by The Psychological Corporation. All rights reserved.
Pages 266-267	*The Merrill Linguistic Reading Program, Catch On, Level C Reader*, p. 22 and *Level C Skills Book*, p. 21, copyright©1980, 1975, 1966 by Charles E. Merrill Publishing Company. Reprinted by permission.
Pages 298-299	Reproduced from the *NFL Reading Kit*, Student Record Form, cards 1 and 2, copyright©1977 by Bowmar/Noble Publishers, Inc. Reprinted by permission.
Pages 334-335	Reproduced from the *Real-Life Reading*, Labels 6-3, published by Instructo/McGraw-Hill, Paoli, Pennsylvania, copyright©1980. Reprinted by permission.
Pages 350	*The Reading Game Sound System*, 5-9 Card 10, developed by American Learning Corporation for Bell & Howell,©℗ ALC 1974. Reprinted by permission.

Published by Charles E. Merrill Publishing Co.
A Bell & Howell Company
Columbus, Ohio 43216

This book was set in Korinna and Clarendon Light
Production and Design Coordination: Deborah C. Damian
Cover Design Coordination: Will Chenoweth

Library of Congress Catalog Card Number: 80–83740
International Standard Book Number: 0–675–08048–7
Printed in the United States of America
1 2 3 4 5 6 7 8 9 10—86 85 84 83 82 81

Other Reading Books of Interest

Principles and Practices of Teaching Reading, 5th edition
Heilman, Blair and Rupley

Diagnosis and Remediation for Classroom and Clinic, 4th edition
Wilson

Teaching Content Area Reading Skills, 2nd edition
Forgan and Mangrum

Programmed Reading for Teachers
Wilson, Hall, Gambrell, Coley, Campbell, Johnson

Phonics in Proper Perspective, 4th edition
Heilman

Locating and Correcting Reading Difficulties, 3rd edition
Ekwall

Analytical Reading Inventory, 2nd edition
Woods and Moe

Phonics for Teachers of Reading, 3rd edition
Hull

Teaching Reading as a Language Experience, 3rd edition
Hall

The Development of Language and Reading in Young Children,
2nd edition
Pflaum

Programmed Word Attack for Teachers, 3rd edition
Wilson and Hall

Contents

Foreword

The author of this book has addressed himself to the children who, in spite of laudatory educational endeavors, have not grown in reading skills according to their innate abilities. The range of reading ability found in any classroom is wide. The better the instruction and the longer it continues the greater will be the variance in reading skills manifested by the children. If instruction is excellent, the average reading level of the class will be improved and the range between the poor and good readers will become wider. *Good teaching widens and highlights the range of reading performance found in any classroom.*

The very fact that an identified number of children are experiencing problems in learning to read is no indictment against the teaching profession. If the condemning public would only look at the facts, it would quickly reach the judgment that the child of today is reading better than his counterpart did a decade ago.

A quick perusal of this book will convince those who plan to use it as main text, as well as those who plan to use it as a resource book, of its timeliness, the scholarship of the author, and the practicality of the tenets presented herein. Also, it will become readily evident that the author, to borrow a saying, has endowed the reader with all his mental goods pertaining to the diagnosis and remediation of reading problems a child may manifest.

As with the third edition, most chapters have been expanded to a significant degree, giving the reader new insights into tests and techniques that have been time tested, as well as tests of recent copyright. A new chapter, "The Handicapped Reader," has been added and is a most welcome addition. Another addition that will be notable to the reader is an introductory section to each chapter, listing chapter emphasis, thus giving the reader a clear-cut purpose for the reading and study of the expanded contents therein. As with the other editions, the main emphasis is upon *diagnostic teaching*, and highlighted are suggestions for changing emphasis in the instructional program to provide for different learning rates and problems manifested by children. Increased content has been provided for both the classroom teacher and the clinician. Thus, each can extract relevant understanding, knowledge and skills from the chapters, so that a program of intervention and therapy can be provided for the child.

In chapter 1, the rather unsavory term *problem reader* has been eliminated and a kinder one *readers who face problems* has been substituted, thereby creating a more wholesome learning atmosphere around the child. Thus the child may escape the ignominy of being addressed as a retarded reader. Another welcome change has been the expanded section on the assessment of the learning environment, that perhaps, has contributed significantly to the problems faced by the reader.

A welcome expansion will be found in chapters 4 and 5. The so-called normative-referenced tests have been criticized by some very astute scholars, especially their misuse. It is gratifying to note that the author has highlighted the criterion-referenced tests, particularly the teacher-made ones, which possibly can assure higher content validity as well as increased reliability. A most welcome section has been added to chapter 5, one that should prove to be most helpful to the classroom teacher as well as the clinician. A hypothetical case study is listed in a cumulative form, thereby demonstrating the different levels of diagnosis.

The teaching of comprehension could well be the bane of a well intentioned, but unskilled teacher's career. There is hope, however, for the novice. In chapter 10 can be found a sophisticated treatise on comprehension and more. Suggested guidelines, if followed, will help not only the beginning teacher, but also the seasoned teacher will find that the strategies suggested reflect some recent findings about the nature of comprehension.

As has been implied throughout this foreword, the fourth revision surpasses those of previous editions. It is mute testimony to the scholarship and integrity of the author. Perhaps it poses more questions than it answers, but is this not what a text can best do? Thus, the reading of this edition, as the author states of comprehension, can be a personal process. If, through the reading of this text, the reader is stimulated to test the validity of some of the tenets presented herein, he/she has grown in professional stature, and such a search fulfills the *desideratum* the author has implied.

I invite your thoughtful and reflective reading of this scholarly manuscript with the sincere hope that it will be as rewarding for you as it was for me.

Donald L. Cleland
Athens, Ohio

Preface

Much has happened in education since the writing of the third edition of this book. Theory and research in the area of reading comprehension have had great impact. Federal legislation has directed new interest to the handicapped. Good reader–poor reader research has forced us to reexamine some of our beliefs about how some readers do poorly in school. These and other changes in education made it necessary to make major changes in the fourth edition.

An author makes certain assumptions in preparing a manuscript for general distribution. As an aid to the readers of this book, I will discuss them briefly.

First, this book is not a beginning text in reading. Rather, it is assumed that the reader will have had some experience with the teaching of reading; a basic course in reading; familiarity with the concepts behind such techniques as the directed reading activities, the language-experience approach, and word-attack skills; and some understanding of current learning theory.

Second, the book may best be seen as a beginning book in diagnostic teaching. It is not designed to answer all of the questions about problems with reading nor is it meant to cover all aspects of teaching reading.

Third, it is assumed that the reader has worked with students experiencing difficulty in reading without knowing exactly what to do about it.

For the reader's information, the ideas in this revision come from experiences with thousands of students and hundreds of teachers, all of whom would like to see learning as a stimulating and pleasant experience. One tends to become leery of generalizations about readers, knowing full well that each case is indeed unique. For this reason, each chapter now includes a short essay written by an individual teacher. These editorials reflect real-life incidences relating to the chapter's content. At the same time, the general philosophy of this book has been tried and found to be effective with most of the students with whom we have worked.

Our clinic at Maryland is an exciting, stimulating environment for students. The staff members have been open to change and are thoughtfully critical of their techniques. This book, to a large extent, reflects the thinking and activities of that staff. Of course, their effectiveness with students who are experiencing extreme difficulty in learning to read goes far be yond technique — it also incorporates a sincere desire to help each reader in a special way to become a happy, successful learner.

And so, while the reader must beware, it is hoped that this book will reflect the practical experience of many persons and the best thinking that those persons can produce. The ultimate measure of the success of such a publication will be determined as you the reader initiate programs based upon these ideas. The successes that your students have as a result of these ideas will be the final test.

For the reader who may lack the necessary background for most effective understanding of this book, the author would like to suggest several books that may well serve as an overview of the reading process.

Three books that overview the reading process, teaching reading, and the foundations in theory and research are:

> Hall, MaryAnne; Ribovich, Jerilyn K.; and Ramig, Christopher J. *Reading and the Elementary School Child.* New York: D. Van Nostrand Co., 1979.

> Heilman, Arthur W. *Principles and Practices of Teaching Reading,* 5th ed. Columbus, Ohio: Charles E. Merrill Publishing Co., 1981. Provides a thorough coverage of the basics of reading instruction.

> Stauffer, Russell G. *Teaching Reading as a Thinking Process.* New York: Harper & Row, 1969. Provides an indepth explanation of how to make reading meaningful for the reader.

The following book provides specific information about reading skills in the areas of comprehension, sight vocabulary, study skills, and word attack. The format is programmed for self-study.

> Wilson, Robert M. et al. *Programmed Reading for Teachers.* Columbus, Ohio: Charles E. Merrill Publishing Co., 1980.

Further readings are suggested at the end of each chapter. Those with limited experiences are encouraged to pursue these sources so that contrasting points of view can be considered.

Acknowledgments

The author wishes to acknowledge the many people who have encouraged and guided him toward the completion of this revision.

The inspiration and memory of my father C. B. Wilson has been a constant source of help.

University of Maryland clinic staff members Bruce Brigham, Beth Davey, Robert Duffey, Linda Gambrell, and Ruth Garner have been stimulating, thought-provoking colleagues. Their ideas are reflected throughout this book.

My three research colleagues Karen D'Angelo, Linda Gambrell, and Walter Gantt have been of great help in clarifying ideas.

Craig Cleland reacted critically to each chapter as it was written and was helpful in clarifying ideas. Ruth Garner and Pat Koskinen read and reacted to several chapters.

The updated Appendix B was developed by Margery Berman and Marcia Wilson. They both work as specialists in Montgomery County Public Schools and spend large quantities of time evaluating materials for instruction.

The photography in this edition is credited to Mrs. Irma D. McNelia. I also wish to acknowledge Janet Gold's work on the index.

Susan Coles, a fine and speedy typist, is hereby acknowledged.

The input of Ward Ewalt, William Druckmiller, Donald McFeely, and Louise Waynant to the content of earlier editions of this book remain with this edition.

William Powell and John Wolinski were very helpful by making constructive criticisms of the content.

I started to write down the names of the theorists and researchers whose writings have influenced my thinking. As the list grew longer and longer I realized how unfair it would be to cite some and not others. This Acknowledgment is to those professionals who cared enough to share their thinking with the reading community.

And to my family, my wife Marcia, Rick and Judy, Jim, Nancy, and Jennifer, and Sharon and Russ, who have always been totally supportive.

R.M.W.
College Park, Md.

Dedication

To Donald L. Cleland

This fourth edition is dedicated to my good friend, Donald L. Cleland. Don was my major advisor at the University of Pittsburgh. Since those days we have remained close professional and personal friends. His concern for the students who meet failure while trying to learn to read is well known. His loyalty to his students, past and present, serves as a model for all to follow. And his concern for the entire field of reading has been documented time and time again. I see it as entirely fitting that this edition be dedicated to him.

When Students Encounter Difficulty

Chapter Emphasis

- Most low-achieving readers face problems that are largely out of their control.

- Many teachers also face problems that are largely out of their control.

- By focusing upon readers' strengths, reading skills are most effectively developed and refined.

- The effects of low achievement in reading are borne by some students throughout life.

- In diagnosis, both symptoms and causes of reading difficulties should be assessed.

It is common for educators to view a low-achieving reader as one who has problems. In fact, they often refer to such readers with labels such as *problem readers, dyslexic, learning disabled,* or *language disabled.* Such labels leave one with the impression that something is wrong with the reader. In most cases of low achievement in reading, however, the problem is not within the reader; it is encountered by the reader. It is the educator's responsibility to help the reader overcome the problem.

In the first three editions of this book, this chapter was entitled "Working With Problem Readers." My experiences and my review of the literature have encouraged me to drop the term *problem readers* and to examine instead the types of problems that readers encounter. Let's look at a few of them.

PROBLEMS READERS ENCOUNTER

Prejudice

When a reader encounters prejudice and receives discriminatory treatment, the motivation to make the effort needed to learn to read is dampened. Some readers encounter discrimination because of race, sex, social status, appearance, or some other perceived difference. Readers of any age, but most certainly beginning readers, can quickly feel that something is wrong with them when they encounter prejudiced treatment.

Instruction

When instruction is geared to the achieving readers, those who are achieving slowly, or not at all, can be quickly left behind. Catching up can be difficult even when the spirit is there. It is almost impossible when the reader gets so far behind that the desire to try is gone.

Grouping

Readers who are assigned to a group in which all are experiencing difficulty with reading can easily become discouraged. They all know that their group is proceeding at a slower pace than the others and may start to believe that they are, in fact, slow.

Labels

When another person affixes a label upon a low-achieving reader, it is difficult for that reader to maintain a positive self-concept. And, it is difficult to remove the label.

Humiliation

Public records of the progress of readers are humiliating to the low-achieving readers. No amount of encouragement can motivate those readers who must sit in a classroom and see their names on a chart that indicates that they are not doing well.

The list could go on and on, adding items such as uninterested parents, problems at home, difficulties with peer acceptance, and inappropriate instructional materials. The point is that some readers encounter serious problems that are not of their doing. As they do, they are likely to get the message that something is wrong with them, become discouraged, and stop trying. Then come the labels, special groupings, special instructional materials, and the message is confirmed.

One of the purposes of a book such as this one is to help educators to examine the problems faced by low-achieving readers and to offer suggestions for avoiding or

Labeling can cause low self-esteem in a student.

overcoming them. It is hoped that all who study the remaining chapters will find that purpose met.

PROBLEMS TEACHERS ENCOUNTER

It is not my intention to leave the reader with the impression that all reading difficulties are caused by inept teachers. Although such is the case in some instances, there are other explanations. Many teachers do not have the controls that would enable them to provide the type of instruction necessary for all readers to be successful. A glance at a few of the problems confronting teachers today should make the point clearly.

Class Size

For no good reason, classrooms have been constructed so that thirty or more students can fit in them. To provide efficient instruction to thirty some students at one time is an extremely difficult task.

Pressure

Parents, administrators, supervisors, and many others can apply great amounts of pressure upon teachers. One of the worst pressures is to satisfy others that all readers are reading on grade level. This expectation is unreasonable, but the pressure is there; consequently, many readers are placed in materials far too difficult for them to use successfully.

Nonteaching Duties

In some schools teachers must spend too much time making reports, managing lunch counts, supervising hall behavior, and other such nonteaching duties. While some are necessary, often these duties interfere with time that should be allotted for instruction.

Materials

Many teachers face their students with inadequate or insufficient materials. Learning suffers in those cases in which the teacher cannot make adjustments to overcome the inadequacy of the materials provided.

Preparation

Some teachers enter their teaching careers with extremely poor preparation. Colleges and universities that do not provide prospective teachers with adequate instruction and experience in reading, language, measurements, and psychology must bear the responsibility for poor teaching. We have known for a long time that a desire to teach well is not enough to make up for poor teacher preparation.

Testing

In some schools testing has reached an unbelievable level. Tests for intelligence, readiness, phonics, spelling, reading achievement, reading subskills, and arithmetic may be required at the beginning, midway, and again at the end of the year. I have received reports indicating that some students spend most of the first month of the school year in testing situations. Appalling. Not only does it cut into instructional time, but it can well lead to a series of frustrating experiences, especially for the low-achieving readers who do not test well.

The point is made. The problems that teachers encounter can cause them to be unable to provide necessary instruction for some readers. So the students suffer along with the teachers.

PROBLEMS READERS TAKE WITH THEM TO SCHOOL

Some students have personal problems that cause difficulty in learning to read. As mentioned before, these types of problems far less often cause low achievement than those just discussed. Illness, physical or emotional handicaps, and limited intellectual ability cause some readers great difficulty with the reading process. Public laws have pinpointed the need for placing such students in the most advantageous learning environment to enhance the development of their academic and social skills. Chapter 3 will provide more detailed information about the problems that some readers take with them to school.

RAMIFICATIONS OF LOW ACHIEVEMENT IN READING

Low achievers not only face obstacles that interfere with achievement, but they must also face the task of overcoming the difficulties that low achievement creates. These difficulties occur in school, with peers, and at home with their parents.

In School

In school, where students often are pressured to achieve a certain grade level of performance, low achievers are a source of never-ending disappointments. Whether the pressure is subtle or direct, both the readers and the teachers sense failure. Teachers may react by giving up on them or by feeling that they are indifferent, lazy, or troublesome. These reactions may be followed by punishment that usually fosters a hostile attitude between the teacher and students who are ill-equipped to accept hostility. Frustrated by the rejection and the labels that they have received, these readers either cannot or will not work independently. As more and more frustrating materials are heaped upon them, they are likely to busy themselves with noneducational activities and finally decide that learning is just not worth the effort. As they fall behind in their classroom work, they may be forced to repeat a grade, with the constant threat of further repetition. Excessive absenteeism and complete rejection of the school program are inevitable as they proceed through school being promoted on the basis of age alone. A brief look at the reading level of high school dropouts tells the remainder of the story. Penty says, "More than three times as many poor readers as good readers dropped out of school before graduation."[1]

Not all low achievers become school dropouts; however, the strained school-pupil relationship raises dropout probabilities. An additional possibility exists, for there are also those who drop out emotionally although they continue to attend class. Psychological dropouts are in every school; they generally create problems for both the teacher and students who are there to work. In either case, the situation is critical.

With Peers

Although peers often treat them kindly, it is not uncommon for low achievers to be teased and taunted. They are not with the "in" group and are often found alone at play as well as in the classroom. Other children are not likely to seek their efforts for committee work since their contributions are limited. Rejection encourages them to seek companionship with others in the "out" group. A further complication occurs with the repetition of a grade, which places them one year behind their peers. They clearly recognize that they do not "belong" either in the group with which they are placed or with their peers. If they continue to meet peer group disapproval, they become highly susceptible to undesirable influences, the consequence of which is seen in the reports of police authorities who handle juvenile delinquents. Summarizing a study from the Children's Court in New York, Harris reports, "Among those tested . . . 76 percent were found to be two or more years retarded in reading, and more than half of those were disabled five or more years."[2] It should not be concluded that all low achievers turn to delinquent behavior, but continued rejection from peers makes these students more susceptible to undesirable influences.

With Parents

Parents become anxious when their children are not succeeding in school. They may try to solve the problem by urging or forcing the children to make greater efforts. This often means piling on more of the same type of frustrating work that makes them reject school. When such children balk, it is not unusual for them to be compared to siblings or playmates. Seemingly ashamed of their children's behavior, parents often will look for someone to blame. Students are not blind to this shame and rejection, and they too will look for someone to blame. Even more important, they are likely to look elsewhere for that acceptance that all children need from their parents.

By observing these readers, it can be concluded that the ramifications of their difficulties are felt not only by them, but also by the school, peers, and family. Their inability to solve their own problem causes the future to look dark indeed.

On Into Adulthood

As low achievers gain adulthood, real problems emerge. Post–high school educational options are usually denied them. Job opportunities must be limited to unskilled labor that requires little reading skill. The problem is a huge one. Right to Read reports, "An estimated 1.4 million adults report that they cannot read or write in any language. More than 20 million are functionally illiterate."[3] *Functional literacy* is defined as having sufficient reading skills for getting along in a reading-based society. At this writing, Right to Read has funded sixty seven literacy projects in thirty five states to the tune of $5.2 million.[4] So, the problem is not just for the reader; we must all face it as a serious gap in the development of human potential. We must correct the problem where it is first encountered—in the schools.

From one point of view, it appears that the reading and writing skills of adults have improved over the years. Weber points out, on the other hand, that the reading demands of our society have increased more rapidly than have the improvements in literacy.[5]

In 1969, Allen reported that 25 percent of the students in school are likely to experience frustration in reading.[6] By adjusting instructional programs so as to minimize problems that readers face, that percentage could be reduced drastically.

Not all of those who experience difficulty in learning to read follow the patterns mentioned above. Many are capable of making reasonable adjustments, usually with the help of understanding teachers and parents. The problem facing these teachers and parents becomes how to help the student maintain self-esteem while adjustments are made to allow for successful learning.

TYPES OF READING DIFFICULTIES

All students who experience difficulty with learning to read are different. For purposes of categorization, I have classified three types of difficulties.

First, students may be experiencing difficulty with reading because, for one reason or another, they do not read as well as their abilities indicate they should. They should not be judged by their reading skills in relation to their grade levels in school, but rather in relation to their potentials. Slow students reading below their grade levels in school may experience learning difficulties, but this does not necessarily imply that they are retarded in the development of their reading skills. On the other hand, more able students, although reading well above their grade levels, may be considered low achievers when their reading levels fall short of their intellectual potentials. Accurate assessment of the reading levels and abilities of students lets the teacher determine whether or not readers are operating below their potentials.

Table 1–1 **Ability Compared to Reading**

Student	Grade Level	Ability Level	Reading Level
Ruth	4	3	3
Beth	4	6	3

Note: Ruth is operating consistently with her ability; Beth is not.

Second, students may have difficulty when, with the exception of a specific skill deficiency, all measures of their reading are up to their levels of potential. They read satisfactorily in most situations, but they have a specific weakness. Although their deficiencies are difficult to locate because most of these students' reading skills appear normal, once located, they are readily corrected through the precise nature of the remediation necessary. For example, since many adults read slowly, they have a specific skill deficiency. They can perform on tests and seem to read very well, but their slow speeds make reading a bore and reduce their inclinations to read. Students, while appearing to read well, also may have specific skill deficiencies, such as speed, oral reading fluency, word attack, comprehension and study skills.

The third type of reading difficulty occurs when, in spite of reading skills consistent with their potential, students lack the desire to read. LeGrand-Brodsky reports that 6 percent of the American population over the age of sixteen do not read anything at all and that 30 percent are non–book readers.[7] Strang points to this problem when she says, "If the book is interesting they read it eagerly and with enjoyment. . . . Students confronted with drab, uninteresting reading material show the opposite pattern. They read reluctantly, they skip and skim so that they can get it over with more quickly."[8] These factors discourage students from using available skills and tend to dampen their desire to read. It is important that a lack of desire to read be considered a reading problem because often no other is apparent. Clinic reports for such students show that they are frequently subject to ridicule and disciplinary action, since it is often assumed that there is no excuse for their poor reading habits. An understanding of the students' reaction to reading, however, will indicate the need for adjustment of the school situation to help develop a better attitude toward reading. *Alliteracy* is the term being used to describe capable readers who do not choose to read.

DIAGNOSE FOR SYMPTOMS OR DIAGNOSE FOR CAUSES?

When a student has been identified as having difficulty with learning to read, a basic decision must be made. Should the diagnosis be based on a survey of the symptoms available, or should it attempt to determine causation? Perhaps this is not an either-or question. Let's look at some possible answers.

If the cause of the problem can be determined, then we surely want to know it. However, causation is often difficult and many times impossible to determine. For example, if the reader cannot organize information read for speedy recall, then strategies are available to correct that cause of the difficulty. If, however, the cause is some type of minimal brain dysfunction, it may never be diagnosed—not even in the best medical facility. To continue diagnosis and withhold instruction in such a case would be foolish. A look at three examples may be helpful as one assesses reading difficulties for symptoms and for causes.

Example 1: Tony

Tony is not alone. He is one of many students across the country who, day after day, sit in an elementary school classroom in which they encounter reading situations well beyond their ability. Tony, however, may be ranked among the fortunate, for his teacher Mr. Coley realizes that Tony cannot read well enough to do fifth-grade work. He quickly discovered that Tony could read accurately at the third-grade level and that he could read only with frustration at the fourth-grade level. He noticed that Tony refuses to attack unknown words, and, on the rare occasions when he does, his pronunciation is inaccurate.

He also noticed that Tony's reading is characterized by word pronunciation without fluency, that he is uncomfortable in the reading situation, and that he seems hindered by what the teacher calls "word reading." A quick check of the school records indicates that Tony is average in ability but that each year he seems less responsive to the reading instruction.

Therefore, after carefully considering the information available to him and his own analysis of Tony's reading performance in the classroom, Mr. Coley set into motion a two-pronged program to supplement Tony's regular reading. First, he encouraged Tony to read for meaning, by providing highly interesting reading material at a low level of difficulty; second, he taught essential phonic skills from the sight words that Tony knew. Realizing that Tony's problem might be deeply rooted, he asked for an evaluation by a reading specialist. This approach to the situation reflects an interested, informed classroom teacher analyzing a student's problem and attempting to correct it, while waiting for the services of the reading specialist.

When the reading specialist Mrs. Ruark saw Tony, she knew that a careful diagnosis would be essential. She realized that, among other things, she needed to have complete information concerning Tony's ability, his knowledge of word attack, his comprehension skills, and his emotional stability. Therefore, the specialist began thorough diagnosis to establish the cause of the problem; without such diagnosis she doubted that she could properly recommend a program of correction.

This example illustrates two different reactions to Tony's symptoms. The classroom teacher used a pattern of symptoms to set into motion a program of correction. The specialist realized that the problem could best be understood by a more careful study of the student. Both the classroom teacher and the reading specialist reacted appropriately! The teacher instituted a program of correction as quickly as possible after carefully considering the symptoms, his basic concern being the continuation of Tony's educational program. The specialist initiated a program of diagnosis, attempting to determine the cause of Tony's difficulty, in order to recommend the most appropriate program of remediation.

To clarify further the difference between symptoms and causes of reading difficulty, we define *symptoms* as those observable characteristics of a case that lead to an educated guess about a reader's problems. Teachers must look for reliable patterns of symptoms so that an intelligent program of correction can be initiated with minimal delay to the student's educational progress. Harris states that "many of the simpler difficulties in reading can be corrected by direct teaching of the missing skills, without an intensive search for reasons why the skills were not learned before."[9] One must consider that average classroom teachers have neither the time, the training, nor the materials to conduct thorough diagnoses. They must use a reliable pattern of symptoms. Their procedure is as follows:

1. Examine observable symptoms, combined with available school data.
2. Form a hypothesis based on the observed pattern.
3. Begin instruction.

With the possible necessity for referral in mind, teachers must formulate and conduct the most effective corrective programs possible within the limitations of the classroom. It becomes obvious that the reliability of a pattern of symptoms has a direct influence on the effectiveness of their instruction. Reference may be made to chapter 2 for patterns of symptoms applicable to the classroom diagnosis of readers.

Causation may be defined as that factor or those factors that, as a result of careful diagnosis, might be accurately identified as being responsible for the reading difficulty. Robinson presents data to support the multiple nature of causation in reading difficulties.[10] The reading specialist is acutely aware that, since there is rarely one cause for a given problem, a careful examination for causation is necessary. Poor home environment, poor physical health, inadequate instruction, lack of instructional materials, personality disorders, and many other factors have been identified as interfering to some degree with the development of reading skills.

The reading specialist realizes that if causes can be determined, programs of prevention are possible; for, as Robinson states, "preventive measures can be planned intelligently only if causes of difficulty are understood."[11] The cause in Tony's case could have been, for example, a lack of auditory discrimination skills for learning phonics or an overemphasis on isolated word drill in earlier grades. The reading specialist, after a diagnosis designed to determine causes, sets the groundwork for a program of correction. For Tony's teachers, this could involve revision of portions of the reading curriculum from grade one on or establishment of a more thorough readiness program in the early grades. Thus, a careful diagnosis is the first step toward the implementation of a preventive program.

The reading specialist may also emphasize causation to find the most effective program of correction, especially with the more seriously retarded reader. Strang states, however, that diagnosis is complex and that causes are difficult to uncover.[12] If Tony's classroom teacher's program of correction is not effective, it is obvious that a more thorough diagnosis will be essential. This is the other function of the reading specialist. By her diagnosis she will be able to assist the classroom teacher with recommendations to implement the most effective program.

That specialists look for causation and classroom teachers for patterns of symptoms in no way prevents classroom teachers from being aware of possible implications and complications concerning the causes of reading problems. Nor does it excuse them from gathering as much diagnostic information as possible. The more informed they become about causation, the more effective they will be in analyzing patterns of symptoms intelligently. As Harris states, they should be "able to carry out the simpler parts of a diagnostic study."[13] At the same time, teachers' major job is to instruct all students in their care, and this obligation generally precludes thorough diagnosis in any one case. It is also possible that after a most careful diagnosis the reading specialist will not yet be able to identify the causes of the student's reading difficulty. Causative factors may be elusive, but the reading specialist will attempt to identify those causes as accurately as possible.

Example 2: Bill

"Bill, how many times have I told you not to hold your book so close to your face?" Despite repeated efforts to have him hold his book at the proper distance, his teacher Ms. Beath noticed that Bill insisted on this type of visual adjustment. Knowing this to be a symptom of a visual disorder, she began to observe him more closely. She noticed unusual watering of the eyes and an unusual amount of blinking, especially after longer sessions involving seat work. Her response was to adjust the classroom situation to allow Bill the maximum amount of visual comfort (i.e., regulating visual activities to shorter time periods and assuring Bill the most favorable lighting conditions). Realizing that he might have a serious problem, the teacher referred him to a vision specialist.

The teacher's job was to recognize the symptoms and react: first, to teach Bill by adjusting the physical setting to enable him to perform as comfortably as possible; second, to refer him to a specialist for whatever visual correction was necessary.

The reaction of the reading specialist Mr. Nash to Bill was a little different. He saw the symptoms of the difficulty and he realized that referral was a possibility. However, in this case, a visual screening test involving near-point vision[14] was administered first to determine whether Bill's problem was one of visual disability or bad habit.

In all physical problems, referral to the proper specialist is the appropriate action for personnel in education; therefore, the reading specialist and the classroom teacher considered referral of Bill for visual analysis. The difference in their approach is important. Ms. Beath observed a pattern of symptoms that told her that there was a good possibility that vision was interfering with his educational progress. Since Bill's education is her first responsibility, the teacher's proper reaction was to adjust the educational climate so that Bill could operate as effectively as possible. She also was obligated to make a referral for visual analysis. The reading specialist, however, was not immediately confronted with Bill's day-to-day instruction; rather, he was obligated to determine as accurately as possible whether vision was the factor interfering with Bill's education. He was justified in his attempt to screen thoroughly before making recommendations for visual referral or for adjustment to educational climate.

Example 3: Craig Craig had the reputation of being a daydreamer. His present teacher Mrs. Wilhoyte confirmed that he seemed to drift off, but also noticed that he did not participate in discussions and was not able to respond to questions about material he had just read. One day she called Craig to her desk and asked him to read orally for her. Craig did so with ease and fluency. She then asked him a series of questions and found that he disliked reading the stories in the reading book. He became very interested in discussing crabbing, his favorite activity. She found that his father took him crabbing every possible weekend on Chesapeake Bay.

Armed with the information that he had the necessary reading skills and was interested in crabbing, Mrs. Wilhoyte conferred with the media specialist to find some interesting books. Luck would have it that the media specialist had two books about crabbing, *Chesapeake* and *Beautiful Swimmers.* She also had several editions of a high school publication named *Skip Jacks.* Craig was delighted with these books. He studied them carefully, not daydreaming now. He still seemed bored by the other reading he was expected to do, so Mrs. Wilhoyte referred him to the reading specialist Mr. Fowler.

Mr. Fowler was impressed with the efforts Mrs. Wilhoyte had made. Craig seemed open and eager to talk about crabbing. Mr. Fowler found that Craig was in command of his reading skills and could read almost anything he wanted. He also confirmed that Craig seemed to be interested only in crabbing. After giving Craig an interest survey, however, he found that Craig was highly interested in boating, soccer, photography, and swimming. This information provided many opportunities to select materials that would interest him. Mrs. Wilhoyte arranged with the media specialist that Craig would always have available at least one book on a topic of his interest. Once he found reading to be enjoyable, Craig's general interest in learning improved.

Again the teacher and the reading specialist assisted each other to determine how best to help Craig. The reading specialist, with instruments available and time to use them, was able to find Craig's range of interests. His recommendations to Mrs. Wilhoyte helped her to get Craig on task. Once started in interesting material, Craig found school to be stimulating and informative.

The three examples above have been developed to illustrate the roles of teachers and reading specialists in diagnosis. The relationship between causes and symptoms is a delicate one and sometimes confusing. Educators, however, must deal with both symptoms and causes as they work to provide the best educational climate for their students. The point is that educators must also be aware of when they are dealing with symptoms and when they are dealing with causes.

SCHOOL SCREENING COMMITTEES

Many schools have organized all resource personnel into screening committees to handle teacher referrals. These committees meet regularly with the principal to make decisions based upon as much diagnostic information as possible. A committee is likely to include specialists in reading, special education, language disabilities, and speech, as well as the school nurse, psychologist, and guidance counselor. Multiple input helps to prevent errors in diagnosis. The referring teacher usually attends. When it has been determined that the child is handicapped, the parent is represented and actively participates in decision making.

When all available information has been considered, an educational plan is developed and responsibilities are assigned to the most appropriate persons for instruction. Periodic reports of progress are reviewed by the committee. When the child is handicapped, the parent must approve the program by signing an agreement. In these cases the plan is called an Individualized Education Program (IEP) and is mandated by federal legislation, Public Law 94–142.

Several advantages of screening committees have been noted:

1. The principal is informed of the work of the specialists.
2. Records are maintained by the principal so that parents can also be informed.
3. Specialists, working together, find less conflict of interests.
4. Overlapping of responsibilities diminishes.
5. All attention is given to bringing the full resources of the school to assisting students to be successful learners.

In each case described on the preceding pages, screening committee action would have been appropriate and helpful.

SPECIAL CONSIDERATIONS

Two groups of students need special consideration as teachers plan for their instruction. They are those who come from cultures different from those of their teachers and those who have been identified as handicapped.

Cultural Differences

Much has been written about students who come from different cultural environments. Some claim these students come to school with a cultural handicap and label them *disadvantaged*. Others attribute their difficulty in school to their cultural background, implying not only differences but undesirable influence as well. Labels such as *"disadvantaged"* and *"undesirable"* hold no value for diagnosis and create assumptions that hurt students so labeled. That numerous children from poor families or minority groups have difficulty in school is a fact. Students from restricted urban environments and isolated rural environments are often far below their peers in reading skills.

However, it is not true that the environment alone has caused the reading problem. Indeed, evidence also points to a lack of equal educational opportunity.[15] Yet culturally different children come to school with a fully developed language and with wide backgrounds of experiences. Teachers who work with these students should be alert to their strengths, not to their degree of difference. Teachers must recognize culturally different students as having distinct and good cultures. They can be taught if their strengths are evaluated and their programs adjusted to

Mrs. Howell, a fourth grade teacher, entered the principal's office for the first School Screening Committee meeting of the year. She went to discuss her concerns about her students based on the first four weeks of school.

In particular, she brought up John, an alert but shy boy who had entered the fourth grade from a school outside the county. Because he was new, no records from the previous school had arrived; but already, Mrs. Howell was worried.

John functioned best in a basal with a stated readability of 2.5; his math and other subject work were on grade level; he was having considerable difficulty with both manuscript and cursive handwriting; he couldn't work independently and had a poor self-concept. John was being privately tutored at home three times a week in reading and handwriting. Mrs. Howell concluded by saying that while she was pleased with his progress in the basal he had been using, she would like to be able to pinpoint specific strengths and weaknesses in his reading and to improve his weak self-concept.

After discussion, the group made these recommendations: 1. Try to obtain records from John's previous school. 2. Obtain results from speech screening (given to all children new to a school). 3. Proceed with an in-school assessment (a Slosson Intelligence Test, a Metropolitan Reading Achievement Test and/or the Woodcock Reading Mastery Test). 4. Try to ascertain the objectives of the after-school tutoring program. 5. Continue to gather information on strengths and weaknesses through the teacher's daily interactions with the student. 6. Try to have all information available on or before the next scheduled committee meeting.

Later, screening showed detailed reading tests necessary. Since the school did not have a reading teacher available for this grade level, the special education teacher and the principal agreed to perform the assessment and prescriptive work.

The next meeting included the principal, the reading teacher, the special education teacher, the school psychologist, the pupil personnel worker, and the nurse. They heard the following assessment results: Slosson Intelligence Test = 115, Metropolitan Achievement Test = 2.2.

Editorial

They then hypothesized that John 1. had above average ability; 2. was functioning at least two years below grade level in reading only; 3. demonstrated a low level of interest and success in school tasks.

They made the following recommendations: 1. Obtain permission to administer the W.I.S.C.–R (intelligence test) to verify ability level and pinpoint specific cognitive strengths and weaknesses. 2. Administer the Woodcock Reading Test to provide a more specific listing of reading strengths and weaknesses. 3. Invite parents in to obtain more information about John's perceptions of himself and school, his home situation and his tutoring program. His parents would also receive anecdotal and assessment information from the school. 4. Be prepared to review all data and make final recommendations to school team and parents at the next meeting.

At the next meeting, both of John's parents were present. The school gave them all the assessment data: 1. W.I.S.C.–R results indicated slightly above-average intelligence with a wide scatter in verbal and performance sections. Strengths were visual discrimination, visual sequencing and common sense reasoning. Weaknesses were in auditory and visual memory and spatial visualization. 2. The Woodcock Reading Test detected weaknesses in comprehension, blends, and short vowels with strengths in long vowels and vowel digraphs. 3. Records from previous school indicated previous placement in a special education program for reading assistance.

His parents said John's learning and attitude problems began when a younger brother was born. His mother said she had been working with John one hour per night (in addition to tutorial help) in reading and handwriting. She said these sessions were frustrating and often ended with John in tears or very upset.

The group concluded that: 1. John's assessment information indicated a disability in one or more basic psychological processes. According to county and federal guidelines, this condition would qualify him for reading assistance from the reading specialist. 2. Since John felt incompetent and frustrated in reading tasks and independent work, it was recommended that the tutoring program either be terminated for a while or closely coordinated with his school program. It was further recommended that the parent replace what appeared to be mutually frustrating nightly work sessions with opportunities to go to a library or bookstore to select high-interest, low-readability material, followed by brief positive (10–15 minute) sessions to share what had been read, to have silent reading sessions, etc. The parents were also involved in a discussion of factors and practices that contributed to feelings of self-worth. 3. When the Individual Education Plan was to be formulated, it was recommended to include a. diagnostic lessons to gain more information on weaknesses and strengths in comprehension; b. remediation in specific phonic skills (consonant blends); c. assignment of tasks that reduced amount of writing and provided high probability of success; d. close coordination with classroom teacher and parent; e. scheduled review of program and progress in thirty days.

Subsequently John began making progress in task completion, self-concept, and skill acquisition. His program was reviewed throughout the school year.

Joseph G. Czarnecki

It is important to remember that different does not mean deficient.

those strengths. For example, since they can talk, they can be taught through the language-experience approach. Therefore, variations in technique are recommended on the basis of diagnosis rather than generalizations. Alan Cohen claims, "Learning disability patterns as measured on clinic tests of disadvantaged retarded readers do not differ markedly from the learning disability patterns of middle-class children who are retarded readers."[16]

In our research with low-income black students in inner-city schools, we found that almost all students produced larger portions of standard English than divergent English.[17] We were impressed by the sophistication of their ability to use standard syntactical structures. We now feel strongly that one or two divergent usages may attract teacher attention even when the student uses as many as twenty standard usages. Concentration on these uses may cause students to feel inadequate. We also found very low correlations between divergent usage and ability to listen to standard English. Apparently the world of the user of divergent English is filled with opportunities to learn to listen to standard English and comprehend it.

When working with these students, it is important to remember that different does not mean deficient. If we can accept the dialect as a natural and effective means of communication, the students can develop positive self-concepts. I do not advocate teaching to the dialect, but I do advocate accepting it when communicating with students.

Another aspect of teaching students from different cultures is related to the values of a given culture. McDermott cites numerous instances of low achievement when ". . . a group in power educates the children of a minority group."[18] He cites such factors as communication interferences, lack of understanding about what motivates, and failure to understand the other cultural values.[19] If teacher-student relations are strained by a lack of understanding, then learning to read can become very difficult. Smith refers to it as *risk taking*.[20] If the readers do not believe that a given reading situation is worth the risk of embarrassment or humiliation, they will not try. One obvious solution is to make risk taking worthwhile: that is, no penalties, no punishment for the risk taker who fails. Another solution is to study the different culture in order to enhance the possibilities of effective teacher-student relationships.

The third aspect of teaching students from different cultures occurs when English is not the student's native language. The difficulty ranges from the situation of a student completely unfamiliar with English and a teacher completely unfamiliar with the student's language to that of a student skilled but not completely comfortable with English. Unfortunately, the students in both situations respond to English slowly and create the impression that they are lacking in intelligence. Not so, obviously, but the teachers in these situations need help. Volunteers or other teachers who know the child's native language must be provided to bridge the gap while the student learns to communicate comfortably in English.

With all groups mentioned, the focus in instruction should be on the student's strengths. Acceptance of the student and encouragement of risk taking are essential strategies for the teacher to adopt.

Handicaps

As mentioned above, Public Law 94–142 has mandated specific educational processes for those determined to be handicapped. Included under that label are the mentally retarded, hard-of-hearing, deaf, speech impaired, visually impaired, seriously emotionally disturbed, deaf-blind, specific-learning disabled, and other types of health impaired.

As teachers diagnose and instruct the handicapped, attention will need to be given to the interpretation of the laws as they appear in the Federal Register.[21] Basically it calls for full educational opportunities for all handicapped children. Individualized education programs (IEPs) must be written for each handicapped child. These programs are to be implemented in as normal a schooling situation as possible. All IEPs are to be evaluated periodically. (See chapter 6 for more information on IEPs.)

Low achievers in reading may or may not be classified as handicapped. Under the term *specific reading disability,* reading is included when it can be determined that the low achievement in reading is due to some type of disorder in the psychological processes.

Teachers and reading specialists need to be familiar with all school policies that concern the handicapped. Who makes the decisions, where everyone's responsibilities lie, and the established procedures for developing IEPs must be understood.

INSTRUCTING LOW-ACHIEVING READERS

As instructional strategies are developed, it is essential to focus upon the strengths of the readers. It is through repeated success that low achievers develop an attitude that they are successful and efficient readers. That attitude is important in development of an "I can do it" self-concept. Reading is a skill. Like all skills, it is developed and refined through practice. Practice activities must be planned so that the readers can complete them with speed, fluency, and accuracy. If they are designed to fit the readers' strengths, then the readers can refine their reading skills. If they are designed to their weaknesses, then it is likely that they will be practicing slow, nonfluent, inaccurate reading. They will be learning to read in that manner. Specifically:

1. Reading material should be selected so that the readers encounter little difficulty understanding the material

and are highly accurate. (See page 108 in chapter 4 for details on acceptable word pronunciation criteria.)

2. Skill activities should be planned so that the student can achieve success with them. Low achievers have often had plenty of failures and need no more.

3. With all activities, alternative strategies should be planned. When the readers stall on an activity, help should be provided immediately or other activities should be initiated. Continued frustration with too difficult an activity leads to negative self-concepts.

4. Student decision making should occur whenever possible. Students are likely to pick those activities that are of most interest to them and those that they can complete successfully.

Suggestions for activities designed to focus upon strengths will be provided in the various chapters that deal with instructional strategies.

The following selected authorities provide additional insight into the necessity of focusing on readers' strengths:

Waetjen stresses that "if a person is accepted and valued and esteemed, he becomes an inquiring person and he actualizes himself."[22]

Raths claims that "if our meanings gained from our experiences are frowned upon, are devalued—it constitutes a rejection of our life, and that is intolerable to everyone of us so treated. . . . "[23]

Bowers and Soar say that "the more supportive the climate, the more the student is willing to share, the more learning will take place. . . . "[24]

Cohen says, "tolerance for failure is best taught through providing a background of success that compensates for experienced failure. . . . "[25]

Prescott puts it, "the unloved child who fails is in double jeopardy . . . to his insecurity is added the feeling of inadequacy, and he becomes more and more reluctant to try again with each failure."[26]

Smith notes, ". . . attention is likely to be focused on what each child finds incomprehensible in order to 'challenge' them to further learning. Anything a child knows already is likely to be set aside as 'too easy.' Paradoxically, many reading materials are made intentionally meaningless. Obviously, in such cases there is no way in which children will be able to develop their ability to seek and identify meaning in text."[27]

While planning work for students experiencing reading difficulty, some time should be spent developing techniques that will help them develop a desire to learn. Perhaps the most crucial factor in successful program adjustment lies in the area of teacher attitude toward students.

If activities can *focus on strengths,* school can be a happy, fun-filled environment for all learners. As Margaret Mead put it, "If learning to read were seen as a path to individual triumphant success . . . each child's mastery of reading could, in its own way, be celebrated,"[28] just as we celebrate learning to walk and talk. As you read on, keep the idea of focusing on strengths in mind and notice how both diagnostic and instructional activities fit the idea.

SUMMARY

When students encounter difficulty in learning to read, the reactions of teachers and parents is crucial. Attempts to apply more pressure, to label, and to focus on weaknesses can complicate the difficulty. Careful diagnosis followed by instruction that focuses upon strengths can enable many low achievers to gain success and develop an "I can do it" self-concept.

NOTES

1. Ruth C. Penty, "Reading Ability and High School Dropouts," *Journal of the National Association of Women Deans and Counselors* October 1959, p. 14.
2. Albert J. Harris, *How To Increase Reading Ability* (New York: David McKay Co., 1970), p. 3.
3. Albert J. Harris, "Adult Illiteracy: Changing the Statistics," *Reporting On Reading* 5, no. 3 (1979): 6.

4. Ibid.

5. R. Weber, "Adult Illiteracy in the United States," in *Toward a Literate Society,* ed. Carroll and Chall (New York: McGraw-Hill Book Co., 1975).

6. James Allen, "The Right to Read—Target for the Seventies" (Address given to the National Association of State Boards of Education, 23 Sept. 1969.)

7. Katherine LeGrand-Brodsky, "Hope for Reading in America: Practically Everyone Reads," *Reading Teacher* 32, no. 8 (May 1979): 947.

8. Ruth Strang, *Diagnostic Teaching of Reading* (New York: McGraw-Hill Book Co., 1969), p. 106.

9. Harris, *How To Increase Reading Ability,* p. 201.

10. Helen M. Robinson, *Why Pupils Fail in Reading* (Chicago: The University of Chicago Press, 1946), p. 219.

11. Robinson, *Why Pupils Fail in Reading,* p. 219.

12. Strang, *Diagnostic Teaching of Reading,* p. 26.

13. Harris, *How To Increase Reading Ability,* p. 201.

14. Distance of eyes from print—twelve to fifteen inches.

15. James S. Coleman et al., *Equality of Educational Opportunity* (Washington, D.C.: U.S. Department of Health, Education and Welfare, 1966).

16. S. Alan Cohen, "Cause vs. Treatment in Reading Achievement," *Journal of Learning Disabilities,* March 1970, p. 43.

17. Walter N. Gantt, Robert M. Wilson, and C. Mitchell Dayton, "An Initial Investigation of the Relationship Between Syntactical Divergency and the Listening Comprehension of Black Children," *Reading Research Quarterly* 10, no. 2 (1974–75): 193–208.

18. Ray P. McDermott, "The Ethnography of Speaking and Reading," in *Linguistic Theory,* ed. Roger Shuy (Newark, Del.: IRA, 1977), pp. 153–85.

19. Ibid.

20. Frank Smith, *Understanding Reading,* 2d ed. (New York: Holt, Rinehart & Winston, 1978), p. 20.

21. *Federal Register* 42, no. 163 (Tuesday, August 23, 1977).

22. Walter B. Waetjen, "Facts about Learning," in *Readings in Curriculum,* ed. Glen Hass and Kimball Wiles (Boston: Allyn and Bacon, 1965), p. 243.

23. Louis E. Raths, "How Children Build Meaning," *Childhood Education* 31 (1954): 159–60.

24. Norman D. Bowers and Robert S. Soar, "Studies in Human Relations in the Teaching-Learning Process," *Evaluation of Laboratory Human Relations Training for Classroom Teachers* (Chapel Hill, N.C.: University of North Carolina Press, 1961), p. 111.

25. S. Alan Cohen, *Teach Them All To Read* (New York: Random House, 1969), p. 231.

26. Daniel A. Prescott, *The Child in the Educative Process* (New York: McGraw-Hill Book Co., 1957), p. 359.
27. Frank Smith, *Understanding Reading*, 2d ed. (New York: Holt, Rinehart & Winston, 1978), p. 166.
28. Margaret Mead, Editorial inside front cover, *Reading Teacher* 28 (October 1974).

SUGGESTED READINGS

Bond, Guy L., Tinker, Miles A. and Wasson, Barbara B. *Reading Difficulties: Their Diagnosis and Correction,* 4th ed. Englewood Cliffs: Prentice-Hall, 1979. Chapter 3 in this book provides a description of disabled readers. For a point of view different from those expressed in this chapter, the reader should examine their chapter 3.

Gambrell, Linda B., and Wilson, Robert M. *Focusing On the Strengths of Children.* Belmont Calif.: Fearon Publishers, 1973. Rationales for focusing on strengths and numerous specific examples are included. The first three chapters provide the basic arguments in support of focusing on strengths.

Smith, Frank, *Understanding Reading,* 2d ed. New York: Holt, Rinehart & Winston, 1978. Essential reading for those interested in understanding the processes in the reading act. Smith brings theory from a psycholinguistic base and applies it to various activities involved in learning to read.

Waetjen, Walter R., and Leeper, Robert R., eds. *Learning and Mental Health in the School.* Washington, D.C.: Association for Supervision and Curriculum Development, 1966. Several chapters by different authors illustrate the necessity for consideration of a theory behind your instructional strategies. Of particular value are the writings of Syngg in regard to the necessity to focus on student strengths.

Introduction to Diagnosis

Chapter Emphasis

- Three types of diagnosis are recommended for reading assessment.

- Assessment of the educational environment is as important as the assessment of the readers' behavior.

- Diagnosis for readers' strengths has many positive features.

If one views diagnosis from the medical point of view, an inaccurate perception of educational diagnosis will occur. Medical diagnosis is the examination of the nature and circumstances of a diseased condition. The notion of a diseased condition causing educational achievement problems is misleading, since such conditions are seldom the cause of low achievement. Educational diagnosis involves the assessment of the home and school environments, the personal health and attitude of the learner, the learner's skills, and the self-report of the learner.

In the classroom, when first signs of difficulty appear, first consideration should be given to the educational environment of reading. Is that environment a favorable one for the readers? Can easy-to-make changes remedy the situation so that learning efforts can be successful? If so, it is not necessary to involve the readers in testing activities; rather, make the changes and continue with instruction. For example, several readers may have had difficulty responding to instruction in a comprehension lesson. By evaluating the instructional procedures in the lesson, the teacher may find that several new terms were used in the text and that they were the key to understanding the material. While planning the lesson, the teacher may have missed the importance of these key terms and made no plans to introduce them. By going back and introducing the new terms, the teacher may note that the difficulty originally noticed has disappeared. Score one for a good teacher.

Teachers need to develop the habit of keeping careful notes about adjustments that are effective, such as the one mentioned. These notes can lead to a pattern of observed student behavior. It is when such patterns are observed again and again that we are able to gain a reliable assessment of student behavior. Occasional observations of a particular type of behavior tend to create unreliable impressions.

SOME MYTHS ABOUT DIAGNOSIS

All teachers use diagnostic strategies as they are teaching. Teacher-made tests, observations of student behavior, and notations in student records are used by all teachers to assist them in understanding their students. Some myths persist, however, that keep teachers from being as effective as they might be:

1. Diagnosis requires the use of specially designed tests. To the contrary, effective diagnosis is usually best achieved by using teacher observation and informal evaluations. The testing situation creates unnatural behavior with some students and the results are often misleading.
2. Group standardized tests provide useful information regarding individual students. Not true. Group standardized test results provide very little useful information on individual students. (See discussion in chapter 4.)
3. Diagnosis requires highly trained personnel As in all other areas of education, there are levels of competence in diagnosis. All teachers use diagnostic procedures every day. Those with more preparation are probably more efficient, but teaching requires continual assessment.
4. Diagnosis calls for a case-study report. Notes from diagnostic observations should be maintained, but they may be in very simple format. Case-study approaches are generally used when the reading difficulty is severe and a reading specialist has been asked to assist.

TYPES OF DIAGNOSIS

By obtaining some clarification of the myths often associated with diagnosis, we can discuss the types of diagnostic procedures. Three types of diagnosis are useful at various times.

Informal on-the-Spot Diagnosis

Teachers are constantly assessing student performances during instruction. Student responses to questions, writing activities, and general class participation provide teachers with informal input about student progress. When difficulties arise, adjustments are made on-the-spot to assist students to reach success.

Classroom Diagnosis

If, after informal adjustments have been made, students continue to have difficulty, more structured diagnostic efforts may need to be initiated. The teacher sets some time aside to work individually with a student to determine what is causing the difficulty. Some testing might be involved in an attempt to determine the degree of skill development in a

Teachers should constantly be assessing student performance during instruction.

given area. Those findings are checked against data in school records. Then classroom instructional adjustments are made to see if the student can now respond successfully.

Clinical Diagnosis

When instructional adjustments are not successful and reading difficulty increases, it may be necessary to ask for help from a reading specialist. Generally, clinical diagnosis will take place outside the classroom and will involve specific skills testing and diagnostic lessons with the student. Recommendations for instructional adjustments will be made and the teacher and reading specialist can evaluate the success of those adjustments. Clinical diagnosis may also involve specialists in speech therapy or special education. It can also involve the referral of the student to an outside diagnostic agency such as a college reading clinic.

SEQUENCE OF DIAGNOSIS

The following sequence will provide a better understanding of the relationships among the types of diagnosis.

The classroom teacher makes an informal on-the-spot diagnosis and adjusts instruction accordingly. If this fails, the teacher conducts a classroom diagnosis and again individualizes instruction. Should this step be unsuccessful, the teacher refers the student to a reading specialist for a more thorough analysis via clinical diagnosis. Instruction is adjusted according to the recommendations of the specialist. If the entire sequence cannot produce the desired results, the necessity for other referrals is likely. It is unlikely that a single failure will result in the teacher's moving immediately to the next type of diagnosis; rather, the teacher will utilize each diagnostic step thoroughly and repeatedly, if necessary, before moving to the next. It should be noticed that at each step in this sequence, referral is possible (See Figure 2–1).

Since all effective learning relies upon informal on-the-spot diagnosis and its subsequent follow-up, it is assumed that this type of diagnosis is normal in good teaching. It is also obvious that the types of diagnosis are not clearly separated. Nor are specific techniques reserved for the reading specialist; classroom teachers may use clinical diagnostic tools when appropriate. All types of diagnosis include observation of the student as instruction is adjusted, to determine its effectiveness.

DIAGNOSTIC PROCEDURES

Specific procedures will vary with the nature of the difficulty and type of diagnosis being initiated. The following treatment of procedures for each type of diagnosis should be viewed as flexible.

Informal on-the-Spot Diagnosis

The procedures used with informal on-the-spot diagnosis are related to the instructional procedures being used. When the teacher notices that students are experiencing difficulty, an immediate instructional adjustment is made in order to facilitate learning. Some examples may be helpful.

Figure 2–1

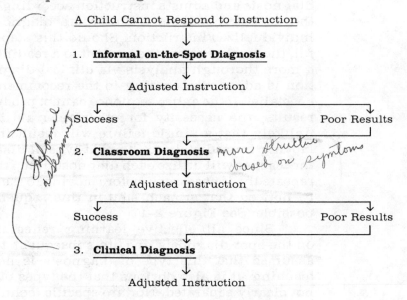

Sequence of Diagnosis

A Child Cannot Respond to Instruction

↓

1. **Informal on-the-Spot Diagnosis**

↓

Adjusted Instruction

Success   Poor Results

2. **Classroom Diagnosis** *more structive based on symtoms*

↓

Adjusted Instruction

Success   Poor Results

3. **Clinical Diagnosis**

↓

Adjusted Instruction

Note: Referral can take place at any step.

1. Margi was not responding well to her teacher's questions on the material she had just read. When the teacher changed the type of question from literal to interpretive, Margi responded very well. Her teacher noted that Margi could deal better with the literal questions after she was successful with the interpretive ones.

2. Roy sounded terrible when he had to read orally. He read in a slow, choppy manner and mispronounced about one word in fifteen. By encouraging Roy to practice reading orally to himself he became fluent and accurate.

3. Catherine was the lowest achiever in her reading group. She knew it and so did the other students. Her self-concept as a reader was poor. Her teacher made arrangements for Catherine to tutor a young child in a lower grade for fifteen minutes each morning. This tutoring made an instant change in Catherine's attitude, as she felt worthwhile helping someone else.

4. Joe was reading well in reading class but he seemed to encounter great difficulty doing assignments in his science text. His teacher noticed that the science text introduced a large number of new words at the beginning of each chapter. By using those new words in contexts that Joe could understand, his teacher could help him with those words before he encountered them on his own. His science assignments improved immediately.

No, it does not always work this nicely. At times, attempted adjustments miss their purpose and the difficulty continues. If repeated informal on-the-spot adjustments do not have the desired effect, then a classroom diagnosis, allowing for a more careful look into the factors causing the difficulty, becomes necessary.

Classroom Diagnosis

Starting with a careful examination of the educational environment, classroom diagnosis suggests a more formal assessment than does informal on-the-spot diagnosis. When students are in a failure pattern and informal adjustments do not help, carefully planned observation and testing become necessary.

The following are procedures for classroom diagnosis.

Identification. The classroom teacher is in the best position to notice potential problem areas. In this way,

The classroom teacher is in the best position to notice potential problem areas.

classroom diagnosis is actually underway by the time the student has been identified; informal on-the-spot diagnosis has previously established certain diagnostic information that the teacher will use in classroom diagnosis.

The tendency for educators to wait until a problem is well developed can be avoided by increased attention to classroom diagnosis at all age levels, including first grade. It is through immediate attention to the first symptoms of reading difficulty that the number of low-achieving readers can be reduced.

Assessment of the educational environment. Notations concerning instructional strategies, grouping arrangements, materials in use, seating arrangements, etc., should be made. Would modifying any of these factors create a successful learning environment?

Gathering available data. The classroom teacher then searches for information about the student and organizes it for consideration during the diagnosis. School records, interviews with past teachers, health reports, and other sources provide considerable data concerning past development, successes, and failures of the student. Notes made during informal on-the-spot diagnosis can be extremely useful, particularly if the teacher making the classroom diagnosis did not conduct the previous one.

1. Limited testing: When necessary, classroom teachers may administer and interpret tests designed to provide information in the area of the difficulty. Testing, of course, is limited by the time that teachers have for individual testing as well as their skill in using the instruments.

2. Direct observations: Using the information available at this stage of classroom diagnosis, teachers will find it advantageous to observe students in various reading situations with particular emphasis on the verification of other diagnostic information. The link to informal on-the-spot diagnosis is clear. When observations and other data complement previous findings, the next step can be taken. When they do not support each other, there is a need for a reevaluation, more observation, possible testing, and new conclusions.

Figure 2–2

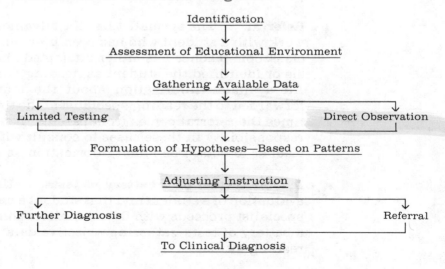

Procedures for Classroom Diagnosis

3. Formulation of hypotheses: From the patterns observed, the teacher will form hypotheses about adjusting instruction for the group or the individual and about the possibility of referral. By looking for patterns, one reduces the chances of error often caused by relying on one observation or one test score.

Once instructional hypotheses have been formed, teachers adjust instruction and test each hypothesis. For example, if the diagnostic hypothesis is "Jack will read more fluently if I reduce the level of difficulty by one grade level," then the teacher finds materials at the level indicated and places Jack in a learning situation. If, in fact, Jack can read fluently in these new materials, then the hypothesis is accepted. If he cannot, then it is back to the diagnostic procedures to develop another hypothesis.

That classroom diagnosis is time-consuming is a fact. However, teachers can minimize the amount of time needed. They can utilize existing records, conduct the diagnosis during times other students are occupied, and collect diagnostic data daily over a period of time. As teachers gain proficiency with diagnostic procedures, they will find them to be less time-consuming. Chapter 4 includes specific strategies for classroom diagnosis.

Clinical Diagnosis

Clinical procedures may be implemented through individual study of the student outside of the classroom. These procedures are listed and described in Figure 2–3.

Referral. The specialist has the advantage of starting to work with a student who has been previously referred. The classroom teacher has either attempted classroom diagnosis or identified the student as needing clinical diagnosis. All available information about the student should be forwarded to the reading specialist at the time of referral. At times the referral comes from parents. It is the specialist's responsibility in these cases to consult with the classroom teacher to obtain as much information as possible.

Administration of a battery of tests. Using a tentative evaluation of a student and that student's needs, the reading specialist proceeds with the administration and analysis of a battery of tests gathering objective data on the student's reading skills.

Figure 2–3

Procedures for Clinical Diagnosis

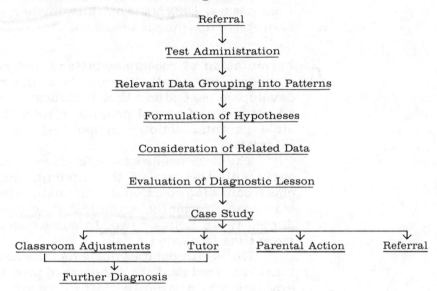

Referral
↓
Test Administration
↓
Relevant Data Grouping into Patterns
↓
Formulation of Hypotheses
↓
Consideration of Related Data
↓
Evaluation of Diagnostic Lesson
↓
Case Study
↓
Classroom Adjustments   Tutor   Parental Action   Referral
↓
Further Diagnosis

Observation of patterns. The reading specialist makes careful observations of behavior patterns during the testing. Combined with test scores and the specialist's analysis of the reading responses on tests administered, these observations will facilitate the grouping of relevant data into meaningful patterns.

Formulation of hypotheses. From the observable patterns, the reading specialist then forms tentative hypotheses concerning the causes of the problem.

Consideration of related data. Once the hypotheses have been formed, the specialist weighs related data with parent and teacher conferences, school records, and previous diagnostic results. When the specialist finds that the hypotheses are supported by related data the diagnosis gains validity; at other times, conflicting information forces reconsideration of the original hypotheses. In many cases, further testing or reexamination of the test results is needed for clearer insights into the difficulty.

Evaluation of diagnostic lessons. The lessons conducted during a clinical diagnosis are brief and specifically related to diagnostic hypotheses. Parts of the lessons should be directed to the student's strengths and parts to the student's weaknesses. Diagnosis is thus further validated through short-term diagnostic sessions.

Formulation of recommendations and referrals. After consideration of all relevant data, the reading specialist develops a case study that includes recommendations for adjustments of school programs, remedial treatment, possible parental action, further testing, and/or necessary referral.

The time needed for effective clinical diagnosis will vary with the age of the student, the effectiveness of classroom diagnosis, and practical matters such as clinician load. Normally, a clinical diagnosis should be conducted in an hour or two. In some cases, however, much more time is needed.

While clinical diagnosis has the advantage of highly individualized study and the use of precise instruments for evaluation by a carefully trained person, it has limitations. One is the relationship of the behavior observed in a one-to-one situation to a student's behavior in the classroom working with others. A second limitation is the reaction of the student to the two different people, the teacher and the reading specialist. A third is that while the specialist may check diagnosis with the diagnostic teaching lessons, the teacher may be unable (for various reasons) to make necessary instructional adjustments. For these reasons, the specialist should discuss the results of the diagnosis with the teacher, in addition to providing a written report. To illustrate the techniques recommended in the report, the reading specialist should offer to work with the student in the classroom for a lesson or two.

Clinical diagnosis often establishes a need for further action for the reading specialist, such as the following:

1. Reporting to a screening committee the results of the clinical diagnosis and the interpretation of those results into recommendations.
2. Reporting and interpreting the results of the diagnosis to parents.

3. Preparing teachers to utilize special instructional techniques through in-service sessions.
4. Consulting with medical or psychological personnel when referrals are made.
5. Instructing the student for a period of time when individual or small-group attention is needed.

SOURCES OF DATA

While conducting any type of diagnosis, teachers need to be aware of the available sources of data. At times one can become so involved with testing that other sources of data are overlooked. Some of the other sources, however, are much more useful than test results.

Informal on-the-spot diagnosis relies heavily upon observation of student behavior, school records, and reports from others. Since most of this diagnosis takes place during instructional time, the only test results available are those of teacher-made tests, which are normally used to assess the effectiveness of the instruction.

Classroom diagnosis relies upon school records, observations of teachers, reports from past teachers, interviews with students and parents, records from home visits, and test results. In classroom diagnosis, the teacher also obtains important data from the assessment of the educational environment.

Data for clinical diagnosis include reports from psychologists, medical personnel, or speech therapists. Data from interviews and questionnaires, diagnostic lessons, and tests are also used. In clinical diagnosis there is a heavy reliance upon a variety of testing instruments. Physical screening tests, intelligence tests, attitude surveys, and a host of reading tests are available for use in clinical diagnosis.

In each type of diagnosis, information from the students can be very useful and is often overlooked. How does the reader see the difficulty? What are the reader's perceived strengths? What is his/her perception of the learning environment? We have found these types of data from readers useful for planning instructional programs.

GUIDELINES FOR DIAGNOSIS

Several guidelines should be understood as one enters into diagnostic activities. While they may not be applicable in every instance, failure to use them when indicated can drastically interfere with student performance.

To Establish Rapport

For students to perform at their best, a situation must be established where tensions are relaxed and they are encouraged into a cooperative attitude. The reading specialist, confronted with conducting diagnosis outside normal classroom situations, must be aware of this necessity. The classroom teacher, through daily contact with the student, has much more opportunity for establishing rapport.

To Provide for Individual Study

Since many group testing situations tend to produce unreliable results, individual study is essential. Individual sessions with students tend to reduce those competitive activities that are frustrating to low-achieving readers.

To Provide for Group Study

Evaluation of students as they interact can offer useful diagnostic insights. Diagnostic results that come from data collected during individual study only are often difficult for teachers to apply. Students' reactions in groups may be quite different from their performances during individual study. Obviously, both types of data are needed for a thorough diagnosis.

To Test, not Teach

By resisting the urge to help students when they experience difficulty during testing, the tester can assure more accurate data. Comments such as "That was almost correct—try again," can serve to encourage some students and discourage others. This guideline applies most directly to clinical diagnosis and test administration. Of course, diagnostic teaching activities involve normal student-teacher interactions.

To Maintain Efficiency

In terms of efficiency, a diagnosis includes only those tests and observations that are likely to help the examiner determine the difficulty. There is a tendency to rely upon a systematic diagnostic procedure regardless of the needs of the student, creating pointless testing situations, which are often frustrating experiences. An efficient diagnosis, then,

I've learned two important and contrasting bits of knowledge about reading diagnosis. First, diagnosis is essential to good teaching. We must provide students with appropriate and meaningful instruction based on the learner's strengths as well as needs. Diagnosis provides this information.

Secondly, I've found that many teachers feel alienated by and isolated from the diagnostic process. They think of diagnosis as formal tests, administered in a formal setting by someone unknown and unaccustomed to classroom realities. These teachers don't realize diagnosis is an inherent part of reading instruction that benefits the learner and teacher.

We need to destroy these myths. Diagnosis is, indeed, more than formal tests, and, without question, can and should be performed by classroom teachers as well as trained clinicians. It is also important for those engaged in reading instruction to realize that certain learning situations, such as oral reading and questioning, are natural opportunities for effective diagnosis.

Further, teachers need to know that while there are times when informal or classroom diagnosis is appropriate, there are also instances when more formal, clinical diagnosis is warranted. Those involved in the teaching of reading should learn about the diagnostic options available to them, and the circumstances under which these options should be applied. Not only does chapter 2 present these options well, but it underlines their differences, similarities and uses.

One of the threads of similarity that runs through all these diagnostic procedures, whether informal, classroom or clinic, is the emphasis placed on the learner's strengths. Such a diagnostic focus should be applauded. For too long I have seen diagnosis perceived as a forum from which only the problems of the reader have been reported extensively. The results of this limited view of diagnosis have been very negative feelings and reactions on the part of parents, teachers and learners. It is time we extolled the strengths of learners and used their strengths as our instructional foundation. This does not mean we ignore a learner's needs, only that we approach them by way of that learner's strengths.

Finally, as so aptly stated by Wilson, "It should be remembered that the student who is the object of the diagnosis is more important that the accumulation of test scores." All those entrusted with the education of others must comprehend diagnosis as the means by which they can help the learner achieve success within the classroom, a success rightly deserved.

Patricia A. Alexander

is one that includes those measures needed by the educator to arrive at a solution; it eliminates those of questionable value to the objectives of the diagnosis.

To Search for Patterns of Performance

Single observations of a reader's performance can lead to unreliable conclusions. A consistent pattern of performance over time, or over different testing situations, increases probability that the results are a true indication of the reader's skills. For example, it would be best to check the student's reading comprehension skills with several passages at the same level. If a student scores well on one and poorly on another, it is difficult to determine whether the difficulty lies in the passage or the reader's comprehension. By checking on a few more passages, the teacher could confirm or reject that suspicion with more confidence.

DIAGNOSIS FOR STRENGTHS

Though a student's weaknesses naturally would be the concern of the teacher, diagnosis for strengths is equally important. Since instructional adjustment should start with areas of strengths, deliberate diagnosis to determine those strengths is necessary. However, as we observe diagnostic reports of students with reading problems, we frequently find no mention of their strengths. All students have strengths. Each student should be made aware of them and teachers should note them during diagnosis. In fact, given a choice, I favor diagnosis for strengths. What students know is important. What they do not know can be assumed from what they do know. As we moved toward strengths diagnosis at the University of Maryland Clinic, we noticed that educators receiving the report felt better about the reports and the students. Parents also appreciated them, for most of them had only negative reports of their child's scholastic performance. Most important was our opportunity to discuss diagnostic results with the students in terms of their skill strengths. Such conferences with students left them feeling worthwhile.

When diagnosing for strengths, teachers must look for student performances that demonstrate comfort, fluency, accuracy, and speed. These can be observed during instruction or during testing. Satisfactory test scores evaluated without these characteristics of performance may be misleading in attempts to identify strengths. The following are examples of diagnostic activities for strengths:

1. Instead of listing skill weaknesses on a phonics test, list those skills that were noted as accurate and well developed.
2. Determine comprehension levels at which students can respond with comfort and accuracy. Report those levels as suggested starting levels for instruction.
3. Note skills demonstrated in oral reading and report them as skills that should be practiced and reinforced.
4. Ask the student to indicate his or her perceived reading strengths. Then set up a diagnostic situation in which those strengths can be demonstrated.

Diagnosis for strengths does not preclude the noting of areas in need of attention. It does add a dimension to diagnosis that is pleasant and positive.

SUMMARY

The three types of diagnosis discussed in this chapter have an important place in reading diagnosis. Each uses data that are available and procedures that are effective in that type of diagnosis. Guidelines for diagnosis are provided to help teachers avoid some of the activities that interfere with effective diagnosis. Diagnosing for strengths is a recommended procedure.

SUGGESTED READINGS

Kennedy, Eddie C., *Classroom Approaches to Remedial Reading*. Itasca, Ill.: F. E. Peacock, 1977. The nature and purpose of diagnosis are discussed in chapter 2. Kennedy approaches diagnosis from a slightly different point of view and is recommended for study.

Rupley, William H. and Blair, Timothy R., *Reading Diagnosis and Remediation*. Chicago: Rand McNally, 1979. The authors make a strong case in Chapter 6 for a study of the educational environment. Included is a teacher effort scale that should be of interest if you plan to assess the environment.

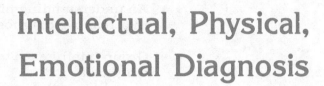

3

Intellectual, Physical, Emotional Diagnosis

Intellectual Diagnosis
Physical Diagnosis
Emotional Diagnosis

Chapter Emphasis

- An understanding of the role of intelligence is critical in a reading diagnosis.

- Group intelligence tests are inappropriate for reading diagnosis.

- Physical disabilities may impair reading progress.

- Symptoms of emotional disturbances can be cause and effect of reading difficulties.

This chapter will assist the educator in identifying potential problems that may be interfering with achievement in reading. It will also assist in making referrals effectively, and recognizing the difficulties involved with diagnosis in each of the areas—intellectual, physical, and emotional.

Diagnosis discussed in this chapter requires specialized training outside the field of reading. However, teachers and reading specialists should be informed about this diagnosis, even if they are unqualified to conduct it.

INTELLECTUAL DIAGNOSIS

Estimates of intellectual potential are useful in diagnosing reading difficulties. An estimate of the student's potential can assist the teacher in setting realistic instructional goals. Such goals should be flexible, however, for the best measures of intelligence are subject to error. Therefore, recognition of the advantages and limitations of measures of intelligence is essential for interpretation of such data in a reading diagnosis.

As a cause of reading difficulties, intelligence is suspect. In fact, intelligence is related to causes of reading difficulties only in relation to the ability of the school to adjust the educational program to the abilities of various types of students. It is important to realize that it is not intelligence—or lack of it—that prohibits students from reading up to their potential; rather, it is that school programs, which are often geared to the majority of average students, do not give ample consideration to those at the extremes (the bright and dull students). The inability of a given situation to provide the necessary adjustments often causes bright or dull students to become low achievers. Although accurate measures of intellectual performance are essential to the diagnosis of reading problems, the intelligence of a given student per se is not the cause of the difficulty.

Complications of Intellectual Testing

Complicating the use of intelligence tests is the educator's tendency to misuse test scores by grasping at high or low scores as the most easily observable division between low-achieving and normal readers. How many students have thus been labeled can only be estimated; that many have been mislabeled is fact. A brief review of the limitations of measures of potential will indicate the difficulties encountered when such data are used in diagnosis.

Reliability.   Has the test measured consistently? Has the test measured by chance? If students were to retake the test, would they obtain the same scores? All test scores are subject to error; therefore, most test constructors provide information about the test error in the teacher's guide. Error information is of two types, reliability coefficient and standard error of measurement. *Reliability coefficients* are usually reported in decimals (e.g., .90). Reliability coefficients below the .90 level cause concern about test reliability.

The *standard error of measurement* is usually reported in terms of the raw score or mental age score on the test (e.g., four months). The basis of the standard error is as follows. If students were to take the test repeatedly, their scores would fall within a range of plus or minus four months of the score obtained with the current administration. Therefore, if a student obtained a mental age score of 9.5 months and the test had a standard error of four months, that student's score would be interpreted as falling somewhere between 9.1 and 9.9 months about two-thirds of the time. For students who score in the extremes, very high or very low, errors of measurement are greater than for those scoring in the middle or average ranges of the test. The necessity for awareness of reliability and standard error scores becomes clear. Without this information, one cannot interpret a given score.

Validity.   Does a test measure what it purports to measure? Validity involves the problem of what intelligence is. Of the many dimensions that intelligence must surely have, most tests measure only a few; some measure only one. Presumably, the most prominent aspects of intelligence have been included in the best-constructed tests. While a test that measures listening comprehension is measuring a significant aspect of intelligence, the resulting score—called a *mental age*—implies more than can be covered by such a narrow measure. Another complication is encountered when a given test also requires specifically learned skills, such as reading. The test's validity is then weakened because the test score is also a measure of the reading achievement of the person taking the test.

Most test constructors attempt to prove the validity of their measure by comparing the results of their test with another test, usually one of established reputation. This is called *concurrent validity*. These figures usually appear as decimals (e.g., .70). For purposes of interpretation the decimal must be squared (.49) to find the percent (49 percent) of the variance measured, in common, by each test.

Validity may also be determined, if the content of the test represents an adequate sampling of the knowledge and skills it is designed to measure. This is called *content validity. Predictive validity* means that a test score can predict some future achievement with accuracy.

When two tests of intelligence are administered, a student probably will obtain two scores that often are quite different. Then the problem is to determine which score is more valid. However, an obvious concern arises. Would the student have scored differently on yet another measure?

To complicate validity further, many tests contain problems that are dependent upon cultural experiences. Students from cultures other than those on which the test was normed may score significantly worse than students from cultures similar to the ones on which the test was normed. In such cases, is the test a valid measure of intelligence? Obviously not.

Test administration, scoring, and interpretation. Despite the efforts of the American Psychological Association, persons other than qualified psychologists administer intelligence tests. Many of these people do so without training and without directed supervision; they often make serious errors in test administration, scoring, and interpretation. Tests administered by untrained personnel must be held suspect and should not be considered useful information in a reading diagnosis.

Group Intelligence Tests

For several reasons, group tests of intelligence are inappropriate for students suspected of having reading difficulty. First, many of the group tests require that students read in order to take the test. Obviously, if they cannot read well, their scores will reflect poor reading as well as intelligence, and the two will be hopelessly confused. Second, rapport is difficult to establish in group testing. For students who have been subjected to considerable failure, any group test may threaten them further and result in a poor performance. Third, the reliability of many of the group tests is very poor, making score interpretation nearly impossible. MacDonald comments on the difficulty with group intelligence tests.

> Because both group-type intelligence tests and reading achievement tests involve reading, the common element present in both kinds of tests represents two measures of the same categories of skill. Poor readers are double penalized with significant underestimation of probable mental ability.[1]

Awareness of the limitations inherent in measures of intellectual performance will lessen the possibility of intelligence test scores' being used or interpreted improperly. For the best assessment of intellectual performance, at least one of the measures of intelligence must be individual and nonreading in nature. Major discrepancies between test scores are justifiable reasons for referral for psychological examination. An accurate I.Q. is not found by averaging conflicting scores.

Considering the limitations of intelligence testing and particularly of group testing, it seems inconceivable that school reading personnel would use such scores to control admission to a program to aid those having reading difficulty. However, many schools limit admission to reading programs to those with group intelligence test scores above a certain score. Such a practice seems indefensible and should be changed, since a student who needs help might well be denied it. Furthermore, that same student might score much higher on an individual measure. Discrimination of this type is not based on a knowledge of the instruments being used.

Instead of relying on such scores, other options are available. What is the nature of a student's reading difficulty? How long has the problem existed? How does the teacher feel about it? How did last year's teacher feel about it? Is there any evidence of school success outside the language areas? Eventually the school will have to deal with such a case, for every student has the right to the best program possible.

Measures of Potential Reading Ability Suitable for Clinical Diagnosis

1. *Revised Stanford-Binet Intelligence Scale.* The Binet test may be administered and scored only by personnel with formal course work and laboratory experience. The test ranges from preschool to adulthood, yielding a mental age and an intelligence quotient. The test measures several aspects of intelligence, is heavily verbal, takes about one hour to administer, is individual in nature, and requires precise administration and interpretation for reliable results.

2. *Wechsler Intelligence Scale for Children—Revised (WISC–R).* Another popular, accurate test of intellectual performance, the WISC–R (page 58) requires individual administration and should be administered by personnel who have had formal course work and laboratory experience. Measuring several aspects of intelligence, the WISC yields performance and verbal scores, with the verbal score normally considered the more valid predictor of performance in reading. With problem readers, however, the performance score probably provides the better measure of reading potential. The students' verbal scores may be limited by the same factors that limit their performance in reading. Deal summarized fourteen studies of WISC subscores and found that the researchers were far from unanimous in their findings concerning interpretation of subscores.[2] Farr, summarizing sixteen studies, found several fairly consistent subscore patterns on the WISC for retarded readers.[3] No cause-and-effect relationship was determined, however. The teacher is cautioned about the use and interpretation of such

subscores for reading diagnosis and subsequent adjustment of instruction. Since WISC scores are best interpreted by psychological personnel, most reading personnel should await their analysis. The *Wechsler Adult Intelligence Scale* (WAIS), also available, may be used with older children and adults. Both the WISC–R and the WAIS take approximately one hour to administer.

3. Quick assessments of intelligence. The Slosson Intelligence Test, The Ammons Full Range Picture Vocabulary Test, and the Peabody Picture Vocabulary Test are examples of easy-to-administer, quick assessments of some of the behavior that is an indicator of intelligence. Such abbreviated measures should be treated cautiously, since their brevity also influences their reliability. If scores obtained on quick tests are exceedingly high or low, a more careful analysis of intelligence is needed. Since the test can be administered quickly, the constructors had to eliminate many of the aspects of intelligence and rely upon, in some cases, only one. This raises the question of validity. Neville, however, found no significant differences between the scores of fifty two children on the Peabody and the WISC.[4] I advocate the use of such tests only as initial indicators of student potential.

4. *Durrell Listening-Reading Series.* As another measure of auding ability, these tests require students to associate words and paragraphs that have been read to them with pictures. The auding scores then are compared to reading vocabulary and reading paragraph scores. Testing time requires approximately eighty minutes and requires little formal preparation for either administration or scoring.

5. Arithmetic Computation. For students who have attended school for two or more years, a test of arithmetic computation, not involving verbal problems, is useful in estimating academic potential. Included as a factor on several intelligence scales, arithmetic computation scores show how well students succeed in school in nonverbal tasks, thus providing an indication of their levels of potential. Arithmetic computation scores verify suspicions of potential that has gone undetected, when they vary noticeably from reading achievement. In some types of more seriously handicapped readers, arithmetic computation scores do not indicate potential. This is especially true when students react against the total

Sample

WISC-R RECORD FORM

Wechsler Intelligence Scale
for Children—Revised

NAME _____ AGE _____ SEX _____
ADDRESS _____
PARENT'S NAME _____
SCHOOL _____ GRADE _____
PLACE OF TESTING _____ TESTED BY _____
REFERRED BY _____

WISC-R PROFILE

Clinicians who wish to draw a profile should first transfer the child's *scaled scores* to the row of boxes below. Then mark an X on the dot corresponding to the scaled score for each test, and draw a line connecting the X's.*

VERBAL TESTS — PERFORMANCE TESTS

Verbal Tests: Information, Similarities, Arithmetic, Vocabulary, Comprehension, Digit Span

Performance Tests: Picture Completion, Picture Arrangement, Block Design, Object Assembly, Coding, Mazes

Scaled Score: 19, 18, 17, 16, 15, 14, 13, 12, 11, 10, 9, 8, 7, 6, 5, 4, 3, 2, 1

*See Chapter 4 in the manual for a discussion of the significance of differences between scores on the tests.

NOTES

Date Tested	Year	Month	Day
Date of Birth			
Age			

	Raw Score	Scaled Score
VERBAL TESTS		
Information	_____	_____
Similarities	_____	_____
Arithmetic	_____	_____
Vocabulary	_____	_____
Comprehension	_____	_____
(Digit Span)	(_____)	(_____)
Verbal Score		_____
PERFORMANCE TESTS		
Picture Completion	_____	_____
Picture Arrangement	_____	_____
Block Design	_____	_____
Object Assembly	_____	_____
Coding	_____	_____
(Mazes)	(_____)	(_____)
Performance Score		_____

	Scaled Score	IQ
Verbal Score	_____*	_____
Performance Score	_____*	_____
Full Scale Score	_____	_____

*Prorated from 4 tests, if necessary.

learning environment with emotional rejection. Arithmetic computation, however, remains a valuable tool as one of the first indicators of intellectual potential.

Other measures of intellectual performance are available for clinical diagnosis; however, most of them require special preparation and laboratory experience, as do the Binet and the WISC–R.

Measures of Potential Reading Ability Suitable for Classroom Diagnosis

1. The Binet and the WISC–R. These are not normally administered by the classroom teacher, but their scores are often found in the school records of the problem readers. The other tests mentioned under clinical diagnosis can be administered by a classroom teacher as part of normal school procedure or as a part of classroom diagnosis.

2. Group Intelligence Tests. Although group intelligence tests are inherently unsatisfactory in reading diagnosis, several of them do separate reading and nonreading factors. The *California Test of Mental Maturity*, for example, provides an M.A. and I.Q. for both language and nonlanguage performance. The teacher who uses this type of test and finds a major discrepancy between the two scores (e.g., nonlanguage I.Q.—125, language I.Q.—100) should be looking for other signs of intellectual performance, for the student may be capable but hindered in the language section by lack of reading ability. Other measures of reading potential, such as those mentioned under clinical diagnosis, should then be checked, or the student should be referred for an individual intelligence examination. However, unless group intelligence tests have nonlanguage features, they are not useful in estimating the reading potential of students with reading problems. Even then, their usefulness is highly questionable.

3. Teacher Observation. The experienced teacher often is able to note characteristics of reading potential through direct observation of the student's response to various school activities. Roswell and Natchez state that a teacher "can form some idea of the child's intellectual ability from his general responsiveness in class."[5] Specifically, noticeable characteristics follow:

   1. Ability to participate effectively in class discussions, both listening and speaking

A student's score on a given test is only a reflection of the student's total ability.

2. Ability to achieve more successfully in arithmetic than in subjects requiring reading
3. Ability to participate effectively in peer group activities
4. Ability to demonstrate alert attitudes toward the world
5. Ability to perform satisfactorily on spelling tests

Admittedly, such observations are not highly reliable indications of reading potential. Teacher observation is limited by the possibilites of teacher bias; they may well see just what they are looking for. For example, a teacher's observation may be controlled somewhat by previous test scores and prior impressions of the student. However, ability in the above areas is often the first symptom to be noted. By such observations, students who have been intellectually misjudged may be referred for more accurate evaluations.

Remember that a student's score on a given test is only a reflection of total ability. The student is always greater as a person than any test score can show. Therefore, teachers are encouraged to look for the best in all students.

Reading Potential and Degree of Retardation

Measures of intellectual performance greatly aid in determining the degree of reading retardation. A comparison of the best estimates of reading potential with the best estimates of reading achievement will result in an arithmetical difference. When potential exceeds achievement, one is concerned that the student is not working up to capacity. The larger the difference, the more serious the degree of retardation.

Perhaps the most common technique for estimating the seriousness of retardation is a simple comparison of *mental age grade equivalent* (I.Q. divided by 100, multiplied by chronological age (C.A.)—5) to reading achievement.[6] This technique is particularly limiting with very young children of high ability, for it assumes a considerable development of reading skills prior to school attendance. A six-year-old child with an I.Q. of 140 entering first grade may be considered to have a mental age of 8.4 $(140/100 \times 6.0 = 1.4 \times 6.0 = 8.4 - 5 = 3.4)$ but should not normally be expected to be reading at the third-grade level because of a lack of social, emotional, and educational experiences for that degree of achievement. Even with older bright students, this technique tends to place reading potential scores unrealistically high. On the other hand, acknowledging these limitations, one can estimate the seriousness of retardation by this technique. Harris recommends a formula that places priority on mental age (Reading Expectancy = 2MA + CA/3) as another alternative.[7]

Bond and Tinker circumvent the limitations mentioned above by using the formula (I.Q./100 multiplied by years in school + 1.0) as compared to reading achievement.[8] The child discussed above would have a reading potential of 1.0 upon entrance to the first grade.

$$(\frac{140}{100} \times 0) + 1.0 = 1.0$$

As children advance through school, this approach expects them to make accelerated progress, so that upon entrance to third grade these same children are expected to be reading at the 3.8 grade level:

$$(\frac{140}{100} \times 2.0) + 1.0 = 3.8$$

Bond and Tinker's research shows that this formula is much more realistic than formulas using mental age, such as that mentioned above.[9] In using this formula, consideration must be given to three factors. First, it must be understood that the term years in school does not mean the student's grade placement, but rather, the actual number of years of school completed. Therefore, for a student who has a grade placement of 4.8 and who has not accelerated or repeated a grade, the appropriate entry would be 3.8 for years in school. (For this formula, kindergarten does not count as a year in school.) Second, the teacher must have accurate data concerning the grades repeated or accelerated. Third, the addition of 1.0 years in the formula is to compensate for the manner in which grade norms are assigned to tests, 1.0 being the zero month of first grade. Despite its obvious advantages, most teachers, lacking complete understanding of it, refrain from using this formula.

Cleland prefers to average four factors, giving equal weight to each, in arriving at a reading potential score that is compared to reading achievement.[10] In this formula, he computes the grade equivalents of chronological age, mental age, arithmetic computation, and the *Durrell-Sullivan Reading Capacity Test:*

C.A.	− 5 = 6 − 5	= 1.0
M.A.	− 5 = 8.4 − 5	= 3.4
Arith. C.		= 1.5
D/S Cap.		= 2.5
		$8.4 \div 4 = 2.1$

This formula has several advantages: first, although mental age is used without the compensation that Bond and Tinker give, it is equalized somewhat by the use of chronological age; second, the use of reading capacity adds auding as a factor (any auding test can be substituted for a capacity score); and, third, the use of arithmetic computation provides measures of the student's ability to do nonverbal school work. It is important to note that grade equivalents of M.A. and C.A. are obtained by subtracting five for the five years the child did not attend school. (Harris recommends subtracting 5.2.) This formula, or variations of it, is commonly used in clinical diagnosis. We find it compares much more favorably to the Bond and Tinker formula than to the mental age formulas.

To compare the child's score on a test of auding with achievement test performance is another relatively easy way of determining the degree of retardation. In this case, the auding score is an estimate of reading potential and may be obtained from tests such as the *Peabody Picture Vocabulary Test* and the *Botel Listening Tests.* On the Peabody, the auding age equivalent may be converted to grade equivalent by subtracting five years.

How large the difference between reading potential and achievement must be to be considered serious will vary with the grade placement of the student. There may be many students who fall slightly short of full reading potential, yet would not be considered problem readers. Older students can manage a larger variance between potential and achievement without the severe ramifications that occur with younger students.

The scale in Table 3–1 may be useful in selecting a cutoff point between a tolerable difference and one that is sufficient to interfere with the child's progress in reading and other subjects. Tolerable differences are presented in this table by individal grade groupings. Although this scale should not be adhered to rigidly, it does provide reasonably useful limits. However, since diagnosis includes considerably more analysis than the estimation of potential and achievement, it would be folly indeed for the educator to evaluate progress in reading by this technique alone.

Table 3–1   **Degree of Tolerable Difference Between Potential and Achievement**

End of Grade:	Tolerable Difference (in Years)
1, 2, and 3	.5
4, 5, and 6	1
7, 8, and 9	1.5
10, 11, and 12	2

Note: Tolerable difference ranges must be used as judgment points, not as absolutes.

When selecting the method for computing the degree of reading retardation, the following factors should be considered:

1. The number and type of students selected as retarded in reading will vary with the method employed.

2. Each method is only as good as the instruments used to obtain the scores for its computation.
3. A student with a specific skill deficiency may not be discovered by these types of formulas.

It is useful to include the standard error of measurement when reporting reading potential scores. In Figure 3-1, the student's chronological age, auding, age, oral reading accuracy score, and silent reading comprehension score have been plotted. The two heavy lines reflect the standard error plus and minus the actual potential score.

Figure 3-1   **Comparing Expectancy Range with Other Reading Variables**

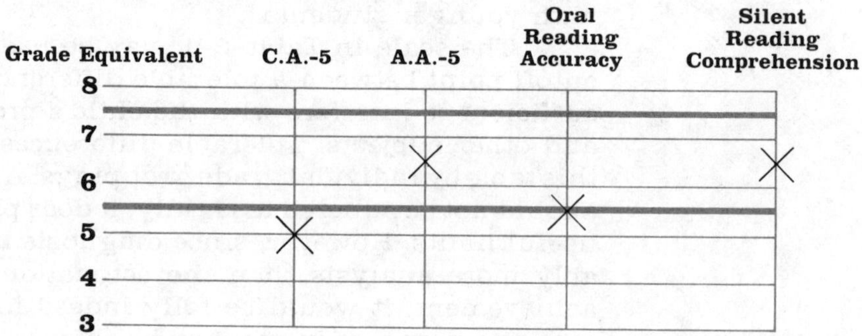

Although neither reading score is as high as the auding age, both of them fall within the standard error of the auding age. This treatment of auding scores expresses to all who receive the report that the score should not be taken as a precise measure.

Some Additional Cautions

Many students could fail to receive the help they need if potential formulas are used as the only indicators of need. Students with specific skill deficiencies or attitudinal problems might well be missed. Students with low potential scores might need a language development program prior to or in conjunction with the start of a reading program.[11] On a given day, a student might well score differently on the reading tests. These and many other problems call for examiners to evaluate the total reader, not just the test scores. Attention to the reader's responses during testing

Editorial

Anthony did not like school. More specifically, he did not like being in my reading class. I took some solace in the fact that records indicated that he had not liked being in previous classes either. But now Anthony was a sixth grader with developing emotional problems. Also, he could not read very well. Standardized tests placed him about four years behind his peers, with a general weakness in most skill areas. Still, Anthony seemed bright. He could argue his case logically in class discussions and he was a leader among his classmates. He took charge of most playground activities, and other children would collect at his desk during any free moments of the day. When it came time for reading, Anthony would often become sullen and look for other things to do. Frequently, he would begin an emotional outburst with a statement intended to hurt or anger a designated target. It was obvious to me that he was embarrassed by his reading problem. Unfortunately, there seemed to be no way to relieve this apparent embarrassment.

One day, however, an interesting thing happened. Anthony came to me and said that his mother's birthday was coming soon and he had saved about three dollars to buy her a present. He asked my opinion as to a gift and I could tell by his expression that he had far more expensive hopes. I suggested an alternative plan. He would surrender his money to me and I would get the ingredients for a cake, a cake he would bake and decorate in school. Anthony liked the idea. The cake was magnificent and it was made with the help of the school secretary and cafeteria staff. No less amazing than the cake was the change in Anthony's attitude over the ensuing weeks. He attempted most of the reading assignments without quarrel and even filled his free time with independent reading. I suspect that Anthony realized that his reading problem did not diminish his value to his teacher and his friends. We liked him just as much anyway! By the end of the year, Anthony was reading in sixth-grade materials and as cocky as ever. I remember a final challenge to me to "pick any book in our room, pick any page" and he would read it. I did and he did.

Gerald L. Fowler

may be more important than the resulting score. How the use of potential fits into classroom and clinical diagnosis is discussed in the following two chapters.

Realistically, the reading specialist should be ready to offer assistance to any teacher who is having difficulty with either assessing or instructing any student. The nature of the resource role is to help when needed. If specialists restrict their assistance to certain types of students, then the teachers will not see the specialist as a helpful resource. If a student is in a non–learning environment, then every effort should be made to change that environment.

PHYSICAL DIAGNOSIS

A physical limitation is considered a cause of a reading difficulty when it interferes with a student's potential and performance. If Sara cannot see a printed page adequately, she cannot be expected to read it as well as her potential indicates she should. Whose job is it to assess the severity of physical disability? Although physical limitations are recognized first in a classroom or clinical diagnosis, medical personnel or other specialists are responsible for specific identification, corrective measures, and recommendations. Both the reading specialist and the classroom teacher can refer students either on the basis of reliable patterns of symptoms or as a result of certain screening devices available to educators.

Specifically, the areas of physical diagnosis of reading problems are general visual, auditory, and neurological health. Limitations in these areas that are serious enough to interfere with performance in reading are also likely to interfere with general educational performance. However, a general educational deficiency does not necessarily indicate physical disabilities.

General Health

Large numbers of students are not healthy enough to profit efficiently from the instruction provided, even under the best of conditions. Educators should know those aspects of general health that interfere with school progress and should be evaluated in the diagnosis of reading problems.

Malnutrition. Malnutrition causes the student to lose weight or to lag behind in physical and mental vitality.

Malnutrition does not necessarily show itself in loss of weight, however. Many suffering from diet imbalance are quite chubby (e.g., those suffering from imbalance of starches). The sluggish behavior that results interferes with school performance.

Glandular defects.   These have also been diagnosed as causing educational problems. When the glands that maintain important balances in the body fail, more than physical discomfort may result.

Mental or physical fatigue.   Caused by lack of sleep, poor sleeping habits, lack of exercise, or overexertion, mental or physical fatigue can cause students to be inattentive and easily distracted in a learning situation.

Poor general physical condition.   Often characterized by frequent illness, poor general physical condition causes a lack of stamina with resulting gaps in the educational instruction. Factors such as overweight, underweight, poor teeth, hay fever, etc., can result in difficulty with school tasks.

Alertness to signs of poor health is essential in a reading diagnosis. Many such cases are first identified by individual attention to a student's performance during diagnosis.

The classroom teacher combines information from school records, reports from the school nurse and the family doctor, information from the parents, and observable symptoms that are characteristic of students with general physical deficiencies. Sluggishness, inattentiveness, failure to complete assignments, apparent lack of interest, sleeping in school, and general lack of vitality often are symptoms that cause a student to be labeled lazy or indifferent. Classroom teachers should observe these symptoms, contact the home to report the problem, and make medical referrals when appropriate. At the same time, they should adjust the instruction to make the learning environment as comfortable as possible for the student. This adjustment may take the form of relaxing the tension caused by the student's apparent indifference, allowing the fatigued student a program of varied activities and necessary rest periods, and, when necessary, following the recommendations of medical personnel. It does not take a medical report to make us aware that all students, not just those with reading problems, need good health for optimal school performance. Necessities such as adequate rest, a balanced diet (particularly a good breakfast), annual physical checkups, and large doses of play activity after school are vital requirements for good school performance.

One of the reading specialist's responsibilities in diagnosis is to evaluate reports received from medical personnel in terms of the total case picture of the student involved and to recommend the appropriate classroom adjustment and/or remedial program.

Visual Diagnosis

The classroom teacher is aware that deficiencies in visual ability and ocular comfort may well impede a student's growth in reading. Reports relate that from 15 to 40 percent of students need professional visual attention. The relationship of vision to low achievement in reading is complicated, since many students with visual problems are not low achievers. The more careful research reports show a relationship between certain types of visual deficiencies and failure in reading and have found that certain visual disabilities and ocular discomfort greatly interfere with students' reaching their reading potentials.[12] In general, functional problems, such as awkward eye movements and poor fusion, more often cause reading difficulty than do organic difficulties, such as nearsightedness, farsightedness, or astigmatism. A review of some of the aspects of vision and ocular comfort clarifies the relationship.

Acuity. Acuity, the clearness of vision, is normally measured at far-point targets (a Snellen Chart twenty feet away from the student). Such screening tests of acuity provide us with information concerning the student's acuity at the far point (e.g., ability to see the chalkboard). The results of this type of visual screening are expressed in terms of what the average person can see at twenty feet. The term 20/20 means that a person can see at twenty feet the same target that a person with normal vision can see at twenty feet. This test, when used alone, however, cannot detect all visual deficiencies. In the first place, we do not normally read targets that are twenty feet from the eyes; neither do we read with one eye at a time. The eyes must efficiently move from one target to another, rather than merely fixing on and identifying a target. Kelley claims,

"The misconception that the Snellen Chart will do an efficient job of screening out students who need visual care is a major block in the road of those trying to establish good school visual screening programs.[13]

Screening devices to measure near-point acuity are desirable in the diagnosis of a low achiever, although they generally take more time and training to administer properly. One who passes the Snellen Chart may still have a visual deficiency that is causing problems in reading. The farsighted reader, seeing far-point targets better than near-point targets, may pass the Snellen Chart yet not see well enough or efficiently enough to read with comfort at the near point. The nearsighted reader, who sees near-point targets better than far-point targets, is likely to fail the Snellen Chart; but, while obviously limited by a visual defect, she may read effectively in most cases. Therefore, effective visual screening must measure both far- and near-point acuity. This need has been partially met by the development of a type of chart for use at a distance of fourteen inches. Additional techniques described below are generally more desirable for accurate near point screening.

Fusion.   Fusion involves the ability of the brain to blend or fuse the image from each eye into an adequate image. A student who looks with one eye and psychologically blinds the other gets a clear image but does not have good fusion. Those with sluggish fusion seldom see a clear target adequately; thus, they experience ocular discomfort and inefficiency that should be identified in a visual screening.

Color recognition.   It is important for the young child to recognize colors accurately. Simple far-point color blindness tests generally are adequate for screening, with the precise measurement of color limitation left to the vision specialist. The reading teacher, with a knowledge of the student's color confusion problems, does not expect the student to perform in tasks requiring color discrimination.

Ocular motility.   The efficient operation of the eye in motion is requisite for effective reading. In particular, ocular motility refers to good left-to-right motion (pursuit), saccadic movement, fixations, and focusing power. Screening devices are available for evaluation in these areas and should be included in a visual screening.

1. Left-to-right motion: In the reading act, the eyes must fix on a target, move to the right, fix on another target, move to the right, fix on another target, then sweep back and take hold of the next line in a manner that is not natural at birth, but learned. Students who are grossly inefficient at this task of left-to-right eye movement or accurate fixation will likely experience difficulty in the reading act.

2. Pursuit eye movement: Eyes should be able to follow a moving target smoothly, not stopping and starting, but following with an effortless, fluid movement. The ability to do so allows students the efficient eye motion between fixations without which they are likely to have trouble following a line of print.

3. Saccadic eye movement: Accurate change of fixations from one word to another or from the end of a line of print to the beginning of the next line is an important ocular-motor skill related to reading. When deficient in this skill, students lose their places, skip words, and read more slowly than is necessary.

4. Focusing power: Prolonged reading demands the power to maintain focus on a target for a long time. The student with deficient focusing power is likely to become fatigued much sooner than others.

5. Binocular vision: During the reading act, some students tend to suppress the vision of one eye and do all the reading with the other. The continuation of this type of reading can lead to serious visual complications that can only be evaluated by the visual specialist.

The areas of ocular motility are seldom investigated in usual school screening; however, when diagnosing a reading problem, the teacher or reading specialist should make every effort to evaluate them.

1. A test using a telebinocular provides near- and far-point screening of acuity, stereopsis, and fusion, as well as a test of color vision. The proper administration and analysis of this test requires supervised experience to assure reliable results. It should be noted that the telebinocular screens the visual skills related to the ability of the eyes to fix only on a stationary target (See photo on page 71 and sample on page 72.)

2. The reading specialist must also be concerned about the

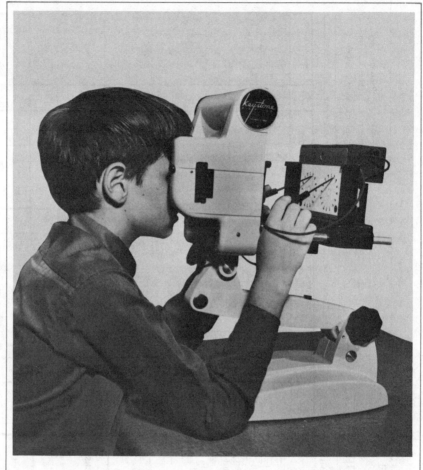

An example of a student using the Keystone Telebinocular.

eyes as they operate in reading situations. The *Spache-Binocular Reading Tests* provide an analysis of binocular vision during the reading act. In these tests, the student looks at a card that has been placed in the telebinocular and reads a story containing some words that only the right eye can see and some that only the left eye can see. By marking the student's responses, the examiner can determine the degree to which each eye operates in the reading act. Referral is based on certain characteristics that are identified in the accompanying manual.

Sample

KEYSTONE
School Vision Screening

FOR USE WITH THE KEYSTONE TELEBINOCULAR
SCHOOL SURVEY CUMULATIVE RECORD FORM NO. 5-B
(CATALOG ORDER NO. 5522-B)

RAPID VISION SCREENING TESTS

	Pass	Fail

DISTANT VISION TESTS

1A. Dog should be seen jumping over pig
The 4 blocks should be seen merged into 3

2A. Balloon No. 2 is farthest away }
Balloon No. 5 is closest
Balloon 2 is red; balloon 5 is green
Letters in Block A: D C Z P T
Letters in Block B: Z P D T C *
Letters in Block C: L D T C Z *   (Training only)

NEAR VISION TESTS (16 INCHES)

3A. Yellow line should pass through white square
The 4 balls should be seen merged into 3

4A. Letters in Block A: L O Z P C   (Training only)
Letters in Block B: T Z O D L *
Letters in Block C: O P T D C *

* Passing score: at least 4 letters

Failure on any test above indicates need for full test at right.

COMPREHENSIVE TEST BATTERY: QUESTIONS

1. What do you see?
2. Does the yellow line go through, above, or below the red ball?
3. To what number, or between what numbers, does the arrow point?
4. How many balls do you see?
4½. In each signboard there are five diamonds (point). In one diamond is a dot. (point to first signboard, show dot in the left diamond.) Ask: Where is the dot in Nos. 2, 3, 4, 5, etc.? Tests 5 and 6 are the same as No. 4½. Ask: Where is the dot?
7. (Point to the top line of symbols and name each one. Show hv pointing that the cross stands out in 3-D.) Ask: Which symbol stands out in each of the next lines?
8. What number is in the upper circle? The lower left? The lower right? (Test 9 is the same as Test 8.)
10. To what number, or between what numbers, does the arrow point?
11. How many balls do you see?
12. In the three circles in the center (point) you see black crossed lines, black dots, and solid gray. Starting with No. 1 of the outer circles, you see black dots. No. 2 has black dots. What do you see in No. 3? Go as far as you can. Tests 13 and 14 are the same as 12: Name what you see in each of the circles.

Copyright 1972 by Keystone View   73-6386

Name _____ Sex _____ City _____
School _____
Grade _____ Room _____ Teacher _____
Date of birth _____ Date of test _____

Wearing glasses? Yes: For reading only _____ No _____
for distance only _____ ; both _____
Snellen Standard (if desired)
With glasses: RE _____ LE _____
Without glasses: RE _____ LE _____

Examined by: _____

TEST	LEFT EYE ONLY	RIGHT EYE ONLY	UNSATISFACTORY (Underconvergence and/or low usable vision)	RE-TEST AREA	EXPECTED RESPONSE	RE-TEST AREA	UNSATISFACTORY (Overconvergence)

FAR POINT TESTS

Test	
1 (DB-10A) Simultaneous Vision	
2 (DB-8C) Vertical Posture	15 14 13 12 11 / 10 9 8
3 (DB-9) Lateral Posture	Arrow only
4 (DB-4K) Fusion	Close — Far apart
4½ (DB-1D) Usable Vision, Both Eyes	Top 32 / Left 79 ; Top 63 / Left 92 ; Right 23 / Right 56
5 (DB-3D) Usable Vision, Right Eye	Numbers only
6 (DB-2D) Usable Vision, Left Eye	Arrow only
6½ (DB-6D) Stereopsis	

Acuity scale (Tests 5 & 6):
1(49%) 1(49%) 2(70%) 3(84%) 4(84%) 5(92%) 6(96%) 7(98%) 8(100%) 9(103%) 10(105%)

NEAR POINT TESTS

Test	
8 (DB-13A) Color Perception	NONE CORRECT — 1 Out of 3 — 2 Out of 3 — ALL CORRECT
9 (DB-14A) Color Perception	NONE CORRECT — 1 Out of 3 — 2 Out of 3 — ALL CORRECT
10 (DB-9B) Lateral Posture	Numbers only
11 (DB-5K) Fusion	Close — Far apart
12 (DB-15) Usable Vision, Both Eyes	
13 (DB-16) Usable Vision, Right Eye	
14 (DB-17) Usable Vision, Left Eye	

Near acuity scale (Tests 12, 13, 14):
1 2 3 ... 22 ; 10% 13% 20% 30% 40% 50% 60% 70% 80% 90% 100% 102% 103% 105%

3. For screening pursuit, saccadic eye movements, and focusing power, a pocket flashlight is used in the following way: holding the light upright in front of the student, approximately eighteen inches from the eyes, the examiner asks the student to look at the light. The examiner then moves the light in a place eighteen inches from the eye in straight vertical, horizontal, and diagonal lines twelve to eighteen inches in length, and, then, in a circle with a radius of about twelve inches clockwise and counterclockwise. Referral should be considered if (1) students cannot follow the light without moving their heads, even after being told to hold still; (2) the reflection of the light cannot be seen in both a student's pupils at all times; or (3) the eye movements are saccadic (i.e., they follow the light jerkily instead of smoothly). To test converging power, the light is again held eighteen inches from the eye, moved slowly to a position one inch directly between the eyes and and held for one second. Since some students do not understand what they are to do the first time, there is justification for referral only if they cannot hold this fixation after three attempts.

Not having any of this screening equipment available, classroom teachers must rely upon a pattern of symptoms observable in the reading act or in other school situations. The check list prepared by the American Optometric Association (Table 3–2) includes a list of these symptoms.[14] Copies of this check list may be secured from the American Optometric Association, 4030 Chouteau Avenue, St Louis, Missouri. Note that this check list recommends that all students who are not performing well in terms of their capacity should be referred for visual examinations.

Students with these symptoms (see Table 3–2) normally will be referred to the school nurse; however, if screening equipment is limited to the Snellen Chart, the classroom teacher should report the observed behavior to the parents, with the recommendation of a complete visual examination by a specialist. Until the student receives treatment, the teacher should make every effort to provide a most comfortable and efficient visual environment. This may be accomplished by placing the student in a position of maximum lighting, by eliminating glare, by adjusting seating to ease board work, or by reducing the reading load.

Table 3-2

Teacher's Guide to Vision Problems with Check List

To aid teachers in detecting the children who should be referred for complete visual analysis, the American Optometric Association Committee on Visual Problems in Schools has complied a list of symptoms—a guide to vision problems. The committee recommends

1. That all children in the lower third of the class, particularly those with ability to achieve above their percentile rating, be referred for complete visual analysis
2. That every child in the class who, even though achieving, is not working within reasonable limits of his own capacity be referred for a complete visual analysis

Following are other symptoms that may indicate a visual problem, regardless of result in any screening test.

Observed in Reading:

  Dislike for reading and reading subjects
  Skipping or re-reading lines
††Losing place while reading
  Slow reading or word calling
  Poor perceptual ability, such as confusing o and a, n and m, etc.

Other Manifestations:

  Restlessness, nervousness, irritability or other unaccountable behavior
  Desire to use finger or marker as pointer while reading
††Avoiding close work
††Poor sitting posture and position while reading
  Fatigue or listlessness after close work
  Inattentiveness, temper tantrums, or frequent crying
  Complaint of blur when looking up from close work
  Seeing objects double
  Headaches, dizziness, or nausea associated with the use of eyes
††Body rigidity while looking at distant objects
  Undue sensitivity to light
  Crossed eyes—turning in or out
  Red-trimmed, crusted or swollen lids

Vocalizing during silent reading, noticed by watching lips or throat
  Reversals persisting in grade 2 or beyond
  Inability to remember what has been read
  Complaint of letters and lines "running together" or of words "jumping"
††Holding reading closer than normal
††Frowning, excessive blinking, scowling, squinting, or other facial distortions while reading
††Excessive head movements while reading
  Writing with face too close to work
  Frequent sties
  Watering or bloodshot eyes
  Burning or itching of eyes or eyelids
††Tilting head to one side
††Tending to rub eyes
  Closing or covering one eye
  Frequent tripping or stumbling
  Poor hand and eye coordination as manifested in poor baseball playing, catching and batting, or similar activities
††Thrusting head forward
††Tension during close work

Only a complete case study will determine whether inadequate vision is a significant factor in nonachievement.

††Found to be particularly significant in a recent study

Visual referral problems.   Referral in vision is complicated by the reluctance of educators to overrefer (i.e., referring a student who may not be in need of help). Kelley views the problem as follows:

> The cardinal purpose of school visual screening procedures is to refer children who may need visual care. It generally is considered more serious for a screening program to *fail to refer* a child in real need of care than for it to *refer* a child not actually in need of care.[15]

Shaw says:

> My opinion is that a child's first opthalmological examination should be given at about age three. . . . The persistence of abnormal symptoms would suggest the need for eye examination regardless of the results of a screening test.[16]

Ewalt sees the problem in overreferral as follows:

> You have heard screening programs seriously criticized because they refer too many youngsters for visual examination. Nonsense! Most of the agencies of this country, dealing with vision, whether they represent the opthalmologists as the National Association for the Prevention of Blindness, or the optometrists as the American Optometric Association agree that every school child should have an annual examination. If all school children need an annual examination, we need not be too concerned with an occasional overreferral.[17]

The schools, through their reluctance to refer, have permitted many students to operate daily with eye strain that leads to more complicated, permanent problems. I believe that all students should have periodic visual examinations by a specialist. Since most schools do not assume this responsibility, it remains a parental obligation. The teacher, then, should not hesitate to refer any student who demonstrates the symptoms in Table 3–2. This in no way implies than an undiscriminating attitude toward referral should be adopted; however, referral is the best way many students can receive necessary visual attention.

The necessity for visual referral is complicated further by changes in the eyes following visual adjustment.

The nature of school, requiring hours of near-point visual activities, may make it necessary for lenses to be changed periodically. Therefore, the teacher should not hesitate to refer students who have symptoms of visual discomfort, even if they are wearing glasses.

A third complication of referral is the strongly motivated student who, regardless of visual strain and discomfort, completes school work and shows no signs of academic deficiency. Again this student, showing symptoms listed in Table 3-2, should be referred without hesitation before the possibility of consequential harm.

Finally, one must choose to whom the referral should be made. The term *vision specialist* has been used to avoid complication. By *vision specialist* is meant an optometrist, an opthalmologist, or an oculist. A competent specialist in any of these fields should be considered satisfactory for referral. Opthalmologists and oculists are medical doctors who have specialized in vision. The optometrist has a doctor's degree in optometry. Each is qualified to prescribe lenses and visual training. In the case of eye disease, an optometrist will refer the patient to the ophthalmologist or oculist. Regardless of the degree held by the vision specialist, educators should make an effort to seek out those who have a special interest in the visual development of students and in the problems of functional vision that relate to reading achievement.

A form such as Figure 3-2 will aid the vision specialists in understanding the reasons for referral and will provide them with basic educational information.

The educator's tone when making a referral is especially important. If the educator's tone is authoritative, conflict with visual specialists and parents may occur. It is best to state the referral in a manner such as "Since Tom appears to be having serious difficulties in reading and since he has not had his eyes checked recently, we would like you to take him to a specialist for an examination. As we start to work with Tom, it will be best to correct any visual disorder first. If he has none, then we will not need to be concerned about visual disability."

In summary, both the reading specialist and classroom teacher should consider students who have difficulties with reading as potential visual problems. Therefore, they should use screening devices and observe symptoms to refer possible problem cases. Under no circumstances

Figure 3–2

> **Visual Referral Form**
>
> _Walter Fowler_ was screened visually and did not
> (Name)
> perform satisfactorily in the following area(s):
> _near point acuity   near point fusion_
> His/her present reading level is _beginning_
> _third grade level_, but his/her reading potential is
> about _upper sixth grade level_
>   Will you please inform us if, after your
> examination, a visual deficiency may have been
> causing this student some difficulties in reading?
>   _Ms. Alexander_
>   Signed

should the teacher or the reading specialist consider a battery of screening devices, no matter how highly refined, as a substitution for a thorough eye examination and visual analysis. Screening tests, at best, are limited to their designed function: the identification of those in need of visual attention.

Auditory Problems

Obviously, students who cannot hear adequately face problems in school. Many students with auditory limitations are placed in special schools or special classes for the deaf and hard-of-hearing so that they can receive specialized educational opportunities. Many others with hearing losses, however, remain in regular school situations. For the most part, school nurses have been able to identify these students early and to refer them to specialists.

Auditory problems affect reading in several ways. In the first place, students with a significant hearing loss are likely to find phonic instruction beyond their grasp because of a distortion of sounds or the inability to hear sounds at all. Most auditory deficiencies concern high frequency sounds; therefore, because of the high frequency of many of the consonant sounds, the most common limitation that a hearing deficiency places upon a reader is in the area of consonant recognition and usage. Students with hearing difficulties are hindered also by inability to follow directions, since they may not hear them clearly. They are, therefore, likely to lose their places in oral reading activities when listening to others, fail to complete homework assignments, and appear inattentive and careless.

It is important to recognize the difference between the student who is unable to hear a word and the one who is unable to discriminate between sounds. In the first case, the student has a hearing loss that is a physical problem, and, in the latter, the student has an auditory discrimination problem that has educational implications. Auditory discrimination will be discussed under educational diagnosis in chapter 4.

Ideally, auditory screening should include a test of pitch (frequency) ranging from low to high and one to measure varying loudness (decibels). This screening can be adequately conducted using an audiometer, (see photo and chart on page 80) an instrument adaptable for either group or individual auditory testing. Although opinions vary concerning a satisfactory audiometer score, it is safe to conclude that a screening score that reports a loss of twenty five decibels at 500, 1,000, 2,000 and 6,000 frequencies, and thirty decibels at 4,000, indicates possible interference with reading instruction and that such a student should be referred.[18]

It is unlikely that the classroom teacher has the time, experience, or equipment to conduct the type of screening mentioned above. Classroom teachers have been advised that a watchtick test or a whisper test is possible in the classroom. However, classroom teachers do not use these tests, perhaps because they have not had enough supervised experience with them and the possibilities of overreferral are too great. Therefore, the classroom teacher should rely upon a pattern of symptoms that, when observed in a student who has failed in reading, is justifiable cause for referral. These symptoms follow.

Physical Symptoms:

1. Speech difficulties (particularly with consonant sounds)
2. Tilting of the head when being spoken to
3. Cupping of the ear with the hand in order to follow instructions
4. Strained posture
5. Persistent earaches
6. Inflammation or drainage of the ear
7. Reports of persistent buzzing or ringing in the head

Behavioral Symptoms:

1. Inability to profit from phonic instruction
2. Inability to follow directions
3. General inattentiveness
4. Excessive volume needed for comfortable radio and phonograph listening

Normally, the student is referred to the school nurse for audiometric screening. Then in an effort to encourage as much success as possible in the classroom for a student with a suspected hearing loss, the teacher should move the student's seat so that it is: in the center of a discussion area; close to the teacher; and away from outside distractions, such as radiators, fans, cars, and traffic noises. A teacher must also be willing to repeat assignments for this student to assure that they have been properly understood. Referral outside the school normally would be made to a general practitioner or to an otologist, a medical doctor who specializes in hearing problems. The medical referral is to be made in terms of the observed symptoms of auditory difficulty, with a request for results of the audiometric examination.

Although the reading specialist may not plan to conduct an audiometric examination with every student, such an examination is called for when the student shows signs of problems in speech and/or phonics instruction. The reading specialist must also attempt to establish the period of time during which the hearing loss first noticeably interfered with school work, and then relate this information to the entire case study. For example, students affected by a hearing loss after the primary years in which oral instruction and basic phonic sounds are presented had the opportunity to learn their basic skills while they had normal hearing. Although such students may be handicapped, remedial techniques will vary in terms of the type of instruction they received prior to the hearing loss.

Neurological Disorders

Neurological disorders include direct damage to the brain and defective neurological systems resulting in either malfunction or disorganization. There is little evidence that neurological disorders are a major cause of low achievement in reading. Bond and Tinker state, "Evidence indicates that brain damage is a relatively rare cause of reading

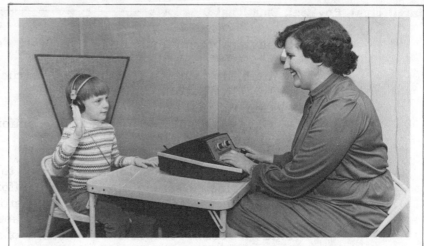

When the audiometer makes a loud sound, the student raises his hand.

Name: Age:

Date of test: Tester:

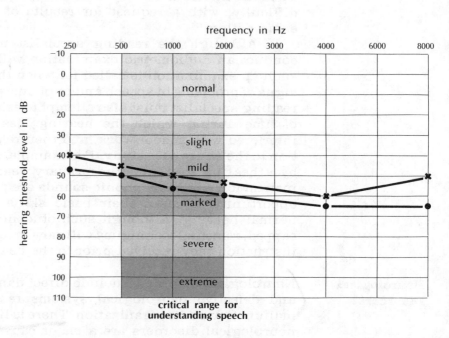

An audiogram charted for a student with a mild hearing loss.
x = left ear   o = right ear

disability."[19] Nevertheless, some believe that many problem readers show symptoms of abnormal neurological patterns. Robinson named neurological disorders as one of the causal factors in 18 percent of the cases in her classic study.[20] In our clinic at the University of Maryland, we have examined over 2000 students referred to us for difficulty with learning to read. We find that much less than 18 percent show symptoms of abnormal neurological patterns discussed on the following pages.

Initially the problem for the educator in this complex area is to identify the student who may be neurologically handicapped. However, precise identification is ultimately the job of medical specialists, who themselves have serious concerns about their accuracy of diagnosis in this area. Let us say simply that most readers are adequate enough neurologically to preclude this area as a cause of reading difficulty; at the same time, let us admit that there remains a small percentage of readers who, in fact, do have these symptoms and need medical referral.

The classroom teacher and the reading specialist are likely to find themselves relying heavily upon a pattern of symptoms for initial identification. Because individual symptoms used for neurological referral are, when viewed in isolation, not peculiar to the neurologically disturbed, it becomes necessary to seek a highly reliable pattern. Without this pattern, the educator may interpret indifference to schooling as neurological disorder. If the identification is made in the initial diagnosis, it is necessary to have a pattern of three or four symptoms to refer a student for neurological examination properly. However, if a student fails to respond after the best diagnosis and remedial instruction, one or more of these symptoms or any history of the following causes of neurological disorders should be considered when deliberating a neurological referral. These causes include:

1. Difficulties at birth—birth complicated by prematurity, use of instruments, or by anoxia or hypoxia
2. Head injuries—blows or accidents in which the head is severely bruised
3. Diseases—those resulting in inflammation and/or pressure in the area of the brain (i.e., rheumatic fever, encephalitis, continuously high temperature, and the like)

Symptoms for neurological problems fall into two categories—physical and educational. Physical symptoms include:

1. Physical incoordination—grossly awkward walking, running, writing, etc., in relation to overall physical development
2. Overactivity—inability to concentrate that causes the child to complete assignments rarely, to annoy others, and to appear uninterested
3. Headaches—history of persistent headaches
4. Speech impediments—persistent blockage of speech or articulation difficulties that are peculiar for age level
5. Visual incoordination—saccadic eye movements, inability of the eyes to focus or to hold a line of print visually

Educational symptoms of neurological problems include:

1. Average or better-than-average intelligence—general educational development deficient in terms of valid measures of intelligence
2. Phonic blending deficiency—knowledge of sounds but inability to blend them into words
3. Poor contextual reader—knowledge of the sight vocabulary but inability to use known words in sentences
4. Slow reading speech—poor reading rate, even with easy, familiar material
5. Poor auditory discrimination—inability to discriminate between sounds of letters, without evidence of a hearing acuity deficiency
6. Distractability—inattentiveness to designated tasks
7. Abnormal behavior—overreaction to stimuli (e.g., laughing long after others have ceased)
8. Poor ability to remember sequences—although apparently normally intelligent, difficulty in remembering sequences, verbal and nonverbal

Obviously, these symptoms in isolation do not necessarily indicate neurological disorder. It is imperative to gather a pattern of symptoms that includes four or more of the above. Students with this quantity of symptoms, whether identified in classroom or clinical diagnosis, should be considered legitimate referrals for neurological examinations. It does not follow, however, that a strong pattern of symptoms leads the educator to a neurological diagnosis, but to a referral.

Clements summarizes the ten most frequently cited characteristics of minimal brain dysfunction from over 100 publications.[21]

1. Hyperactivity
2. Perceptual-motor impairments
3. Emotional lability
4. General coordination defects
5. Disorders of attentions
6. Impulsivity
7. Disorders of memory and thinking
8. Specific learning disabilities in reading, arithmetic, writing, spelling
9. Disorders of speech and hearing
10. Equivocal neurological signs and electroencephalographic irregularities

Many educators seem reluctant to make neurological referrals, for they are overly concerned about either the psychological effects of such referral or the great possibility of overreferral. An understanding of the procedure generally followed in a neurological examination may reduce the educator's hesitation to refer. Neurological referral normally will include an office appointment during which a detailed neurological examination and case history will be obtained. If, at that time, the medical specialist finds symptoms of abnormal tendencies, another appointment will be made for a more involved neurological examination, often requiring hospitalization. For those interested, Clements discusses diagnostic evaluation in more detail.[22]

When educators use patterns of symptoms, they should not be reluctant to refer. If, in fact, they should overrefer, they should be relieved to find that the student's problem is not neurological in nature, and they can proceed with an educational diagnosis.

The reading specialist, upon receipt of the neurological report, relates the findings to other information gathered for the case study. The relationship of neurological problems to the entire case history must be considered in the recommendations for educational adjustment.

The classroom teacher, while waiting for the neurological report, should relieve the student from unnecessary frustration by relaxing tension and providing reading experiences in the area of the student's strengths. If the report indicates that the student does not have a neurological problem, the teacher will continue with a classroom diagnosis in an effort to find the area where correction should start. However, if the report does reveal a neurological problem, the classroom teacher should refer the student to a reading specialist, who will conduct a careful case evaluation, noting all educational aspects and precise recommendations concerning remedial techniques.

Medical personnel should write reports so that educators can understand them. A neurological report stating the findings in technical terms is difficult to interpret and of little value to most educators. Reports written for educators, however, are of value. For example, a recent report stated in relatively simple terms that the student had a receptive problem in the tactile areas, although auditory and visual receptive areas were normal. Such a report leads to effective educational adjustment, which, in this case would not include the tracing or VAKT technique (to be discussed in chapters 7 and 8).

The final analysis of all physical difficulties is the responsibility of medical personnel; however, since physical problems frequently interfere with reading efficiency, the educator often identifies a physical problem first. The educator refers to the medical specialist and, while awaiting that diagnosis, makes practical classroom adjustments. The educator then considers medical recommendations carefully in terms of the student's total diagnosis.

EMOTIONAL DIAGNOSIS

Emotional difficulties, when considered as causes of reading difficulties, create cause-and-effect confusion. Sometimes emotional disturbances cause reading difficulties; however, many emotional problems are not the cause but the result of failure in reading. Unfortunately, there is often no clear line of distinction. When emotional disturbances cause reading difficulties, performance in all learning areas suffers. Often, it is in the diagnosis of a reader that this area of difficulty is first uncovered; however, assessing the severity of the difficulty is properly the task of psychological personnel. Conversely, although emotional reactions may complicate a reading diagnosis, they are often not the cause, but rather an effect of the reading failure itself. Most students who encounter difficulty in learning to read exhibit some symptoms of emotional conflict, and these symptoms often diminish or disappear with effective instruction after the diagnosis. In summarizing the research, Bond and Tinker conclude, "Examination of all the evidence, however, does make it pretty clear that the emotional maladjustment is much more frequently the effect than the cause of reading disability."[23] An effective diagnosis may result in relieving the student of some home and school pressures by exposing the fact that the student's difficulty is not due to a poor attitude or a low level of intellectual potential, but rather to a skill deficiency, which, when corrected, will permit the student to perform as expected.

The classroom teacher and the reading specialist must be aware that most students with reading difficulties react emotionally to their failure through such behavior patterns as refusing to read, not enjoying school, disliking their teachers, or causing problems at home. Furthermore, emotional reactions to specific situations may be different within a given student at a given moment, and they may be different between two disturbed students. For example, when frustrated, an emotionally disturbed student may withdraw and be quiet, or lash out in defiance. In comparing emotional diagnosis to intellectual diagnosis, Carroll states: "Personality traits are more complex and less consistent than intelligence and so more difficult to measure objectively."[24] The more thorough an understanding the teacher has of the intrafamilial, peer, and school relationships, the more likelihood exists of an effective diagnosis. The examiner must anticipate certain types of emotional reactions, note them, include them in the diagnosis, and consider them in the recommendations; however, it is with caution that these reactions should be labeled as causative, for their presence does not necessarily make the student a candidate for referral.

Realistically recognizing their limitations as detectors of emotional difficulties and at the same time recognizing the emotional entanglement of these types of students, the reading specialist and the classroom teacher follow similar diagnostic procedures. Through the cooperation of all the educators in contact with the student, information may be gleaned concerning the student, the home, the school situation, and the student's reactions in peer group situations.

Information Concerning the Student

Due to their daily contact with the student, classroom teachers are in a unique position to obtain valuable information about the student's reactions to many situations. The reading specialist is obligated to rely upon the information supplied by the teacher and parents or to obtain it from a personal interview. Desirable information should include the following:

1. The student's attitude toward family, school, teacher, and friends
2. The student's awareness of the problem and the student's suggestions for its solution
3. The student's attitude and reaction to reading
4. The student's development of worthwhile personal goals

Gathered informally by the classroom teacher or formally by the reading specialist, all information in doubtful areas must be checked for reliability. One can do this easily by comparing reliable sources. A student may have claimed to be earning Bs and Cs in school. The educator will rely more readily on the student's other statements about school if, when checking the school records, one finds that the student does indeed make Bs and Cs.

Personality testing of a formal nature is available. *The California Test of Personality,* one of the more popular instruments for classroom use, provides standardized evaluations of the student's reactions to questions concerning personal and social adjustment. This test may be administered individually or in classroom-sized groups. Since adequate performance requires the student to possess reading skills close to the grade level of the test, the seriously handicapped reader will be unable to read the questions. In evaluating the *The California Test of Personality,* one is cautioned against the tendency to place undue emphasis on any low set of scores; however, such scores may be considered indicative of areas of potential personality problems. Scores indicating the necessity for referral are

Classroom teachers are able to obtain valuable information about their students' reactions to many situations.

described in the test manual. Final verification will not come from this type of testing, but rather from careful teacher observation and referral to psychological personnel.

Personality testing through the use of incomplete sentences is an informal way of obtaining valuable information. The student is expected to respond to several incomplete sentences, some examples of which might be the following: "I like books, but . . ." "My home is . . ." "I like my brother and . . . ." Strang provides an example of responses in informal inventories including some advice on the techniques of interpretation.[25] The most reliable use of this type of information is to note patterns of responses and to verify them by direct observation of the student in situations where these responses may be reflected in the student's behavior. Again, the examiner is cautioned against excessive analysis of any slightly deviate responses and urged to leave to psychological personnel the final assessment of the emotional stability.

Personality tests of the paper-and-pencil variety are considered inherently weak, since students often anticipate what they consider to be acceptable responses. These tests tend to record "of-the-moment" responses. Those who have had bad days may score poorly on such tests; however, twenty four hours later, they may score many points higher. When this occurs, it is obvious that the scores obtained have severely limited use in the diagnosis of emotional problems.

A technique for noting personality characteristics in a more natural situation is to observe the students at play. An investigation of play behavior may be based on the following type of questions. Do they play with others their own age? Does it appear that they are accepted by their peers? Do they play fairly? Do they play enthusiastically? Answers to such questions provide further analysis of the total behavior pattern without the limitations of paper-and-pencil tests. Shafer and Shoben feel that the analysis of free play has definite advantages in emotional diagnosis. "Many diagnostic suggestions may be drawn from watching a child in free play. . . . The communications of very young children tend to be symbolized only in the activities of play. . . ."[26] Forest also feels that such observation of play is desirable. "Emotional release through play activities due to a sense of competency and mastery may be observed in normal groups of children."[27] Note that both of these authorities suggest that play analysis has particular value with younger children.

A Study of the Home

Although the home usually is not visited as a result of a reading diagnosis, under certain circumstances such a visit is profitable. When it appears that situations at home are impeding the student's language and/or emotional development, the educator who hopes to improve these conditions must make a home visit. In cases where a home visit would be of little value, one may gather information concerning home conditions through parental interviews or questionnaires. These are constructed to obtain the following types of information: socioeconomic status of the home, availability of books, intrafamilial relations, parental efforts to assist the child, general family activities, and overall acceptance of the child in the home.

Abnormal home conditions should be brought to the attention of appropriate personnel (school officials, home-school visitors, social workers, and psychologists). Neither the classroom teacher nor the reading specialist is justified in offering unsolicited advice to parents about home conditions unrelated to the student's educational progress. There are times when parents will turn to an educator and ask for consultation. Although it depends upon the individual situation, it is my opinion that an educator is normally acting outside the proper professional role in offering advice in such cases. Offering advice concerning domestic affairs implies that one has training or information about "best" solutions.

The educator will want to contact the social worker when home problems appear to be a basic source of difficulty for the student. These professional persons are skilled in working with parents and investigating home situations. Many schools have found it worthwhile to have social workers on their professional staffs.

A Study of the School

The classroom teacher gathers relevant data for a classroom diagnosis and submits it to the reading specialist for case analysis. From the school it is necessary to obtain information relating to attendance, behavior, ability to work and play with others, and reactions to various types of failure. School records do not always contain this type of information, although teachers are often encouraged to write comments concerning outstanding characteristics of students. When such notations are available, they should be included in the diagnosis; when not accessible, the information should be gathered through interviews or questionnaire responses from the teacher.

While students are reading, teachers should note peculiar reactions that reflect anxiety, frustration, and emotional disturbance. Roebuck found that the emotionally disturbed tend to read orally with tense voices, to react more definitely to the material being read, and to read compulsively.[28] In compulsive reading, the students never stop or hesitate; rather, they read on whether they know the words or not, skipping and/or mispronouncing unknown words. Other noticeable symptoms are refusal to read aloud, profuse sweating of the hands during oral reading, and refusal to complete assignments.

If the educator is to be effective in obtaining such information, students and parents must be assured that it will be handled confidentially and will not find its way into the hands of irresponsible people. A confidential approach on the part of both parents and educators is necessary for reliable data collection.

After psychological referral has been made, the classroom teacher adjusts instruction to avoid further complicating potential emotional difficulties while awaiting referral recommendations. Adjustments include avoiding placement of the student in failing situations that cause unnecessary embarrassment, avoiding implications that the student is lazy or stupid, and providing a sensible program of discipline by which the student can gain a degree of composure and self-reliance. Carroll points out some of the difficulties involved with discipline for students with these symptoms:

> The causes of misconduct insofar as classroom conditions are concerned are not hard to identify. Every child needs to succeed. If the academic tasks set for him are too difficult, he feels frustrated. Frustration is uncomfortable, and he feels driven to do something about it. . . . Denied the opportunity to satisfy his need for scholastic achievement, he strikes out against environment.[29]

He also says that they must have their successes recognized by the group and by the teacher, whether the successes are large or small. Furthermore, he states, "She (the teacher) will be more lavish with praise than criticism. She will help every child to maintain his self-respect."[30] In discussing the control of the group when this student is disruptive, Carroll points out that the teacher will have to take disciplinary measures but adds, "She should never use fear as a technique of control."[31]

The classroom teacher must consider this student to be one who needs and deserves special considerations; negative reactions can only drive the student to reject further the learning processes and the environment. At the same time, the teacher has an obligation to the other students in the room to provide an environment conducive to learning. If disruption occurs, alternative strategies for dealing with the emotionally disturbed student will need to be considered.

Prevention of complex emotional disorders is also in the hands of classroom teachers. Their reactions, for example, to the initial signs of frustration and failure of an individual student may cause the students' acceptance of their temporary situation or a reaction against it. Although students must be challenged in school, not all will meet these challenges with the same degree of success. Teachers may relax tensions and feelings of failure by their attitudes toward the efforts of the less successful. All students must succeed in school. The successes of all, but particularly the less successful, should be highlighted. Beware, however, of false praise—students resent it. Instead of false praise, one should structure situations in which, with a little effort, a student can legitimately succeed and be praised. More of these types of techniques are discussed under remediation in chapters 6 and 10.

All information and notations concerning the student's emotional behavior should be included and evaluated in the case analysis. The reading specialist should apply the recommendations for the necessary educational adjustment. If the classroom teacher, after the institution of these recommendations, finds further complications, the student should be referred to the reading specialist.

A note of caution concerning emotional referral may be helpful. Teachers are prone to interpret obscure symptoms as signs of emotional problems in certain students: if they are only children, if they do not talk much, if their parents are divorced, or if a parent is under psychiatric care. While such observations should be noted, they do not constitute a legitimate referral; the student's behavior must call for it. Nor should emotional diagnosis be made on the basis of test performance alone. Abnormal scores do not call for psychological evaluation unless observed performance confirms the test score. Referring on too little evidence clogs the referral system with those who are not in need. Many times this causes parents needless anguish and expense.

SUMMARY

As we understand the educators' role in these complex areas of diagnosis we see that they must be aware, informed, and skilled in making observations of various types of behavior. Generally, they attempt to make immediate adjustments of the learning environment and refer the students to appropriate specialists. Team effort that brings all of the resources of the school to assist those students who are experiencing difficulty is the recommended procedure.

NOTES

1. Arthur S. MacDonald, "Research for the Classroom," *The Journal of Reading* 8 (November 1964): 115–18.
2. Margaret Deal, "A Summary of Research Concerning Patterns of WISC Subtest Scores of Retarded Readers," *The Journal of the Reading Specialist* 4 (May 1965): 101–11.
3. Roger Farr, *Reading: What Can Be Measured?* (Newark, Del.: International Reading Association, 1969), pp. 93–94.
4. Donald Neville, "The Relationship Between Reading Skills and Intelligence Test Scores," *The Reading Teacher* 18 (January 1965): 257–61.
5. Florence Roswell and Gladys Natchez, *Reading Disability* (New York: Basic Books, 1964), p. 27.
6. Albert Harris, *How to Increase Reading Ability* (New York: David McKay Co., 1970), p. 211.
7. Harris, *How to Increase Reading Ability*, p. 212.
8. Guy L. Bond and Miles A. Tinker, *Reading Difficulties: Their Diagnosis and Correction* (New York: Appleton-Century-Crofts, 1973), p. 92.
9. Bond and Tinker, *Reading Difficulties*, p. 94.
10. Donald L. Cleland, "Clinical Materials for Appraising Disabilities in Reading," *The Reading Teacher* 17 (March 1964): 428.
11. John J. Pikulski, "Assessing Information about Intelligence and Reading," *The Reading Teacher* 29 (November 1975): 162.
12. Charles R. Kelley, *Visual Screening and Child Development* (Raleigh, N.C.: North Carolina State College, 1957), p. 11.
13. Kelley, *Visual Screening and Child Development*, p. 11.
14. *Teacher's Guide To Vision Problems* (St. Louis: American Optometric Association, 1953).
15. Kelley, *Visual Screening*, p. 11.
16. Jules H. Shaw, "Vision and Seeing Skills of Preschool Children," *The Reading Teacher* 18 (October 1964): 36.
17. Ward H. Ewalt, Jr., "Visual Problems of Children and Their Relationship to Reading Achievement," *The Optometric Weekly,* October 22, 1959.
18. Darrell E. Rose et al., *Audiological Assessment* (Englewood Cliffs, N.J.: Prentice-Hall, 1971), p. 150.
19. Bond and Tinker, *Reading Difficulties,* p. 118.
20. Helen M. Robinson, *Why Pupils Fail in Reading* (Chicago: The University of Chicago Press, 1946), p. 218.
21. Sam D. Clements, *Minimal Brain Dysfunction in Children,* (Washington, D.C.: GPO, 1966), p. 13.
22. Clements, *Minimal Brain Dysfunction*, pp. 14–15.
23. Bond and Tinker, *Reading Difficulties*, p. 129.
24. Herbert A. Carroll, *Mental Hygiene* (New York: Prentice-Hall, 1947), p. 246.

25. Strang, *Diagnostic Teaching of Reading*, pp. 262–63.
26. Laurance F. Shafer and Edward J. Shoben, Jr., *The Psychology of Adjustment*, 2d ed. (Boston: Houghton Mifflin Co., 1956), p. 508.
27. Isle Forest, *Child Development* (New York: McGraw-Hill Book Co., 1954), p. 64.
28. Mildred Roebuck, "The Oral Reading Characteristics of Emotionally Disturbed Children," *International Reading Association Proceedings* 7 (1962): 133–38.
29. Carroll, *Mental Hygiene*, p. 210.
30. Carroll, *Mental Hygiene*, p. 210.
31. Carroll, *Mental Hygiene*, p. 211.

SUGGESTED READINGS

Cleland, Donald L. "Clinical Materials for Appraising Disabilities in Reading." *The Reading Teacher* 17 (March 1964), 428. This interesting, easy-to-read article presents summaries of the various appraisal materials available for clinical diagnosis. Of particular interest is the discussion of reading capacity and appropriate techniques for determining it.

Clements, Sam D. *Minimal Brain Dysfunction in Children.* Washington, D.C.: U.S. Department of Health, Education, and Welfare, 1966. In fifteen pages, Clements summarizes terminology to clarify several issues and to offer a blue print for action on minimal brain dysfunction. The information contained in this monograph will be useful to those who have not read widely in this area.

Harris, Albert J. & Sipay, Edward R. *How to Increase Reading Ability* Sixth Edition, New York, David McKay, 1975. Harris & Sipay discuss several techniques for the use of mental age in determining reading expectancy scores. For a review of alternate methods, the reader is encouraged to refer to these pages.

Kelley, Charles R. *Visual Screening and Child Development.* The North Carolina Study. Raleigh, N.C.: North Carolina State College, 1957. This book reports a little-known, but carefully organized study concerning the scope and sequence of vision and scholastic effectiveness. The reader who is interested in a more detailed study will find it worthwhile.

Money, John. *The Disabled Reader.* Baltimore, Md.: The Johns Hopkins Press, 1966. A book of readings collected by Money under the topic of dyslexia. Attention provided to medical and psychological opinion as well as to educational opinion. Essential reading for those working with the seriously handicapped.

Reeds, James C.; Rabe, Edward F.; and Maniken, Margaret. "Teaching Reading to Brain-Injured Children." *Reading Research Quarterly*. Summer 1970, p. 379. An excellent review for those interested in brain-injured children. Claiming a lack of evidence for specific program adjustments for brain-damaged children, the authors review several of the most highly respected sources.

Robinson, Helen M. *Why Pupils Fail in Reading*. Chicago: University of Chicago Press, 1946. Robinson presents a discussion of the multiple causation theory in terms of the most prominent authorities and also in terms of her research in this area. Of particular importance are the conclusions that she reaches through her technique to determine causation.

Strauss, Alfred A., and Lehtinen, Laura E. *Psychopathology and Education of the Brain-Injured Child*. New York: Grane & Stratton, 1947. This book provides the rationale for the syndromes of distractability and perseveration. It is a basic book for those who are interested in more thoroughly understanding the aspects of minimal brain injury. Explanations are given in terms designed for educators.

Stuart, Marion. *Neurophysiological Insights Into Teaching*. New York: Pacific Books, 1963. This book provides relatively elementary explanations of diagnosis and treatment of readers with neurological limitations.

Classroom Diagnosis

Chapter Emphasis

- The first task is to assess the learning climate.

- Classroom diagnosis involves the observation of student behavior, limited testing, and assessment of interests and attitudes.

- Equal attention should be given to student strengths and needs.

- Records of classroom assessment are essential.

  Note: All tests mentioned in this chapter are included in Appendix A, which provides a detailed check list indicating each test's characteristics.

The classroom teacher, who has a relatively long acquaintance with a student, relies heavily upon informal observation, systematic observation, informal testing, and self-assessment by the student for educational diagnosis of difficulties in reading. The classroom teacher considers the learning climate, the various causes of reading difficulties, the possible instructional adjustments that can be made, and the continuous assessment of student progress.

THE LEARNING CLIMATE

When teachers notice that certain students are experiencing difficulties in reading, a quick assessment of the learning climate is a logical first step. While it would be impossible to note all aspects of the learning climate in each teacher's classroom, a brief look at some important factors may prove to be helpful.

1. Is the climate one in which students are comfortable? Are such aspects as ventilation, lighting, and room cleanli-

ness appropriate for learning? Since reading requires vigorous attention to the tasks at hand, physical discomfort can easily cause difficulties. Most of the physical aspects of discomfort can be adjusted easily if noticed.

2. Is the climate one that fosters communication? Are there any signs that students are experiencing difficulty communicating with the teacher or with other students? The threat of ridicule or failure can discourage some students from even attempting to communicate. Students are well aware of the risks involved in attempting to communicate. When risk taking is not worthwhile, communication becomes difficult and it may appear as though the students are not able to respond. Risk taking and communication can be improved by the following:

a. Starting comprehension discussions with personal questions that all students can answer without the fear of being "wrong." For example, if the starter question is, "What did you like most about this story?," all students can respond without the fear of being wrong.

b. Focusing on a discussion about what has been read, as opposed to a teacher-questioning session. For example, after using a *personal starter question,* the teacher and students can discuss agreements and disagreements about the responses of others. By staying away from a questioning session in which the students are penalized for being wrong, the spirit of communication can be developed.

c. Keeping at the eye level of the students instead of standing in front of them

d. Encouraging student-to-student communication and teaching students to regard the thoughts of others as important even when there is disagreement

These and other aspects of facilitating risk taking and communication will be discussed in detail under the topic of comprehension in chapter 10.

3. Are the materials for instruction appropriate? Are the materials suited to the reading levels of the students who are experiencing difficulty in reading? If not, then there may be no need for further assessment. The materials should be adjusted and the students observed to see if the difficulties disappear.

4. Are there opportunities for individualizing portions of instruction? Do all students have to complete the same assignments in the same amount of time or are there alternatives? If alternatives do not exist, can they be developed? Many readers appear to be having difficulty when they are attempting activities that are not appropriate for them, either because the activities are not geared to the student's strengths or the time allotted for completion is not sufficient.

There are numerous aspects of the learning climate that may be assessed to determine if reading difficulties can be attributed to the climate instead of to the student. The four mentioned above are common causes of difficulties that appear to be within the student when they are not. Other common aspects that may be examined are inappropriate class size, inappropriate instructional strategies, discriminatory treatment of students, and the effect of labels that are attached to certain students.

Observing Student Behavior

If the learning climate seems appropriate and if the students are not able to respond when the climate is adjusted, then the classroom teacher needs to observe and assess the students' behavior to determine where the difficulties might lie.

1. Do the students have difficulty with reading comprehension activities? If students are not effectively gaining meaning from their reading, then they are reading nonsense. When reading without gaining meaning, the student makes many errors that may appear to be vocabulary problems or problems with word attack skills. In this chapter several approaches to assessing comprehension skills will be presented.
2. Are the difficulties most apparent when the students are reading in the content areas? Many students do satisfactory work in teacher-directed reading lessons but seem to have considerable difficulty with independent reading in content-area books. The particular books, the assigned activities, and the nature of the difficulty need to be assessed. For example, the answers to the following questions would be helpful:
    a. Are students having difficulty with all content books or just certain ones? If certain ones, why?

Appropriate classroom climate is important for independent reading time.

    b. What features of the books creating the difficulty can be identified? Are readability levels too high?

    c. Can the assigned activities be changed to make the reading of content books an easier task? Are new concepts introduced prior to independent reading? Are new vocabulary words discussed?

    d. Are study guides available for student use? If not, are the students certain of the specific tasks in the assignment?

3. Do oral reading activities seem to be difficult for these students? Many students can read silently and answer questions but cannot read that same material orally with fluency. The assessment of the nature of the difficulty is necessary in such instances before further oral reading activities are planned.

4. Do these students read accurately and with good comprehension but so slowly that they never finish their reading when others do? A cause of real problems for the teacher is the slow reader. Slow readers hold up the entire group while others wait until they finish their

reading. The assessment of slow reading is difficult, but important.

These four areas of assessment are discussed in this chapter. They are examples of the most common difficulties that students experience in reading. Other related difficulties will also be discussed in this chapter.

IMPLEMENTING CLASSROOM DIAGNOSIS

Classroom diagnosis can take place before, during, or after instruction. Each technique has distinct advantages and limitations and most teachers use each of them at times.

Diagnosis before Instruction

It is important to know the state of development of various skills students have prior to planning instruction. These data can be collected from past school records, student self-assessment, and from tests.

School records contain a variety of types of information ranging from very useful to completely useless. When using this information, teachers should first try to assess the reliability of the data found on school records. Teacher comments, test scores, health information, and past scholastic performance are usually found on school records. Unfortunately, much of this information is in the form of global information and is of little use. For example, test scores usually indicate total test scores and give little indication of how those scores were obtained. A low score of an I.Q. test may appear in the records as an intelligence quotient; however, if the test itself were available it might show that the student did satisfactorily on all but one section, and that section pulled down the total score. In many instances, however, useful data are found in school records and they should be examined prior to initiating testing. If, for example, you are curious about a given student's intellectual ability, the school records may contain several indicators of that ability, making additional testing unnecessary.

Student self-assessment provides useful information, many times of an unexpected nature. Numerous professionals utilize self-report as one of the first steps in diagnosis. The doctor wants to know how you are feeling,

[handwritten annotations in left margin:]
A — Student self assessment
B — test
1. standardized
2. prepared informal inventories
3. teacher made inventories
4. cloze tests
5. maze tests
6. Criterion-referenced

the dentist wants to know which tooth hurts, and the lawyer wants to know your opinion of the problem. In our clinic, we have found that many students have very accurate perceptions of their difficulty and are willing to discuss those perceptions. We use the following questions to get the students thinking about how reading is working for them:

1. Do you think you read better, worse, or about the same as other students in your class?
2. What do you do best when reading?
3. What causes you most difficulty when reading?
4. Are you reading a book for fun? (If yes, ask for the name of the book.)
5. If you were to describe reading to a kindergarten child, what would you say?
6. Why do you read books of your choice?

☐ for information ☐ for fun ☐ have to ☐ other

After assessing the reading skills of the students who have already provided us with a self-report, we are more able to help them understand themselves as readers. We have found that students make accurate self-reports more than 50 percent of the time. Accuracy is determined by comparing student self-report with data collected during diagnosis. Many teachers attempt to determine the strengths and weaknesses of their students by testing them before instruction. They use these test results as they plan future instruction and as they plan for grouping students. Six basic types of testing instruments are available for classroom diagnosis: standardized tests, prepared informal inventories, teacher-made informal inventories, cloze tests, maze tests, and criterion-referenced tests.

The selection of the testing instrument must be in terms of the information needed for the diagnosis. Some instruments are designed to measure the progress of groups of students. Others are designed to provide information on individual students. Some help teachers obtain information concerning the reading levels of students. Others provide information on skill development. By first determining what type of information is needed, teachers can make intelligent choices of instruments. The following descriptions provide an overview of the various types of instruments available for classroom diagnosis.

Standardized tests. Most schools test regularly with one of the major standardized tests *(Iowa Test of Basic Skills, California Reading Test, Comprehensive Test of Basic Skills, Stanford Reading Test, Metropolitan Reading Test,* or the *Gates MacGinitie Reading Test).* Each of these tests is in common use, and many teachers have student scores available to them. The tests usually yield total reading, vocabulary, and comprehension scores. Students usually take these tests in class-size groups, and their performance is to be completed within specified time limits; most of these tests can be administered within a half hour or hour. Some of the tests have subscores relating to various types of reading vocabulary and comprehension skills. Standardized test scores are norm-based, i.e., the scores obtained are compared to the score distribution obtained from the population upon which the test was normed. This procedure necessitates that approximately equal numbers of students will score above and below the test's normed mean for a given grade level.

Standardized test scores are nearly useless for classroom diagnosis.[1] The tests' limitations have been discussed by many authorities in reading. First, that they are administered to groups necessitates multiple-choice answers and encourages guessing. Second, the standardizing procedures are subject to error, a fact that causes considerable concern about their reliability. Third, their ability to match the student with a given reading level is constantly under question. Finally, the use of subtests has been discouraged because of the extreme lack of reliability of these measures.

However, since schools administer tests to determine how well students are doing generally, two diagnostic uses of standardized test scores are recommended.

1. While the earned scores do not reflect accurate reading grade levels, extremely low scores usually indicate reading difficulty. Therefore, prior to instruction, teachers can gain an idea of which students may experience difficulties; they may be able to identify those students most in need of informal diagnosis. If the scores in Table 4–1 were obtained at the beginning of fourth grade, Jack and Portia logically would be selected as those most in need of further diagnosis due to their extremely low performance.

Table 4–1   **Standardized Test Grade Equivalents**

Student	Word Meaning	Paragraph Meaning
Jack	1.3	2.3
Portia	1.9	2.0
Larry	3.4	3.5
Marcia	2.7	3.7
Cheryl	3.5	3.8
Judy	3.6	3.7
Pat	3.7	3.9
Don	4.1	4.0
Robin	4.2	3.9
Dolores	4.1	4.1

2. While subtest scores do not meet reliability standards, extreme differences in subtest scores can serve as indicators of possible skill difficulties. For example, in Table 4–1, Jack and Marcia exhibit extreme differences between word-meaning and paragraph-meaning scores. The teacher should not accept these scores at face value. Instead, the scores should suggest that something may be wrong. The teacher should continue the diagnosis, usually through the use of informal techniques.

Teachers will find standardized test scores recorded in either grade equivalents, percentiles, or stanines. Since grade equivalents are often confused with grade levels (which they are not) and since they do not reflect a student's relative position with other students, the use of stanines or percentiles is preferred. Stanine scores range from 1 to 9, 1 being low and 9 being high. Percentiles range from 1 to 99, 1 again being low.

These two uses of standardized test scores are suggested only if scores are available. Tests should not be administered solely for the purpose of obtaining such scores, however, since they are more reliably obtained from other sources.

Prepared informal inventories.   Several publishing companies and many school districts have prepared informal testing instruments that are useful for classroom diagnosis. Informal inventories are usually developed by teachers from the actual materials the students will be expected to use during instruction. Inventories already prepared for teachers generally use a sampling technique, i.e., words are selected from a sampling of commonly-used reading materials. Other inventories include paragraphs for oral and silent reading. Teachers using these instruments can obtain measures of the student's oral reading accuracy and silent reading comprehension as well as skill development. The paragraphs are usually evaluated through the use of readability formulas or taken from materials that have been graded previously.

One informal instrument is the *Botel Reading Inventory* (Revised). Three sections of this inventory are useful for reading diagnosis: word recognition—the student reads graded lists of twenty words aloud to the teacher; word opposites (reading)—the student identifies antonyms from graded lists of ten words (see sample on this page); and phonics—the student identifies graphemes as the teacher pronounces words. Both the word opposites and the phonics sections are group tests. The two group measures can be administered in about thirty minutes. Using prepared informal inventories can result in a teacher's obtaining results that assist in the identification of students' skill strengths and weaknesses and that yield estimates of reading levels.

Sample

BOTEL READING INVENTORY **B**

Word Opposites Test (Reading)

Directions: Pick a word in each line which means the opposite or nearly the opposite of the numbered word. Draw a line under it.
Example:
1. work   find   <u>play</u>   stop

Name _____

Date _____

Teacher _____

	A	**a**	**b**	**c**
(First)	1. father	birthday	<u>mother</u>	children
	2. boy	shoe	train	<u>girl</u>
	3. in	eat	one	<u>out</u>
	4. big	away	<u>little</u>	around
	5. here	live	find	<u>there</u>
	6. morning	please	<u>night</u>	horse
	7. up	there	from	<u>down</u>
	8. him	bag	ask	<u>her</u>
	9. go	<u>stop</u>	boat	kitten
	10. yes	saw	<u>no</u>	fish

Score _____%

Table 4–2   Botel Reading Inventory

Student	Word Recognition	Word Opposites	Phonics* % Correct		
			Consonants	Blends	Vowels
Betty	2–1	2–2	90	80	80
Jim	2–1	2–2	50	40	20
Janet	2–1	2–2	75	60	40
Les	2–2	2–2	80	60	70
Mae	3–1	2–2	90	80	50
Linda	3–1	3–1	90	90	70
Joe	3–1	3–1	100	100	90
Jane	3–2	4–1	90	60	90
Joan	3–2	4–1	60	50	40
Bill	4–1	4–1	90	90	80

*The Botel phonics section has many more categories.

Results, such as those in Table 4–2, can be useful in matching students to books and in making decisions about skills that they have or need. The word recognition column indicates how well students can decode certain levels of words. The word opposites column reveals how well the students can obtain word meanings. The phonics columns show how well they have mastered the various phonics skills. Although in columns one and two, Betty and Jim appear to be operating on the same levels, their phonic skills development is entirely different. And, while Joan appears to be reading better than most of the others, her phonic skills are deficient.

The usefulness of the data from the *Botel Reading Inventory* is obviously greater than the data on Table 4–1, because it relates more closely to instruction. When teachers add data concerning oral reading and comprehension, it can be even more useful.

Early in the school year teachers can administer these types of inventories to help make instructional adjustments. Group tests can be administered first to survey students' strengths and needs. Oral reading testing is, of course, done individually. Using the score from the group test, teachers can obtain supplemental data by asking students to read aloud from material at those levels. Silent reading comprehension can also be tested from materials available for instruction. See Appendix A for a listing of prepared informal inventories.

Teacher-made informal reading inventories (IRIs). Obviously, teachers can develop informal tests having the same features as those prepared commercially. Using the material from which they intend to teach the students, teachers can assess a reader's abilities to recognize words, to read orally, and to read silently for comprehension. Many school systems develop IRIs for use by their teachers. The construction of such instruments can be time-consuming and requires considerable knowledge of both the reading process and test construction. Interpretation can be even more difficult. Powell raises serious questions concerning traditional norms used on informal inventories.[2] Others also have found the subject of norms for informal inventories rather perplexing.[3] Betts is acknowledged as creator of the IRI as a functional measurement instrument.[4] Since then, Powell has conducted numerous studies attempting to establish criteria that teachers can utilize when interpreting informal inventories.[5]

Powell's latest study of criteria for interpretation of informal Reading Inventory results can be applied by a study of comprehension, word recognition, and other systematic behavior. Powell states, however, "The comprehension dimension is the most important of the three in determining final placement. When comprehension drops below the criterion for a given level, then it matters not what happens on the other two dimensions."[6]

Powell contends that the comprehension and word recognition criteria will vary with the difficulty of the material. His criteria can be seen in Table 4–3.[7]

These criteria are based upon oral reading at sight. The criteria were determined by comparing IRI scores with scores on cloze tests. It should be noted that word recognition errors in oral reading include insertions, omissions, mispronunciations, substitutions, unknown words, and transpositions. Other errors such as repetitions, disregard of punctuation, nonfluent reading, etc., should be noted and evaluated diagnostically, but should not be used for determining word recognition scores for IRIs.[8]

A student reading a second-grade book would be considered to be reading at an independent level when making one word recognition error per seventeen running words. A student reading from a fourth-grade book would be considered to be reading at the frustration level when making one or more word recognition errors for every

Table 4–3   **Informal Reading Inventory Scoring Criteria
by Performance Level—for Diagnosis**

	W/R	Comp.
Independent		
Level		
1–2	1/17	80+
3–5	1/27+	85+
6+	1/35+	90+
Instructional		
Level		
1–2	1/8–1/16	55–80
3–5	1/13–1/26	60–85
6+	1/18–1/35	65–90
Frustration		
Level		
1–2	1/7–	55–
3–5	1/12–	60–
6+	1/17–	65–

nineteen running words. Powell checked this criterion against a dependent criterion, on a test of comprehension at each level cited above. Test results can be used in much the same manner as that suggested for commercially prepared informal inventories. A major advantage of teacher-made inventories centers around the ability to make the test cover a wider range of reading materials than do many commercially prepared tests. The larger sampling tends to produce more reliable results. However, two serious problems occur with their construction. Can the teacher select materials and ask questions that are accurate measures of the student's development, and are the materials accurately graded?

The answer to the first question is yes. With some training, teachers can select materials and ask questions that are accurate measures of the student's development. Also, they are more capable of interpreting the results when they have developed the instrument. However, without training and without a thorough knowledge of the skills of reading, many sloppy, inaccurate, relatively useless instruments have been developed.

The answer to the second question is probably not. Publishers tend to pay little attention to the readability level of materials even if they place grade-level numbers on the books.[9] Even then the readability level is generally an average of the readability levels of the individual pages. Through readability checks on several basals, teachers become aware that a "fifth-grade" basal can range in readability from second- to eighth-grade level.[10] If the teacher uses these materials for an informal inventory and happens to select pages that are at the extremes of the ranges (second- and eighth-grade levels in the above examples), the assessment of a student's reading ability will be inaccurate.

The *Autobiography of Malcolm X* was rated as having a readability level of fifth grade, eighth grade, and tenth grade.[11] In this study, the examiner used three different readability formulas. The question is what factors are considered when one discusses "readability level"?

A problem exists with matching performance prior to instruction with any given material. In fact, mismatching probably occurs all too frequently. That a student's reading ability tends to change with the material's content contributes to the mismatching. Books tend to be inaccurately marked, particularly in the content areas. Informal inventories, even when considering their limitations, provide more useful information than do standardized tests. With teacher-made inventories, mismatching is held to a minimum since the student is being tested from samples of the same material in which instruction will take place.

Cloze tests. One approach, closure testing, may help circumvent the problem of mismatching and labeling. Cloze tests constructed from the types of materials students are expected to use can provide relatively useful information concerning the students' abilities to work with various types of printed materials. The procedures for closure testing are as follows:

1. Select several passages of at least 150 words from the various books to be used.
2. Retype the selection, deleting every fifth word. Do not delete proper nouns.
   Mary had a little lamb. Its fleece was white _____ snow. Everywhere that Mary _____ the lamb was sure _____ go. It is recommended that the first sentence contain no deletions, permitting students an opportunity to pick up on the author's meaning.

3. Have the student read the selection, supplying the omitted word. Older students can write the words in; younger students can read the passage to you.
4. Determine a score by counting as correct responses the number of words actually used by the author.

A score of about 40 percent or better indicates that the book should be one that the reader can handle.[12] A score below that level indicates that the book is probably too difficult. The student will need more help reading it or should be permitted to use easier material. The use of closure eliminates the necessity of matching a grade-level score with a book, for the test derives from the various types of material that the student will be expected to read. Closure tests are easily constructed, scored, and interpreted. While they are not without flaw, they may be the most useful type of testing instrument for use prior to instruction that is available to the classroom teacher. A word of caution is necessary. Considerable research is being conducted with closure testing materials. Adjusted norms will be reported indicating possible differences from the 40-percent criterion mentioned above. As one works with students of different ages and materials from different content areas, adjusted norms can be expected. The reader should watch for reports of such changes for the most useful application of closure in reading diagnosis.

Two problems arise with the use of cloze tests for reading diagnosis. First, the tests are usually very frustrating to students who are operating in material at and beyond the instructional level. If, after five or six deletions, the student has made serious mistakes concerning the meaning of the passage, then the reader is working with nonsense. Many give up—refuse to try any more items because they know that what they are doing does not make sense.

The second problem has to do with grading a cloze test. The exact word of the author must be presented in order to be counted as correct. Synonyms do not count and creative entries do not count. This scoring procedure is annoying to many teachers who must mark an entry as an error when they know that the student has obtained the meaning of the author. Try this one.

Test item: The owner of the _____ dog was Mike.
Correct response: The owner of the *huge* dog was Mike.
Student response: The owner of the *big* dog was Mike. Wrong

The student is not helped at all if, in the next sentence, the clue is: Mike's big dog likes _____. Now the response "big" looks to be accurate. And what person would write "ice cream" in the second blank? And so it goes.

Maze tests.   An adjustment to cloze tests called *maze tests* [13] has been made to overcome some of the objections raised above in relation to cloze testing. As in cloze tests, every fifth word is deleted. Three alternatives are given, however, so that guess work is reduced. So, given the sentence, "The men were working at the oil well," a maze test would look like, "The men were working in the oil well."

at
big

Two of the alternatives are the same part of speech so that they would both be syntactically correct. The other is not acceptable syntactically and makes nonsense out of the sentence.

Maze tests require the students to obtain scores of 70 percent or better for the material to be appropriate for their instruction. We have found that scores around the 70-percent mark, 65–75 percent, are an indication that teacher direction is necessary for successful utilization of the material.

We have worked with school faculties to develop maze tests for all of their basic texts. Assembled by a faculty, these tests can be constructed easily and placed in the school office for future use. New students can be given a few of these and be placed with a high degree of accuracy. When other students are experiencing difficulty with working in a given book, a quick use of a maze test can provide data concerning the difficulty of that material for those students.

When a maze test seems to indicate that the material is above students' instructional level, a new sample of material can be selected and an alternate form of the maze test for that material can be developed.

Criterion-referenced tests (CRTs). "CRTs are designed to measure specified behavior performed by an individual toward mastery of a specific skill."[14] Unlike standardized norm-referenced tests that compare students with one another, CRTs get at how much of a specific skill a student can demonstrate. The effectiveness of CRTs for use in reading diagnosis is limited to whether or not the objective of the test is important and whether or not the test can measure the objective.

For each objective that is judged to be important, several test items are developed. The student's ability to respond to the test items in relation to that specific objective will become one indicator of the degree to which the student has learned the objective. It is easier to develop items for some objectives than others. For example, it is easy to construct a test item to determine if a student can substitute the initial consonant *t* to make new words from mop, sip, and sin. But it is much more difficult to construct a test item to determine if a student can obtain the main idea from a complicated paragraph.

Numerous CRTs are finding their ways into classrooms. Table 4–4 shows Stallard's[15] report on some of the variables that need to be considered when choosing a CRT for classroom use. The wide range of objectives and items for sampling each objective, and the variance in what is considered mastery make test selection and interpretation difficult. The tests are often justified as a management system for teachers; however, unless interpreted cautiously, they can lead to mismanagement, calling for the teaching of unimportant subskills and locking all students into the identical path to reading. It is up to the teacher to utilize only those parts of such tests that relate to what they think is important. In the area of phonics subskills in particular this is true.

One advantage of CRTs, when teacher-constructed, is that the teacher has the opportunity to develop large numbers of items to sample the students' behavior. Large sampling tends to increase the reliability of tests. When few items are included to measure a given type of behavior, CRTs have the same reliability problems as do standardized tests.

Table 4–4 **Characteristics of Fifteen Objective-Based Reading Programs**

	1[a]	2 A/B	3	4
Rationale presented in book or booklet form			X	X
Grade levels included in program	K–Adult	K–6 K–6	1–6	1–6
Categories of skills included in program				
Bilingual reading skills				
Comprehension skills	X	–/X	X	X
Creative reading skills		–/X		
Interpretive or critical reading skills		–/X		X
Oral reading skills				
Readiness skills	X	X/–	X	X
Secondary or content area skills	X	–/X	X	
Self-directed or independent reading skills				
Study skills		–/X	X	X
Vocabulary skills	X		X	X
Word attack skills	X	X/–	X	X
Total number of objectives in program	450	32/31	428	343
Percent of test items correct which demonstrates skill mastery	95%	100/ 84%	75–100%[c]	50–80%
Average number of test items per skill	2–3	17/12	3	5
Average number of specific activities for teaching each skill		10+/ 20+		
Consultant services available		X/X	X	X
Inservice training of teachers available	X	X[f]/X[f]	X	X[e]
Procedures for including teacher-made objectives in tests	X	[e]		
Purchaser selects desired objectives from catalog				

[a]Each number designates a particular program.

  1. Criterion Reading
2A. Croft Word Attack
2B. Croft Comprehension
  3. Fountain Valley
  4. IPMS
  5. Performance Objectives

  6. PRI
  7. Read-On
  8. SCORE
  9. SOBAR
10. ICRT

11. Wisconsin Design
12. ORBIT
13. PLAN
14. High Intensity
15. SARI

5	6	7	8	9	10	11	12	13	14	15
X	X		X			X	X	X	X	
K-6	K-6.5	1-4	1-8	1-6	1-8	K-6	K-12	K-12	1-Adult	K-8
				X						
X	X	X	X	X	X	X	X	X	X	X
						X				
	X		X	X	X	X	X	X	X	
							X		X	X
	X	X	X				X			
X			X	X		(X)^b	X	X	X	
						X		X	X	
			X	X	X	X	X	X	X	
X		X	X	X	X	X				X
X	X	X	X	X	X	X	X	X	X	X
312	172	60	800+	463	329	309	335	1100	475	95
	80%	90%	66.7 75,100%^{d}	d	d	80%	75%	66–80%^{d}	80%	90–100%
	3–4	15–20	3+	3	4	12–25	4	3–4	10	20
	8					14+		5+		2+
X	X^e		X			X	X		X^e	X
X	X		X	X		X^f	(X)^b	X	X	X
			X						X	
X			X	X		X		X		

^{b}Being developed. ^{c}75% is "proficiency" level, 100% is "mastery" level; individual user chooses criterion level desired for the class. ^{d}Mastery level is established by individual user of program. ^{e}Available on request. ^{f}Inservice programs are also designed to be training sessions for district personnel who intend to conduct inservice training for others in their district.

STALLARD: *Comparing Objective Based Reading Programs*

It was the end of another school year, and the IOWA tests had again shown our third and fifth graders six to two years behind state averages. Why?

In a meeting between the principal and the fourth- and fifth-grade teachers, we examined possible causes. Factors included socioeconomic level, materials, and organization. As test and teacher data were analyzed, several patterns began to emerge. First, fifth-grade classes had children below grade level, with few children above grade level. Second, the achievement range of the class was typically broad, spanning the levels second grade through eighth grade, with most children at the lower end of the scale. Third, the distribution of ability appeared normal and class sizes for the past few years had been in the mid to upper twenties. Certified teachers using approved material had taught the upper level program for years.

Two facts were more relevant to depressed achievement than the others: the failure of the above-average ability children to perform above grade level and the wide range of achievement levels exhibited by the classes.

Since classroom teachers can rarely handle more than three relatively fixed reading groups, it appeared that the seven achievement levels extracted from test and teacher data would not have their needs met when condensed into three instructional groups. Because of this problem and the existence of classes with under thirty children, it was decided to look at a teaming format for fourth and fifth grade, whereby the children in both classes would be reassigned for the upcoming school year into one of six different reading level groups. The fourth and fifth grade teachers would take responsibility for three different groups. Tentative assignment to each group would be based on past school and test performance and teacher judgment.

It was agreed that the county reading skill sequence would be followed, rather than the skill sequence appearing in commercial basal readers. The county skill sequence was fairly specific, yet did not require mastery of skills at specific grade levels.

As a new organization began to emerge, other areas became affected. Flexibility in grouping, accurate record keeping, and a multi-text approach seemed very desirable.

A workshop was planned to 1. Establish criteria for assignment to instructional groups. 2. Create a record keeping system that would reflect a skill-based rather than basal-based program. 3. Select materials to match both identified needs and the county skill sequence. 4. Explore other instructional strategies that might include diagnostic teaching, use of pre tests, individualized reading instruction, etc.

The workshop evolved an excellent fall plan. Importantly, the staff grew in confidence in being able to better meet individual needs.

Joseph G. Czarnecki

Editorial

**Diagnosis
during
and after
Instruction**

The advantages and disadvantages of diagnosis before instruction make an obvious case for diagnosis during and after instruction. In classroom diagnosis, observation of the student's ability to respond to instruction is of prime importance. Through the direct observation of the student's responses, the teacher can avoid some of the time-consuming, costly, and sometimes questionable testing commonly linked to diagnosis. Also of prime importance is the continued assessment of the learning climate. That climate can change rapidly and without notice by the teacher unless there is a continuous assessment procedure. Student self-assessment should also be a continuous activity. As students' attitudes and self-concepts as readers change, it is important that teachers note the changes and adjust instruction according to those changes. Instead of the formal questionnaire, as was suggested in diagnosis before instruction, self-assessment can be informal and can occur during and after instruction. A simple, "How well do you think you did on this activity?" can provide important information for the teacher. If the students think they did very well and the teacher assessment is that they did very poorly, then it is conference time. During the conference it can be determined whether the students understood the assignment, the expectations, and the form of the final product.

Skills assessment during and after instruction rests heavily upon the ability of the teacher to observe various types of student behavior. Obviously, the products produced by the students are a valuable source of data as are the results from a teacher-made test. Of equal importance, however, is the student behavior during instruction. Attention to task, enthusiasm, cooperative spirit, and efficient study habits can only be observed during instruction. At times teachers are too busy to make accurate observations during instruction and the cooperation of others is needed. Other teachers, the principal, the reading teacher, an aide, or a parent volunteer can be asked to help. If the concern is with three or four students, then these students can be observed using a check list for several minutes apiece. If an observation is made every fifteen seconds for five minutes, the teacher will have twenty pieces of data. Information from observations can be noted on a form such as the following:

Table 4–5   **Example of Systematic Observation Record Keeping**

Student's Name	Paula			Date	May 4	
Activity a	independent		b		c	

Observation	On Task	Off Task	?	Working with Letters	Words	Sentences
1	✓					✓
2	✓					✓
3		✓		✓		
4		✓		✓		
5	✓					✓
6	✓					✓

Using this form, an entry for each activity is used to indicate whether the student is working with the teacher in a group, with the teacher individually, or independent from the teacher. Only two check marks are needed for each observation: (1) is the student on task, off task, or was it not possible to determine and (2) with what type of materials was the student supposed to have been working? If the pattern in the example were to continue, it would tell the teacher that Paula goes off task when working independently with letter-type activities, but is on task when working with sentences.

The teacher can now examine those letter exercises and see if they can be made more appealing; conference with Paula and discuss her on-task and off-task behavior to see if she has any ideas about how to improve things; or change to more sentence exercises so that Paula can benefit as much as possible from her school activities. Obviously, any behavior could be substituted for those shown; however, it is important to observe as few as possible at one time. Trying to observe too much behavior at one time tends to be confusing and produces unreliable results.

To assess reading behavior during and after instruction, the teacher will want to identify the context in which that behavior occurs. Is behavior during teacher-directed instruction the same as behavior while working independently or with an aide? Does a given student work better alone or with another student? When working alone, does the type of activity seem to generate different kinds of behavior? For example, some students may work quite well with the teacher, be completely inadequate when working at assigned work independently, and then work quite well again when working with a buddy. If the only sample of behavior were taken when working at assigned seat work, a distorted perception of the student's reading behavior would be obtained.

For the purpose of diagnosis, student behavior will be assessed in four reading situations.

1. Behavior while working with word recognition and word meaning activities
2. Behavior while reading orally
3. Behavior while reading silently
4. Behavior while responding to silent reading to demonstrate understanding of what has been read

The order of these activities does not indicate their importance. Usually the last one will be the most important source of data. Given a specific objective, however, any one of the four may be the most important in a given situation. For each activity, the teacher will try to obtain answers to the following questions:

1. What is the instructional level? It must be determined at which level each student can respond most effectively to instruction; normally, it is a point at which the student makes errors but does not fail completely. Teachers have numerous opportunities to observe students reading different types of materials. They realize that students do not have one instructional level, but several. In social studies materials, a given student may read at levels considerably above materials read in other areas. As a student encounters materials that are obviously too hard, instructional adjustments are necessary in either increased assistance through word introduction and concept development prior to reading, or reduction of the difficulty of the material by selecting different books.
2. Specifically, what types of skills do the readers possess? (What are their reading strengths?) Diagnostically, the teacher looks for those skills that the students have apparently mastered. For example, if a student always attacks the initial portion of the word accurately, initial consonants may be listed as mastered. The teacher also notes observed patterns of errors. Thus, both strengths and needs are credited.

3. What classroom adjustment can be used to teach to the students' strengths? What adjustments can be made to assist students in areas of needs? By starting with adjustments that will permit students to demonstrate strengths, success experiences can be developed. Awareness of adjustments that will help students in the areas of need will help teachers plan for continued student development.

4. Which activities seem to generate the most enthusiasm on the part of the student? The expression of interest or enthusiasm for learning is important to note, since all teachers need to know which types of activities motivate their students and which types seem to be boring or frustrating to them.

To answer each of the above questions, teachers directly observe students in three reading situations: word recognition and word meaning exercises, oral reading, and silent reading. Reading situations differ from skill areas in that each situation requires the use of one or more of the skills for acceptable performance. Improvement in the skill areas results in improvement in reading situations when the diagnosis has been effective in establishing the instructional strengths and needs of students. Word recognition exercises provide teachers with information concerning the ability of a student to handle words in isolation. Since almost all reading activities call for dealing with words in context, word recognition diagnosis is of little value. However, it does give the teacher some insight as to the word knowledge of a student. Word meaning exercises focus on the various meanings of words. Again, in isolation most word meanings are vague. What does *bank, ball, run, happy,* or *awkward* mean without a sentence of support? And service words such as *if, and, on,* and *when* carry meaning only as they relate to other words. Observation of students in oral reading provides teachers with the best insight into their overt reading behavior. It provides teachers with their only observation of the overt reading behavior of students when reading in context. That oral and silent reading require somewhat different behavior is a given fact. Probably oral and silent reading are more similar for beginning readers and become less similar as readers gain maturity. Silent reading provides teachers with the best situation to determine the comprehension performance of students. Observations in each situation provide information that is important for the complete picture of students' reading performances. Teachers add these observations to any testing information that they may have and formulate diagnostic hypotheses that they will attempt to interpret into intructional adjustments.

Word recognition and word meaning. Scores from word recognition– and word meaning– assessment activities can be used as a basis for selection of passages for initial diagnosis in oral and silent reading. Some analysis of performance with words in isolation can be conducted. Patterns of performance need to be observed in the various reading situations in order to develop sound diagnostic hypotheses. Each pattern of behavior observed should be followed by a statement of diagnosis, looking at both strengths and weaknesses. Strengths generally indicate areas in which a student is making a positive effort; therefore, attitudes as well as skills are reflected. The following are examples of observed student behavior and possible assessment implications.

1. The student refuses to pronounce words even after a delay of up to five seconds.
    strengths: unknown
    weaknesses: may not know the word;
    may have no apparent use of word attack skills
2. The student hesitates to pronounce a word but finally pronounces it after a delay of between two to five seconds.
    strength: may be using word attack skills or delayed recall of word form at sight
    weaknesses: may not be in sight vocabulary
3. The student partially pronounces the word but fails to pronounce entire word accurately (e.g., *ta . . .* for *table*)
    strength: uses graphic cues for portion of word pronounced, in this case, initial consonant and vowel sound
    weaknesses: may not be in sight vocabulary; may have difficulty in word attack with unpronounced portion of word, in this case, word ending
4. The student substitutes one word for another while maintaining the basic word meaning (e.g., *kitten* for *cat*)

> *strength:*   may have clue to word meaning through association
>
> *weakness:*   may be disregarding graphic cues

5. The student can pronounce a word accurately but does not know its meaning.

> *strength:*   uses graphic cues
>
> *weaknesses:* may need concept development;
>   may have worked so hard to pronounce the word that attention to meaning was not possible

6. The student confuses letter order—reversals (e.g., *was* for *saw, expect* for *except*).

> *strength:*   may be observing graphic cues
>
> *weaknesses:* may have directional confusion (orientation); may not know the word

Observations noted during word-recognition activities should be verified by observation in oral and silent reading activities.

Oral reading.   Observation during oral reading adds the dimension of the use of context. Teachers can observe how students use graphic and semantic (meaning) cues. The first three types of behavior discussed below are considered to be minor and are often the signs of thoughtful oral reading:

1. The student repeats words or phrases. Four types of repetitions should be considered.

   a. Student successfully changes first response to match text:

> *strengths:*   may be using context (semantic) cues; may be using graphic cues
>
> *weaknesses:* unknown

   b. Student attempts to correct but is unsuccessful:

> *strength:*   may be aware of semantic cues
>
> *weakness:*   may be unable to utilize graphic cues in this semantic setting fully

   c. Student simply repeats portion that was initially correct:

> *strength:*   may be attempting to improve intonation
>
> *weakness:*   may be biding for time to attack forthcoming segment of the passage

    d. Student changes an initially correct response:

        strength: may be changing passage into a more familiar language

        weakness: may be biding for time to attack forthcoming segment of the passage, searching for meaning.

2. The student omits words. Two types of omissions should be considered:

    a. The omission distorts meaning:

        strengths: unknown

        weaknesses: may not be reading for meaning; may not be in sight vocabulary

    b. Omission does not distort meaning:

        strength: may be reading for meaning

        weaknesses: may have too large an eye-voice span; may not be in sight vocabulary

We found that omissions occurred infrequently and account for less than 7 percent of oral reading errors and that 93 percent of the time they did not distort the meaning of the sentence.[16]

3. The student inserts words. Two types of insertions should be considered:

    a. The insertion distorts meaning:

        strengths: unknown

        weakness: may not be using semantic cues

    b. The insertion does not distort meaning:

        strength: may be embelling the author's meaning

        weakness: may have too large an eye-voice span

We found that insertions also occurred infrequently and accounted for less than 6 percent of oral reading errors and that 94 percent of the time they did not distort the meaning of the sentence.[17]

The remaining observations during oral reading take on more important diagnostic implications:

4. The student substitutes a word or nonword for the word in the passage. Substitutions account for more than 87 percent of oral reading errors.[18] When such a substitution occurs, it can be analyzed according to these types of information: graphic, syntactic, and semantic. These types of behavior were presented in a theoretical argument by Goodman.[19] Such an analysis considers qualitative as well as quantitative considerations. The qualitative aspects rest heavily with the student's reaction to the passage in a meaningful context.

Example: Student reads: "the big title was"
Text was: "the big table was"
Graphic initial—accurate
        medial—error
        final—accurate
Syntactic: accurate, a noun for a noun
Semantic: error, major change in meaning

Example: Student reads: "boy hurried down"
Text was: "boy hustled down"
Graphic: initial—accurate
        medial—variance
        final—accurate
Syntactic: accurate, a verb for a verb
Semantic: not accurate, but acceptable

These three types of oral reading behavior need to be considered in terms of how they relate to one another. Individually the strengths and weaknesses include these:

a. Student fails to use all graphic cues:

strengths: uses graphic cues for portions of words accurately pronounced;

                may be using syntactic and semantic cues

weaknesses: may fail to use all graphic cues available;

                may not be in sight vocabulary

b. Student fails to use syntactic cues:

strength: may be using graphic cues

weaknesses: may fail to use syntactic cues in the language;

                may not be in sight vocabulary

c. Student fails to use semantic cues:

strength: may be using graphic and syntactic cues

weaknesses: may not be in sight vocabulary;

                may be concentrating on pronunciation instead of meaning;

                may not be familiar with concepts

5. The student fails to observe punctuation:

strengths: unknown

weaknesses: decoding may be so difficult that punctuation is ignored;

                may be unaware of the function of punctuation

6. The student observes all punctuation via pauses and inflection:

       strengths: using semantic cues;
                     knows cues implied by punctuation
       weaknesses: unknown

7. The student loses place during oral reading:
       strengths: unknown
       weaknesses: may have directional confusion;
                     may be reading meaninglessly;
                     may have visual problem;
                     may be overconcentrating on decoding

8. The student reads word-by-word (all words pronounced accurately, but slowly with pauses between them and with much expression):
       strength: may be using graphic cues
       weaknesses: may not be using semantic cues;
                     may not have sufficient sight vocabulary

9. The student exhibits difficulty when asked questions although he accurately pronounced all words:
       strength: may be using graphic cues
       weaknesses: decoding may be so all-consuming that comprehension does not occur;
                     may have inadequate conceptual development; may have poor verbal memory

Normally reading assessment does not include oral reading comprehension as an important skill, especially when the reader is reading orally without reading silently first. We do recommend asking a question or two after oral reading to help the readers know that all reading should be purposeful. Errors in comprehension of passages read orally should always be confirmed in silent-reading situations.

Symptoms observed during oral reading should be based upon materials that the student can handle fairly well (accuracy 90–95 percent). All symptoms observed during attempts to read frustrating material are invalid due to the difficulty of the material, creating unnatural error patterns. (Readers tend to depend more heavily on graphic information when reading frustrating material.)

Silent reading. Assessment of silent-reading tasks takes place in two situations. First, during the silent reading itself and second, in comprehension activities that follow

The important diagnostic aspect of silent reading is the student's ability to demonstrate an understanding of the author's message.

silent reading. Comprehension assessment is difficult, but very important. If all other reading skills are functioning well but the readers are not obtaining meaning, then they are not reading. On the other hand, if other reading skills are incomplete but the readers are obtaining meaning, then they are functioning as readers. During silent reading, teachers can observe several instances of overt behavior that may aid in the total diagnosis:

1. The student moves lips and makes subvocalized sound during silent reading:
   strength: appears to be working on graphic cues
   weaknesses: may be overworking decoding;
   may be trying to remember what is read;
   may be a habit carried over from excessive oral reading
2. The student points to words with fingers:
   strength: may be using touch to keep place or to emphasize words
   weaknesses: orientation skills may need touch sup-

port; may be having decoding difficulties
3. The student shows physical signs of reading discomfort (e.g., rubbing of eyes, extreme restlessness, constant adjustment of book):
    strength: may be persevering with task
    weaknesses: possible difficulty of material;
                   possible physical defect—vision, nutrition, and the like;
                   possible emotional reaction to frustration

The important diagnostic aspect of silent reading is, of course, the ability of the student to demonstrate an understanding of the author's message. Five important considerations must be noted.

1. What types of questions are to be asked: literal questions that call for facts and details; interpretive questions that call for paraphrasing and drawing inferences; or problem-solving questions that call for critical and creative response and evaluative thinking?
2. What situation is the student facing when answering questions? A recall situation calls for the reading material to be unavailable during questioning. A locate situation encourages the student to find the answer in the reading material. Locating opportunities appear to have a great effect on a student's ability to respond to questions at all levels.
3. Was the student aware of purposes for silent reading?
4. How much exposure has the student had to the reading material? Are the responses expected after a single reading or after study and reexamination of the material? It is obvious that different performances may be expected depending on the amount of exposure to the material.
5. How much time has elapsed between the reading of the material and the student's response to it? If long-term memory is expected, comprehension responses can be expected to be less accurate.

The following procedure is suggested for silent-reading comprehension diagnosis.

1. Have the student read the story for a set purpose. At times the purpose is set by the teacher and at other times it is set by the students.
2. After the students have finished reading, give them a few moments to think about what they have read and then ask them to retell as much of the story as they can. From this the teacher can assess the personal meaning that various students were able to derive from the story.
3. Start questioning in a recall situation and with interpretive questions. Davey found that students answer literal questions more accurately when questioning starts with interpretive questions than they do when questions start with literal questions.[20] Then ask literal and problem-solving questions.
4. On all questions missed in the recall situation, permit students to return to the passage and locate the answers.

From steps 3 and 4 teachers have six types of comprehension scores from questioning. Using the number or percent of accurate responses, these scores can be charted as in Table 4–6.

Table 4-6   **Example of Comprehension Record Keeping Form for Diagnostic Use**

	Reading Situations	
Type of Response	**Recall**	**Locate**
Interpretive		
Literal		
Problem Solving		

The following behavior can be observed during the question-reaction period of a silent-reading lesson.

5. The student can decode the material but cannot respond to literal questions in a recall situation:

   strength: may be using graphics, semantic, and syntactic cues
   weaknesses: may have poor (visual) memory;

may need concept development related
to material read;

may be overconcentrating on graphic
cues

6. The student can decode the material and can respond to
literal questions in a locate situation:

strengths: may be using graphic, semantic, and
syntactic cues;

may be able to locate literally stated
ideas

weaknesses: unknown

7. The student can respond to literal understanding
questions but cannot interpret those ideas into own
words:

strengths: may be using graphic, semantic, and
syntactic cues;

uses literal understanding

weaknesses: possible overconcentration of graphic
cues; possible load difficulty;

possible failure to reflect on the author's ideas

8. The student can respond literally and can interpret the
author's ideas but cannot apply ideas to problem-solving situations:

strengths: may be using graphic, syntactic, and
semantic cues;

uses literal understanding;

uses interpretation

weaknesses: may have problem-solving skills;

possible misunderstanding of the
problem

9. The student can retell the story accurately but cannot
answer teacher-made questions relating to it:

strengths: shows literal understanding;

uses sequence skills

weakness: may have inability to anticipate teacher questions

10. The student can answer teacher-made questions when
allowed to study and reexamine passage, but not after a
single reading:

strength: gains meaning when allotted sufficient
time

weakness: may need repeated exposure for comprehension

11. The student can answer teacher-made questions immediately after reading but is unable to do so a day or so later:
   strength: may have short-term memory
   weakness: may not have adequate long-term memory

12. The student can answer questions covering short passage but is unable to do so on longer passages:
   strength: may have short-term memory
   weaknesses: may have inadequate long-term memory;
                   may lack organizational skills

Teachers should collect observational data relating to comprehension over a period of time. A given comprehension failure might be as attributable to story content, reader interest, or reader motivation on a given day as it is to reading ability. Once a consistent pattern is observed, teachers can make diagnostic hypotheses and start to make adjustments in the instructional aspects of the reading program.

Three Cautions

First, observation of reading behavior is a learned skill. Consistent practice, the habit of keeping careful records, and double and triple checking of findings are musts. Obviously one repetition in an oral reading situation cannot become a diagnostic hypothesis. A danger also exists that classroom observations will lead to a fractionalized view of the reader. Every reader is more than the sum of skills listed on the preceding pages—a lot more. The classroom teacher in a diagnostic role needs to pull back periodically and observe the whole reader. Such observations may reveal that the reader is always on-task, enjoying the reading activities, helping others, and happy. Perhaps such observations are more important than a listing of skill strengths and weaknesses. At least they should be recorded as equally important information.

Second, many readers do very poorly during the initial efforts to respond in a diagnostic setting. They are attempting to determine what is expected of them and may be quite nervous since they do not know what is going to happen next. For this reason, it is recommended that students respond to a practice passage of relatively easy material. In this case, student performance on the first passage read orally would not be counted in the assessment. Likewise, the student response to the first silent reading passage would not be counted. Our interest is in determining how well these students can read, so we want to provide the best assessment situation that we can.

Third, in comprehension assessment the reader's prior knowledge of the content of the passages being read is going to have an effect upon how well that story is comprehended. It is possible to be fooled completely about a reader's comprehension skills or the lack of them. For example, most of us have considerable knowledge about the events surrounding the assassination of President Kennedy and would feel very comfortable reading a passage or two about that day in Dallas. If, however, the passages to be read were about the Battle of Hastings most of us would be a bit uncomfortable because we cannot bring much prior knowledge to that event in history. If your comprehension were to be assessed using one of these two events in history, undoubtedly, most of you would choose the passages about the assassination of President Kennedy. In classroom assessment of reading comprehension it is therefore helpful to assess comprehension over a period of time using a variety of passages.

QUESTIONS TO PINPOINT DIAGNOSTIC FINDINGS

From word recognition, oral reading, and silent reading data, teachers should seek answers to the following questions:

Skill Area: prereading-readiness skills. If answers to questions in this area are yes, remedial suggestions can be found in chapter 1.

1. Do language skills appear to be underdeveloped?
2. Do speech skills appear to be underdeveloped?
3. Does dialect usage appear to cause difficulty?
4. Do visual or auditory problems appear to be causing discomfort?
5. Do visual discrimination skills appear to be underdeveloped?
6. Do auditory discrimination skills appear to be underdeveloped?

7. Do reversals occur frequently enough to cause confusion?
8. Does student frequently lose place during reading?

Skill Area: sight vocabulary. If answers to questions in this area are yes, remedial suggestions can be found in chapter 8.

1. Does student miscall small, similar words?
2. Do words missed represent abstract concepts?
3. Do word meanings appear to be confused?
4. Does student know words in context but not in isolation?
5. Does student appear to know words at end of a lesson, but not the next day?

Skill Area: word attack. If answers to questions in this area are yes, remedial suggestions can be found in chapter 8.

Phonics:

1. Does student use graphic cues? Which graphic cues are used?
2. Does student attack small words accurately, but not larger ones?
3. Does student seem to know sound-symbol relationships but seem unable to use them during reading?

Structural:

1. Do words missed contain prefixes or suffixes?
2. Are words missed compound words?

Contextual:

1. Does student appear to ignore syntactic cues?
2. Does student appear to ignore semantic cues?
3. Does student appear to ignore punctuation cues?

Skill Area: comprehension. If answers to questions in this areas are yes, remedial suggestions can be found in chapter 9.

1. Do large units of material seem to interfere with comprehension?

2. Do comprehension difficulties occur with some types of comprehension and not others? (Literal comprehension is weak but interpretive is good.)
3. Does student respond when given opportunities to retell stories from a personal point of view?
4. Does student have difficulty using locating skills?
5. Does student have difficulty understanding material read in content areas?
6. Does student reorganize what has been read so that it makes sense from a personal point of view?
7. Does student fail to comprehend most of what has been read?

INTERESTS, HABITS, AND ATTITUDES

An evaluation of student interest, habits, and attitudes is an important part of classroom diagnosis. Teachers, through regular observation of student performances, are in the ideal setting to note changes in interests, habits and attitudes. An effort should be made to note effective and ineffective habits that seem to very considerably from those of the average student. The classroom teacher is likely to be asked by the reading specialist for information concerning interest, habits and attitudes; therefore, observations should be noted carefully. Specifically, classroom teachers should obtain answers to the following questions:

1. What uses do students make of free reading opportunity? Do they appear eager to use free time for reading, or is reading only the result of constant prodding?
2. Do students appear anxious or reluctant to read orally? Silently? Does there appear to be a difference in attitude between oral and silent situations?
3. Are signs of reluctance noticeable in reading situations only or in all learning situations? Students who hesitate in all learning situations must be motivated; whereas those reluctant in reading alone need success and reward in reading.
4. In what reading situations are students most or least effective? Do students tend to enjoy providing answers orally as opposed to writing them? Do questions that call for summaries get better results than specific questions?

Students often develop habits as a result of what has been expected by other teachers.

5. Do students have to be prodded to finish reading assignments? If they cannot work without supervision even when specific assignments have been made, unsupervised reading situations should be avoided in initial remedial instruction.
6. What types of book selections do the students make in the library? Considerable information can be obtained about interests by noticing the types of books chosen from the library. Remedial efforts should start with the type of material in which students have indicated an interest.

Answers to the above questions will become important guides to the initial remedial sessions. Teachers will find it useful to record these findings so that they will have a record of accurate data and be able to inform the reading specialist. Although these questions will be answered for the most part by informal observation, teachers should give them special attention and become active agents in collecting information.

At times, it is not possible to obtain precise yes or no answers to such questions. In these cases, teachers should continue to observe the readers until they can substantiate accurate patterns of errors. Specifically, teachers may provide students with individualized exercises to do independently, go over their responses, and have a short conference about their responses. As a part of informal, on-the-spot diagnosis, this technique can be useful in verifying classroom diagnosis. Suppose, for example, that one has diagnosed irregular patterns of difficulty with final consonant sounds. Several carefully prepared exercises with final consonant sounds can be developed, administered, and analyzed for the purpose of verification. Further verification can come from information available in school records, from parental interviews, from past observations, from classroom diagnostic tests, and from subsequent instruction.

Pencil-and-paper interest surveys can be used to obtain information about areas that are motivating to the students. However, interests change rapidly, creating a situation in which the results of a survey may not be appropriate several weeks from the time it was administered. Sample questions for an interest survey might include:

1. What things do you like to do when you get home from school?
2. If you could wish for three things for your future, what would they be?
3. Name three of your favorite television shows.
4. Do you enjoy participating in sports? If so, which sports?
5. Do you have any hobbies? If so, what are they?

Such questions tend to provide the teacher with natural areas of interests. Books and articles about these areas can now be read in the classroom by these students. Lessons can be planned to feature activities related to the interests of the students.

RECORD KEEPING

Classroom diagnosis effectiveness will rest to a large extent upon the records teachers keep. The type of records will vary with the purpose of the diagnostic activities. Several examples of record-keeping procedures follow:

1. Table 4–7 is an example of group record keeping. An entire class can be monitored by this type of record using no more than two sheets of lined $8'' \times 11\frac{1}{2}''$ paper .
2. Another type of group record can be used to monitor student progress over time. The teacher can determine what data are available and periodically assess student behavior in those areas. One we have found useful is shown in Table 4–7:

Table 4–7   **Example of Group Record Keeping**

Name	Botel WO	Oral Reading Accuracy	Comprehension	Placement Reader Level
Pat	3^2	97%	Good	3^2
Warren	4	99%	Good	4
JoEtta	3^1	95%	Fair	3^1
Ron	3^1	90%	Poor	3^1

Students in this record were placed according to the *Botel Word Opposites (Reading) Test*. The teacher periodically asks individual students to read orally a 100-word passage. Their oral reading accuracy is sampled in this

Table 4–8   **Example of Individual Record Keeping Form**

Name *Marianne Harvey* Age *12* Teacher *Dolores Pfieffer*

Grade *6* Date record initiated *October, 1980*

	Date *Oct., 1980* Score	Date *May, 1980* Score
Scores:		
Word Recognition	*3.5*	*4.5*
Oral Reading Accuracy	*4.0*	*5.5*
Silent Reading		
Recall Comp.	*4.5*	*6.0*
Locate Comp.	*6.0*	*7.0*

Strengths:	**Strengths**	**Strengths**
Word Recognition		
Oral Reading Behavior		*greatly improved*
Silent Reading Comp.	*comprehension using locating skills*	*recall comprehension greatly improved*

Weaknesses:	**Weaknesses**	**Weaknesses**
Word Recognition	*pronouncing words in isolation*	*improved*
Oral Reading Behavior	*oral reading accuracy*	
Silent Reading Comp.		

Interests and
Attitudes   *She is very interested in camping, backpacking, and outdoor activities. She plays center on school basketball team.*

Comments: *She is very sensitive about her reading, seems embarrassed to talk about it.*

manner. Note that in Table 4–7, Ron appears to be having considerable difficulty with his accuracy in the 3^1 reader. Then, over time, the teacher jots down impressions received about each student's responses during comprehension lessons. Ron again seems to be doing poorly. Having obtained this type of information, the teacher may consider placing Ron in material that he can handle with better comprehension and better oral reading accuracy. Using this type of record and updating the data several times during the year will assist in keeping students in appropriate materials for instruction.

3. A third type of record keeping involves a detailed account of the reading-skill development of individual students. Such records are time consuming to develop and probably would be maintained only on the students about whom you have the most concern. These records would include test scores and data from teacher observations and would be collected periodically. Table 4–8 can be adapted for individual record keeping.

4. Records can be kept on an informal basis. Using a 5 × 8 index card for each student, the teacher can jot down important behavior noted during any lesson. Dates and behavior observed serve as a suitable record of student progress. Table 4–9 shows the types of entries that may be recorded:

Table 4–9	Example of Informal Record Keeping

9/12 Administered Botel Word Opposites Test—Jim scored at 3^2 level.

9/15 Jim comprehended well in the 3^2 material.

10/3 Jim appears to have trouble completing assignments in his social studies book. I'll try to introduce new concepts.

10/7 After introduction of new concepts, Jim comprehended material in his social studies book well.

As the teacher makes decisions about record-keeping formats, care should be taken to assure that the records do not create unreasonable time demands. It is suggested that careful records be maintained on a few important types of behavior instead of inaccurate records on many types.

FOUR FINAL QUESTIONS

Teachers should reflect upon the answers to the following four questions to complete an effective classroom diagnosis and to assist them in establishing more clearly the validity of their findings:

1. Did the students make the same error in both easy and difficult material, or did the observed errors indicate frustration with the material? We are most interested in the errors made at the instructional level, the level at which we hope to make improvement. All readers make errors when reading at their frustration level; these errors, however, normally do not lead to diagnostic conclusions, for these are not the errors upon which remediation is based.

2. Were the errors first interpreted as slowness actually an effort on the part of the reader to be especially careful and precise and to be reflective? Beware of diagnostic conclusions drawn from the students' responses to questions on material read due to slowness, especially when timed standardized tests are used or when testing situations make the reader aware of being evaluated. Many students have been taught to be impulsive with their responses when, in fact, reflective behavior may be considerably more desirable.

3. Can students be helped as a result of classroom diagnosis, or is further diagnosis necessary? Further testing with any of the instruments mentioned under clinical diagnosis may be in order and is appropriate when the teacher has the knowledge of their proper usage and interpretation and the time to use them. At this point, however, the services of a reading specialist may be required.

4. Did the students appear to concentrate while being directly observed, or did they seem easily distracted? Children who appear to be distracted during observation may have produced unreliable symptoms.

The diagnostic task has been to observe individuals through analysis of symptoms, to associate the symptoms to appropriate skill areas, to determine the significance of the errors, and to organize the information in terms of practical classroom adjustments. On only a few occasions will diagnosis be concluded at this point. An ongoing process, diagnosis will normally continue during the remedial sessions, always attempting to obtain more precise information concerning the readers. Morris feels that this is the important advantage for the classroom teacher. He states, "To the teacher . . . the challenge is to get to grips more directly with the problem and by working with the individual pupil try to understand what is leading him astray."[21] To this can be added: and to determine more precisely the skill, *strengths*, and deficiencies of the student.

EARLY IDENTIFICATION

Teachers are capable of making early identifications of children who are likely to experience difficulty in school. In Maryland, a multidiscipline task force worked two years to develop assessment instruments to identify children with potential learning handicaps. They found the best device for such identification to be systematic teacher observations.[22] At the University of Maryland reading clinic, we found a similar result when asking teachers to identify potential reading problems. They identified them more accurately than did the tests that we administered. In some schools, early identification occurs in kindergarten. When accompanied by specific symptoms, such identification assists teachers to modify educational programs to increase the possibilities of success. Some children might best start with a phonics-based program; others might profit from one that stresses sight learning. Some succeed best when the initial program uses the language-experience approach, and others need multisensory techniques. Such programs have the potential to assist children to get a successful start in school and to avoid several years of failure.

Several problems are related to early identification programs. First, if they stop with identification, they may do more harm than good. Second, when tests are relied upon heavily, many children become identified erroneously, and others are not identified when they should be. Thirdly, providing teachers with check lists of behavior that may cause learning problems may result in self-fulfillment. For example, if a teacher is told that children in first grade who make reversals may have serious reading problems, teachers might react to children so identified in such ways that create nonlearning. Finally, parents can be aroused to such a state of anxiety as to alarm the child.

If early identification programs are to be implemented, several safeguards can be applied to avoid the above-mentioned problems. Early identification should never be made using a single testing instrument. Children who have been initially identified should be reevaluated periodically. Early identification programs should be accompanied by instructional adjustments. Parents should be informed of the program and the advantages it offers their children. All early identification programs should be carefully monitored and periodically evaluated to be certain they are effective.

SUMMARY

Classroom diagnostic assessment involves the observation and testing of student behavior. It also involves the assessment of the learning climate. Classroom diagnostic assessment can take place before, during, or after instruction. Teachers are encouraged to diagnose for strengths as well as for needs. Evaluation of student self-appraisal is a recommended tactic for classroom diagnosis.

Teachers should develop some type of record keeping to reflect classroom diagnosis. These records are used to assess skill development, to aid in communication with other teachers and parents, and to evaluate the success of instructional adjustments.

NOTES

1. Roger Farr, *Reading: What Can Be Measured?* (Newark, Del.: IRA, 1969), pp. 97, 212–18.
2. William R. Powell, "The Validity of the Instructional Reading Level," *Diagnostic Viewpoints in Reading* (1971): 121–33.
3. William K. Durr, ed., *Reading Difficulties* (Newark, Del.: IRA, 1970), pp. 67–132.
4. Emmett A. Betts, *Foundations of Reading Instruction* (New York: American Book Co., 1946).
5. William R. Powell, "Revised Criteria for the Informal Reading Inventory," (Speech presented at International Reading Association, New Orleans, La., May 3, 1974).

6. Ibid., p. 11.
7. William R. Powell, "Measuring Reading Informally," (Paper presented at International Reading Association, Houston, Texas, 1978) p. 9.
8. Ibid., p. 8.
9. Robert E. Mills and Jean R. Richardson, "What Do Publishers Mean by Grade Level?" *Reading Teacher* 16, no. 5 (March 1963): 359–62.
10. Mae C. Johnson, "Comparison of Readability Formulas" (Ph. D. diss., University of Maryland Reading Center, 1971).
11. Lowell D. Eberwein, "The Variability of Basal Reader Textbooks and How Much Teachers Know About It," *Reading World* 18, no. 3 (1979): 259–72.
12. Earl F. Rankin and Joseph W. Culhane, "Comparable Cloze and Multiple Choice Comprehension Test Scores," *Journal of Reading*, December 1969, p. 194.
13. John T. Guthrie et al., "The Maze Techniques to Assess, Monitor Reading Comprehension," *Reading Teacher* 28, no. 2, (November 1974): 161–68.
14. William H. Rupley, "Criterion Referenced Tests," *The Reading Teacher* 28 (1975): 426.
15. Cathy Stallard, "Comparing Objective Based Reading Programs," *Journal of Reading* 21, no. 5 (Oct. 1977) 36–44.
16. Karen D'Angelo and Robert M. Wilson, "How Helpful is Insertion and Omission Analysis?", *Reading Teacher* 32, no. 5 (February 1979): 519–20.
17. Ibid.
18. Ibid.
19. Kenneth S. Goodman, "Analysis of Oral Reading Miscues: Applied Psycholinguistics," *Reading Research Quarterly* 5 (Fall 1969): 9–30.
20. H. Beth Davey, "The Effect of Question Order on Comprehension Test Performance at the Literal and Interpretive Levels," Faculty research paper, University of Maryland, Reading Center, 1975.
21. Ronald Morris, *Success and Failure in Learning to Read* (London: Oldbourne, 1963), p. 159.
22. *Reading in Maryland* (Baltimore, Md.: Division of Instruction, Maryland State Department of Education, 1974-75).

SUGGESTED READINGS

Deboer, Dorothy L., ed. *Reading Diagnosis and Evaluation.* Newark, Del.: International Reading Association, 1970. Emphasis is on the diagnostic aspects of reading. This IRA collection features early identification, use of testing, and formal approaches.

Durr, William K., ed. *Reading Difficulties.* Newark, Del.: International Reading Association, 1970. The second section, "The Informal Inventories," includes six articles by different authors on the various aspects of informal inventories. Readers who are unfamiliar with informal techniques will want to study this section.

Farr, Roger. *Reading: What Can Be Measured?* Newark, Del.: International Reading Association, 1969. An excellent paperback that looks at the value and limitations of the various measuring instruments used in reading. Farr has prepared a valuable resource for teachers.

Geyer, James R., and Matanzo, Jane. *Programmed Reading Diagnosis for Teachers: with Prescriptive References.* Columbus, O.: Charles E. Merrill, 1977. For those who want practice coding and analyzing reading behavior, this book may be interesting. Aside from specific practice exercises, case studies are included for prescription writing. Suggested answers are provided throughout.

Goodman, Kenneth S. Analysis of Oral Reading Miscues: Applied Psycholinguistics." *Reading Research Quarterly* 5 (Fall 1969): 9–30. Goodman states his case for oral reading analysis in this article. This view of the reader as a processor of language cues is important for those who wish to become skilled diagnostic teachers.

Stallard, Cathy. "Comparing Objective Based Reading Programs." *Journal of Reading* 21, no. 1. (Oct. 1977), 36–44. Stallard discusses criterion-referenced testing programs and instructional programs. The coverage is useful for those considering a commercial program for their students.

Clinical Diagnosis

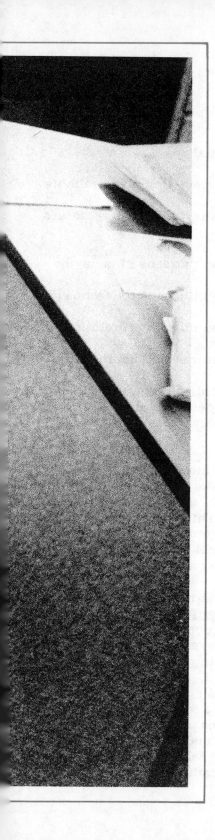

Chapter Emphasis

- Clinical diagnosis is individual

- Clinical diagnosis is both systematic and unreliable

- Clinical diagnosis involves varying levels of assessment

- Clinical diagnosis relies upon patterns of behavior

- Clinical diagnosis relies upon diagnostic lessons

- Clinical diagnosis relies upon data interpretation

- Clinical diagnosis relies upon record keeping

   Note: All tests mentioned in this chapter are included in Appendix A, which provides a detailed check list indicating each test's characteristics.

Clinical diagnosis is conducted by a reading specialist using a variety of assessment techniques to collect the data needed to plan instruction or make recommendations for instruction. In clinical diagnosis, the student is usually evaluated out of the classroom. This involves taking the student to a testing area in the building or to a testing facility out of the building. Clinical diagnosis features an individual evaluation of the reader and the reading situation.

   The purposes of clinical diagnosis are the same as those for classroom diagnosis. The questions asked are the same questions asked in classroom diagnosis. Clinical diagnosis is required when the best efforts at the classroom level have not resulted in helping the student to be a successful reader. It is assumed, therefore, that all or portions of the classroom diagnosis were not effective and that the classroom teacher makes a referral request. This is not always the case, however, since parents, other resource people, and other teachers may make the referral. Occasionally a student will make a self-referral, asking for specific help in some aspect of reading.

The major advantages of clinical diagnosis are these:

1. It is individual in nature.
2. It is conducted by specially trained professionals.
3. It utilizes the best assessment instruments available.
4. It relieves the classroom teacher for other responsibilities.
5. It utilizes a variety of professional resources.
6. It utilizes data from a variety of sources.

These advantages may make clinical diagnosis sound superior to and more desirable than classroom diagnosis. And sometimes it is. But clinical diagnosis is complicated with rather severe limitations. Some of those follow:

1. Evaluation of a reader in an individual setting does not necessarily provide information about that reader's behavior in a group setting.
2. The matching of clinical data with instructional procedures and materials is an error-ridden procedure.
3. Conflicting clinical data can lead to confusion instead of enlightenment.
4. Clinical diagnosis tends to focus upon the deficiencies of the reader and may well overlook deficiencies in the learning climate.

As we discuss clinical diagnosis we will attempt to offer suggestions to overcome, or, at least, minimize, these limitations. Our experience with over 2,000 clinical cases leads us to advise that clinical diagnosis be a continuous activity. That is, once the initial assessment recommendations are made, the reader's progress should be continuously monitored to assure a successful outcome. Although most readers who receive adjusted instruction recommended by a clinical assessment make spectacular progress, some do not. And some of those do not respond even after continued instruction adjustments and continued assessment. In other words, we do not know all of the answers to failure in learning to read. We know more now than we did in previous editions of this book and, with continued study, expect to know more in the future. But some of the difficulties are caused by subtle, untestable problems in the learning climate or within the reader, not the least of which is the development of an "I-can't" attitude. As discussed in chapter 1, when the failure syndrome is severe; when the reader has seldom or never experienced success in reading; and especially when the reader has been in this situation for three or more years, it is possible that there is sufficient damage to the reader's self-esteem that remediation will not be effective. As we approach clinical assessment, we do so with these thoughts in mind.

Although there is great variation in the steps taken to conduct a clinical diagnosis, the following suggestions can be adapted to the uniqueness of a specific situation.

REFERRAL

Readers are referred to reading specialists through some type of referral system. This system not only refers the readers but is the starting point of data collection for the clinical diagnosis.

In the school setting, a screening committee might well be the referral agency. That committee gathers all available information concerning the referred readers and forwards those data with the referral. When referrals are made outside the school (to a college reading clinic, for example) the receiving agency usually asks for data from the referring agency. The referral form (on pages 149–151) is one that we are now using when parents refer their children to the University of Maryland Reading Clinic. It provides us with important preassessment data and often prevents us from making serious mistakes in our assessment activities. For example, we recently examined a deaf child. By using the information on the form we knew in advance that this child was deaf so we were certain to have a "signer" at the initial evaluation session.

Besides obtaining information from referring parents, outside agencies should take advantage of existing school records. Scores on tests, information from classroom diagnosis, health records, and progress in school are types of data available in school records that can be helpful in a clinical diagnosis.

University of Maryland   College of Education   Reading Center

Date *September 9, 1981*

Child's Name *Daniel C. Wagner* Birthdate *02-08-71* Grade *6*
Mother's Name *Frances E. Wagner* Occupation *store manager*
                                   Business Phone *1-203-445-8394*
Father's Name *James E. Wagner*   Occupation *Cabinet Maker*
                                   Business Phone *1-203-445-8394*
Home Address *222 Poquonnock Rd.* Child's School _____
College Park, Ct. 06340   Address _____
　　　　　　　　　　Zip Code
　　　　　　　　　　　　　　　　　　　　　　_____
Home Phone *445-4216*   Principal *Mrs. Mildred Brown*

Reason for referral to University of Maryland Reading Clinic
Classroom teacher suggested it. They have met with no success at his school.

Please be sure to fill out the attached questionnaire and return
all of this to the University of Maryland, College of Education,
Reading Center, College Park, Maryland 20742.

Place an X on the line following each question and add comments
when appropriate.

	Not at all 1	Perhaps 2	Certainly 3
1. Do you believe health problems have affected your child's reading?	X		

If 2 or 3, please comment _____

_____

	Not at all 1	Perhaps 2	Certainly 3
2. Do you believe attitude problems have affected your child's reading?	X		

If 2 or 3, please comment _____

_____

	Not at all 1	Perhaps 2	Certainly 3

3. Do you believe teaching procedures have affected your child's reading?

    [X marked between Perhaps and Certainly]

If 2 or 3, please comment *They use the same set of readers for all children even when a given set does not work well.*

	Not at all 1	Perhaps 2	Certainly 3

4. Do you believe teacher attitude has affected your child's reading?

    [X marked at Not at all]

If 2 or 3, please comment _____

	Not at all 1	Perhaps 2	Certainly 3

5. Do you believe problems at home have affected your child's reading?

    [X marked at Perhaps]

If 2 or 3, please comment *I never learned to read well. Maybe it is my fault.*

	No 1	They tried, but 2	Very well 3

6. Do you believe the school authorities have responded to your child's problem?

    [X marked at No]

Please comment *The teachers seem to care but the school does not even provide special help for those having trouble with their reading.*

	No	Yes

7. Is this your first referral of your child for help with reading problems?

    [X marked at Yes]

If no, please explain _____

8. How many schools has your child attended? ① 2 3 4 5
9. If your child was retained a grade, what grade? *2nd*

10. Do you believe your child believes that reading is valued in the home?

Not at all	Some	A lot
	X	

11. How frequently did you read to your child when he/she was:

	Not at all	Occasionally	Almost daily
2–4 years old?		X	
5–6 years old?		X	
7–8 years old?	X		
9+ years old?	X		

12. Is your child now reading a book that is not a school requirement?

No	Yes
X	

If yes, what book _____

a. Is the mother?

No	Yes
X	

If yes, what book _____

b. Is the father?

No	Yes
	X

If yes, what book _Beautiful Swimmers._

13. Have there been other reading problems in the family?

No	Yes
	X

If yes, please comment _As I mentioned, I never learned to read well._

14. Do you help your child with his/her reading at home?

Not at all	Some	A lot
X		

If ''some'' or ''a lot,'' what do you do? _____

Use back side to tell us anything not included on this side.

INITIAL SCREENING

Since most reading specialists have less time than they need to service all of the students referred to them, a screening procedure needs to be established. The purpose of the screening is to obtain a rough estimate of the reading skills possessed by the reader. The screening results can be evaluated by the referring committee and plans for future help can be made. Screenings in out-of-school clinical agencies save hours of diagnostic time. We have found, for example, that about one-third of the students referred to us for clinical diagnosis have no reading difficulties. These referrals are usually based on a decline in school grades, a concern raised by an article in the press, or an interest in the reader's development without concern that there are difficulties. Obviously, there is no need for a full-blown clinical diagnosis in such cases.

We recommend that screenings include some indication of mental ability, oral reading behavior, comprehension after silent reading, word-attack skills or study skills, and a diagnostic lesson. Screenings take about an hour and a half to two hours. A running example, a reader named Walt, will help to illustrate the type of data collected in an initial screening. The following steps are examples of initial screening procedures.

Establishing Rapport

Purposes: a. Relax the reader and develop a communicative atmosphere.
b. Obtain information from the reader.

Procedures:
a. Using the referral form, discuss areas that appear to be strengths.
b. Use the self-assessment procedure discussed on page 102.
c. Use an interview guide form to gain interest information.

Time needed: Generally, about five minutes. At times a very shy student may need more time to relax and feel comfortable.

Walt example:
Age 12   Grade 7
Likes school, football, mathematics, cooking, and skateboards

Establishing rapport helps relax the reader and develop a communicative atmosphere.

Does not care for water sports or history
Says he has few friends

Indication of
Mental Ability

In a screening situation all we can obtain is an indication of mental ability. The careful testing of mental ability would take more time than the entire screening. As such, the indication must be evaluated liberally. We suggest using the standard error for a range score.

Purposes: a. Determine a reading expectancy (level or range).

b. Determine the need for further testing of intellectual ability, i.e., excessively high or low scores or scores that do not fit other available data (teacher observation, listening comprehension, other scores on tests of mental ability). In these cases, further testing is recommended.

Procedures: In a screening we will generally use a quick test of mental ability, but this will be supplemented with reading specialist observation during the screening. For example, if a reader scores poorly on a test of mental ability, but has a good speaking vocabulary and scores well in reading comprehension, then the ability score is in doubt.

Examples of types of tests:
    Listening section of the Diagnostic Reading Scales (Test 4)
    Peabody Picture Vocabulary Test
    Slosson Intelligence Test
    Verbal Opposites of the Detroit Tests of Learning Aptitudes

Time needed: Five to fifteen minutes

Walt example:
    Age 12   Grade 7
    Likes football, school, mathematics, cooking, and skateboards
    Does not care for water sports or history
    Says he has few friends.
    Ability range: Age 10–12

Oral Reading Testing

This testing can be divided into two subsections, oral reading of isolated words and oral reading in context.

Oral reading of isolated words.   (Word recognition)

Purpose: To obtain a quick estimate of reading level to determine the starting point for further testing.

Procedures: Many word recognition tests are available. A few examples are:
    Botel Word Recognition
    Diagnostic Reading Scales (see sample on page 156)
    Woodcock Reading Mastery

Time needed: Five to ten minutes

Walt example:
    Age 12   Grade 7
    Likes football, school, mathematics, cooking, and skateboards
    Does not care for water sports or history
    Says he has few friends
    Ability range: Age 10–12
    Word recognition: Grade 4

Note: Some authorities suggest rather sophisticated procedures be used in testing word recognition using timed and untimed responses. Others suggest an analysis of word recognition errors. In a screening situation we feel that such procedures are too time-consuming and are not warranted. These two procedures will be discussed under the topic of extended diagnosis. Note that the only purpose for word recognition testing in a screening is for placement in other tests.

Oral reading in context.

Purposes: a. Determine oral reading level.
         b. Determine oral reading comprehension.
         c. Evaluate oral reading behavior to gain insight into the reader's oral reading strategies.

The procedures for purpose c are different from those for purposes a and b. Since a given screening may utilize all three purposes, the procedures for each will be presented. Procedures for purposes a and b: Many test instruments are available for these two purposes. Examples are:

Diagnostic Reading Scales
Gilmore Oral Reading Tests
Gray Oral Reading Test
Informal reading inventory
Slosson Oral Reading Test

Although the directions for administration of these tests vary, they have the following basic ingredients: the student reads aloud from graded selections, ranging from simple to difficult; the examiner records the reader's responses as outlined by the manual; scores are based on a frequency count rather than a qualitative analysis; several comprehension questions are asked that normally provide a measure of the reader's ability to recall specifically stated facts from the story. The value of oral-reading comprehension scores is subject to question. During oral reading, most readers are concentrating on pronunciation and fluency. The valuable insights we get from an analysis of oral reading relate to those processes that the reader demonstrates. The skills of comprehension are best measured after silent reading. Why, then, ask questions after oral reading? Starting with purpose-setting questions and following oral reading with those questions helps the students see purpose in their reading.

Sample

_____	1.	look	_____	26.	good
_____	2.	come	_____	27.	girl
_____	3.	in	_____	28.	name
_____	4.	the	_____	29.	away
_____	5.	you	_____	30.	this
_____	6.	one	_____	31.	bed
_____	7.	she	_____	32.	call
_____	8.	mother	_____	33.	time
_____	9.	me	_____	34.	sleep
_____	10.	yellow	_____	35.	fish
_____	11.	pig	_____	36.	morning
_____	12.	it	_____	37.	seen
_____	13.	big	_____	38.	children
_____	14.	milk	_____	39.	live
_____	15.	dog	_____	40.	around
_____	16.	tree	_____	41.	barn
_____	17.	are	_____	42.	other
_____	18.	day	_____	43.	under
_____	19.	run	_____	44.	cry
_____	20.	all	_____	45.	chicken
_____	21.	father	_____	46.	breakfast
_____	22.	door	_____	47.	chair
_____	23.	like	_____	48.	rain
_____	24.	ball	_____	49.	asleep
_____	25.	eat	_____	50.	peep

total score _____

placement _____

Number Correct	Grade Placement
11-13	1.3
14-20	1.6
21-32	1.8
33-44	2.3
*45-50	2.8

*If student achieves this level, administer List 2.

A portion of word recognition test from Diagnostic Reading Scales.

As with word recognition, many reading specialists prefer to construct informal tests of oral reading. Using the graded materials that the student may be expected to read, passages are selected. Accuracy, if a level of oral reading is desired, is recorded as it is on standardized tests of oral reading. Using informal tests of oral reading during diagnosis offers the advantages of larger selections and a variety of content. A major disadvantage is inherent in the assumption that the graded materials used for the tests are, in fact, accurately graded. For example, if a given selection taken from a fifth-grade book is actually at the sixth-grade level, diagnostic conclusions that come from it are faulty. Another limitation relates to how such tests are interpreted. Pikulski states that an informal inventory's usefulness in diagnosis is related to how well the testing material matches the material to be used for instruction.[1] Obviously, if they are mismatched, interpretation of results is difficult.

Oral reading tests as diagnostic tools are plagued by several limitations. In the first place, there is considerable disagreement about what an oral-reading error is. Certainly, one would recognize mispronounced words, hesitancy on unknown words, or disregard of punctuation marks as obvious limitations to effective oral reading, at least as far as the listening audience is concerned. But is it an error when a reader repeats words to correct oral reading mistakes? Is it an error when a student stops to use word-attack skills on words not known at sight? Or are these examples of the type of behavior that we want readers to display? Are all errors of equal importance, or do some interfere with reading efficiency more seriously than others? If weights could be developed for various types of errors, would the same weight hold at various grade levels? For example, would a vowel error made by a first grader be as serious an error as a vowel error made by a fifth grader?

Test constructors, in an effort to standardize oral reading tests, have had to establish some easily recognizable arbitrary standards of accurate and inaccuate oral reading. Although these arbitrary systems vary, most of them include markings similar to those listed in the *Gilmore Oral Reading Test.*[2] Substitutions and mispronunciations are written above the word for which the substitution was made; omissions are circled; repetitions are underlined; words inserted are put in the appropriate place; punctuation that is disregarded is marked by an *x*;

hesitations of two seconds or more are marked by a check mark above the word; at five seconds, these words are pronounced for the reader, and two check marks are indicated. Diagnosis, of course, depends upon the accurate marking of errors and a valid interpretation of them. Naturally, the marking system will somewhat control the type of information available for interpretation.

The following paragraph has been marked according to the system discussed:

A spaceman has stepped onto the surface of the moon.

He is very careful as he steps from his capsule. Live

television brings the moment to the entire population of

the earth. It is an exciting moment.

With such marking, a student's reading is recorded. This student hesitated on the word *has* and failed to pronounce the word *stepped* in five seconds, mispronounced *surface* and disregarded the period after *moon,* repeated *He is very,* substituted *telephone* for *television* and *a* for *an,* omitted *entire,* and added *very.* The above paragraph illustrates not only the marking system but also the fact that all errors are not of equal importance. For example: hesitation on the word *has* is not as serious an error as is the failure to pronounce *stepped.*[3] One can also observe reader strengths.

Another limitation of oral-reading tests concerns the ability of the examiner to hear and record accurately the errors that the reader is making. Supervised practice is necessary to obtain proficiency in oral reading test administration. It is obvious that if the examiner is not able to hear or record the responses accurately, the results of testing will be invalid. Through practice, competency can be developed to assure satisfactory administration and interpretation of oral reading. However, unsupervised testing without adequate practice can lead to extremely unreliable results.

Time needed for oral reading testing for purposes a and b: It depends upon how well one estimates the appropriate starting place. Time needed for accurate estimates can range from five to ten minutes. When one starts at an inappropriate place, time can go up to twenty or twenty-five minutes because the student will be reading more passages.

Walt example:
    Age 12   Grade 7
    Likes football, school, mathematics, cooking, and skateboards
    Does not care for water sports or history
    Says he has few friends
    Ability range: Age 10–12
    Word recognition: Grade 4
    Oral accuracy: Grade 5
    Oral comprehension: Grade 5

Procedures for purpose c, evaluation of the student's oral reading behavior: Testing for this purpose should be conducted on longer passages than passages in the tests mentioned for purposes a and b. Goodman and Burke[4] have developed passages for this purpose. Teachers can select passages from materials that students would normally be expected to read in school.

As discussed in chapter 4, the work of Kenneth Goodman has influenced the way many are using oral reading in clinical diagnosis.[5] This influence is away from using oral reading to obtain reading-level information and toward using it for linguistic processing information. Student responses during oral reading are classified qualitatively in terms of the appropriate use of cues. The coding system mentioned above is also changed to reflect the qualitative classifications.

Many have made adaptations of the ideas of Goodman[6] for clinical use. Staff members at the University of Maryland Reading Clinic, for example, have adapted his ideas as a way of looking at *oral reading behavior (ORB)*. Those ideas that most directly affect the ability to make useful recommendations to teachers were modified and used. Basically, with this approach, every response that is in variance to the text is recorded, leaving one word of text on each side of the variant word, for example:
    Text: in *the* street
    Student response: in *a* street
Then a judgment is made to classify the student variance as a regression, insertion, omission, or substitution. Regressions are further analyzed to determine:

1. Did student change first response to make correction?
2. Did student appear to attempt a correction but without success?
3. Did student simply repeat a portion that was initially correct?
4. Did student change a response that was initially correct?

With such an analysis, one can see that a regression may be classified as good oral reading behavior as well as poor.

Omissions and insertions are judged in terms of whether or not they changed the meaning. If they do not change the meaning, we can assume that the reader is using semantic cues. See limitations of omission and insertion analysis, page 123.

Substitutions, the most important student response to be studied, are evaluated as follows:

1. When making the substitution, did the reader use graphic cues? In what way did the reader display knowledge of phonics or structural analysis?
2. Did the reader use semantic cues? In what ways did the reader demonstrate use of the context?
3. Did the reader use syntactic cues? In what ways did the reader show knowledge of grammar? If the reader uses semantic cues, one assumes the use of syntactic cues. However, if the reader does not use semantic cues but does use syntactic cues, valuable information is obtained about the student's awareness of language.

Obviously, each of these analyses involves some judgment. But with them the reader can be given credit for oral reading strengths even when responses are at variance with the text. Each of these responses is recorded; then all responses in a category are totaled. As a result, the specialist can say how much of the time a student demonstrates a specific type of oral reading behavior; for example, when the reader makes substitutions, semantic cues are used effectively 75 percent of the time.

The use of this type of oral reading behavior analysis calls for considerable practice. Examiners are urged to use tape recorders, at least during initial efforts, to record variances for this type of analysis.

The work of Goodman and Burke may be referred to for those who want to obtain a detailed explanation of oral reading miscue analysis.[7] It should be cautioned that oral reading diagnosis is of most value for students reading between second- and seventh-grade reading levels. Beginning readers' responses may be related to the method used for instruction. If language experience has been used, the reader may rely heavily upon semantic cues; if a phonics method has been used, the reader may indicate heavy reliance upon graphic cues. Once the reader is beyond the initial stages of learning to read, one can better determine which cues the reader has picked to rely upon. Older readers probably use very different behavior in oral and silent reading. Perhaps oral reading analysis becomes less useful as an insight into silent reading behavior as the reader matures. Diagnostic information from oral reading should be interpreted with this caution in mind.

Time needed for purpose c: Usually oral reading behavior analysis is conducted on one passage and takes little testing time (5–10 minutes); however, if the passage is one upon which the reader either makes no errors or makes so many that she is reading nonsense, another passage needs to be selected and more time allotted.

Obviously, a screening can be conducted using all three purposes. If so, time will be added to the screening. Most reading specialists will want to decide which oral reading purpose best suits their needs and evaluate oral reading accordingly.

Walt example:

    Age 12   Grade 7

    Likes football, school, mathematics, cooking, and skateboards

    Does not care for water sports or history

    Says he has few friends

    Ability range: Age 10–12

    Word recognition: Grade 4

    Oral accuracy: Grade 5

    Oral comprehension: Grade 5

    Oral-reading behavior: High use of semantic cues at fifth-grade level

                        Low use of graphic cues at fifth-grade level

Comprehension after silent reading. Comprehension diagnosis is difficult because so much depends upon the diagnostic procedures utilized. Ranges of comprehension level can vary several grade levels when different procedures are used. The content of the passages being used, the setting for silent reading, and the assessment procedures can all influence any reader's comprehension performance. Purposes: a. Determine the reader's skills in responding to each of three settings for comprehension.

    b. Determine the reader's skills in understanding passages at varying degrees of difficulty.

    c. Determine the reader's skills in responding to varying types of questions.

As in oral reading, the procedures needed to attain these purposes will vary; however, the procedures can be combined so that each purpose is attained in a screening situation. By using an informal reading inventory, the reading specialist has the flexibility to manipulate the reading setting so that important diagnostic information can be obtained.

Procedures for purpose a: Since our procedure for assessing comprehension has an effect on the reader's responses, it is suggested that we intentionally assess comprehension in three settings, when using an informal reading inventory.

a. Have the reader read for the purpose of retelling the story in the passage. Retelling is a personal response that indicates what the reader saw as most meaningful.

b. Have the reader respond to questions about the story from recall, i.e., without the printed material available for referral.

c. Have the reader respond to questions that could not be answered in recall by locating the answers in the material.

At each passage level, the assessment should include the reader's performance in each of the above settings. Procedures for purposes b and c, determining comprehension level and skills with varying types of comprehension: The reading specialist will need to decide what type or types of instrument shall be used to assess comprehension. These instruments include prepared tests, informal inventories, cloze or maze tests, and criterion-referenced tests. These happen to be the same types of instruments that are available for classroom diagnosis. In clinical diagnosis, remember, the testing is done on an individual basis allowing for different tests and more careful evaluation of the reader's behavior.

Testing in clinical diagnosis. Several examples of prepared tests that are available for clinical diagnosis are the Diagnostic Reading Scales (see sample on pages 164 and 165), Gates McKillop Reading Diagnostic Tests, Durrell Analysis of Reading Difficulties, and Woodcock Reading Mastery Tests.

Tests such as these provide information about the reader's ability to understand material at different levels. They can also provide information about the reader's ability to respond to varying types of questions. The reading specialist will want to examine the types of questions asked to be certain that different types of questions are provided. Some tests provide questions that ask for literal responses only.

When selecting a test, the reading specialist should make certain that it is reliable and valid. Information concerning validity and reliability can be found in the technical manual that accompanies the test. Tests that lack validity do not reflect the variables that the test was constructed to measure. Tests with low reliability are measuring too much chance score and the results are not dependable.

Informal inventories. Informal inventories, whether prepared commercially or prepared by teachers, provide clinical diagnosis with flexible instruments to assess reading comprehension. The flexibility is feasible because the tests are not standardized, allowing for the types of assessment suggested under purpose a. The manipulation of standardized tests interferes with their norms so that the results are meaningless. Some prepared informal inventories are:

> The Classroom Reading Inventory
> The Standard Reading Inventory
> Pupil Placement Tests
> Analytical Reading Inventory

Each of these is presented in detail in Appendix A. The reading specialist will want to examine each of these and make selections most suited to their school situation. Considerations should include:

Sample

PUPIL RECORD BOOKLET

FORM **1**

GATES-McKILLOP
READING DIAGNOSTIC TESTS

ARTHUR I. GATES
Professor Emeritus of Education
Teachers College, Columbia University

ANNE S. McKILLOP
Professor of Education
Teachers College, Columbia University

Pupil's Name _____ School _____ Date _____

Pupil's Age _____ Birthday _____ Grade _____ Examiner _____ Teacher _____

AGE, GRADE, INTELLIGENCE	1 Raw Score	2 Grade or Other Score	3 Rating	READING AND OTHER TESTS Date Given	1 Raw Score	2 Grade or Other Score	3 Rating ( ) ( )
1 Chronological Age				1			
2 Grade Status (A.G.)			(Date Given)	2			
3 Binet __ I.Q. _____ MA				3			
4 _____ I.Q. _____ MA				Average Silent Reading Gr. (ASRG)			

READING DIAGNOSTIC TESTS

I. Oral Reading (OR)			( ) ( )	V. Knowledge of Word Parts			(OR)
Total Score				1. Recognizing and Blending Common Word Parts			
Analysis of Total Errors				2. Giving Letter Sounds			
a. Omissions, Words		%		3. Naming Capital Letters			
b. Additions, Words		%		4. Naming Lower-Case Letters			
c. Repetitions		%		VI. Recognizing the Visual Form of Sounds			
d. Mispronunciations (g through k)		%					
Analysis of Mispronunciations				1. Nonsense Words			
e. Full Reversals				2. Initial Letters			
f. Reversal of Parts				3. Final Letters			
g. Total Wrong Order (e+f)				4. Vowels			
h. Wrong Beginnings							
i. Wrong Middles				VII. Auditory Blending			
j. Wrong Endings							
k. Wrong Several Parts							
II. Words: Flash Presentation			( ) ( )	VIII. Supplementary Tests			( )
III. Words: Untimed Presentation				1. Spelling			
				2. Oral Vocabulary			
IV. Phrases: Flash Presentation				3. Syllabication			
				4. Auditory Discrimination			
				5. _____			

I. ORAL READING

To examiner: Continue until child makes 11 or more errors on each of two consecutive paragraphs. Try to finish the first four paragraphs no matter how many errors.

Analysis
of
Errors

1.

_____ The boy had a dog.

_____ The dog's face was black.

_____ The dog's body was brown.

_____ He had no tail at all.   Errors _____ Raw Score _____

2.

_____ Once the dog saw a rat.

_____ It was a bad rat.

_____ The dog did not like the rat on his place.

_____ So he ran the rat into his hole.   Errors _____ Raw Score _____

3.

_____ After the rat got into his hole, he began to peek at the dog.

_____ This drove the dog nearly mad.

_____ He said: "I like raw meat to eat.

_____ If you do not stop, I will eat you."

_____ Then he left the rat alone.   Errors _____ Raw Score _____

4.

_____ This talk only made the rat smile.

_____ He could not stop smiling.

_____ He stuck out his chin and cried:

_____ "You are as dull as a donkey.

_____ You are as silly as a monkey.

_____ Let me give you a good tip.

_____ You had better find a doctor now, before it is too late.

_____ Maybe he can do something for your head."   Errors _____ Raw Score _____

Form I

1. Are alternate forms available? Alternate forms provide flexibility needed for pre- and posttesting, use of alternate passages for starter examples, and use when there is doubt about the performance on a given passage.
2. Do the questions reflect varying types of comprehension? As was discussed previously, varying types of questions are needed to assess purpose c.
3. Do the passages reflect the type of reading material being used in the reader's school? If the reader is placed in content materials and the passages are narrative, then a mismatch has occurred.
4. Have the readability levels of the passages been checked? If so, how? Passages with unchecked readability levels should be held suspect. It is not enough that the passages have been taken from graded books. See page 110.
5. Are the cutoff scores realistic? Since the work of William Powell (see page 109) was made available in 1978,[8] some inventories may be using outdated cutoff scores.

Teacher-developed informal inventories have long been used to assess reading comprehension. Generally these inventories are developed using the materials that the students will be reading in school, eliminating the problem of matching test materials with instructional materials. For best results it is suggested that a group of reading specialists work together to develop the informal inventory. By checking and double checking the passages and the questions, easy-to-make errors can be avoided. Passages should be field tested and replaced when they do not yield accurate results. Inventory developers should apply the same questions to their tests that we asked them to apply to commercially-developed informal inventories.

The following steps are suggested for developing an informal inventory for clinical diagnosis:

1. Select passages from instructional material. Passages should be varied in topic, complete in thought, and of interest to the grade level of the students. Passages should be between 125 and 175 words, in order for error pattern to stabilize.
2. Develop questions on each passage. It is suggested that about ten questions be developed to assess comprehension. Questions should elicit literal, interpretive, and problem-solving responses. The number of each type of question will vary with the passage content.

3. Field test each passage on students who you know are reading satisfactorily at the grade level of the passage. When reading silently most students should be able to answer 70 percent of the questions. If they fall below that, the questions should be reworked. If the students are tested after oral reading the acceptable correct response level is lowered to 55–65 percent. How one field tests the inventory will depend upon the purposes one has for developing it in the first place. We prefer to use the inventory as a measure of silent, not oral, reading comprehension. If they answer all of the questions, then it may be that the questions are too easy. If adjusting the questions does not change student performance, the problem may be with the readability level of the passage. Even though it was selected from instructional material, it may be that a given passage is higher or lower than that listed on the instructional material. In such cases, a different passage should be selected.

4. After making necessary adjustments, utilize the inventory, keeping notes on its effectiveness.

5. If difficulties occur, make further adjustments.

Cloze and maze tests.   Cloze tests are constructed directly from the material to be used in instruction. Every fifth word is deleted, and the student is to supply the missing word. Accuracy scores of 40 percent reflect the 70-percent mark (or instructional level) on the tests previously mentioned. Fifty deletions are suggested. These tests are very frustrating, especially when the student is doing poorly.

Cloze tests can be used more informally to determine how well students use syntactic and semantic cues when reading. In these cases, certain words are deleted (for example, all verbs) to see if the students can supply appropriate words.

Maze testing is a modification of cloze procedures. In maze tests, instead of deleting every fifth word, a three-word choice is provided. For example:

street
The boys walked down the house.
run

The student is to select the most appropriate word. In this type of testing, students are expected to score 70-percent accuracy to determine instructional levels.

Many will find cloze and maze tests useful to supplement information obtained from informal inventories. See discussion of cloze and maze test on pages 110–112.

Criterion-referenced tests.   As with classroom diagnosis, Criterion Referenced Tests (CRTs) can be used in clinical diagnosis. Usually they are more useful for classroom diagnosis since they are group instruments. Reading specialists often develop short CRTs for use in screenings to measure one or more specific objectives. For example, if a screening indicates that the student is having difficulty grasping the author's major ideas, the reading specialist may select several paragraphs and have the student read the paragraphs to obtain the author's main idea. By adding these data to that which was already available, the reading specialist would be adding reliability to the findings of the screening. (See discussion on CRTs on page 113, chapter 4.)

From the above-mentioned possibilities for comprehension diagnosis, the reading specialist will need to make a decision concerning what would be most useful. No one decision is appropriate for every case; however, the following suggestions have proven to be useful in most.

1. Select a good informal reading inventory.
2. Administer it for the retelling purpose.
3. Ask specific questions in a recall situation for important items missed in retelling.
4. Ask specific questions in a locating situation for important items missed in recall questioning.

Time needed: about twenty minutes
Walt example:
　　　Age 12　　　Grade 7
　　　Likes football, school, mathematics, cooking, and skateboards
　　　Does not care for water sports or history
　　　Says he has few friends
　　　Ability range: Age 10–12
　　　Word recognition: Grade 4
　　　Oral accuracy: Grade 5
　　　Oral comprehension: Grade 5
　　　Oral-reading behavior: High use of semantic cues at
　　　　　　　　　　　　　　　　fifth-grade level
　　　　　　　　　　　　　　　　Low use of graphic cues at
　　　　　　　　　　　　　　　　fifth-grade level

Comprehension using Informal Reading Inventory

4th-grade passage retelling good, recall 90% + locate 10% = 100%

5th-grade passage retelling fair, recall 70% + locate 30% = 100%

6th-grade passage retelling poor, recall 50% + locate 20% = 70%

7th-grade passage retelling poor, recall 20% + locate 30% = 50%

Note: By adding the recall and the locate percentages, we are able to obtain a picture of the percent of questions answered accurately. These data tell us that Walt's retelling dropped off immediately after the fourth-grade passage and recall dropped off after the fifth-grade passage. Therefore, his retelling comprehension level is fourth grade, his recall level is fifth grade, and his locate level is sixth grade.

At this time in the screening a decision must be made. Is further testing desirable? If so, in what direction should it go? Since Walt scored into the fourth-, fifth-, and sixth-grade levels on all tests, it was decided to extend the screening to include an assessment of Walt's study skills. If he had scored at the first-, second-, or third-grade level, we would probably have continued with an assessment of his word-attack skills.

Study-skill assessment

Purposes: a. Determine if the reader can utilize reading skills in content materials.

b. Determine if the reader utilizes effective study techniques.

It is difficult in a screening to obtain an accurate assessment of utilization of reading skills in content materials. Generally this assessment would be obtained in an extended diagnosis or during instruction.

Procedures:

a. Collect interview data from content teachers.

Types of questions for content-teacher interviews:

1. Is Walt able to complete independent assignments for your class?
2. In what areas does Walt show strengths?
3. What is your assessment of Walt's weaknesses?
4. What adjustments have you been able to make for Walt's lack of reading skills?

b. Collect interview data from student.
Types of questions for student interview:

1. How much homework do you get each evening?
2. How long do you work on your homework?
3. Where do you do your homework?
4. What do you find easiest to do?
5. What is most difficult for you?

c. Sample of the student's reading in content material at her instructional level: By taking a content book at the student's instructional level, the reading specialist can teach a directed lesson and note the student's ability to respond.

Time needed: five to ten minutes
Walt example:

Walt and his teachers believe that Walt can work independently in mathematics and is unable to complete social studies and science assignments. Spelling is very weak.

Word-attack assessment

Purposes: a. Determine if important word-attack subskills may be causing reading comprehension difficulties.
b. Identify those important word-attack subskills that are the reader's strengths.

Procedures: The usual procedure is to administer a test of identified important word-attack skills. The word *important* is used here because many word-attack tests include the assessment of skills that are not useful to the reader. The reading specialist will need to determine which word-attack skills need assessment and then select an instrument or a portion of an instrument that assesses those skills. Some instruments that can be considered are:

Botel Reading Inventory (revised): Phonics section
Diagnostic Reading Scales
Roswell-Chall Diagnostic Reading Test of Word Analysis Skills
Sipay Word Analysis Tests
Woodcock Reading Mastery Tests

Each of these tests is described in Appendix A. Note: the amount of time needed to administer the tests varies greatly. At this point in a screening time becomes crucial, since the reader is likely to be weary of testing. Perhaps the selection of a short survey-type test would be most appropriate, saving the more time-consuming tests for extended diagnosis, if necessary.

Time needed: ten minutes

Walt example:

> We had already decided that Walt did not need a word-attack assessment. But, if he had, perhaps the results would show:
>
> Knowledge of initial consonants: excellent
> Rhyming-word skills: excellent
> Syllabication skills: weak

Diagnostic lesson.   The final step in the screening is to test out the hypotheses developed from the available data through an instructional lesson. In Walt's case, the data available look like this:

Walt example:

> Age 12   Grade 7
> Likes football, school, mathematics, cooking, and skateboards
> Does not care for water sports or history
> Says he has few friends
> Ability range: Age 10–12
> Word recognition: Grade 4
> Oral accuracy: Grade 5
> Oral comprehension: Grade 5
> Oral-reading behavior: High use of semantic cues at
>   fifth-grade level
>   Low use of graphic cues at
>   fifth-grade level
>   Comprehension using IRI

4th-grade passage retelling good, recall 90% + locate 10% = 100%

5th-grade passage retelling fair, recall 70% + locate 30% = 100%

6th-grade passage retelling poor, recall 50% + locate 20% = 70%

7th-grade passage retelling poor, recall 20% + locate 30% = 50%

Study skills assessment
Good in completing mathematics assignments
Weak in completing social studies and science assignments
Weak in spelling

From these data several hypotheses may be developed:

1. Although Walt is having some difficulty with reading, he has a good attitude toward school and likes mathematics, so we ought to try to develop opportunities for Walt to demonstrate his math skills.
2. Walt comprehends best when using both recall and locate situations. We ought to encourage the use of both recall and locate situations for comprehension in all school subjects.
3. Since Walt is using semantic cues in oral reading, we are not grealy concerned. It may be useful, however, to determine which graphic cues are used and which are ignored. This analysis may help explain some of his difficulty with spelling.

What lesson could be useful in this situation? We would recommend one of two possibilities:

1. A directed lesson with content material, using locating skills
2. A lesson directed toward Walt's locating comprehension skills, using different passages

Of these two, the first is clearly preferable, since Walt is in seventh grade and independent work in content areas is needed. In other cases, the diagnostic lesson could be used to:

1. Determine if the student can respond to the language experience approach
2. Determine if the student can respond to the VAKT technique
3. Determine if the student can respond to different types of questioning procedures
4. Determine if the student can read in a teacher-directed lesson when unable to do so in a testing situation

The goal is obvious. The diagnostic lesson is used to verify the working hypothesis generated from the data of the screening. If it does verify the screening data, then recommendations can be made with assurance. If it does not verify the data, then extended diagnosis is recommended.

Caution on Initial Screenings

The data collected in this brief manner lead to the formation of working hypotheses that must be tested through extended diagnosis and instruction. The results are NOT conclusive. Although every effort is made to be thorough, there is simply too much involved in the reading process to be thoroughly evaluated through a screening. As we approach the interview session with the parents and possibly the student, caution is urged. No pronouncements of cause and effect and no absolute conclusions are given. What we have here is our first careful look into the situation.

THE INTERVIEW

Now for a most important step in the screening—the interview through which the reading specialist and the parents seek to obtain more information about the student's reading difficulties.

Parents come to the interview with a lot of information about their perceptions of their child's reading difficulties. They will have difficulty listening until they have the opportunity to share these perceptions. We recommend, therefore, that the interview be started with a solicitation of information from the parents. Some starter questions might be:

1. Why do you think Walt is having difficulty with his reading?
2. What has the school personnel told you about Walt's difficulty?
3. Why did you refer Walt for this screening?

It has been our experience that most parents will take these types of questions and willingly unload their concerns. We recommend that the person conducting the interview listen carefully, showing interest, but not showing approval or disapproval. When the parents pick up signals that they are on acceptable or unacceptable ground, they tend to become guarded and less communicative.

The interview between the parent and the specialist should start with information from the parent.

It is our experience that most parents are very perceptive about the difficulties their child is experiencing. Often their comments reinforce or clarify the findings of the screening. In these cases, the interview is a confirming activity. In some cases, the parents tend to concentrate on one aspect of reading, one teacher, or one instructional activity (usually phonics). This type of concentration keeps them from gaining a broad perspective about their child's reading. In these cases, the interview becomes an enlightening activity.

After the parents have expressed their concerns it is time for the reading specialists to discuss the results of the screening. The following procedures have been tried and found to be useful:

1. Explain each test, giving an example of an item, and discuss the student's performance on that test. The test score and its interpretation should be given.
2. Summarize all observed behavior.
3. Present implications in the form of working hypotheses.

We do not recommend suggesting conclusions as a result of a screening. Rather, we state that these adjustments would be the first things to try and then we will reevaluate.

4. Ask for questions from the parents.

Here are several do's and don'ts about interviews following initial screenings:

1. Do not take notes during the interview. Wait until the parents have gone and then write down a record of what transpired. Note taking during an interview tends to make parents uneasy.
2. Do not tape record an interview. Tapes make parents uncomfortable. If you must tape the interview, be certain that all involved know that it is being taped.
3. Do not take sides with the parents against a teacher or a school program. Taking sides in these matters is unethical because we do not have both sides of the story.
4. If the screening is to be shared with other school personnel, be certain that the parents know this. An out-of-school agency should have written permission from the parents to share any report of testing.
5. Attempt to offer plausible recommendations. When possible, make the recommendations so that the parents have some decisions to make. For example, it may be that the school could offer some service or that a private tutor could be found.

A written report of the screening data with implications and suggestions for instruction or extended diagnosis is usually prepared. This report generally is forwarded from private agencies to the referral persons, i.e., the screening committee in the schools or the parents.

This edition includes much more detailed information about the screening procedures because reading specialists in the field tell me that this is the type of diagnostic request they are most likely to receive. Seldom, they tell me, is there a request for testing in more detail than what has been described here as an initial screening. Therefore, much more attention has been given to the aspect of screening in the hopes of being more helpful in areas of expressed need.

HYPOTHESIS FORMATION

After measuring the strengths and weaknesses of the reader in sight vocabulary, oral reading, and silent reading, tentative hypotheses are made. From these hypotheses, the reading specialist obtains clues to the reader's strengths and weaknesses in the skill areas and plans further diagnosis. The procedures here are identical to those used by the teacher in classroom diagnosis. Although the questions asked in relation to each skill area are those asked in classroom diagnosis, the resulting conclusions may culminate in further diagnosis, since the reading specialist has more diagnostic tools available and is more qualified to interpret the results. Using these tentative hypotheses, the reading specialist may need to extend the diagnosis to those skill areas that have been identified as needing further analysis.

One of the basic considerations for clinical diagnosis concerns the possibiliy that a student may have a certain strength in mode of learning. For example, a reader who may learn effectively when tactile experiences are combined with visual stimuli, may not learn through visual stimuli alone. These strengths and weaknesses should serve as guides for instruction.

Learning Modalities

To assess learning modalities, the reading specialist has such tests as the *Mills Learning Methods Tests,* the *Monroe-Sherman Group Diagnostic Reading Aptitude and Achievement Tests,* the *Detroit Tests of Learning Aptitude,* the *Gates Associative Learning Test,* and the *Illinois Test of Psycholinguistic Abilities.* These tests attempt to identify strengths in visual or auditory sensory systems; the Mills test adds tactile and combination techniques. For the severely handicapped, identification of strong learning modalities seems to be especially helpful. Modality identification is illusive, however. The examiner must realize that scores from such tests are just that and that students may have many strengths not noted when using a specific instrument.

Intellectual Abilities

Diagnosis may also be extended into the area of intellectual abilities. As discussed in chapter 3, the WISC and the Binet are most commonly used for these purposes. The *Illinois Test of Psycholinguistic Abilities* (ITPA) claims to provide a

Summer clinic was only a week away, and we were still screening the few stragglers whose applications were the last to arrive. I had done several before and felt downright cocky about my ability to correctly diagnose reading problems.

My last screening of the day was Gary, a thirteen year old boy who was to be retained in the sixth grade for the second time. I carefully studied all of the notes written by his teachers and the parent referral form. They made Gary sound like Attila the Hun with a week-old sinus headache and aspirin yet to be invented. I suspected by reading between the lines that if his teachers had been asked to list his strengths, about the only thing they could have offered would have been that Gary didn't show up very often. His mother wrote that he was unpopular with other kids and rude to adults. Although she tried to be positive in her description of his behavior at home, I suspect he wouldn't have been her first choice for a Dale Carnegie award. According to everything I read, not only did Gary have the personality of a pit viper, but the poor kid couldn't read either.

You can imagine how overjoyed I was at the thought of spending the next hour or so in his company. Just like the referrals said, Gary really turned on the "charm" as soon as he came in. He didn't respond to my half-hearted attempts to establish rapport before beginning the testing. I, not being a masochist, decided that a longer interview was a waste of time, so we plunged directly into the testing. Now I had the situation under control; Gary wasn't recalcitrant, and the testing was quickly finished. According to the preliminary findings, Gary definitely had a reading problem. His silent comprehension was 3^1 in a recall situation and 3^2 in locate. I completed all of the paperwork and thought to myself, "God help the poor sucker who has to work with him for the next six weeks."

Being a terrible conniver, I explained to my partner that Gary and I had a personality conflict at the screening and talked her into spending more time working with him. I certainly didn't bother to recite chapter and verse of his past history to her.

Gary made some progress socially and academically almost daily after an initial week of negative behavior. It was soon obvious that he could read with comprehension far above what the initial screening indicated. Thanks to my partner acting as a buffer, Gary and I worked out a tentative truce by the end of the third week. He turned out to be likeable and enjoyed clinic. By the fifth week my conscience and curiosity got the best of me. I retested Gary with amazing results. He could now recall on a fifth-grade level and locate on sixth.

After the initial unjustified feeling of euphoria that we had accomplished so much in five weeks, we had to look at the results realistically. Try though we might, it just wasn't possible for us to take credit for the jump in his scores. I finally asked Gary why he had performed so poorly at the initial screening. Three years later, I'm still ashamed to tell you his answer. Gary said, "I could tell right away that you didn't like me, so I tried to finish the testing as fast as I could."

For the moral of this story, turn to page 189 and re-read the seventh pitfall of diagnosis.

Darryl Quinn Henry

different look at the student's linguistic functioning. Newcomer and Hammill caution, however, that the ITPA's value is limited to gathering broad, descriptive information and is seriously limited for specific educational diagnosis.[9] Furthermore, correlations between ITPA subtest scores and reading achievement are very low.

Visual Discrimination

If visual discrimination skills appear to be deficient, the *Monroe-Sherman Group Diagnostic Reading Aptitude and Achievement Tests,* standardized readiness tests, or informal measures can be used for further diagnosis. The clinician should be certain that diagnostic data will aid in the development of an educational prescription. Generally informal measures are of most value. Informal testing, using a simple passage or an experience story, can be conducted by asking the reader to circle all words that begin with a specific letter after showing the letter, by asking the reader to underline all words that have a certain ending, or by finding specific letters in a paragraph. The advantage of such informal testing is that the actual reading passage is the testing medium.

Auditory Discrimination

If auditory discrimination appears to be the problem, further testing through measures such as the *Wepman Auditory Discrimination Test* appears to be of value. Here, auditory-discrimination abilities are further identified as initial sounds, medial sounds, or final sounds. Informal measures are equally useful and easily constructed. The clinician can read lists of words in pairs ("cat"—"fat") and ask the student to indicate whether they are the same or different. Perhaps a better way to determine auditory-discrimination skills is to ask the student to repeat the two words. This eliminates confusion about what is meant by same or different.

Orientation

If the tentative hypothesis identifies the orientation area as a problem in reading, diagnosis often is extended through an evaluation of eye motion during the reading act, normally through careful observation of the student during both oral and silent reading. Do the eyes appear to move with a reasonable number of fixations across the line of print? Do the eyes move backwards, making many regressions? Everyone makes regressions in reading; without experience in observing students in the reading act, it is

difficult to diagnose this area accurately. Reading specialists should observe groups of good, fair, and poor readers so
that they can learn what is expected in the observation of eye
movements. Other observations can lead to suspicions
about orientation: for example, behavior such as peculiar
reading position, turning the book, and losing one's place.

**Dominance
Preference**

Another extension of diagnosis of orientation often focuses
on the area of dominance preference. After screening
thousands of cases of severely-handicapped readers, the
staff of the University of Maryland Reading Clinic found no
relationship of dominance to orientation problems, nor did
they find any remedial solutions based upon such diagnosis. While many students have symptoms of confused
dominance, such cases are not restricted to reading problems. Their conclusion about diagnosis in this controversial area is that there is no justification for continued efforts
to link reading difficulties to dominance problems. In fact,
such diagnosis often leads educators away from the symptoms that will best offer solutions to the student's educational difficulties.

**Sight
Vocabulary**

If the tentative hypothesis identifies sight vocabulary as the
problem area, a more careful analysis of tests previously
administered may determine consistent patterns of sight
vocabulary errors (See chapter 4). Durrell suggests that the
word not known at sight should be used to see if the reader
can analyze the word using word attack when time is not a
factor.[10] In such cases, the word recognition answer sheet
will have two columns, one for instant pronunciation and
one for delayed pronunciation. Obviously if the reader does
not know the word at sight but does know it when permitted
to examine it, that reader has skills to attack the word
properly but has not overlearned it to the extent that it can
be called a sight word.

Word Attack

If the tentative hypothesis finds the area of word attack in
need of further diagnosis, the specialist should analyze the
errors made in word recognition and oral reading, as was
done in the classroom diagnosis (See chapter 4). There are
also tests available for clinical diagnosis that measure
specific word attack–skill performance. The *Botel Reading
Inventory: Phonics Mastery,* the *Diagnostic Reading Test*
by Bond, Balow, and Hoyt, the *Roswell-Chall Diagnostic*

Reading Test of Word Analysis Skills, the *Doren Diagnostic Reading Test,* and the *Sipay Word Analysis Tests* are five well-known, quite different evaluations of word-attack skills. Each of these tests may be administered to groups of students who respond to oral presentations by the teacher. The Botel test is quite short; the Bond, Balow, and Hoyt test takes about forty five minutes; and the Doren test takes three hours. The Sipay test can be given in sections taking ten to twenty minutes per section. The various diagnostic-test batteries also contain an analysis of word-attack skills; however, they heavily emphasize phonics. Teacher-made, criterion-referenced tests of the various word-attack skills often provide the best insight into skill strengths and needs in this area. For example, if analysis of word recognition and oral reading responses indicates that the student is having difficulty with word endings, then a test can be constructed that measures only those skills dealing with word endings. A standardized word-attack test would seem to be a waste of time in such a case.

Reading specialists generally want to see how well a student with specific word-attack problems performs on a spelling test. A test of this nature should be given at the student's instructional level. Through an analysis of spelling errors, the reading specialist can extend the diagnosis and verify previous findings.

The reading specialist is cautioned that many readers have learned to attack words adequately in isolated drill-type exercises but are not capable of performing the same task when they see these words in context. It would be erroneous, therefore, to conclude that students do not have word-attack deficiencies simply because they perform successfully on diagnostic tests of word-attack skills. Evaluation must be made in an oral reading situation where the student is faced, not with the single unknown word, but with the unknown word in a group of familiar words.

Comprehension

If the tentative hypothesis identifies the comprehension area as needing further diagnosis, attention must again be directed to those questions asked in classroom diagnosis (See chapter 4). Clinical diagnosis will be extended to review the history of the basic types of approaches used in the student's reading instruction. From this type of analysis, it often is possible for the reading specialist to understand gaps in areas of instruction and to suggest remedial programs to fill these gaps. In the area of comprehension, the specialist should establish the answers to four additional questions before proceeding to remediation:

1. Is the reader's poor performance on a comprehension test due basically to weak comprehension skills, or is it more closely related to inadequate vocabulary? One technique for determining the answer to this question is to make a careful comparison between word-meaning and paragraph-meaning scores. Poorer performance in word meaning usually indicates that a student's vocabulary skills are prohibiting maximum performance in comprehension.

2. Is there a need for further comprehension testing to verify scores upon which there is conflicting evidence? It may be necessary to administer a test that has more items, one that has a better variety of items, or one that measures a certain type of comprehension skill not measured in the previously administered silent reading test. When students have serious comprehension difficulties, the reading specialist seldom will find one silent reading test satisfactory. If another test is administered, the results of that test should undergo the same diagnostic scrutiny as did the previous test. Scores of such tests should not be averaged, however. When more than one test of silent reading is used to diagnose skill strengths and weaknesses, analysis of the responses to types of questions rather than a composite score is critical to clinical diagnosis.

3. Is the reader's poor performance on a comprehension test due basically to reading speed? In classroom diagnosis, the ability to complete the reading assignments in a specific time period is considered; in clinical diagnosis, equal consideration must be given to the reader who fails to complete reading tests in the allotted time or is very slow on untimed tests. There is no possibility of obtaining this information from the grade scores on silent reading tests; rather, a careful inner test analysis will reveal the amount of material covered. A test now is available to determine the flexibility with which a student attacks print designed for different purposes. The *Reading Versatility Test* is designed to provide this type of information.

4. Is the reader's poor comprehension on specific text

exercises caused by the lack of experiences in the area of the content of the material being read? It is easy to understand that a city student unfamiliar with farm life may score poorly on a story test about farming, yet be quite capable of comprehending a similar story about city life. Diagnosis, however, is not so easy. While broad areas of experience may be identified, a reader's background of experiences is quite personal and involved.

Reading Habits and Attitudes

If the tentative hypothesis identifies reading habits and attitudes as the problem area, the reading specialist has found that the student has the basic skills to read adequately but does not care to read. This diagnosis involves a careful consideration of the information from the areas of emotional and physical diagnosis. The student may indicate a poor attitude toward school-type tasks and books or physical discomfort. Two study-habit questionnaires are available to assist in the extension of diagnosis in this area. They are *California Study Method Survey* and *Survey of Study Habits and Attitudes* (SSHA). See *Form H* for grades 7–12 of *SSHA* on page 184. Further evaluation is needed of past efforts made by the school to encourage the student to read, the availability of books in the school and at home, and the general atmosphere that may encourage or discourage reading in these situations. A student who can read but normally doesn't is not considered in need of a specialist's attention. The reading specialist's obligation is to make specific recommendations to the classroom teacher. Fully aware that interests are of the moment and always changing, the reading specialist, nevertheless, will attempt to assess the student's interests: formally through an established interest inventory or informally through interest inventories and/or a personal interview with the student, his parents, and his teacher. Many students, although they are reading as well as can be expected, are placed in frustrating reading situations daily in school. It does not take a specialist to realize that reading is not much fun for these students and that they may easily develop a negative attitude toward reading. Information gleaned in such a manner will be important to include in the diagnostic report of a problem reader.

Diagnostic Batteries

There is available for clinical diagnosis a group of tests that, used in a single unit, constitutes a diagnostic battery.

These tests are designed for use as a rather complete reading analysis. The more prominent of these batteries are the *Durrell Analysis of Reading Difficulties, Gates-McKillop Reading Diagnostic Test, Diagnostic Reading Scales,* and *Monroe-Sherman Group Diagnostic Reading Aptitude and Achievement Tests.*[11] The first three are individual in nature, while the last is a group test. A careful examination of these diagnostic batteries is essential for an appropriate selection for clinical diagnosis. The only items that all these tests have in common are measures of silent- or oral-reading and work-attack skills. Some tests also include word recognition, oral reading, arithmetic, spelling, auditory and visual discrimination, and auding. The main advantage of using a diagnostic battery is that the scores of the subtests are more comparable, since they are standardized on the same population. Another advantage is that there is one manual and one test to learn to administer and interpret; one does not have the overwhelming job that occurs in some other types of testing combinations. The resulting information will provide an individual analysis of how a student is reading and how the student's skill development is related to total reading scores.

These diagnostic batteries are not without limitations, however. Some are too brief and some are standardized on very small populations, thereby causing reliability problems. Most important, possibly, is the fact that reading specialists will find that the tests do not measure the types or quantities of skill that they wish to measure, thus causing validity problems. Therefore, in clinical diagnosis, it is unlikely that any one of these diagnostic batteries will be adequate for a complete diagnosis. Note that subtests of diagnostic batteries are recommended for use in specific areas of diagnosis, not for precise scores, but for indicators of strengths and weaknesses that can be studied in more depth.

Diagnostic Teaching

Formulating diagnostic hypotheses from data based on testing situations can lead to a distorted view of the reader. How does the reader operate during instruction? An instructional session provides additional important data for extended clinical diagnosis.

Specifically, reading specialists should provide lessons that check their findings concerning reading level, major skill strengths, and major skill needs. For example, if

DIAGNOSTIC PROFILE FOR SURVEY OF STUDY HABITS AND ATTITUDES

W. F. Brown and W. H. Holtzman

Name __Benson, Susan__
    Last   First

School __Burtonsville Jr. High__ Date __6-10-83__

Age __13__ Sex __F__ Form of SSHA __H__

Circle Grade or Year in School:

High School: ⑦ 8 9 10 11 12   College: Fr. Soph. Jr. Sr.

Profiling Your SSHA Scores

To find out how you did on each scale of this survey, look at the numbers in the row marked "Percentile." Your percentile on each scale shows your relative standing in the group of people described on the "Norms Used" line at the bottom of the chart. For example, if your norms group is college freshmen and your percentile on the TA scale is 45, it means that 45 per cent of the freshmen received lower scores than yours on the TA scale, while 55 per cent of them received higher scores. Thus, your percentile tells where you rank in comparison with others in your norms group.

You can complete your profile by making a heavy line across each column at the level which corresponds to your percentile rank on that scale. For example, if your percentile rank on the DA scale is 65, make a heavy line across the DA column halfway between 60 and 70. Draw a line corresponding to your percentile rank for all seven scales.

Then start at the horizontal line you have drawn and black in each column up to or down to the 50th percentile line. Since the 50th percentile line represents the score made by the middle student of your group, the vertical bars above that line on your profile show those scales on which you have scored higher than the middle student and the bars below that line show the scales on which you scored lower.

What Your SSHA Scores Mean

High scores on SSHA are characteristic of students who get good grades; low scores tend to be characteristic of those who get low grades or find school work difficult. Therefore, your scores on the SSHA scales can indicate your strengths and weaknesses in the areas measured by the survey, and also help to predict future academic achievement.

What the SSHA Measures

(DA) DELAY AVOIDANCE—your promptness in completing academic assignments, lack of procrastination, and freedom from wasteful delay and distraction.

(WM) WORK METHODS—your use of effective study procedures, efficiency in doing academic assignments, and how-to-study skills.

(TA) TEACHER APPROVAL—your opinions of teachers and their classroom behavior and methods.

(EA) EDUCATION ACCEPTANCE—your approval of educational objectives, practices, and requirements.

(SH) STUDY HABITS combines the scores on the DA and WM scales to provide a measure of academic behavior.

(SA) STUDY ATTITUDES combines the scores on the TA and EA scales to provide a measure of scholastic beliefs.

(SO) STUDY ORIENTATION combines the scores on the SH and SA scales to provide an overall measure of study habits and attitudes.

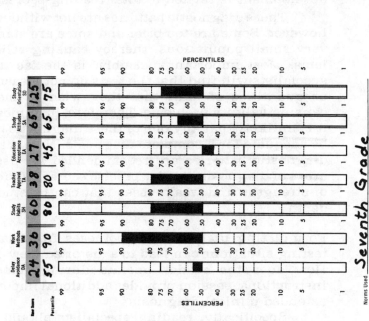

PERCENTILES

	Delay Avoidance DA	Work Methods WM	Study Habits SH	Teacher Approval TA	Education Acceptance EA	Study Attitudes SA	Study Orientation SO
Raw Score	24	36	60	38	27	65	125
Percentile	55	90	80	80	45	65	75

Norms Used: Seventh Grade

the diagnosis supported an instructional level at 3–1, skill strengths in beginning consonants and directly stated recall, and skill weaknesses in vowels and problem solving, a lesson should be designed to see how the reader operates in each of these areas. Several books—one at the 2–2 level, one at the 3–1 level, and perhaps one at the 3–2 level—can be selected with silent reading followed by questioning in the area of strengths and needs. A short phonics lesson can be developed to see how well the reader handles consonants and vowels.

If the hypotheses are confirmed, the diagnosis becomes more certain. However, if the student can perform during instruction, new hypotheses will need to be formulated and tested. Rarely are all hypotheses confirmed. Clinicians who skip the step of diagnostic teaching place themselves in the position of drawing faulty conclusions. Preparing a report on a student that contains faulty conclusions has serious consequences. If specialists expect teachers to use their reports to adjust instruction, they should test their findings in instructional situations. In the reading center at the University of Maryland, we have found diagnostic lessons that follow testing to be of the utmost value. Occasionally a full case study seems necessary to complete a diagnostic evaluation. To develop a full case study, in-depth testing is required in the areas of intelligence, verbal performance, auditory skills, visual skills, word recognition, oral-reading behavior, silent-reading comprehension, and word-attack skills. To these are added medical reports and a developmental history, as well as detailed information from the school and the home.

The decision to proceed with a full case study will stem from lack of information on the student and failure of the initial screening to identify satisfactorily the student's strengths and weaknesses. Every aspect of the student's educational development, along with an evaluation of intellectual, emotional, and physical development, is needed. Because of the time needed, the expense, and the coordination of efforts, case studies are reserved for those students in most need.

CASE REPORTING

As in classroom diagnosis, the information accumulated in

a clinical diagnosis is useless unless it can be organized so that it is readily understood.

A case report is the typical approach to preparing diagnostic information for clinical use. Although the precise form may vary, the following format should be used so that persons unfamiliar with this student can make optimum use of case information:

1. The first page should contain a concise summary of the essential data included in the report (that is, name, age, address, and school of the student, degree of reading retardation, and a summary statement of the diagnostic findings, including intellectual, physical, emotional, and educational diagnosis).

2. The first page should be followed by as many pages of explanation as necessary. The explanation should include all test scores, the dates upon which they were administered, and the name of the test administrator, as well as diagnostic interpretations of the test performance and evaluations of the student's responses. It also should include data from screening tests and referral reports. It is here that the relative importance of each piece of data is evaluated and interrelated and that causative factors may be identified.

3. A page or two of complete description of the successes of the diagnostic lesson should be the content of the third section.

4. The last page of the case report should be reserved for specific recommendations and referrals. Recommendations should include those to the clinic, the classroom teacher, and the parents specifying preventive as well as remedial procedures.

It is useful to explain the report to the teacher in a face-to-face interview. Teachers nearly always have questions about the report that can be answered during the interview. It is more likely that the report has been understood by the teacher if it has been discussed.

Not long ago, parents were not given specific information concerning test results. Today that has changed. Not only have parents become aware of the need for such information, they have rights to it. It is essential to give parents copies of anything sent to teachers. If reports are misfiled or lost, parents must have copies to replace those lost. Furthermore, parents can often implement adjustments at home to assist with the correction of difficulties.

Since reports often contain technical language, it is helpful to parents to give them the report during a conference. In this manner, technical language can be explained and questions can be answered.

Pitfalls of Diagnosis

Both clinical and classroom diagnosis may be plagued by certain pitfalls. They include the following:

Overgeneralization. The tendency to use total test scores without examination of the pattern of test scores; the tendency to draw conclusions before all facts are in; the tendency to rely upon the first significant symptom; and the tendency to hazard guesses outside the professional field are all examples of overgeneralizing in diagnosis. Overgeneralizing can be controlled, in part, by making couched statements when all data are not available. For example, instead of saying that a student has a poor home life, one can say that from the data available the home conditions bear watching as a possible cause of the student's educational development. More than merely playing with words, couched statements protect the educational diagnostician and lead to more accurate reporting of diagnostic results.

Overextension of diagnosis. Extending diagnosis beyond that which will help arrive at an accurate picture of the student may cause the student to become overconcerned about the reading problem and is therefore a waste of time. In commenting on the disadvantages of extended diagnostic periods, Strang concludes, "He may feel more strongly than ever that something may be wrong with him.[12] Overextension of diagnosis occurs more commonly in the clinic than in the classroom, for it is in the clinic that the most careful study of the reader is conducted and a variety of tests are available. Some clinics suggest that each student receive a complete diagnostic analysis regardless of need. This can only be justified in the interest of gathering research data; however, the expense to the student must always be considered, for not all students can accept large quantities of diagnosis. Nevertheless, every effort must be made to arrive at a true picture of the difficulty. Through the use of initial screenings, selective studies, and in-depth case studies, diagnosticians have choices available and can avoid overextension of diagnosis.

Abbreviated diagnosis.   A hurried diagnosis often does not investigate a given reading difficulty properly. Insufficient diagnosis is most common in the classroom, where lack of time and materials exert constant pressure upon the teacher's efforts. Regardless of the limitations of the classroom situation, the teacher must use all available data to insure that the information obtained is reliable and valid. Through abbreviated diagnosis, it is common to jump to wrong conclusions and, in effect, to waste large amounts of time that would have been saved through a more thorough diagnosis. If diagnosticians include the diagnostic teaching lesson as part of their diagnosis, the chance of an abbreviated diagnosis is lessened, for in a diagnostic lesson unknown factors come to light.

Overstepping professional boundaries.   There is a tendency for educators to make statements that are beyond the professional boundaries of their preparation. The diagnostician must refrain from playing psychiatrist or medical doctor and, instead, must refer willingly when necessary. As with overgeneralizing, couching terms in a diagnostic report that goes beyond the field of education will help avoid overstepping professional boundaries. For example, if a telebinocular examination indicates the need for referral, the clinician may write that poor performance on test four of the telebinocular indicates the need for a professional visual examination. That type of statement is more appropriate than one stating that the poor score on the telebinocular indicates visual problems that need professional attention.

Unfounded statements of fact.   In direct relation to the preceding pitfalls are positive, factual statements made by educators based on evidence that does not justify so strong a statement. The couching of terms to indicate areas of suspicion where more testing may be needed or areas where referral is necessary will be beneficial to all those who are attempting to arrive at a student's area of difficulty. An examiner must be certain that positive statements concerning a student's observed difficulties are backed by highly reliable data.

Isolation of factors: Isolated pieces of diagnostic data, test scores, and the like must not be examined without consideration for their relationship to the entire diagnosis. It is not unusual for the significance of particular data to be lessened when they are placed in the total picture of a student's reading difficulty. A single group of data or a single test score used in isolation is likely to lead to a distorted picture of the difficulty. Even in the classroom, where time and materials are at a premium, this pitfall should be avoided.

Previous bias. The examiner must be alert to the possible interference of data that are tainted by bias. Bias is often found in the remarks of parents or teachers and can have a definite effect on the direction the diagnosis may take. To circumvent this effect, the examiner may intentionally avoid the evaluation of data from the parents and teachers until tentative hypotheses are reached.

Difficult Diagnostic Problems

The so-called nonreader. Unfortunately, not all diagnosis falls into neat packages of specific skill deficiencies. Some students appear unable to profit from even the best instruction in any of the skill areas. They cannot learn to read by conventional methods. Abrams estimates this population to be less than 1 percent of the total population of disabled readers.[13] While diagnosis of these students may be the basic responsibility of the reading specialist, the entire resources of the school should be consulted.

Commonly referred to as dyslexic, neurologically deficient, minimally brain damaged, or as possessing a specific reading disability, nonreaders have disabilities complicated by multiple factors. They are almost always emotionally involved in their gross failure. They are likely to be physically deficient and may appear to be dull. Trying to please the teacher often is no longer of interest to them. Diagnosis has failed to identify a consistent pattern of behavior. Educators have attempted to teach them by all known methods; each of these methods has failed.

Effective diagnosis calls for an interdisciplinary approach to these students. Every effort should be made to seek out the sources of difficulties. It is often necessary for these students to be diagnosed in clinics that have been established to work efficiently with them. Diagnosis and initial remediation will be accomplished most effectively in these clinic-type situations. Many school districts are establishing special schools for such students. Carefully trained teachers work in coordination with personnel from other disciplines to establish meaningful educational programs for these very troubled learners.

In some cases, despite all efforts, these students continue to fail. Multidisciplinary efforts are continuously explored in hopes of establishing new areas of diagnosis and remediation for them. Screening committees assure that the most appropriate resource personnel work to diagnose and remediate these students. Early identification programs followed by early intervention hold some promise. Multisensory techniques are often employed effectively. But the search continues for diagnostic and instructional techniques that will make school life more pleasant and successful for these students.

The culturally different. Another group who appear to be experiencing severe difficulty in traditional programs are those who come from culturally different backgrounds. Their language and their experiences are not likely to correspond to the instructional materials that they are expected to use. Mismatching students from poor-income homes with books designed for middle- and upper-class children has been common.

Diagnostic instruments that use stories based on middle-class concepts (Dick and Jane going on a vacation in the suburbs) put poor students at a disadvantage in the testing situation. Interpretation of low reading and intelligence scores must be in terms of the different cultural backgrounds of the students.

Aside from considerations such as these, culturally different students should be diagnosed using the questions suggested in this chapter. Strengths should be noted and utilized. Deficiencies should be worked with through the students' demonstrated strengths. The philosophy of accepting and challenging is extremely important for establishing good diagnostic and remedial relationships with these students.

In all likelihood these students will be urged to try harder and make more effort, and continue to be compared with successful students from the cultural majority. McDermott, discussing the high rate of failure among some groups, states, "Almost invariably, such problems arise when a group in power educates the children of a minority group."[14] He attributes the problem to lack of communication and failure to understand what motivates those who are different from ourselves.

Confirming McDermott's position are Williams and Associates who developed the BITCH test (Black Intelligence Test of Cultural Homogeneity).[15] They found that city black students could perform well on this test but suburban whites found it impossible. The test is used by many to help develop an awareness of the cultural bias that exists in many of the commonly-used tests.

Diagnostically, the point is that if some students come to school and hear a strange language and experience strange customs, it is likely that they will not enter into a situation conducive to communication. The error one can make is to assume that their silence is an indication of lack of ability. Once that error is made, the entire diagnostic effort becomes invalid.

SUMMARY

Clinical diagnosis is normally conducted on individual students. It relies heavily upon the use of observations of student behavior and the results of testing. Clinical diagnosis has obvious advantages and several severe limitations.

The understanding of the purposes and procedures involved in an initial screening is crucial to clinical diagnosis. Initial screenings involve interviews, questionnaires, testing, and diagnostic lessons. Initial screenings are followed by instruction with continuous evaluation or extended diagnosis. Extended diagnosis is heavily reliant upon testing.

The reading specialist must avoid the seven pitfalls that can lead to erroneous diagnostic conclusions and invalid diagnosis. The reading specialist must also be aware of the difficulties in diagnosing nonreaders and readers from different cultural backgrounds.

If clinical diagnosis is seen as a part of an ongoing diagnostic and instructional program, not as an end in itself, then successful learning can be provided for many readers who do not now experience it.

NOTES

1. John Pikulski, "A Critical Review: Informal Reading Inventories," *Reading Teacher* 28 (November 1974): 143.
2. "Gilmore Oral Reading Test," *Manual of Directions* (New York: Harcourt Brace Jovanovich, 1952), pp. 8-9.
3. For opportunities to practice oral reading coding, see James Geyer and Jane Matanzo, *Programmed Reading Diagnosis for Teachers: with Prescriptive References* (Columbus, O.: Charles E. Merrill Publishing Co., 1977).
4. Yetta M. Goodman, and Carolyn L. Burke, *Reading Miscue Inventory—Manual* (New York: Macmillan Publishing Co., 1971).
5. Kenneth S. Goodman, "Analysis of Oral Reading Miscues: Applied Psycholinguistics," *Reading Research Quarterly* 5 (Fall 1969): 9–30.
6. Ibid.
7. Yetta M. Goodman and Carolyn L. Burke, *Reading Miscue Inventory—Manual* (New York: Macmillan Publishing Co., 1971).
8. William R. Powell, "Measuring Reading Performance Informally," (Paper presented at International Reading Association, Houston, Texas, 1978.) p. 2.
9. Phyllis L. Newcomer and Donald D. Hammill, "ITPA and Academic Achievement: A Survey," *Reading Teacher* 28, no. 8 (May 1975): 731–41.
10. Donald D. Durrell, *Manual of Directions: Durrell Analysis of Reading Difficulty* (New York: Harcourt Brace Jovanovich, 1955), p. 14.
11. The Woodcock Johnson Psycho Educational Battery is another useful instrument.
12. Ruth Strang, *Diagnostic Teaching of Reading* (New York: McGraw-Hill Book Co., 1969), p. 8.
13. Jules Abrams, "Minimal Brain Dysfunction and Dyslexia," *Reading World* 14, no. 3 (March 1975): 219.
14. Ray P. McDermott, "The Ethnography of Speaking and Reading" in *Linguistic Theory,* ed. Roger Shuy (Newark, Del.: IRA, 1977), p. 176.
15. Robert L. Williams, "Misuse of Tests: Self Concept," in *Report of the Tenth National Conference on Civil and Human Rights in Education* (Washington D.C.: NEA, 1972), pp. 17-19.

SUGGESTED READINGS

Abrams, Jules. "Minimal Brain Dysfunction and Dyslexia." *Reading World* 14, no. 3 (1975): 219–27. A useful discussion, this article places these terms in perspective for reading teachers and classroom teachers.

Buros, Oscar K. *Reading Tests & Reviews, 1 & 2.* Highland Park, N.J.: Gryphon, 1975, 1968. This publication is a listing of all available reading tests available as of 1968. Most tests receive critical reviews. An essential book for those selecting testing instruments in reading.

Farr, Roger. *Reading: What Can Be Measured?* Newark, Del.: International Reading Association, 1967. Chapters 2 and 3 discuss the use and misuse of available testing instruments in reading. Readers are encouraged to study Farr's discussion.

Geyer, James R., and Matanzo, Jane. *Programmed Reading Diagnosis for Teachers: with Prescriptive References.* Columbus, O.: Charles E. Merrill Publishing Co., 1977. The opportunity for specific practice in various parts of diagnosis and prescription is provided in this book. Reading specialists would do well to work through all aspects presented by Geyer and Matanzo.

Goodman, Kenneth S. "Analysis of Oral Reading Miscues: Applied Psycholinguistics." *Reading Research Quarterly* 5 (Fall 1969): 9–30.

Harris, Albert J. *How To Increase Reading Ability,* 4th ed. New York: David McKay Co., 1970. Chapters 7 and 8 present rather interesting discussions of the topics discussed under educational diagnosis. Harris's book is considered required reading by all those seriously interested in the diagnosis of reading problems.

Kolson, Clifford J., and Kaluger, George. *Clinical Aspects of Remedial Reading.* Springfield, Ill.: Charles C. Thomas, 1964. Chapters 3, 4, and 6 discuss diagnosis of reading problems from the most difficult to the not so serious. This book limits itself to clinical diagnosis and would be most interesting to the reading specialist.

McDermott, Ray P. "The Ethnography of Speaking and Reading" in *Linguistic Theory,* ed. by Roger Shuy. Newark, Del.: IRA, 1977, pp. 144–52. Presents an interesting case for the ways in which readers are treated differently. He cites instances when both communication and motivation are missed, causing certain groups of readers to fail.

6

The Handicapped Reader

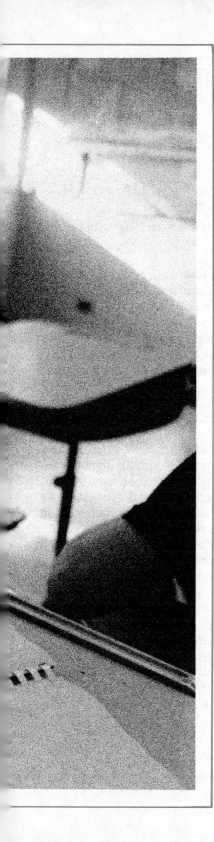

Chapter Emphasis

- There is a need for teachers to be knowledgeable about the laws that affect them.

- The reading teacher should assume a major role in assessing the skills of special students and in helping to design their instructional programs.

- Many of the same approaches and techniques that are used with other students in the regular classroom may be adapted for use with the handicapped student.

- Public Law 94–142 has radically changed the manner in which many special students are being educated.

Increased attention is being given to the educational programs of handicapped students. Federal legislation such as the Rehabilitation Act (PL 93–112, Section 504) and the Education for All Handicapped Children Act (94-142) add legal authority to this increased attention. All educational agencies must provide free, appropriate, public education for all handicapped students between the ages of three and twenty one. Teachers are expected to be familiar with the requirements of the law so that they can function within the law.

Since PL 94-142 provides detailed requirements for the education of the handicapped, we shall use it as an example of how such legislation affects the role of reading personnel in the schools. It should be understood that PL 94-142 is one piece of important legislation but that teachers need to be aware of other legislation that affects them, as well as legislation that is yet to come.

MAJOR PROVISIONS OF PL 94-142

In order to understand the impact of any legislation, one must first understand the major provisions of that legislation. The following is a brief overview of the major provisions of PL 94-142.

Handicapped

Includes those children evaluated as being mentally retarded, hard-of-hearing, deaf, speech impaired, visually impaired, seriously emotionally disturbed, orthopedically impaired, other health impaired, deaf-blind, multihandicapped; or as having specific learning disabilities, who because of those impairments need special education and related services.

The last category, specific learning disabilities, will naturally include many children experiencing serious difficulties with learning to read. Reading teachers, however, must be prepared to be involved with the assessment and instruction of all handicapped children.

Free and Appropriate Public Education

A free, appropriate, public education that includes special education and related services is required. This education should be designed to meet the special needs of the students. It provides safeguards for the rights of handicapped students and their parents and it provides for periodic evaluation of the program to assure its effectiveness.

Individualized Education Program (IEP)

An IEP will be developed for each handicapped student. It will be developed after an evaluation by a multidisciplinary team. IEPs take a variety of forms in different educational agencies, but they must all include:

a. A statement of the student's present levels of educational performance
b. A statement of annual goals as well as short-term instructional objectives
c. A statement of special education or related services to be provided, as well as the extent to which the student will participate in regular education programs
d. The projected dates for initiation of services and the expected duration of those services
e. Appropriate objective criteria and evaluation procedures and at least an annual evaluation to determine whether the objectives are being achieved

An IEP must be in effect and approved by the parents before special education and related services can be provided. (See sample on next page.)

IEP Accountability

Educational agencies and teachers must make good faith efforts to assist students to achieve the objectives and goals of the IEP; however, Part B of the Act does not require anyone to be accountable if the student should not achieve the growth expected. Parents have the right to complain and ask for revisions in the program if they believe that sufficient efforts have not been made.

Parental Consent

Parental consent is required for the initial placement of the child in a program that provides special education or related services. They must also approve of the IEP. If they do not approve it, they have a right to an impartial due-process hearing. Parents must also approve changes in the program.

Assessment

Assessment of a student identified as handicapped will be conducted by a team including at least one teacher or other specialist with knowledge in the area of suspected disability. Testing materials and procedures are to be selected and administered so as not to be culturally or racially discriminatory. No single procedure can be used to determine a student's placement or program.

Least Restrictive Learning Environment

Handicapped students should be placed, when possible, with students who are not handicapped. Placement decisions are to be made on an individual basis using information from the assessment. When possible, students are to be placed as close to home as possible and in the school they would have attended if they were not handicapped.

Specific Learning Disability

Children may be classified as having a Specific Learning Disability if they do not achieve commensurate with their age and ability levels in one or more areas. Several areas are specifically listed in the law, including difficulties with basic reading skills and reading comprehension. This type of definition allows for a very broad interpretation and may result in many children being listed as handicapped when they are not. Reading-skill deficiency, however, certainly handicaps a student as far as success in school is concerned.

Sample

Individual Education Program

Child's Name *Margi Kraus*

School *12ᵀᴴ St.* **Grade** *5*

Date of Program Entry *Nov. 3, 1983*

Long-Term Goals:

1. *Develop comprehension in 2ᵈ reader.*
2. *Develop word attack system.*
3. _____

Summary of Present Levels of Performance

Comprehends well in 2ᵈ reader
Knows all initial consonants
Knows many rhyming syllables
Does not attack unknown words
_____
_____

Short-Term Objectives	Specific Ed. or Support Services	Person(s) Responsible	Percent of Time	Beginning and Ending Date	Review Date(s)
1. Margi will use non-questioning activities to further develop comprehension skills.	classroom	classroom teacher	5	Nov. 3, 1983 – April 1, 1984	April 1, 1983
2. Margi will substitute initial consonants to -AT, -IN, and -ING to form new words	Title I Resource	Title I Resource Teacher	5	Nov. 3, 1983 – March 1, 1984	March 1, 1983

Committee Members Present

Mrs. King – Principal
Mrs. Kraus – Parent
Mr. Fowler – Teacher
Mrs. Dayhoff – Title I Resource
Mr. Czarnecki – Vice Principal

Parent Approval ✓ **Yes** ___ **No**

Louise Kraus
   signature

Objective Evaluation Criteria: _____
1. *Reading comprehension evaluation by vice principal*
2. *CRT now in use in school for initial consonant substitution.*

CONFIDENTIAL INFORMATION:

Percent of Time in Regular Classroom _____

Placement Recommendation
   Grade 5, Mr. Fowler

Committee recommendations for materials, techniques

use initial consonant substitution with Durrell Speech to Print Phonics. Use non-questioning strategies – Wilson, p³¹²

RESPONSIBILITIES OF THE READING TEACHER IN ASSESSMENT

The reading teacher's contribution to the multidisciplinary assessment is an important one. Careful preparation and careful data interpretation are necessary. While the suggestions mentioned below are relevant to the diagnosis and remediation of all students, they are deserving of special attention when dealing with students who have been identified as handicapped.

According to the law it is necessary to have data from more than one source in planning an IEP for a handicapped student. The reading portion of the assessment should not rely upon the results of a single test score, either.[1] The tendency to rely upon one's favorite instrument can be especially misleading when dealing with the handicapped. Often such students perform poorly in certain conditions, but do well in other situations. For example, a hearing-impaired child may perform poorly when questions are asked orally, but do well when responding to written questions.

Handicapped students should be placed, when possible, with students who are not handicapped.

As the time approached for my first IEP conference, I somewhat nervously shuffled through the papers in front of me. After all, the workshops that I had attended on Public Law 94-142 had elaborated at great length concerning the parents' legal rights to challenge a special class placement or an Individualized Education Program (IEP) of which they disapproved. In my mind IEPs were linked with due process, legal requirements, and court proceedings. Further, although Albert had been enrolled in my special education class for over a year, this would be my first meeting with his parents. Repeated attempts to meet them the previous year had failed and even telephone overtures had proved unsuccessful.

As I shook their hands, I told Albert's parents that I was pleased that they had been able to come to the school to discuss plans for his education in the coming year. Albert's father gruffly replied that they wouldn't have attended if they hadn't received a registered letter from the school that made it sound important. I remember muttering that I thought that they would indeed find the meeting to be important, as I ushered them into a conference room.

Albert's parents were introduced to the other participants at the meeting, our principal, guidance counselor, speech therapist, and school psychologist. I began the meeting by explaining that the major purpose of an IEP conference was to review a student's educational progress to date and to cooperatively plan the goals and objectives that would guide instructional efforts in the coming year. I then outlined Albert's strengths in various subject areas. As I was describing his strengths in reading, his mother began to cry. She explained that doctors and school officials had always told them what Albert couldn't do, but that I was the first professional to emphasize Albert's abilities. From that point on, the meeting took on a decidedly positive note. We outlined to the parents the school's plans for Albert in the coming year and asked them if our goals seemed to be challenging yet realistic for Albert. Based upon input from his parents, we revised our goals and also formulated objectives for Albert in two other areas of paren-

Editorial

tal concern, behavior and citizenship. We then fielded questions from the parents concerning the instructional program and things that they could do at home to be of help. Albert's father was particularly interested in things that he could do with his limited reading ability to aid Albert in developing his reading skills. At the end of the conference, the parents signed the tentative IEP and agreed to come to the next PTA meeting to discuss Albert's progress toward the goals that had been established. As they left, they sincerely thanked each of us for our efforts in Albert's behalf.

In the remaining two years that I knew them, Albert's parents continued to be interested supporters of the school program. I had always intuitively recognized the value of focusing on strengths in contacts with students, but Albert's IEP conference compellingly demonstrated to me the importance of that approach with parents, too!

Craig J. Cleland

Test information coupled with direct observation of student behavior in learning situations is recommended.

Diagnostic assessment of the handicapped student should focus on strengths. Traditionally, diagnosis of the handicapped tends to focus largely upon weaknesses. You may be the only person on the multidisciplinary team to advocate an assessment of strengths. The need for looking at the strengths of handicapped students is highlighted by the fact that many view such students as weak because of their handicap. Let us ask what reading skills a hearing-impaired student has developed. Let us be certain to know how well a mentally-retarded student reads. As strengths are identified and communicated to the student, the parents, and the teachers, a new view of the capabilities of the student emerges. In some cases this will be the first notation in school records regarding the strengths of a handicapped student. When the IEP is developed, program adjustments for a student's strengths will be just as important as those adjustments made because of weaknesses.

Subskill assessment is a routine procedure used by some professionals, but it can lead to misplacement if all aspects of the reading process are not assessed. For example, we recently received a report on a visually-impaired student that indicated severe weakness in several of the visual discrimination skills. Upon assessment of the student's oral reading skills and silent reading comprehension, we found that the student was reading above grade level and up to potential. Upon further evaluation we found that the student was doing well in reading class and was considered by the teacher to be a fine student. The use of a visual discrimination subtest on a student with visual impairment seems logical; however, in this case, the student had overcome those deficiencies although unable to perform on a given test. Had the total reading behavior not been assessed, this student would have been misplaced into a program to improve visual perception.

Other subskill-evaluation instruments can lead to similar misevaluation. For example, some readers cannot perform well on phonics subskill tests, yet they can read very well. Others may not do well with tests of auditory discrimination, yet they also read very well. Total reading performance must be assessed as well as specific subskills.

The multidisciplinary team will make placement decisions based upon the interpretation of the data used in the assessment. Test instruments that are used for such decision making should be defendable in terms of reliability and validity. All team members should be able to attest to the reliability and validity of the tests that they use. They should also have evidence that the test is a useful assessment instrument for students with specific handicaps. For example, an auditory discrimination test would not be useful for assessment of a deaf student. They must also be able to demonstrate that the test is not culturally or racially biased. When data are derived from questionable testing instruments, misplacement may well result. Correct placement is the responsibility of the team that develops the IEP. The multidisciplinary team has great responsibilities for all handicapped students. Each team member must approach the team meeting well prepared. The team will be relying upon the reading teacher for important data relating to the reading development of the handicapped student. If one is ill-prepared, then one's input will be of little value to the team.

RESPONSIBILITIES OF THE READING TEACHER IN IMPLEMENTING THE IEP

Once the IEP has been prepared and approved by the parents, the reading teacher will be involved in implementing the reading portion of the program. This involvement can take the form of helping the classroom teacher or working directly with the student.

When helping the teacher, the reading teacher can provide materials for instruction, work with one group while the teacher works with others, demonstrate effective techniques suitable for a specific type of handicap, or simply offer suggestions. The teacher should be able to call upon the services of any of the interdisciplinary team; however, one team member will normally assume the major responsibility to help the classroom teacher. When the difficulty is primarily a reading one, the reading teacher will usually be that person. At times, due to load consideration or when dealing with a multihandicapped child, the resource may be someone other than a reading person. In such cases the reading teacher should have direct input into the implementation of the reading section of the IEP.

In the team assessment meeting a decision will be made about which team member will work with the student outside the classroom. It is a common (but not desirable) practice that personnel with little reading training will be providing reading instruction for students with multiple handicaps. Since such personnel may have limited understanding of the reading process, there is a tendency to rely upon commercial materials that focus on subskill development. The reading teacher may be in the position of offering suggestions for approaches and strategies that reflect a more complete understanding of the reading process.

It would be better, of course, if the reading teacher were assigned the responsibility for the reading portion of the IEP. The instructional program needs to be coordinated with the classroom teacher who is responsible for most of the other instruction. As in all instructional programs that pull students from the classroom, effectiveness is highly related to a coordinated effort with all involved.

Keep in mind that the overall objective is to make program adjustments so that a disability does not handicap the student or that an existing handicap can be minimized. Ramps are constructed so that children confined to a wheel chair can enter a building without aid. Signers are assigned to the deaf so that they can profit from instruction in regular classrooms. In reading, the emphasis should be on obtaining meaning. Every effort should be made for the students to obtain the view of reading as a meaningful process. To facilitate instruction in meaningful reading, special adjustments may be needed for handicapped students. A few examples include:

Individualization Adjust assignments so that they are practicable and meaningful. Design assignments toward the strengths of the handicapped students. For example, minimize the visual work for the visually impaired by having their instructions available on tapes. Make certain that instructions are understood and that the students will know when they have completed the expected work.

Oral Reading By reading orally with the students, the teacher has an opportunity to help them feel fluent and accurate in their reading. Fluency and accuracy facilitate comprehension. Read passages with students several times until they can read them fluently alone.

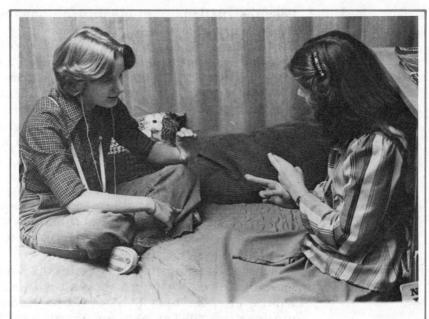

A deaf child can teach other students to sign.

It is common practice to have readers read orally by themselves. This practice, however, often causes laborious, nonfluent oral reading. When that happens, the readers are practicing poor oral reading and are learning to read poorly. Reading with the students gives practice in fluent reading and lets attention be given to meaning.

Support

The addition of three handicapped students to a regular classroom may necessitate the need for help. Help can come from:

Resource personnel in the school.   These people have special training to help special students. They are usually delighted to be asked to help and they can relieve some of the extra load.

Learning pairs.   Letting students work on activities in pairs lets them help each other. Paired learning is especially important when students are working independently from the teacher.

Peer instruction.   Students who have mastery of a skill can often help others learn it. Sometimes it takes that extra two or three times through a process to learn a skill. The student can be strong in one area and not in another, so that different students can be peer instructors at various times. And remember the handicapped student when selecting peer instructors. For example, a deaf child can teach other students to sign. By looking for the strengths of handicapped students, you will find areas in which they can be the helper.

Community volunteers.   People with special skills or with extra time can participate in the classroom for a portion of the day. They may assist a handicapped student who needs individual attention in order to complete some activities.

Personal Learning

Use student strengths to maximize the personal nature of all learning. Find out what they already know and utilize it whenever possible. Utilize those nonquestioning techniques discussed in chapter 9 with handicapped students. Let them feel the success that results from personal reactions to material that has been read.

AREAS OF POTENTIAL DIFFICULTY

The passage of PL 94-142 has created some situations that may prove to be difficult for many teachers. These difficulties can result in teacher frustration and discomfort. A discussion of a few of those areas follows.

Lack of Services while Awaiting the Approved IEP

Since IEP approval is needed before special educational services can begin, there may be a waiting period at the beginning of the school year. At times this waiting period extends to months. Teachers will need to provide instruction during that waiting time. They should assess strengths, help handicapped students feel comfortable in their classrooms, and plan programs that are practicable. They should ask for help in terms of materials and program suggestions.

Lack of Teacher Training

Regular classroom teachers are usually not trained to work with specific types of handicapped students. Teachers should ask for inservice programs, resource assistants, and recommendations for materials and procedures. In these cases teachers should not feel inadequate when asking for help. As they strengthen their teaching skills with the handicapped, their frustrations will diminish.

Lack of Time

Teachers have reported that they feel a lack of time to help their regular students when they must individualize for handicapped students who have been placed in their classroom for portions of the day. They feel pulled in too many different directions. Teachers should ask for help to relieve them of this time problem. They can utilize one or more of the suggestions on page 000 in this chapter to get some help so that they will have more time.

Distorted IEP

Teachers may be asked to work on the implementation of an IEP in which the reading section is distorted. This usually occurs when the IEP lists objectives in terms of subskills. Teachers should make note of the difficulties with the implementation of the IEP and ask for a reassessment of it. Notes can be taken regarding the frustration that results when the student tries to complete the activities. They may relate to materials inappropriate to implement the IEP. They may deal with the lack of time to help the student feel success with the objectives of the IEP. Once they have given the IEP a reasonable effort and have collected their data from the notes, a team meeting can be called to reassess the program.

Class Size

Some teachers have class sizes controlled by national, state, or local rules and regulations. Most teachers of regular classrooms do not. As handicapped students find increasing opportunities to participate in classes with the nonhandicapped, some attention will need to be given to class size control. If not, there is likely to be severe teacher resentment of the additional responsibilities placed upon them without the support system needed to make the delivery of those responsibilities a reality.

SUMMARY

The impact of PL 94-142 is dynamic. Students who otherwise saw themselves as odd or different are now seeing themselves as a part of regular education. Nonhandicapped students are working beside the handicapped and learning about the handicaps of others. Some of those with disabilities are finding that they are not as handicapped as they once thought they were. Parents of the handicapped are finding their children to be more able to deal with regular classroom instruction than they once thought.

Of course the picture is not all positive. The severely and profoundly handicapped do not work in regular classrooms. The teasing and harassing of the handicapped has not stopped. The problems mentioned in the above section are not yet solved. School agencies need to deal with these and other problems to make PL 94-142 work smoothly. New priorities need to be set and funding systems need to be adjusted. But, from now on, the handicapped students will be finding a new type of schooling waiting for them.

NOTE

1. IRA Board of Directors, "A Position on Minimal Competencies in Reading," *Reading Teacher* 33, no. 1, (October 1979): 54–55.

SUGGESTED READINGS

————, *A Teacher's Guide to PL 94–142,* Washington, D.C.: National Educational Association, 1978. Uses a situation-response approach to explain some of the major implications of PL 94-142. Tackles controversial as well as legal implications. May be reproduced for teacher use.

Joseph Ballard. *Public Law 94-142 and Section 504—Understanding what they are and are not.* Reston, Va.: Council for Exceptional Children, 1977. Uses a question-answer approach to assist one in understanding PL 94-142 and Section 504. Provides detailed information and suggested additional references.

————, *Education for All Handicapped Children.* Washington, D.C.: National Educational Association, 1978. Uses a case-study approach to examine the impact of Section 504 and PL 94-142. Provides both positive and negative reactions of teachers, parents, and other school officials.

7

Remediation—Some
Insights

Guidelines for Remediation

Chapter Emphasis

- Effective remediation is based upon careful diagnosis.

- Remedial programs should seek to guarantee and illustrate success to the student.

- Techniques used in classroom and clinical remediation do not differ from one another.

- Important insights into remediation can be gained from several recent research findings.

- Remedial programs that are successful require careful planning and skilled implementation.

Remediation of reading difficulties is not, as many believe, based upon mysterious techniques that are impossible for the classroom teacher to understand. Rather, remediation is based upon sound instructional principles focused upon the strengths and needs of the students on the basis of careful diagnosis. Since remediation calls for skillful teaching, it is assumed that anyone who works in a remedial program is a skilled teacher who keeps up-to-date by reading and studying.

As previously discussed in diagnosis, there is seldom one cause of reading difficulties; therefore, there is seldom one approach to their solution. On this point, the public has often been led to believe the opposite, thereby causing pressure to be placed upon educators to teach by certain methods. That there is seldom one satisfactory remedial approach, however, in no way justifies using a little of all known teaching techniques; this is called the "shotgun" approach. Rather, remediation should be in direct response to diagnostic findings, necessitating the use of the most suitable educational techniques as solutions to the diagnostic findings. These findings contain information concerning skill strengths as well as needs.

GUIDELINES FOR REMEDIATION

By adhering to the following three guidelines, teachers will find remediation most effective.

✦ Remediation must guarantee immediate success. In the remedial program, initial instruction should culminate in a successful, satisfying experience. In this way, students who have experienced frequent failure in reading begin the remedial program with the attitude that this educational experience will be both different and rewarding. Without this attitude, the best remedial efforts are often wasted. Successful learning situations also are assured by directing activities toward those learning activities that the diagnosis has indicated are the students' strengths and interests. It is recommended that all the early lessons be directed toward student strengths. As remediation progresses, the percentage of time devoted to strengths is likely to decrease. When the students start to ask for instruction in the areas of their weaknesses, changes in instructional strategy can take place. However, it is recommended that throughout the entire program, a large portion of every lesson be directed to strengths.

✦ Remedial successes must be illustrated to the student. It is not enough that a reader be started at the right level and experience success; successes must be presented so that awareness of them is assured. As students progress, charts, graphs, word files, and specific teacher praise comments can be used to illustrate successes.

Remediation must provide for transfer to actual reading situations. There will be occasions in a remedial program where isolated drill in various areas will be required; however, drill activities should always come from contextual reading material and should always conclude in contextual reading situations. The overlearning of all skills takes place best in actual reading situations.

Types of Remediation

Unlike diagnosis, classroom and clinical remediation involve the same teaching strategies. The students need individualized instruction. Instruction is based on sound learning theory, and is constantly adjusted to students' responses. While remediation in a clinical setting may be easier because of small group size, the strategies used do not differ. There are no materials, no techniques, and no

Students need individualized instruction.

learning theories that are reserved for the clinical setting. In fact, the opposite may be true. Many teachers are able and willing to apply skills learned in a clinical setting to their classrooms. Many reading specialists find it useful to conduct remedial efforts without taking the readers from their classrooms. In this manner, teachers can easily pick up teaching strategies used by the reading specialist. And, to the surprise of some, reading specialists can often learn a great deal from the classroom teacher's teaching strategies.

Implications from Research

The findings of the following five research reports are cause for alarm as we consider the plight of those experiencing difficulty with learning to read. We can channel that alarm into constructive use if we consider the implications of these studies as we plan remedial lessons.

1. Allington found that poor readers read very little during remedial reading classes.[1] The mean number of words read during a given session was forty three. He recommends less skill instruction and more reading time—a lot more.

2. Clay observed first graders and found that good readers read 20,000 words during the year and poor readers read 5,000 words.[2] These findings support Allington's, in that poor readers do not get much reading practice. Clay also noted that good readers would correct one error in three, whereas poor readers would correct only one error in twenty. If poor readers made nineteen errors without correction, it would appear that they were not reading for meaning.

3. Allington also found that good readers and poor readers are treated differently during instruction.[3] When good readers made oral reading errors, they were interrupted by the teacher 24 percent of the time. Poor readers were interrupted 68 percent of the time. With good readers the interruptions were made at the end of a meaningful unit; poor readers were interrupted at the point of the error. Two implications can be gleaned from these data: good readers get to read more because they are interrupted less; and poor readers, interrupted at the point of the error, have difficulty understanding what they read and are not given the opportunity to self-correct.

4. Durkin conducted observational research and found almost no comprehension instruction in grades 3 and 6.[4] Comprehension was assessed, but not taught. She also found almost no instruction in the area of study skills. Content knowledge was assessed, but the skills to acquire that knowledge were not being taught. If readers can comprehend what they read, they do well in assessment; and if they cannot comprehend they will do poorly in the assessment sessions.

5. We found that good and poor readers were treated differently in an observational study of fourth graders.[5] Good readers were all reading in material that was very easy (their error rate was one in 100 running words). Poor readers were placed in material that was very difficult (one error in nine running words). Good readers were observed reading 57 percent of the time; poor readers were reading only 33 percent of the time. Poor readers spent twice as much time in phonics skill activities as good readers. Finally, good readers were observed to be on task 92 percent of the time but poor readers only 81 percent of the time. These findings may be explained as follows: poor readers are placed in difficult material and sound inaccurate. The teacher

therefore increases the skill work, thereby decreasing reading time. Skill work tends to be meaningless, so the poor readers go off task.

Considerations for Starting Remediation

Several types of planning strategies need to be considered as one enters into remedial programs. These strategies have been found to make a difference between success and failure when instructing handicapped readers.

Assure positive attitude. Remedial activities, while based on diagnosis, should concentrate on the interests of students. The sense of self-worth must be developed early. Helping readers to realize success with materials that are of interest has tremendous impact. The "I-can't-do-it" attitude quickly turns around to "I can do it." We don't talk handicapped readers into feeling good about themselves; we make certain that success experiences are realized. We also make certain that those experiences are important to the student. The use of newspapers, auto magazines, model construction, and cooking are examples of reading activities that generally have high interest. One student, reportedly not able to read above the third-grade level, could read football articles in the *Washington Post* at a high level of comprehension. The following suggestions can be used as starter ideas.

1. When students perform successfully, let them teach the activity to another.
2. Provide rewards for successful performance.
3. Build small-group rapport: "We can read—we are worthwhile."
4. Provide teaming situations for successful learning. Let pairs of readers work toward an objective.
5. Make certain the students know the objectives and know when they have reached them.
6. Keep parents and other teachers informed about successes so that they may reinforce them.

Plan for a balanced program. Two types of balance make remedial programs effective. The first type is balance between reading narrative types of material and reading content material. As students see reading skills transferred to content material, the realization develops that they can be

Remedial activities should concentrate on the interests of students.

successful in science and social studies activities and that success in school is possible.

Another type of balance is that of skills and reading. Each skills lesson must result in a successful reading activity. Actually, three steps are appropriate:

1. Skills lessons
2. Practice lessons utilizing those skills
3. Free reading, applying those skills

From the research previously cited, it would appear that reading time to apply skills should be a major portion of each remedial lesson.

Without these types of balance, remedial instruction can become segmented and can distort the purposes for learning to read well. Success in phonics lessons is useless unless those learned skills can be applied in free reading. Teachers need to plan for balance in order to assure a complete remedial program.

√ **Encourage risk taking.**   Years of unsuccessful attempts to respond to reading activities tend to discourage students from trying. It is too risky. They get corrected, ridiculed, embarrassed, and defeated. If they decide not to try, there is no risk of failure. Remedial lessons must encourage risk taking by:

a. Assuring that there will be no penalty for inaccurate responses
b. Placing students in material that they can handle with ease
c. Encouraging students to work together toward an answer to a problem
d. Creating a discussion atmosphere during comprehension lessons rather than a teacher-questioning session in which the teacher holds the correct answer (See chapter 10)
e. Setting attainable goals for each student; when the goals are reached, the student should be recognized for those successes.

Plan for student decision making.   There is no better way for a student to be enthusiastic about the lesson than to be involved in setting objectives, selecting activities, and participating in evaluation. Many handicapped readers sit through activities designed to improve their reading skills but have no idea where the lesson is designed to lead them.

During orientation activities to a given lesson, students should be free to add objectives and question others. This is not to say that students make all decisions, but they can have input. Generally students are inclined to put forth more effort once they understand why they are doing a given activity.

Contracting to complete a certain number of activities in a certain amount of time has great impact. The teacher provides a list of possible activities that will satisfy skill drill, skill practice, and free reading. From this list, the students and teacher pick those that are of most interest and appear to be most possible for them. The concept of negotiation is important. Both the students and the teacher have input. At times certain activities are required; at other times, two activities are selected from a list of five. At other times, students may have completely free choice. A form such as Figure 7–1 is useful.

Realizing the need to provide for alternatives and student involvement was easy—but identifying an organizational plan that could account for the varying strengths and needs of thirty heterogeneously grouped third graders seemed overwhelming to me as a classroom teacher. However, as the time progressed, I was continually unable to deny the frustration I witnessed as many handicapped readers tried and failed with reading, writing, and spelling activities that were too difficult for them. The need for individual students to become aware of and involved in the setting of attainable goals convinced me to try contract teaching.

There are many observations I can reflect upon, at this time, that have convinced me that contract teaching is a viable and desirable way for teachers to provide for decision making, student involvement, and individually paced instruction—but there is one instance that was so delightful that I'm sure I'll remember it vividly for a long time to come.

I had a class of thirty third graders who were mastering the concept of contract spelling. My class included students who on the Botel Word Opposites Test, scored everywhere from below pre-primer level to sixth-grade level. The spelling book issued to me contained twelve words—a number that had proved to be very easy for some children and totally unreachable to others.

We had passed the stage where children had learned to select, with teacher involvement, those words that they felt they could successfully learn by Friday. We had also talked about various study methods that could help us learn to spell new words, and we were currently experimenting with a limited variety in order to identify those specific techniques that were most beneficial to each individual student.

On Friday, the class was taking the post-test with each student writing only those words that he or she had contracted to learn. While I was reading the list, I realized that some students, while waiting for me to read a word they had contracted for, had free moments when they could sit back and wait, or look around . . . .

Being familiar with the efforts to copy that can occur if students are frustrated, I immediately requested the students to please cover their papers and remember to keep their eyes on their own working area. No sooner had the (thoughtless) remark left my mouth when one student looked up at me and said, "*Why* would anyone cheat in this room?"

That question caused me to think about and isolate the following changes that were occuring in my room: 1. Being involved in the attainment of a task that was attainable was removing the syndrome of failure and reducing the negative effects of unrealistic competition. 2. The development of an atmosphere where success was possible for all had created an atmosphere where students were encouraging and supportive of one another. 3. Continued experience with success was encouraging students to become "risk takers." 4. "Involvement" of students had developed an awareness of the need for learning as well as a commitment toward learning.

Not only did contracting offer me, as the teacher, a manageable system for offering differentiated learning opportunities, but it proved to be a technique that resulted in a learning climate that was positive and assured success. Had I taken the time to put words to the changes I was witnessing, I might have had a better answer for the boy who asked me, "Why would anyone cheat in this room?"

Marcia M. Wilson

The student is instructed to self-evaluate by placing a smile or frown in the little box beside the activity completed. When all agreed-upon activities are completed, no further work is assigned. The payoff for completing assignments must not be more assignments.

The teacher and students now discuss the quality of the completed activities and plan for tomorrow's lessons. Activities positively evaluated should be discussed in terms of what made the students feel good about them. Those negatively evaluated should also be discussed. The important point is that students should not be made to feel badly about an honest evaluation. Use their reactions as clues in future planning. Experience with such contracts shows that many students become more and more positive about reading, and it is not uncommon for them to ask for more activities—a good sign that reading is becoming interesting and worthwhile.

The students now feel very involved with their lessons. They become trusting and enthusiastic. The teacher, always in control, now knows what does and does not interest the·students; therefore, better planning results.

Conduct task analysis. When students have difficulty with a given activity, task analysis can be used as a diagnostic teaching tool. Task analysis asks the teacher to consider which subskills may be missing in order for the student to complete the given task. Since all students master skills in very personal ways, pat formulas for why a given student cannot respond are of little use. The efforts in this direction by the University of Maryland's reading center were stimulated by the ideas of Ladd.[6] Here is how we have applied those ideas:[7]

Step 1 A problem is identified.
    Example: A student cannot respond satisfactorily to questioning about the material read, even when reading silently.
Step 2 The teacher is to determine the strengths and weaknesses the student has in this skill area.
    Example: Can read orally with satisfactory accuracy at the fourth-grade level.
    Cannot answer literal questions asked of him from this material.
    Can answer literal questions when working from the third-grade level.

Figure 7-1

Name_____ Date_____
Pick one activity from box 1, 2, 3.
Pick one activity from box 4, 5, 6.
Pick one activity from box 7, 8, 9.
Activity 10 is required.

1. Play initial consonant game. ▢	2. Teach consonants to your partner. ▢
3. Complete skills sheet on consonants. ▢	4. Find words beginning with *s, t, c, b* on page 34. ▢
5. Read story about Pat the Rat. ▢	6. Read aloud with teacher. ▢
7. Read story from book on library shelf. ▢	8. Make display advertising book you are reading. ▢
9. Read aloud with your partner from book of your choice. ▢	10. Participate in ten-minute sustained silent reading. ▢

Step 3 The teacher makes a series of hypotheses concerning the possible reasons for this difficulty.
Example: The student is not interested in the material.
The passage is too long.
The questions are threatening.
The student does not have purpose for reading.

Step 4 Through diagnostic teaching, the teacher tests each hypothesis.
Example: For the first hypothesis, the teacher may attempt to determine the student's interest areas and find material at the fourth-grade level that is of interest. For the second hypothesis, the teacher may break the passage into smaller parts, asking the questions following each part.

Step 5 The teacher keeps a record of each diagnostic lesson and forms a tentative conclusion to be tested in further instruction.
Example: This student responded well when material was in the area of sports and motorcycles. He also

responded better when he jotted down his purposes for reading before he started. Passage-length adjustment did not change his ability to comprehend, and the questions did not seem threatening in this new situation.

Of course task analysis is a strategy that has been used by good teachers for a long time. But we have found it helpful to formalize the process in this manner so that all can profit from its power as a diagnostic tool.

The value of task analysis for reading diagnosis is increased by the fact that people do not all learn through the same set of subskills. What stops one person from comprehending a given passage is different from what stops another. And what one person needs as a subskill to read better may well be a subskill that another person does not need. Task analysis provides a highly suitable, flexible strategy for getting at the unique learning styles of each reader.

Get others involved. Teachers must use all possible resources when their students are having difficulty in learning to read. The answer to a given student's problem may best be solved by involving a physical education teacher, a speech therapist, the parents, a psychologist, or the family doctor. Even if others do not have suggestions for helping such students, communication channels should be open so that all involved are informed. Many a good instructional program has become ineffective when members are working at crossed purposes.

Peers can work with a reader by teaming together on activities that the reader cannot do alone. They can also conduct some of the time-consuming, drill-type activities; they too can profit from the student's strengths. For example, I worked with a boy who always was the poorest in every activity. He always saw himself as a follower, never as a leader. As a field trip approached, he was taken on a "dry run" to familiarize him with the features of the field trip. He became excited and served as a group leader on the actual field trip. The other children appreciated his leadership and assistance. By getting everyone involved, the teacher can change a student's life from one of failure and frustration to one of success and excitement.

By considering these ideas prior to initiating a

remedial program, teachers can make adjustments that provide for a greater chance of success.

The older handicapped reader. Secondary school students who encounter serious problems while learning to read require special consideration in planning a remedial program. Materials for instruction and instructional techniques need to be selected in terms of appeal for the secondary student. Driver's manuals, job information, consumer education materials, and newspaper articles are examples of appealing materials. We have found it best to let these students bring to class the materials they need to be able to read.

Secondary students who have many unsuccessful experiences tend to be very poor risk takers. If they decide not to try, they cannot fail again—but they won't learn either. The lessons must be planned so that risk taking is encouraged, not punished.

Contracting with these students also has appeal. The contracts differ from those used with younger students, in that the secondary students are more involved with the decisions made in each part of the contract, i.e., planning, selecting activities, and evaluating. We have also found secondary students with severe reading difficulties to be excellent tutors for younger students. They take great pride in such roles and obtain excellent results. As is commonly reported, they probably learn more than the student being tutored. It also helps to organize instructional activities around problems that the students have identified as important to them. Secondary students can get turned on to reading when the learning activities have immediate application in their lives.

Continuing to teach the same reading skills that these students have had forced upon them for years is seldom effective. Instead of isolated phonics, keep instruction at the word and phrase level at a minimum. Instead of seeking to retain details, engage the student in discussion of important ideas. Relate reading skills to those academic subjects that are of interest. Help them see reading as a key to success in school.

While all of the above suggestions have application to students of all ages, they have particular application to secondary students with severe reading problems, because almost all of these students have been turned off to school and to reading. The teacher has to work first on attitude and self-concept. A little reading success with the right types of materials can start changing negative attitudes.

SUMMARY

Effective remedial programs focus on the self-concept of the student. Strengths must be practiced, recognized, and approved. Students must be decision makers in their instructional activities along with the teacher. All school resources must be utilized to assist readers to realize they can and do read.

NOTES

1. Richard Allington, "If They Don't Read Much, How They Ever Gonna Get Good?", *Journal of Reading* 21, no. 1 (October 1977): 57–61.
2. Marie Clay, *Reading: The Patterning of Complex Behavior* (London: Heinemann Educational Books, 1972) p. 102.
3. Richard Allington, "Are Good Readers and Poor Readers Taught Differently?" American Research Association, Toronto, March 1978.
4. Dolores Durkin, "What Classroom Observations Reveal About Reading Comprehension Instruction," *Reading Research Quarterly* 14, no. 4 (1978–79): 481–533.
5. Linda B. Gambrell, Robert M. Wilson, and Walter N. Gantt, "An Analysis of Task Attending Behaviors of Good and Poor Readers," unpublished research.
6. Eleanor Ladd, "Task Analysis," *Reading: What Is It All About* (Clemson, S.C.: Clemson University, 1975), pp. 68-77.
7. Robert M. Wilson, "Comprehension Diagnosis Via Task Analysis," *Reading World* 14, no. 3 (March 1975): 178-79.

SUGGESTED READINGS

Durkin, Dolores. "What Classroom Observations Reveal About Reading Comprehension." *Reading Research Quarterly* 14:481–533. A detailed description is presented that concerns the observed behavior of teachers during reading and social studies lessons. This article should be studied by all who are planning remedial lessons.

Gambrell, Linda B., and Wilson, Robert M. *Focusing on the*

Strengths of Children. Belmont, Calif.: Fearon Publishers, 1973. Detailed accounts for techniques for focusing on strengths of all students are provided. Ideas for making school enjoyable are throughout.

Kaluger, George, and Kolson, Clifford J. *Reading and Learning Disabilities,* 2d ed. Columbus, O.: Charles E. Merrill Publishing Co., 1978. In chapter 8, the authors suggest techniques for starting a reader in a remedial program. With an approach differing from those suggested in this chapter, the authors explain the necessity for establishing rapport.

Smith, Frank. *Understanding Reading,* 2d ed. New York: Holt, Rinehart, and Winston, 1978. Chapter 2. The problems of risk taking are discussed in this and other chapters. This book is important reading for those who are going to work with students who have experienced large amounts of failure.

Wilson, Robert M., and Gambrell, Linda B. *Contract Teaching.* Paoli, Pa.: Instructo/McGraw-Hill, 1980. Numerous examples of contract teaching with detailed explanations are included. Record-keeping strategies and reinforcement techniques make this a useful source.

8

Readiness Activities

Language

Auditory Difficulties

Visual Difficulties

Orientation

Chapter Emphasis

- Language differences reduce students' inclinations to take risks.

- Instructional programs should start where the developing student can respond with success.

- Auditory and visual discrimination skills are best taught with written passages.

- When students seem to be disoriented, be certain that the difficulty is not in the learning climate.

  Note: All instructional materials cited in this chapter are listed in Appendix B, giving details.

Some readers need help in the basic readiness areas of reading—language, auditory, visual, and orientation. These readers often appear to be slow, immature, and limited intellectually. With effective instruction, however, these characteristics tend to disappear. In some cases the decision will be made that the reader needs time to develop. Most of the time, however, waiting will not accomplish the development of readiness skills and instruction will be necessary.

Readiness activities for readers experiencing serious difficulties with reading are similar to readiness activities for beginning readers, the difference being that the materials for instruction will be adjusted to assure student interest.

LANGUAGE

When students develop an awareness that their language is different from their peers' they tend to withdraw from oral communication. It's too risky. I imagine we have all searched our minds for a synonym rather than attempt to use a word about which we are unsure of the proper pronunciation. We avoid the criticism that usually follows. Imagine, then, the students who have developed that feeling about every utterance they make. If you don't attempt oral communication, you don't get the criticism. Risk taking is essential, however, for language development. Teachers must develop a climate in which oral communication is enjoyable and rewarding. By reducing the threat of criticism the teacher increases the risk taking and facilitates the use of oral communication. Language difficulties can result from three different causes: the student's language does not match the language of the school; it is underdeveloped through limited experiential language background; or it reflects limited intellectual development.

Language Mismatching (Dialect)

Students whose dialect differs from that used in school and in the materials of instruction are often found in remedial reading classes. Their difficulty lies in attempting to learn to read a language that differs to some degree from the one they speak. How seriously the problem of dialect mismatching affects reading ability is uncertain; however, one may safely assume that it causes a degree of discomfort that, when coupled with other learning difficulties, can interfere with learning to read easily. Of course, many students with mismatched language do learn to read effectively.

Instruction must start with acceptance of their language by the teacher. Genuine respect for the language that students take to school is extremely important. Attacks and criticisms of language differences are intolerable, for they attack not only the students but their families and friends. Specifically, the teacher should demonstrate acceptance by the following:

1. Responding to language differences without initial correction.
2. Responding to the students' thoughts with enthusiasm regardless of their language form.
3. Not repeating the students' response in a correcting effort.

The premise upon which such suggestions are based is that anyone can work better and faster with a student who feels comfortable and accepted. However, teachers demonstrate considerable concern about these techniques because they feel that they are responsible for improving language.

Randy was a very shy first grader. He rarely talked to the other children and often responded to me with gestures rather than words. When he did speak, the sounds were often garbled and the messages limited to one or two phrases. By the end of the first month of school, Randy still seemed bewildered and approached every experience as though it were his first. A referral to our speech therapist came back with the response that Randy had the language capacity of a "two or three year old." My own experiences had shown me that he had no knowledge of letters (names or sounds), few labels for common objects, and limited visual discrimination ability for graphic constructions. Also, Randy was not doing well in the readiness program designed to lead into the basal readers used in our school.

Further background information revealed that he lived with his father and a sister who was a few years older than he. His family was very poor, having few modern conveniences. There were no phones, radios, televisions, or books in his apartment. His father had to leave Randy and his sister alone while he worked. They were given strict instructions to keep the door locked and talk with no one during his absence.

I decided that Randy needed a rich language-oriented program to become a successful reader. I began using the language-experience approach with him. In this way we could begin with the few words he already knew and use them as building blocks in many skill areas. Randy enjoyed this approach. He spent another year in first grade, and four years later I happened to be visiting the school (I had since left) and discovered he was doing quite well in grade five. Not the top of the class but well enough to read comfortably in groups and do many of the content-area assignments that required reading.

Gerald L. Fowler

But the concept of "improving" in itself implies nonacceptance. The teacher must recognize the students' language as being good for them and acceptable for their purposes.[1] The teacher also can help students to become aware of language forms other than those more commonly used in school. Most importantly, students must feel accepted so that they can receive further instruction. Specifically, the following instruction techniques are useful:

When using prepared materials, accept students' use of dialect.   If the sentence is "I see two dogs," and a student says, "I see two dog," accept it without correction. By so doing, meaning is being stressed and language is accepted.

Use language-experience stories that students can dictate to you.   (See chapter 9 for specifics on the use of language experience.) In writing student contributions, be certain to spell words accurately (e.g., if a student says, "da dog," write "the dog"). When the student reads the story aloud and says "da dog," it should be acceptable. Teachers should not change the syntax. (For example, if a student says, "I ain't got none," it should be written as spoken.) To change the syntax to "I don't have any" is a correction, denies the principle of acceptance, and reduces risk taking.

Structure numerous opportunities for students to hear and to respond to language commonly found in books and used in other segments of our society.   Read to them. Read every day. Read good literature. Talk with them about what you have read. Let them discuss it with you. Always serve as a model. Enunciate precisely and use standard English forms. Teach students to respond to your language. Use of tape recorders to provide stories and directions for activities can provide even more modeling opportunities.

Provide structured lessons to develop students' abilities to use the language they will find elsewhere in society and particularly in school.   Feigenbaum suggests the following three steps:[2]

1. *Auditory discrimination:* Help the student to hear differences in language form. Take one type of difference (negation, for example) and say, "Tell me whether these two sentences sound exactly alike or different: 1. I ain't

got none. 2. I don't have any." As the students develop auditory discrimination skills between their language and school language, move to step two.

2. *Identification of school language:* From the two sentences, help the students to pick the one they are more likely to hear the teacher use or to read in books. Auditory awareness of school language is not difficult to develop, but is not to be assumed merely from the ability to discriminate auditorily.

3. *Dialect transfer:* Say one sentence and have the students respond in the other language. Such transfer should be practiced both ways (i.e., from home language to school language and the reverse). For example, the teacher says, "I ain't got none," and the students attempt to put the expression into school language ("I don't have any"). Then the teacher uses school language, and the students respond in their language. When conducting structured lessons, the teacher should start with a structure common to the students' language and stay with one structure until dialect transfer is mastered before selecting another. All lessons must be conducted without reference to right and wrong or good and bad.

Once dialect transfer is mastered, the teacher should encourage the students to use school language in school but should not encourage them to use it in their informal conversations at play or at home. De Stefano refers to the use of different dialects in different social situations as the use of registers.[3] We all use different registers at times. We adjust to the social situation. The register I pick for use at a football game is quite different from the one I pick to use when teaching a class. It seems reasonable to discuss the use of registers with students and to use one's self as the example. As students with language mismatch problems gain skill in dialect transfer, instruction with materials using school language can be used effectively.

Language Mismatching (Foreign)

Numerous students come to school with a native language other than English. Their mismatch with the language of school is nearly total. Even if they become skilled at getting the printed code into a spoken code, nothing makes sense.

The difficulty depends somewhat upon whether English is a second language and whether the students are fluent in English. If they are fluent in English they can be taught with regular school materials even though they might be more comfortable in their native language. If they know little English and are nonfluent, a major block is in the way of successful reading. For example, the Puerto Ricans who are recent immigrants and live in Puerto Rican communities in New York may well go to school with little knowledge of English. In such cases, beginning reading instruction should be in Spanish, not English. As these students become fluent in Spanish, transfer can be made from Spanish to English. In this way these students can become successful readers of two languages.

Instructional assistance should be obtained through programs offered by the schools. If no program is offered in a given language, attempts should be made to enlist community volunteers who are fluent in the students' native language.

The dilemma is that if we try to teach them in English and fail they cannot read English and cannot read their native language. If they return to their native country after three years of failure in learning to read English, they will now have difficulty in reading their native language because that language was not used to teach reading.

Underdeveloped Language

Students who come to school seriously deficient in experiences simply do not have the conceptual framework to work effectively in reading. The importance of language development in reading is stressed by Sticht as follows. "Reading ability is built upon a foundation of language abilities both developed and expressed largely by means of oracy skills of auding and speaking."[4] Those students from isolated rural poverty areas and those from severe poverty areas in large cities may be considered to represent these types of students. In the following discussion, it is assumed that they lack experiences but not mental ability. They may appear to lack mental ability because they fail to understand situations that are comprehended easily by others. They may lack primary experiences with mountains, lakes, automobiles, and airplanes. The teacher may make specific educational adjustments such as the following:

Emphasize language experiences. Everything that happens during the school day can be discussed. Linking language directly to the experiences of students helps them to develop concepts for the things they are encountering.

Trips, pictures, films, and tapes can be used in the development of language experiences. Activities within the classroom, special programs in the school, and visitors in the classroom also stimulate language. Every experience must be discussed, for language should be a constant part of the experience. For example, it is not enough for a class to make a trip to the zoo. The students should talk about what they are experiencing, and the teacher should bombard them with language explanations of what they are experiencing.

Start with the language-experience approach. As it does for students with different dialects, the language-experience approach assures a successful start in reading, since the concepts students encounter are their own.

Use available commercial programs. Several companies have commercial programs designed to facilitate language development. Most of these programs involve stimulation with pictures, tapes, or films. Teachers are directed to help students explain what they are seeing or hearing. Vocabulary is developed as they listen to each other and to the teacher. Synonym and antonym activities also stretch students' conceptual framework. (See Appendix B for a listing of such programs.)

Facilitate continuous language exposure. Activities that permit students to talk with one another and to listen to the teacher make language improvement possible. Activities may include these:

1. Role playing in which students are encouraged to act out roles of story characters or persons whom they admire stimulate students to talk with each other.
2. A telephone corner with toy phones can be used to stimulate talking.
3. Perhaps an older buddy can come to the room to talk about an exciting experience.
4. Activities that stimulate one-to-one conversations are needed in abundance for those with underdeveloped language backgrounds. Activities through which teachers can encourage students to talk include: a question chair placed close to the teacher's work area (a student with a question comes to the chair, and the teacher

discusses the concerns with the student); simple repetition games that call for students to repeat what the teacher has said; and eating lunch and chatting with several students every day.

Activities such as these place value on language as communication and expose students to modeled language. However, since reading is not withheld until large vocabularies are developed, it is important to remember that the language bombardment technique must continue for several years.

Intellectual Development

There are some who have language problems that stem from slow intellectual development. They may be six years old but have slowed intellectual development, so that they react to language like four year olds. Many of these children have compounding problems, such as poor motor coordination or physical defects. Although many find their way into programs for the mentally retarded, many others are mainstreamed into regular classrooms, and teachers must learn how to work with them.

As a first suggestion, every teacher should be urged to view each student as a developmental human being. As such, we accept all students as being as developed as they can be. Instructional programs are planned in accordance with where students are, not where we would like them to be. Categorizing them under labels of locking them into slow-moving groups indicates a lack of acceptance and is of little educational value. At the same time, expectations in terms of rate of learning, quantity of learning, and retention ability should be realistic. Programs must be adjusted for these students in order to utilize their strengths. Patience and many rewards for successful performances should be predominant. Successes must be highlighted, and failures must be minimized or ignored.

One strategy that we have found to work well is that of contracting. Contracting permits the teacher to adjust the amount and type of learning for each student. The completion of the contract is regarded as educational achievement and is recognized as a success. For example, students may be contracted to learn X (X is used to indicate that it could be any number and would vary from student to student) number of words each week. Words could come from any context, i.e., teacher talk, books, other students, posters,

Use of children's language to develop stories focuses on their strengths.

food labels, etc. The objectives are to develop vocabulary and develop success experiences. The teacher pays attention to the rate and type of learning that will allow each student to be successful. Contracts can be renegotiated when students or the teacher believe that the rate or type of learning is no longer appropriate. For best use, a contract should not be longer than a week for these students.

Regardless of the type of language deficiency, the students' education must continue. No excuses, no "cop-outs." Starting points must be identified, and progress should be documented. The teacher should keep in mind that all students can learn and that all can profit from reading programs if the programs are adjusted to their strengths.

The classifications for language deficiencies suggested in this chapter are not as clear-cut as they may seem. Many students may be handicapped by two or all three types of language limitations. But these students can learn. Educators cannot use the lack of language development as an excuse for not teaching; students cannot use it as an excuse for not learning.

The developmental nature of language is obvious. That students have language indicates that they have developed their language to some degree. Teachers must start with what the students have, make them feel comfortable, illustrate to them that learning is possible and fun, and be pleased with successes that occur.

AUDITORY DIFFICULTIES

Hearing Problems

Some students enter school without the necessary auditory skills to profit from normal instruction. When ignored by the teacher, these auditory skills can remain undeveloped, thus causing considerable discomfort to the struggling reader. For this discussion on remediation, auditory skills will be classified in two general areas: hearing problems and auditory discrimination problems.

While teachers can do nothing to correct hearing problems aside from referring the student to a hearing specialist, they can make temporary classroom adjustments to facilitate a comfortable learning situation.

1. They can arrange the seating so that the students with hearing problems are close to the teacher during group instruction.
2. Teachers should stand close to those students' desks during group instruction and should increase their volume so that students with hearing problems can hear the instructions. They can also face the students, thereby providing opportunity for lip reading.
3. Creating a buddy system is helpful. When a student does not hear the teacher or the other students, the buddy can repeat the information and help that student to understand it.
4. When possible, visual learning activities (i.e., reading instead of listening) should be stressed. Instruction for independent work should be written, as should rules, regulations, and announcements. The writing can be on the board, on chart paper, or in personal notes to students with hearing problems.

Auditory Discrimination

It is common to find students with normal hearing skills but underdeveloped auditory discrimination skills. They have difficulty distinguishing one sound from another. Their difficulty is likely to be easily recognized as speech impairment or trouble with phonics. That students come to school with most speech skills developed would lead one to believe that their auditory discrimination skills are also developed. However, for teachers with students whose articulation skills are underdeveloped or who are not in the habit of listening carefully, the following suggestions can be of value:

1. Request the assistance of a speech therapist who can work with the students, help you to diagnose the child's difficulty, or offer suggestions for classroom adjustments.

2. Serve as a speech model. Enunciate distinctly and read with articulate speech patterns.

3. Provide exercises that stress gross auditory differences. For example:
   Tell me whether the words that I repeat are the same or different:
   > catch—catch
   > big—dog
   > many—some

   Tell me whether the first sounds you hear in the words that I repeat are the same or different:
   > big—big
   > butter—lettuce
   > boy—sail

4. Gradually provide exercises involving finer auditory discriminations. For example:
   Tell me whether the words that I repeat are the same or different:
   > catch—catch
   > corn—scorn
   > can—tan

   Tell me whether the first sound you hear in the following words is the same or different:
   > big—pig
   > bite—tight
   > best—best

5. Provide exercises that demand longer auditory memory. For example:
   Listen to the first word that I give you. Then

tell me whether the following words are the same or different:

pig: pig—small—big—pig—dig

Listen to the first sound in the word I give you. Then tell me which of the following words have the same beginning sound:

pig: bite—pick—pencil—dig—picnic

6. Provide exercises that call for listening for sound in different parts of the word.

For example:

Listen for words that end in the same sound as the word *pig*:

dig—ditch—park—twig—dog

7. Provide exercises that indicate the ability to hear rhyming words. For example:

Listen to the first word I give you and tell me whether the following words rhyme with that word:

cat: rat—sat—pot—pat

8. Provide a stimulus word and ask the student to say some words that rhyme. For example:

Listen to the first word I give you and tell me some words that rhyme with it:

cat:

Techniques for conducting drill lessons such as those suggested above can include: placing items on tape and having students do the exercises independently, having an aide or a skilled student read what you have prepared, calling the students who need such work to you while the others are working independently. The point is that the students need daily practice to assist them in the development of the auditory-discrimination skills. As the skills are mastered, periodic review is necessary. It is also necessary to review the skills prior to the development of phonics lessons. Auditory-discrimination skills are easily developed. Furthermore, skills that have been taught can be reinforced through game activities.[5]

Some students will not respond to the activities suggested above due to serious problems in auditory orientation. These students need in-depth training in a cooperative effort among the reading teacher, the classroom teacher, and the speech teacher. Phonics instruction for them should be withheld until a thorough program in auditory sequencing has been completed. They have difficulty distinguishing initial, medial, and final sounds as they hear them. They also have difficulty associating auditory with visual sequences. Understandably these are different skills. Auditory sequences occur in time; visual sequences occur in space. That most students come to school with these skills in hand causes some teachers to assume that all students have them. Programs such as *Auditory Discrimination in Depth* provide instruction in sound formation, sound sequences, and sound placement.[6] These programs require one-to-one instruction and complete cooperation of all who work with the student. The results have been rewarding in the few times I have seen the program in operation.

VISUAL DIFFICULTIES

As is true of auditory problems, visual problems also can be grouped into two categories: those dealing with the skills and functions of vision and those dealing with visual discrimination. Numerous students find giving visual attention difficult, either as the result of a physical disability or of a developmental lag.

Problems in Vision

Visual problems can be adjusted and corrected by vision specialists. The teacher, in the meantime, must work with those students daily. Several suggestions are offered for helping students with vision problems:

1. Arrange seating so that the reader has the best light, the least glare, and the optimum distance for easy viewing. Those who are farsighted can sit in the back of the instructional area and those who are nearsighted can sit in the front.
2. When writing on the board, use larger letter size than usual.
3. Supplement writing on the board or on chart paper by providing auditory reinforcement.
4. Use the buddy system. By working with a student who has normal sight, a student with visual difficulties can seek help when visual difficulties interfere with getting needed information.
5. Stress auditory learning. A student with visual problems

may respond better to a phonics approach or to sound reinforcement. Tracing also helps, for it develops opportunities for reinforcing weak visual skills.

6. Make visual activity periods of short duration. When students show signs of discomfort (e.g., rubbing of eyes and inattentiveness), they should be released from the visual tasks involved in reading.

Adjustments such as those suggested above are not the answer to the basic problem but are adjustments that can make learning both possible and comfortable for a student.

Visual Discrimination

Difficulties with visual discrimination skills are usually the result of a lack of experience or an inability to attend to the task. In either case, successful experience can usually develop comfort in visual-discrimination skills. The following suggestions can be of value in developing them:

Start with the language of the students. As they talk, write down what they say. For example, if a student wants to talk about what was seen on the way to school, the following story may develop:

> I saw a big dog.
> His name was Rex.
> The dog frightened many of us.
> But I picked up a stick and scared the dog.
> Everyone thinks I am very brave.
> Do you?

Once the story is written, two copies are prepared for each student, one to use for visual-discrimination activities and one to save for reading. On the copy that the students can mark, the following activities can be tried:

1. Ask the students to pick words that they know. Write the words on cards and then have them find the words in the story. They do not need to say them, but they do have to match them.
2. Write the letter *s* on a card and ask the students to underline that letter every time they see it in the story.
3. Ask the students to circle all the words that begin with the letter *a*. (Give them *a* cards.)
4. Write a phrase on cards. Have the students find it in the story and draw two lines under it.

5. Ask the students to draw a box around every word that ends with the letter *e*. (Give the students *e* cards.)

From story copy that has been duplicated, have the students cut out words and phrases and match them with the story on chart paper. Such an activity enhances transfer from activities at the seat to activities at the board. Depending upon the story, there are many visual-discrimination activities that can help students develop the required skills. Matching, seeing letters in words, finding letters in specific parts of words, and finding groups of words in a certain order are but a few examples. By asking the students to do something different in each activity (underlining, circling, drawing a box, and so on), the teacher can see easily how well each activity has been completed. As is true with auditory discrimination, start with gross discriminations and move to fine discriminations. For example, beginning with the letter *s* is easier than starting with *d*. Finding a word is easier than finding a letter; finding a letter or a group of letters in a certain position in a word is even more difficult. Discover where the students are in the development of visual discrimination abilities and work from there. It is also important to give a stimulus with which the students are to work visually. Auditory reinforcements are fine, but the activities must be visual to visual (i.e., the students see a word on a card and match it with a word on the board).

Word cards (i.e., cards on which the students have written words mastered) can be used to develop visual discrimination skills. For example, ask the students to complete these tasks:

1. Find all the words in their files that end in *e*, like at*e*.
2. Find all the words that end in *ing*, like walk*ing*.
3. Find all the words that have double consonants, like te*ll*. The suggestions for such activities could be endless, but two points about them are important: (1) you are working with visual clues and from words that the students know; and (2) through teaching from strengths, students can develop strong visual-discrimination skills.

Provide an area in the room where several magazines are collected.   Instruct the readers to look through the magazine ads for examples of certain kinds of words (e.g., words about people, words that describe things, etc.). Provide a visual stimulus (e.g., a pair of scissors or some paste, and a place to post these words when found).

Game-type activities hold considerable merit in developing visual discrimination, just as they do in developing auditory discrimination.   Suggestions can be found in Sullivan.[7] For example, give the students a set of cards with letters on them. Start with a small group of letters, such as *s, t,* and *w.* Hold up a letter and have them hold up the same letter. Then hold up two letters and have them hold up the same two letters in the same sequence. Such an activity gradually can be increased in difficulty, thus developing the attention to detail and visual-discrimination skills needed for reading. Once the game idea is developed, students can play without direct teacher supervision.

Use newspapers to develop visual skills.   The newspaper is useful because of its availability, its expendability, and its motivational appeal. Have students work at the following:

1. Make a collage of all the various forms of a given letter that they can find in advertisements and headlines.
2. Circle all the occurrences of a given letter in the comic strips after a lesson on that letter.
3. Conduct word hunts for words that are in their word banks. Cut them out and paste them on their word-bank cards.
4. Find words in advertisements that have unique features and make a collage out of them. For example, all words with ascending letters or all words that end in *s.*

These and numerous other ideas can be developed from available newspaper supplies and are motivational in themselves. The students notice that they are working with the same type of material that they see adults in their home using.

Commercially prepared materials are available in several forms.   Workbook-type activities, spirit duplication master sheets, and pencil-paper activities are common. Many such activities start with form identification. For example, five balls are placed on a sheet; four of them are green and one is red. Students are to mark the one that is different. However, such activities should be reserved for only the most severely handicapped and even then seem to be of questionable value in the reading process. Several of the more popular commercial materials are listed in Appendix B. However, teachers themselves can make materials that are more relevant to the reading process with relatively small commitments of time and energy. Students respond very well to such homemade materials.

While making materials for students to use in visual discrimination activities, several precautions are necessary:

1. Printing should be done very carefully; however, typing is preferred.
2. Only printing should be used on working copies. These copies should contain no art work, pictures, or other types of distractions.
3. At first, small amounts of print should be used on a page. Do not smother the reader with too many words and sentences.
4. Make activities short and, if possible, self-correcting. Provide answer keys or models of marked copies.
5. Make the print of beginning activities look like that which the children are accustomed to seeing. For very young children, each new sentence should start a new line. With older students, material can appear in paragraph form. To make the material too much like a preprimer is insulting to older students.
6. Always end the activity with a reading of the story. If the students cannot read it, read it to them. Always take the activity back to reading for thought. Discuss the story and its meanings with the students.
7. When students do well, tell them so. Praise for legitimate successes is important in all drill work, but do not praise incomplete or inaccurate work. Instead, restructure the activity so that students can complete it and then praise them.

Continue with visual-discrimination activities as the students begin to read. Review as well as more advanced activities should be part of the visual-discrimination program until students are operating with comfort.

ORIENTATION

Orientation difficulties are reflected by inability to follow the print in words or sentences visually. Orientation skills are commonly listed under visual discrimination; however, difficulties in this area seem to be peculiar enough to justify separate classification. As has been stated, visual-discrimination skills are related to seeing likenesses and differences; orientation skills are concerned with the left-to-right controlled visual movements necessary for effective reading.

It is generally acknowledged that readers' orientation errors cannot be corrected by simply calling the errors to their attention. Remedial procedures in the area of orientation skills are most effective when they help students feel the comfort and success that accompanies correct orientation and when they provide practice to extend the skill into a habit.

Three specific questions are pertinent to correction of orientation problems:

1. Does the student exhibit visual difficulty in following the print from left-to-right?
2. Does the student habitually reverse words and letters?
3. Does the student habitually lose his/her place?

The framework of remediation will involve dealing with these questions in terms of instruction.

The symptoms suggested by these questions are closely related at times, for they all pertain to directional attack on the printed page. As a result, remedial techniques are often quite similar. However, these areas are differentiated here in an effort to make remediation as understandable as possible.

Failure to Move Left-to-Right This difficulty normally can be traced to a faulty habit and, therefore, is usually alleviated by concentrated practice to correct the habit. Many suggestions for improved left-to-right movement across the printed page are available in the manuals of the basal readers. The following specific suggestions have worked well with those who need more practice than that suggested in these manuals:

Utilize opportunities for writing experience.   It is through writing that students can clearly see the necessity of the left-to-right formation of words across the line. Students should observe the teacher writing on the board, and those who are able to write should be given every opportunity to do so.

Illustrate that sentences involve a left-to-right progression of words.   An initial approach would be to have the students write sentences containing their sight words, thereby actively involving them in developing effective left-to-right sequence. Understanding of this concept is demonstrated when students are able to create their own sentences from their resource of sight words.

Have students point to words while reading.   In this respect, the finger is used as a crutch until the habit of left-to-right eye movements can be developed more fully. Clay discusses the issue of pointing to words under the topic "Is Pointing Good or Bad?"[8] While most of us have heard about the many ill effects of pointing to words while reading, Clay points out that most students have adequate left-to-right behavior. Some, however, reveal gross difficulties when asked to point to the words they are reading. When this type of difficulty is noted, some time can be spent instructing students to point to the words they are reading to fix the concept of left-to-right eye movements.

Utilize choral reading activities.   A dividend added to the obvious advantages of choral reading is the opportunity for students to experience in a group a feeling for the flow of words from left-to-right. Reading orally in unison with the teacher or with others also is helpful in the same way. There should be one good model of oral reading in the group. Sentences from experience stories can be cut into word cards and reassembled to match the original sentence.

The Michigan Tracking program (Figure 8–1) has been useful in working with students with severe orientation problems.   These materials are constructed to teach readers to move from left to right and from the top of the page to the bottom. Students must complete the entire activity in order. If they miss one item, the materials are constructed so that they cannot finish.

The concept of tracking can be adapted to any materials. For example, take any unit of print and provide a sentence to look for these:

Look for: See the dog run
Unit of print: I have a dog. You can *see* him on Saturday. He can run into *the* house. My *dog* can *run* very fast.

Mechanical aids are available to help students with orientation skills.   Tracking, for example, can be reinforced by the use of the *Controlled Reader.* Students watch a story from a film that is paced either a line at a time or by a left-to-right exposure control, and that can be regulated for speed. Mechanical aids can help motivate the students to attempt activities that are otherwise rather dull. However, when one considers the costs of such devices and the excitement that can be created with teacher-made materials, it would appear that the use of machines in remedial reading is of a seriously limited value. First, they place readers in reading situations that are unreal. Reading is not a mechanically-paced activity; rather, it is a stop-and-go activity. Readers stop to use word-attack skills and to reread certain passages; they then go quickly to other sections. That all words and phrases deserve the same amount of reading time must be seriously questioned. When mechanical aids are used, they should be followed by practice with normal reading materials without the use of the aid. In such a way, students are assisted in transferring from practice situations to real reading situations.

Tendency to Reverse Letters, Words, and Phrases

While normal for some beginning readers, the tendency to reverse letters, words, and phrases is one of the common orientation difficulties, particularly with young readers. Different from following left-to-right across a line, reversals involve inappropriate left-to-right progression in words and phrases within a line. The reader not only must consciously attack words from left to right but must develop this attack into a habit. After awareness is developed, the problem can be solved by specific practice.

Figure 8-1

Sample of Word Tracking

1. **The man walked.**
   She This The Them
   me may mad man
   talked waked walked walled

2. **Joe ran here.**
   Jim Joe John Jack
   run ray ran ram
   there then head here

3. **Dad is big.**
   Day Dad Dab Dog
   it at as is
   bag buy big bog

4. **Boys play ball.**
   Bugs Bays Buys Boys
   plan play park page
   bill pull ball balk

5. **I saw birds.**
   A I It As
   was say way saw
   bids birds burst birch

Fill in:

Boys	ball.	saw birds.
Joe	here.	Dad is
The man		Min Sec

6. **Girls, go home.**
   Grills Girls Guys Goods
   go got get golf
   house horse home come

7. **Look at him.**
   Cook Lake Took Look
   it as at is
   his her him hem

8. **Are you there?**
   Car Are Far Tar
   one your you once
   here then were there

9. **Who was that?**
   Why How Who What
   saw was way wash
   this then that they

10. **Call her up.**
    Came Tell Tall Call
    him her has his
    up on down in

Fill in:

Who was	?	at him.
Call her	?	Are there?
Girls,	home.	Min Sec

SOURCE: *Word Tracking* by Donald E. P. Smith. From the Michigan Tracking Program. Ann Arbor: Ann Arbor Publishers, 1967. Reprinted by permission of the author.

Kindergarten and first-grade teachers should emphasize directional progression both directly and subtly. Through writing on the board in front of students and calling their attention to the direction that the letters flow to form a word, the teacher can give the children opportunities to grasp this concept. The students may also write on the board, for there is less tendency to make directional errors when doing board work. It should be noted that this is a more difficult concept for some to grasp than is the left-to-right movement across a line of print, especially when whole-word techniques have been stressed in initial instruction. The sense of touch involved in writing easily confused words reinforces the left-to-right progression within words. When individual language-experience stories are being written, the teacher should sit beside each child so that the child can watch the words being formed. Sitting across the table, the child watches the words being formed right-to-left instead of left-to-right. If the teacher types the story, the child should sit at the typewriter to watch the words form.

Phonics lessons also provide opportunity for the reinforcement of proper progression through words. This is particularly true in initial-and final-consonant substitution activities where the position of the letters in words is emphasized. In phonics lessons, where stress is being placed upon the initial sounds in words, it is often possible to place words on the board to illustrate the similarities or differences in the initial sounds. This practice, of course, emphasizes the left-to-right concept as it applies to word attack.

Spelling activities are excellent times for reinforcing the proper image of the word. This is so because the concept of the position of the letters in each word is of primary importance. Through the spelling of confused words, the teacher is able to reinforce the proper sequence of letters.

Students also may be encouraged to trace words that are missed so that they may feel the left-to-right progression. As the students trace the words, they are expected to pronounce them correctly. If they cannot do this, the problem is more likely one of inadequate sight vocabulary. Special instructions for the kinesthetic technique follow:[9]

1. The reader is exposed to the word symbol and its

pronunciation. (That these words are usually taken from the reader's experience stories implies that he knows their meanings.)

2. The reader is directed to trace the word while saying it. (This tracing procedure is to be repeated until it appears that the reader has mastered the word. The teacher demonstrates as often as necessary when beginning this approach.) Fernald notes that finger contact with the letters is essential, especially in these early stages.

3. The reader then is directed to reproduce the word without the copy, again pronouncing while saying it. It should be noted that this technique is not one in which the reader spells the word or sounds the letters; rather, it is a whole-word technique. The advantages of the tracing technique are not limited to orientation skills; other uses will be noted under sight vocabulary and word attack where a more detailed explanation is presented.

Teachers will find several variations of the kinesthetic technique in the literature. Some prefer that all tracing be done in sand; some prefer the use of a blackboard; others feel that tracing the word in large copy is entirely adequate. Some suggest that the word be printed, providing the best transfer to actual reading. Others prefer that the word be written in script to reinforce the flow and connection between the letters. Regardless of the system, the left-to-right progression of the words is reinforced, and the reader, sensing the total results of his efforts, often learns to pronounce words properly. Teachers will find many opportunities in other reading activities to reinforce left-to-right progressions. Teachers need to help students with meaning cues when reversals are made. "Did that make sense to you?" "Did that mean anything to you?" Since the ultimate check on reading accuracy is always in terms of making sense from the passage, meaning cues are always appropriate.

Tendency to Omit Words Without Distorting Context

Omissions seldom distort the meaning of the passage. Apparently readers keep their mind on the context and make sense out of it while not necessarily reading every word. While such an omission is not in itself worthy of much concern, the habit of omitting words is of concern, for one day the word omitted may be a very important one. For example, on a medicine label, the message "Do not swallow" may be read "Do swallow." We are interested, therefore, in developing an awareness in students that all the words on the page should receive their attention. The following suggestions should do the job.

Effective utilization can be made of a tape recorder for students with this type of difficulty. Having taped an oral-reading selection, the students listen carefully to the tape while following the story with their eyes. They then mark each word that was omitted. (Students are generally surprised to find that they make the many omissions that they do.) Then the students attempt to reread the story without omitting any words. They listen to the new tape while following the story; again they mark omissions. We often find that students are able to make conscious corrections, although this technique may need to be repeated several times to develop satisfactory performance.[10] Self-diagnosis helps to emphasize to the students their reading strengths and needs. Followed by practice and reevaluation, it tends to correct most omission errors.

The reading-impress technique for oral reading has value for students who make many omissions.[11] The teacher and the student(s) read in unison. The teacher is the leader and sets the model. The model is one of fluency and accuracy. The student(s) follow, reading with the teacher and obtaining the feeling for fluent, accurate oral reading. The teacher may want the student to read the passage alone once it has been read with the teacher. If accuracy is not obtained, then the process should be repeated.

Habitual Loss of One's Place

This reading behavior may be related to a visual problem; therefore, it first would be advisable to check for signs of ocular difficulty manifested by other symptoms (see chapter 3). If there is no indication that the difficulty is visual, the student should be given instruction.

When readers lose their places during reading, they may be having difficulty with following the line of print or with their return sweep. As a reader moves from line to line, his eyes sweep back across the page. Many readers find that movement difficult.

For either of the above reasons, use of a line holder of some type is suggested. An index card will do just fine. Some instruct students to point to the first word in the line.

Skill instruction should always end with silent reading time.

It is more desirable to use line holders than to encourage the student to point to individual words; however at times pointing is necessary. Pointing to words can lead to word-by-word reading and can slow the pace of reading greatly. The use of all line holders should be dropped as soon as the student becomes comfortable and is able to read without losing his place.

Those who lose their places during reading may also be indicating a lack of interest and may not be paying attention. They need to be involved in setting the objectives for their lessons and in selecting materials for instruction. These are attention-getting strategies and tend to increase reader awareness of the need to stay with the lesson. At other times, the tempo of the lesson encourages some minds to wander. As the teacher stops to assist a reader having difficulty, other students may mentally slip away. Teacher attention to the lesson tempo should help to alleviate such problems.

The Seriously Disoriented Reader

Some students display serious difficulties in all of the readiness areas. Their orientation to the printed page is so distorted that there is little chance of their learning to read.

Their problem is usually complicated by inability to remember sight words, to understand the relationship between letters and sounds, and to make any sense out of the passage. Several suggestions are offered for working with students who have these types of problems:

1. The first step is to reexamine the learning climate. Are there any distractors that may be keeping the student from giving full attention to the reading activity? If so, adjustments to those distractors should precede any of the following suggestions.
2. Physical and psychological assessments should be conducted so that problems in these areas can be understood and adjustments can be made. If no problems are identified as a result of these assessments, the problem is with the school program.
3. A school screening committee should gather as much data as possible including observation of the student during instructional periods. With all of the resources of the school available, the screening committee makes decisions concerning which resources can best assist the student. A plan is implemented and periodic evaluation of progress keeps the screening committee informed and able to make future decisions.
4. Some schools have special programs for those experiencing serious difficulties. Instructors with special training direct the learning of such students. Experienced nursery-school and kindergarten teachers may have highly useful instructional suggestions. Local college personnel who operate clinics and who work with seriously handicapped readers may offer program suggestions and work with specially identified children.
5. Means for providing large amounts of individual attention often need to be developed. Teacher aides, parents, volunteers, and, at times, a peer tutor can assist the teacher. They can help students as they work independently from the teacher. They can assist them to avoid practicing faulty learning habits, and they can help build a sense of self-worth and success that these students need so badly.
6. Teachers will need to provide communications with parents. Naturally parents become anxious about their children's difficulties. They also become easy targets for people who have all the answers. Expensive tutorial

programs, often operated in the interests of profit instead of the reader, are easy to find. By helping the parents to understand the problem and realize the efforts being made by school personnel, much of the anxiety can be reduced.

SUMMARY

The activities involved in readiness instruction are not limited to primary-grade teachers. Teachers at all levels must be skilled in identification and treatment of the types of problems discussed in this chapter. Reading specialists must know how to obtain maximum help for teachers who can't reach students because of readiness limitations. In most cases, there is no reason why reading instruction, directed to the strengths of students, cannot proceed while readiness programs are being conducted. Of course, the effort must be to assist the student in becoming the most successful learner possible.

NOTES

1. Kenneth S. Goodman, "Dialect Rejection and Reading," *Reading Research Quarterly* 15 (Summer 1970): 603.
2. Irwin Feigenbaum, "The Use of Nonstandard English in Teaching Standard: Contrast and Comparison," in *Teaching Standard English in the Inner City* (Washington, D.C.: Center for Applied Linguistics, 1970), pp. 87–104.
3. Johanna S. De Stefano, *Some Parameters of Register in Adult and Child Speech* (Washington, D.C.: Institute of Applied Linguistics, 1972).
4. Thomas Sticht et al., *Auding and Reading* (Alexandria, Va.: Human Resources Research Association, 1974), p. vi.
5. David Russell and Etta E. Karp, *Reading Aids Through the Grades* and *Listening Aids Through the Grades* (New York: Teachers College, Columbia University, 1951).
6. Arthur Heilman, *Phonics We Use, Learning Games Kit* (Chicago: Lyons and Carnahan, 1968).
7. Dorothy Sullivan, Beth Davey, and Dolores Dickerson, *Games as Learning Tools* (Paoli, Pa.: Instructo/McGraw-Hill Book Co., 1978).
8. Marie Clay, *Reading: The Patterning of Complex Behaviour,* (London: Heinemann Educational Books, 1973) pp. 56–57.
9. Grace Fernald, *Remedial Techniques in Basic School Subjects* (New York: McGraw-Hill Book Co., 1943), pp. 35–39.

10. Robert M. Wilson, "Oral Reading Is Fun," *Reading Teacher* 18 (October 1965): 41–43.
11. Paul M. Hollingsworth, "An Experiment With the Impress Methods of Teaching Reading," *Reading Teacher* 24 (November 1970): 112–14.

SUGGESTED READINGS

Clay, Marie. *Reading: The Patterning of Complex Behaviour.* London: Heinemann Educational Books, 1972. Part II of this book discusses early reading skills in detail. Chapter 6 provides interesting reading regarding directional learning.

Fernald, Grace. *Remedial Techniques in Basic School Subjects.* New York: McGraw-Hill Book Co., 1943. The advantages and specific techniques of the tracing technique are presented in chapter 5. The reader will find this presentation interesting and complete.

Hall, MaryAnne. *Teaching Reading as a Language Experience*, 3d ed. Columbus, O.: Charles E. Merrill Publishing Co., 1981. This book provides a basic background for those unfamiliar with the possibilities for using the language-experience approach in remediation. Chapter 7 deals specifically with the teaching of prereading skills through the language-experience approach.

Hymes, James L., Jr. *Before the Child Reads.* New York: Row, Peterson & Co., 1958. Hymes presents the point of view of an experienced educator of young children. His chapter "You Do Not Have to 'Build' Readiness," while concerned with preschool children, should be considered required reading.

Kephart, Newell C. *The Slow Learner in the Classroom.* Columbus, O.: Charles E. Merrill Publishing Co., 1971. The reader will find interesting reading covering completely the motor readiness needs of youngsters. Particular attention is given to motor skills, which the author sees as being related to success in learning.

Monroe, Marion, and Rogers, Bernice. *Foundations for Reading.* Chicago: Scott Foresman and Co., 1964. The authors have presented a series of chapters (chapters 1–5) relating to the beginning processes of reading. The educator who is attempting remediation without a thorough understanding of this initial process will find this reading very profitable.

Sticht, Thomas G. et al. *Auding and Reading.* Alexandria, Va.: Human Resources Research Association, 1974. For a thorough discussion of the place of language in the reading process, this book is recommended. The authors take a position about the place of language and have developed a model for its conceptualization.

9

Word Identification

Chapter Emphasis

- The language-experience approach is useful in developing personal sight vocabularies.

- Sight vocabulary and word-attack activities can be developed from word-bank words.

- Sight vocabulary and word attack lessons should be short and crisp and end with reading in context.

- Phonics instruction can be abstract and therefore very difficult.

- Learning centers are useful reinforcement materials for sight vocabulary and word-attack activities.

- Some students need a system for attacking unknown words.

    Note: All instructional materials cited in this chapter are listed in Appendix B, giving details.

Sight vocabulary and word-attack skills are needed for successful reading. It is difficult to make sense out of a passage in which there are many unknown words. The purpose of remedial work in sight vocabulary and word attack is to improve comprehension. Some programs would lead you to believe that the purpose is to learn a large set of isolated words or skills, since there is no emphasis upon understanding. As we discuss remediation in these areas, repeated attention will be given to stress—the relationship between the activities and comprehension.

THE LANGUAGE-EXPERIENCE APPROACH

An understanding of the language-experience approach is essential for the teacher and reading specialist who are planning remedial activities in the area of sight vocabulary and word attack. This approach stresses reading as a meaningful, communicative activity. For students who have experienced difficulty in reading, an approach that stresses personal meaning has numerous advantages.

1. Usually they have had many lessons that stressed isolated skill development. The language-experience approach focuses first upon meaning, so it is different and has motivational appeal.
2. The words used in developing language-experience stories all have personal meaning for the students who developed the stories. The teacher can assume that the students have at least one meaning for the words used.
3. The syntax of the stories is familiar to the students who developed them. No strange grammatical structures are used to interfere with understanding.
4. The content of the stories is personally meaningful to the students. This assures comprehension and facilitates motivation.

As we recommend the use of language-experience stories as a basis for remedial activities in sight vocabulary and word-attack skills, we also recommend that the lessons start and end with the words in context so that the students are continuously reinforced with the concept that all of this effort is toward reading for meaning. The following suggestions can serve as possible techniques for the use of language-experience stories for developing sight vocabulary and word attack skills:

1. Following an experience with one student or a group of students, generate a discussion concerning the experience. Encourage the students to talk about what they saw or did, about how it made them feel, and about the meaning the experience had for them.
2. Following free discussion, direct the students to tell a story about the experience. Ask for contributions and write exactly what they say. Always spell words correctly but do not change the contributor's sentence structure. Some guidelines for writing stories follow.
   a. Encourage all students to contribute.
   b. In the beginning, use some type of identification for each individual's contribution [e.g., "Donald said, 'I see a big dog' " or "I see a big dog" (Donald)].
   c. Read what has been written immediately following the writing of each sentence. Next, have the student who gave the sentence read it; then, the entire group.
   d. For very young readers, start every new sentence on a new line. For older readers, write in paragraphs.

PIZZA

1. Preheat oven to 425° F.

2. Put pizza flour mix in a small bowl.

3. Add ½ cup very warm water to mix. Stir with spoon until all flour particles are moistened. Then stir vigorously for 25 strokes.

4. Cover bowl. Let stand in warm place for 5 minutes.

5. Using shortening, grease well a 14" pizza pan or a 14"x11" rectangle on a cookie sheet.

6. Grease fingers then lightly spread pizza edges of pan up edges ¼" to rim.

7. Pour canned sauce over t

Following direction activities can come naturally from the language-experience approach.

    e. Begin by making stories rather short. If the students have more to say, write the story on two pages with only a few lines on each page. Those with serious reading problems can become discouraged with too much print on a single page.

    f. Have students watch as the story is written. Call attention to the formation of words as they are written.

    g. As students develop skill with beginning consonants, invite them to help with the spelling of words (e.g., "How would I begin the word *boy?*").

3. After the story is written, have the students read it in unison several times.

4. Duplicate the story as soon as possible, making at least two copies for each student. One copy can be placed in a folder to become the reading material for the students. The second copy can be used for skill development.

5. Skills can be developed from language-experience stories in a variety of ways. In chapter 7, using language-experience stories to develop visual discrimination, auditory discrimination, and orientation skills

was discussed. Skills in vocabulary can be developed as follows:

a. Have the students mark all the words that they know. Then have them put several of these words in a private word box or word bank. The students' word banks provide a natural opportunity for meaningful word drills. On the front of the word bank card print the word. On the back write a sentence given by the student using the word.

$$\boxed{\text{tiger}} \qquad \boxed{\text{The tiger is strong.}}$$
(front) (back)

b. Students can practice their known words in pairs or in small groups. They can match words in their word bank with words in their stories. They can select words for classification as action words, as naming words, as people words, as words beginning with specific letters, and so on.

c. Once a group of words is developed, students can use their word banks to help them with spelling activities. They can use them to build sentences, make crossword puzzles, and in many other activities.

d. Add words to the students' banks occasionally. When the word *and* or *the* occurs again and again in a story, but has not been chosen for placement in the word banks, call it to the students' attention. Such service words will be needed in future reading and in vocabulary activities.

6. Word-attack skills can be developed as follows:

a. Using word bank words, make a collection of rhyming words, e.g., "Collect all words in your word bank that rhyme with *cat*." Then have students share their rhyming words. Write them on the board and discuss how all of the words found are the same and how they are different. See if the students can brainstorm to build more *-at* rhyming words.

b. Search word banks for all words that begin with a given consonant. Share what they have found. See if they can brainstorm to add words that fit.

c. Search the word bank for words with common prefixes or suffixes. Again share and brainstorm.

d. After studying syllabication generalizations, use word-bank words to serve as examples and exceptions to the generalization. For example, if the

generalization being taught is vc/cv, then the students would find words such as *window, picnic, pencil,* and *problem* as examples that match the generalization, and a word such as *father* that is an exception.
7. Comprehension activities can also be developed from language-experience stories (See chapter 10.).

The suggestions listed above in no way cover all the possibilities for uses of the language-experience approach in remediation. Additional specific suggestions are provided under various remedial areas in this and other chapters. Those unfamiliar with the language-experience approach will want to study the books of Stauffer or Hall listed in the Suggested Readings at the end of this chapter.

REMEDIATION IN SIGHT VOCABULARY

Sight vocabulary involves the skills of instant word pronunciation and identification of word meaning. While the remedial approaches to sight vocabulary problems are presented in terms of the questions asked in diagnosis, it must be remembered that the goal of sight vocabulary study is comprehension, which involves the decoding and association of the word in a line of print, in a sentence, or in a paragraph, rather than in isolation; for word meaning depends on relationships with other words.

Remedial procedures will be developed in direct reply to the questions asked under the diagnosis of sight vocabulary difficulties. Specifically, those questions are stated below:

1. Does the student miss small, graphically similar words?
2. Do words missed represent abstract concepts?
3. Do word meanings appear to be confused?
4. Does the student know words in context but not in isolation?
5. Does the student appear to know words at the end of a lesson but not the next day?

These difficulties seldom appear alone; rather, they are interrelated. The purpose in establishing the answers to the questions is to determine in which areas the interrelationship has taken place and to emphasize these areas in remediation. Through examination it can clearly be seen, for example, that small, graphically similar words are often words with abstract meanings that require dual remedial considerations.

Small, Graphically Similar Words

Do the students miss small, graphically similar words or do they falter on words that are obviously different? Quite often, readers will miss small words that are minimal in configurational differences (e.g., *when* and *where*) while effectively attacking larger and more obviously different words (e.g., *elephant* and *Christmas*). The latter is considered a skill in sight vocabulary, while the former is normally a problem in word attack, especially if the words missed are at or below the instructional level. The major point is to work from the readers' strengths. If the students can work with words of maximal differences, the teacher should provide more exercises with those types of words, moving gradually to words that are more similar until skill with those words is developed. Then the students should move to words even more alike until skill with words that have minimal graphic differences has been developed.

Ultimately, the student must receive instruction in the discrimination of words that are minimally different. These exercises should be conducted in phrase and sentence form so that the reader realizes that the minimal difference distorts not only the pronunciation but the meaning of the words as well: "We took the dig [instead of *dog*] for a walk." To clarify these similarities and differences in minimally different words, it is sometimes feasible to pull these words from context for study (*dig-dog*). Any exercise, however, should be followed by returning to context.

In the early grades, the teacher may use experience charts to illustrate the need for careful visual discrimination of minimally different words. In these situations, the teacher should take every opportunity to emphasize how words of similar configuration actually differ in both form and meaning, using the reader's own language contributions as examples. For instance, when writing a student's story, the teacher should look for opportunities to demonstrate how certain words look alike or different.

Using words from the students' word banks (i.e., words that are already known) illustrates teaching to strengths. Locating words in the banks that look very much alike, pronouncing them, noting meanings, using them in sentences, and noting how they look alike and different is extremely useful. Attention should be given to differences in all parts of the words—initial, medial, and final.

Programmed materials are available that are particularly adaptable to the classroom for use in remediation of this type of skill difficulty. These materials can aid the student to observe differences in words that are alike except for minimal graphic differences (e.g., *hat* and *bat*). As an example of these materials, *Programmed Reading* contains a series of exercises through which the reader can develop skill with a minimum amount of teacher supervision. Note the sample on page 268. The student must look at the pictures, read the sentence or partial sentence, and use closure to obtain the correct code and message. These exercises progress from the elementary type seen in Figure 9–1 to complete stories. The forced-choice closure concept is maintained at all levels (i.e., the reader selects from a limited number of appropriate responses).

The student is reinforced by the appearance of the correct answer after each frame or after each page, depending upon how much material the teacher feels the reader can handle without reinforcement. The skills developed in the workbooks are transferred to reading in prepared *Storybooks*, containing stories with minimally different words. It is unlikely that these materials will satisfy the total reading needs of the reader. We found that programmed materials such as these can be supplemented with the language-experience approach, allowing students to develop their personal word bank of meaningful words.

The linguistic approach can be adapted to almost any type of material, for example, word banks that add a personalized aspect and the programmed materials mentioned above. The *Let's Read* books and *The Merrill Linguistic Readers* (see samples on pp. 266 and 267) are prepared linguistic materials for beginning reading, appropriate for individualized instruction of students with serious reading problems. Both of these approaches have in common a controlled vocabulary of minimally different words, the controlled initial presentation of words with consistent vowel and consonant sounds, and an absence of pictures, so that correct visual perception is necessary for accurate decoding. A similar approach, *The Linguistic Readers*, varies somewhat from those mentioned above but does maintain the necessity for visual perception of minimal differences. An example of adaptations of the above for instruction is thoroughly described by Botel.[1]

**Abstract
Concepts**

It is common for students to find it particularly difficult to remember words that represent abstract concepts (e.g., *when, these, if, those*). Emphasis in remediation for students with this type of difficulty should focus on the word as it appears in context, for it is from context that the function of these words can be understood. Furthermore, since there is seldom a reading situation in which these words are used in isolation, they should not be taught in isolation.

Once again, experience-story approaches are of particular value in the development of this type of reading sight vocabulary. Students use these words to formulate their experience stories, gaining a natural opportunity for instruction in the service and function of these words as they use them. Although the experience-story approach will probably be used more frequently with the younger reader, considerable success with this type of approach has been found with older students as well. It is in experience-story reading that we can be certain that all words used have meaning for the readers since they are their contributions. Through these materials, the use and nature of abstract words can be effectively illustrated.

Again, word-bank words that carry little meaning of their own (*and, the, of,* and the like) are known to students and can be developed into meaningful activities. For example, using *and, the,* and *of* from a word bank, ask which word would fit in the blank: bread _____ butter, I see _____ man, and on top _____ the table. The use of such modified closure activities develops skills in the use of abstract words.

Sight vocabulary drills with abstract concepts are most effective when the words are used in phrases (e.g., *in a good spirit*). Prepared phrase cards with the more commonly used word combinations are available in the *Dolch game* (e.g., *Match, Basic Sight Cards*) series. There is little or no justification for sight-word drill with these words in isolation, for when they are extracted from context, any meaning the word contains is lost.

After a certain amount of sight vocabulary has been developed, students may build sentences from word cards. Here emphasis should be placed upon the function of the

A Little Red Hen

A little red hen is in Ben's pen.

Pam looked at the hen and said,

"Can I have the red hen

for a pet?"

Ben said, "If you can get a box

for it, you can have the red hen."

Pam ran and got a red box

with a lid.

She fed the hen and led it

to the box.

The little red hen got into its

little red box.

A sample page from the reader and skills book of the Merrill Linguistic Reading Program, Catch On, Level C.

| 5 | The little red hen got into its box. |

| 2 | Pam said, "Can I have the hen for a pet?" |

| 4 | Pam ran and got a box with a lid. |

| 1 | A little red hen is in Ben's pen. |

| 3 | "If you get a box for the hen, you can," said Ben. |

Use after page 24 of Unit 5. **Arranging Events in Sequence:** Pupils should carefully read the story on page 22 before doing this exercise. Then have pupils read all of the sentences on this page. Have them find the number **1** and read the sentence that tells what happened first. Then have them decide which event happened next and write the number **2** in the correct box. Repeat for the remaining sentences having pupils work independently. Notice that the last one is done for the pupil. Pupils may copy the sentences in correct sequence on a separate sheet of paper.

Figure 9–1   Sample Page of a Programmed Reader.

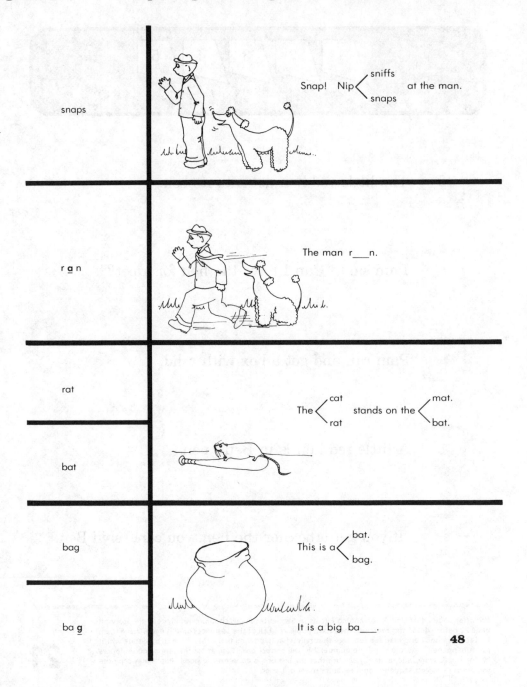

snaps

Snap! Nip⟨ sniffs / snaps ⟩ at the man.

r <u>a</u> n

The man r___n.

rat

The ⟨ cat / rat ⟩ stands on the ⟨ mat. / bat. ⟩

bat

bag

This is a ⟨ bat. / bag. ⟩

ba <u>g</u>

It is a big ba___.

48

abstract word as created by the student. With this activity, the unknown word is not placed in a definition situation; rather, it appears in a functional situation, the sentence. Intentional distortions of these types of words in context may be used to illustrate their importance. For example, the text reads, "In the table is a lot of money." We change it to read, "On the table is a lot of money." The students either describe or illustrate how the slight change has affected the meaning of the sentence.

Such word games as Word Lotto that use abstract words can be used successfully to reinforce words that have been previously learned (i.e., words from students' word banks). Word games are highly motivating and tend to take the drill atmosphere from reinforcement activities. Games such as Checkers can be used with words taped on each square. As players move or jump opponents, they are expected to pronounce the words on the spaces involved. Students become so enthusiastic about such activities that they ignore the drill nature involved.

Confused Word Meanings

Remedial instruction in this very important area must be precluded by the following two considerations:

1. There are situations in which students, for one reason or another, fail to develop a background of experience that permits them to associate the meaning with the word they have pronounced. If this deficiency is chronic, remediation, of necessity, will consist of experiential language development rather than instruction in sight vocabulary.
2. We find numerous students who have little trouble pronouncing the words they see in print. Although they know the meaning of a word and can use it in a sentence, they fail to associate the word with the correct meaning, apparently because of preoccupation with word pronunciation. Remedial activities with these students, then, should be in the area of sight vocabulary, where they must be taught to be conscious of what the word *says* as well as how it *sounds*.

As has been stated previously, every word drill should end with the word in context. In this way the precise meaning and function of the word are best understood; readers with this deficiency must have context emphasized even more precisely. The students begin by reading easy material and demonstrating their knowledge of the words in question by paraphrasing the author's words. This technique will be discussed in chapter 9.

It is often useful to establish whether the students know the meaning of a word through definition. If they do, it is not the meaning of the word as such that is causing the problem, but the use of the word in a particular contextual situation. The presentation of the word in various settings is then appropriate.

Since students already understand the meaning of the pronounced words, experience stories using the students' own wording again play an important role in remedial efforts. Teachers of elementary school children are urged to provide numerous opportunities for group-experience stories in which there is an association between the experiences of the group and the words that represent those experiences. This is a golden opportunity to create situations in which students learn from one another. Frequently we find students reacting better to the responses of their peers than to teacher efforts. Two sources of activities to assist students to develop word meaning skills are Heilman and Holmes[2] for the younger student and Dale and O'Rourke[3] for the more mature student.

Although frequently not included as a remedial technique, the dictionary is of particular assistance to older students. Their knowledge of the correct pronunciation of a word in print permits them to use the dictionary to find meanings efficiently; they may, incidentally, develop a habit of consulting the dictionary for unknown words. Techniques for use with the dictionary are discussed in the section "Remediation in Word Attack."

Although it is fine to talk about building experiences to develop listening and speaking vocabularies, it is another thing to build such a program (refer to chapter 8). The *Peabody Language Development Kits* contain programs for numerous lessons in language development. Teachers may find this type of program a guide for the entire school year. Among the experiences included with these kits are following directions, brainstorming, critical thinking, memorizing, rhyming, and listening. Pictures, objects, and tapes are used to enrich the child's experiential background.

The *Building Pre-reading Skills Kit-A-Language* provides the teacher with another program for language development. It consists of pictures through which vocabulary can be stimulated, synonyms developed, and language-experience stories drawn.

For the reader seriously handicapped by the inability to associate, the *Non-oral Reading* approach may contain the requisites for initial instruction. This approach bypasses completely the vocalization of the printed word and emphasizes instead the word's association with a pictured concept. The task is to match the printed symbol with a picture representing the concept for that symbol. This direct association from print to concept minimizes the importance of pronunciation for those who have been overdrilled in it.

Teachers will also find it useful to have the student respond directly through physical activity to such printed word commands as "jump up," and "shake hands." This approach also minimizes vocalization of the printed word, emphasizng again the meaning of the word through the student's response. The *Nichols Tachistoscope Slides* developed for this purpose appear to be effective in establishing the importance of the concepts covered by words.

By placing word bank words on a checker board, it is possible to make drill exercises an enjoyable activity for students.

Most handicapped readers avoid reading and have developed skills of avoidance much as other students have developed skills in reading. These avoidance skills have become strengths for these students and must be approached and used as such.

In an Improve Your Reading Club in high school, I found that these very handicapped readers could consistently beat top students (and their teachers!) at a nonreading game, checkers. Many of these same students also had a great need—to be able to read the Driver's Education manual and apply its contents.

My concern was not just that they be able to pass the driver's test, but that they become good, safe, knowledgeable drivers.

Analyzing the task, I recognized that there were three areas where reading skills were involved: vocabulary, symbol recognition, and theory application. Once these areas were identified it became a simple matter to put on index cards words, symbols, or situations in the form of questions. Over seventy-five cards were compiled, each asking for a specific bit of information. These cards contained questions such as these:

What is a <u>pedestrian</u>? (vocabulary)

What does a sign of this shape mean? (symbol identification)

What would be the best speed for driving on a rainy night on a road with this sign? (theory application)

```
┌──────────────┐
│ SPEED        │
│ LIMIT        │
│ MAXIMUM      │
│   55         │
│ MINIMUM      │
│   45         │
└──────────────┘
```

The final task was to "marry" the strength to the need. Since checkers playing was an obvious strength and overlearning of material the goal, the obvious course was to incorporate the driver's education cards into a checkers format. The simplest solution was best; students could play checkers as much as they wished; but, before taking a turn, they had to draw an index card and answer the question correctly. I did prepare an answer booklet so that disputes could be solved by the players independently; since they'd go through all the cards at least once in an average game, it wasn't needed for long.

The goal of over-learning was achieved by simple repetition; boredom did not become a factor. Checkers are meant to be played fast, so the students became very adept at responding rapidly with the correct answer. And, of course, becoming knowledgeable in a subject which was important to them was very motivational.

Since an error in answering a question led to forfeiture of a turn, the students stayed alert and on-task while playing, hoping that their opponent would make a mistake. These cut-throat checkers players were so evenly matched in that skill that often the outcome of a game depended on who made an error on the driver's manual questions.

Mary Jo Comer

Collecting words from the word bank in categories can also help to stress word meanings. For example, to collect action words, the student must think of word meaning, not just pronunciation. Words that are names of things can be matched with the action words to make short sentences (e.g., *dogs run, ducks talk, horses jump*). Students can look at the sentences they have built to determine which ones make sense. This is an extremely meaningful activity. In addition, stimulating students with incomplete sentences, such as "I like to _____" makes the learning personal and, therefore, more interesting.

Teachers also may use initial sight-vocabulary exercises consisting of nouns, adjectives, and verbs that can be pictured. The Dolch *Picture Word Cards,* containing ninety-six of these types of words, may be used. Several matching-type games involve a student's matching a picture with a printed word, thereby indicating understanding of the meaning of the word in a gamelike activity that is self-motivating. *Picture Word Puzzles* provides similar reinforcement with children having association deficiencies.

Active participation can be achieved by having students build sentences from the words that they know. After known words are placed on cards, the cards are scrambled and the students are asked to build specific sentences or to build sentences of their choosing. The *Linguistic Block Series* can be used in the same manner with the blank block for words in the students' personal vocabularies.

Meaning in Context

Students who know words in context but not in isolation are telling you that context aids their reading. Being aware of the function of words in their language and aware of sentence meaning, these students are using desirable word-attack processes. Since most words are encountered in context, this difficulty should not be considered critical.

Occasionally, however, a word is faced in isolation and recognition is crucial, e.g., *stop, danger, women*. Such words should be taught in context, then pulled from context and attention placed on meaning. Since meaning clues seem to aid this type of reader, the stress on meaning should also help. These words should also be encountered in real life whenever possible. Locate a stop sign and see if students know the word when they see it at a street corner.

Sometimes the reverse is true: the student recognizes

Pupils can build sentences from their word cards that have been scrambled.

the word in isolation but not in context. While such cases are rare, some consideration should be given to the problem. Usually this happens when the use of the word has been changed from what students had known. If students learn the word *bank* as a basketball term and then encounter it in the following sentence, "I can *bank* on you," they may not understand it. In such a case it would be correct to say that the students did not have the word *bank* as used in the sentence above as a sight word; so they did not know the word in isolation. Some readers have difficulty with certain types of print. Small print on a crowded page can cause them some confusion. The teacher can encourage these students to frame the word by blocking out all of the other words. If the other words were distractors, the student should then be able to read the word and proceed with the reading of the passage. By starting vocabulary instruction with words in context, this problem should not occur.

Learning not Retained

Of all the problems with sight vocabulary, students' knowing words at the end of a lesson but not the next day is surely the most frustrating to teachers. Thinking that the students have learned the words, the teacher plans the next lesson using those learned words as a base. Then the students become confused, for they had not remembered those words from the previous lesson. The solution for such problems in elusive because there are several causes that may be operating alone or in combination.

Teachers may be asking the students to learn too many sight words in a given lesson. If so, pacing then must be adjusted. In remedial situations, the teacher and the student should negotiate the pace of sight words to be learned. If the teacher feels that a student can learn about four words a day and the student says, "I think I can learn three a day," three words should be the accepted goal with an added, "And be certain to learn them well." If this adjustment helps the students to know their sight words, a suitable pace for successful learning has been found. Of course there are easy words (*elephant, Halloween*), and there are difficult words (*there, their*). Pace, therefore, may need to be adjusted daily depending on the difficulty of the words to be remembered. The point is to be certain that the students learn what they study. The resulting success is not contrived, but real, and can be acknowledged as such.

Another problem may be that the students have not had enough opportunities to encounter the new words. We have all encountered the problem of thinking we had mastered something only to find out that it had slipped our memory. Repeated exposure to such information enables us to recall it clearly. For students who forget easily, it is often necessary to structure extra practice. Games, learning centers, and working with peers can be ways of helping students retain what they respond to initially. Remembering that some need more exposure to sight words than others, such practice should be individually prescribed.

Still another possible explanation is that the teacher has assumed too much when planning to use yesterday's words as a base for today's lesson. A quick review of the materials assumed to have been learned will quickly let the teacher know if the base is solid or not. If not, a brief review lesson should strengthen the ability of students to recall the sight words so that the base for the lesson is established.

Some students need more sensory reinforcement for learning sight words than do others. The VAKT technique, for example, can be used to help some students remember sight words. This technique is discussed in detail on pages 249 and 250.

Finally, one wants to be certain that the students have learned the words in a contextual situation. If the students' word cards have only the word in the front of a card, then sentences using the word created by the students should be placed on the back. If students do not seem to be able to respond to a word, they can turn the card over and see it in a familiar context. In this manner, they can work with word cards without teacher help even when they run into difficulty.

Additional Considerations in Sight Vocabulary

The following aspects of remediation of sight vocabulary problems should be carefully understood by any person conducting remediation in this area.

Segmentation of skills. Students often see no connection between the learning of sight vocabulary and reading. I recall the student who asked if the difference between second and third grade were three work sheets a day instead of two. While a humorous account of a student's perception, it is also distressing. Efforts to link sight vocabulary training to actual reading situations are essential. Students should be asked why they think they are studying these words. Their verbalization of how sight vocabulary fits into reading helps teachers to know how well their students understand the purposes for a given activity.

The need to tell students the word. The teacher will find many situations in which it is advisable to tell the students unknown words. Although normally teachers should not provide unknown words, they will often find that students are in situations where they simply do not have the skills needed to attack unknown words. In these cases, telling them the word will permit them to move along with the context of the story, focusing attention on those words they have the skills to attack effectively. In such cases, the teachers need not feel guilty about telling students words, nor should they make the students feel this way.

The need for overlearning. The very nature of sight vocabulary (instant recognition and meaning) implies that it must be overlearned. Overlearning, not to be conducted in isolated drill activities, is most effective when the reader has opportunities to use the word again and again in context. Many remedial efforts fail because they do not provide for the overlearning of sight vocabulary words in context. Experience stories, trade books, and similar materials are available to facilitate overlearning.

Reinforcement of sight vocabulary through the use of word banks exemplifies the concept of "focusing on strengths" and meets the need for overlearning. Several suggestions for the use of word banks as reinforcers follow.

1. Find all the words that begin like _____ or end like _____.
2. Find all the words that rhyme with _____.
3. Find all the words that are one-syllable words or two-syllable words, and so on.
4. Find all the words that are examples of _____ (a given generalization).
5. Find all the words that contain silent letters or blends or digraphs, and so on.

Likewise games, either commercially developed or not, make overlearning exciting and funfilled. Games that follow the pattern of a race track and involve the spinning of a wheel or the rolling of dice can be used. Each block on the race track can require the student to demonstrate a skill: initial consonant substitution, syllabication, or vowel knowledge. Remember that the element of chance enters into game activities; a loss is not a matter of intellectual inability but luck. Teachers should be certain that the chance factor is obvious in all games used for these purposes.

Every remedial session should provide opportunities for the students to read materials of their own choosing. Perhaps as much as 25 to 50 percent of the remedial time can be wisely spent on such activities. It is through a great deal of reading that readers become comfortable with words that they will meet over and over again. Overlearning is often interpreted as a drill-and-grill type of activity. Obviously, the more motivating the activity, the less it will be viewed as a chore.

Word length and sound length. Some seriously handicapped readers may look at a word such as *mow* and call it *motorcycle*. These readers have not made an association between sound length and word length. Consequently, they have a slim possibility of making progress in sight-vocabu-

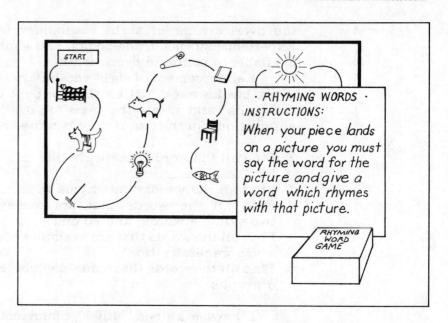

Competitive games add enrichment to otherwise boring phonics activities.

lary development without an intervention program in awareness of sound and graphic relationships. We are not talking about phonics here, rather an awareness that long-sounding words will appear to be longer in print than short-sounding words. While it amazes mature readers that some students have difficulty in this area, the fact remains that they do. Instruction is directed to the problem by discussing the facts with the students and then providing exercises with extreme examples (*mow—motorcycle*) and moving toward instruction with minor changes (*mow—mower*).

Need to know word boundaries. Some immature readers have difficulty identifying word boundaries even though they sound as though they are reading accurately. Clay reports this type of phenomenon and attributes it to memorizaton of the passage.[4] The students listen to others and repeat what they have heard. They sound as if they are reading, but they are not. If one is concerned that some of the readers are doing just that, it may be worthwhile to ask the readers to frame several of the words. If they frame the word *house* as follows, then they do not recognize the boundaries of the word *house.*

> I went into (the house to) see Jim.

The students should be shown the word *house* on a card and asked to read a sentence. They should be able to find it in the sentence and frame it. In this way, they can learn the boundaries of the words.

Motivation Techniques

The often subtle development of power in sight vocabulary needs to be illustrated to problem readers so that they may be encouraged by their progress. The following techniques have been found to be particularly helpful.

1. Transferring every lesson to contextual situations illustrates that the effort the students are making in sight vocabulary is, in effect, making them better readers. Particularly with older students, this in itself is often ample motivation.

2. Recording experience stories in booklet form is interesting to younger students, for they can see progress merely by the quantity of the material they have been able to learn to read. The sight-vocabulary implications of that quantity can be pointed out if need be to the student.

3. Charts illustrating the goals toward which the student will work in sight vocabulary seem to trigger some students' efforts to achieve better performance. Ultimately, it is desirable that intrinsic motivation fulfill the function of such charts, and they should never place one reader in competition with another. An illustration of success through the use of charts must be carefully planned. Objectives must be short-term and within the realistic grasp of the student. Charts that emphasize long-range goals can discourage as well as encourage students. During a moon shot, University of Maryland clinicians led their students in a vocabulary development race against the astronauts. The students won the race, and the short-term nature (eight days) of the chart made it worthwhile. Such charts should never place one reader in competition with another.

4. Sight vocabulary cards maintained in a file or on a ring illustrate visually to students that they have accumulated a number of useful words through which they can become better readers. These words should not be listed

in isolation; rather, they should appear in a sentence with the word highlighted.

In several of the techniques above, games have been suggested for teaching purposes. These appear to hold a student's interest and to establish a degree of motivation, while assisting the student to develop sight vocabulary.

As has been mentioned, the use of contracts through which students regulate their learning to some degree are of particular value. The completion of a contract is motivation in itself. Of course, specially constructed rewards and motivational devices can be built in. For example, contract completion can result in an immediate reward through free-reading time, praise, and other encouragement. The motivation to strive for future efforts is built-in and automatic.

REMEDIATION IN WORD ATTACK

Word-attack skills include those techniques that enable students to pronounce words not in their sight vocabularies and to understand them as they are used in contextual situations without teacher assistance.

Many readers have serious difficulties with word-attack skills, so many remedial programs concentrate upon them heavily. Consequently, an abundance of materials is available to teachers for use in word attack, and there are many approaches to the problem recommended in the professional literature. With this wealth of information, it is very easy for teachers to overemphasize instruction in word-attack skills. Heilman proposes, "The optimum amount of phonics instruction that a child should receive is the minimum amount he needs to become an independent reader."[5] Following such advice should lessen the possibilities of overemphasis. Another danger related to word-attack instruction is that it often occurs in isolation—away from context. Students often fail to see the purposes for such lessons and interest starts to lag. Ending all word-attack lessons in context where students can see how what they have learned has helped them to read better is strongly advised.

Perhaps, in light of the research on good and poor readers (chapter 7), reading specialists and classroom teachers should assure all readers of ample time to practice the reading act. This is especially to be remembered as one develops lesson plans in the area of word attack.

In the discussion on the use of criterion-referenced tests in chapter 4, teachers were warned against testing too many objectives. Some programs that accompany CRT lock students into learning a specific set of subskills prior to moving to the next level. Since these subskills lessons seem to concentrate on word-attack skills, the problem is greatest in this area. The fact is that different students need different amounts and types of phonics instruction. Care should be taken to avoid use of programs that lock students into specific learning sequences. Remedial programs in word attack should be designed to foster independence in reading, not mere proficiency in word attack drills.

Because there are various methods for attacking words not known at sight, educational focus should be on those word-attack skills that assist the reader in attacking words most efficiently in terms of time and most consistently in terms of application. Once overlearned, efficiency in word attack should have the same aims as did sight vocabulary (i.e., to decode the word and associate its meaning instantly to the context in which it occurs).

As indicated in the diagnosis chapters, word attack falls into three major categories: phonics clues, structural clues, and contextual clues. Dictionary skills, a fourth category of word attack that normally is not considered of remedial necessity, at times need development in remedial programs.

Discovery Technique

It must be assumed that most students referred for remedial help have had instruction in word-attack skills. That those skills have not been mastered indicates clearly that the instructional efforts have failed. Therefore, part of the reason for failure in learning word-attack skills must be attributed to the technique of instruction. Throughout this chapter, the *discovery technique* will be mentioned as a solution to specific problems.[6] A brief review of the discovery technique and some of its possibilities are included as a preface to the discussion of remediation in word attack:

1. Present word patterns that contain the visual clues desired for instruction. For example (using known words):

   index   picnic   pencil   chapter

2. Direct the students to observe visually the patterns in the words. For example:

   a. Place a *v* above each vowel.   v   v
                                            index
   b. Place a *c* above each consonant   vccv
       between the vowels.   *index*
   c. Divide the word into   vc cv
       syllables.   *in/dex*

3. Have the students form generalizations in their own words. For example, one student may say, "vc/cv"; another might say, "When you have vccv divide between the c's," concerning the patterns and the syllabication above. Any appropriate response is acceptable. Teachers should avoid forcing their wording on the students.

4. Have the students turn to material that they are reading to collect words that fit the pattern. For example, refer to a specific page in a book on which you know there are five words that fit the pattern. The students may also find words in their word banks that fit the pattern.

     The major advantages of the discovery technique include the active response of the students, acceptance of their generalizations, and the impact that results from forming a generalization through the use of visual clues. Teachers may choose to vary the approach at times; in fact, Botel suggests that steps three and four be reversed. Other variations may include: a discussion of exceptions to the generalization; help in beginning the wording (e.g., "When a word contains the pattern . . ."); and activities directed from word lists to determine the ability of the students to discriminate the visual pattern. Although the discovery technique takes more time than simply telling the students, the lasting effects of the learning are extremely valuable.

Phonics   Remedial efforts in the area of phonics will be in terms of the questions asked after diagnosis.

1. Does the student appear not to use graphic cues?
2. Does the student attack small words accurately but not large ones?
3. Does the student seem to know sound-symbol relationships but seem unable to use them during reading?

Although in diagnosis the skills of phonics have been delegated to three precise areas (sound of letters, syllabication, and blending), it is necessary that the remedial program combine these areas for instructional purposes. The functional use of phonics skills involves the ability of the reader to divide the word into syllables, sound the letters, blend the sounds into a recognizable word, and check the derived pronunciation in the context from which the word was taken.

Auditory-discrimination skills are considered essential to success in phonics instruction. These skills were discussed in chapter 8. However, with seriously handicapped readers any phonics instruction should start with auditory discrimination activities. Make it a policy not to assume prior learning in this area.

We must continue to remind ourselves that phonics instruction is the most abstract, and therefore most difficult, learning for students. Lessons, therefore, should be short, crisp, and related to some contextual situation.

Graphic cues.   Does the student appear not to use graphic cues? Which graphic cues are used accurately? For each student, the teacher should have a list of all known strengths in the area of phonics. This information has been accumulated during oral-reading testing and specific testing in the area of phonics. All phonics lessons should start with these strengths. As new skills are mastered, an adjustment should be made to the list of strengths for each student. In this way, the teacher always has an accounting of each student's phonics knowledge.

Make a plan for instruction. Plans should include the approach to be used to teach the skills, methods for practicing the skills, and procedures for using them.

Plans for teaching the skill.   The decision whether to teach phonics from whole words or in isolation basically is reserved for the teacher. In either case, the major decision concerns which approach best suits the student's strengths. Both will call for providing ample opportunity for all students to demonstrate their skills rather than their weaknesses, and the suitability of either approach will depend upon the following:

1. The teacher's familiarity with a given technique combined with the availability of materials and results

obtained through its use. Although teachers generally work best with familiar techniques and materials, new methods and ideas should not be overlooked. Inflexible and inappropriate teaching can result from the failure to adapt. It is therefore very important for teachers to be as objective as possible in their assessments of the materials and techniques that can be used most effectively.

2. The student's previous experience and reaction to that technique. If, after good instruction, a student fails with a given technique and develops a negative attitude toward it, another approach may be more desirable.

By using these two factors to help make decisions about what approach to use, no doors are closed. It must be remembered, however, that working from known words has the distinct advantage that the instruction is related to something already meaningful to the students. That fact makes working from known words a heavy favorite from my point of view.

Students should be alert to the idea that each time they decode a word, the sounds that are uttered should be associated with a meaningful concept. As part of each phonics lesson, techniques must be used to facilitate this alertness. The students may be required to put the pronounced word in a sentence, or the teacher may present words in which classification is possible (e.g., things we do at school and names of animals). In either case, attention is called to the fact that the pronounced word has meaning as well as sound.

Several approaches for instruction are outlined here.

1. *Discovery approach.* In phonics instruction the discovery approach is used to help students develop an awareness of the consistent sound-graphic relationship. The teacher starts with visual and auditory stimulation:

Let's read these words:

      see   sit   sox   sun

Listen carefully to the first sound in each word. They all start with the same sound. Let's hear it. What letter does each of these words start with?

Once the students have an awareness of the relationship between the letter *s* and the sound it represents, the teacher has several choices:

Look in your word banks and see how many words you can find that start with the letter *s*.

Pronounce these words and see if they all have the sound that *see, sit, sox,* and *sun* start with.

Look in your book on page____. There are three words that start with *s*. Find them and let's see if they start with the sound we hear at the beginning of *see, sit, sox,* and *sun.*

Or, I'll give you some word endings. You place the *s* sound in front and let's see which ones make real words:

s-and   *s-at*   *s-im*   *s-oz*

Tempo is important. These steps can be dragged out to a point that makes instruction boring. Make this instruction snappy and move on the generalization step:

Let's all try to say in our own words what we have learned today.

Teachers should check each effort and help students to clarify the generalization. A student may write, "When a word starts with the letter *s*, it will start like the word *sat*." At this point, instruction is over and students go into a practice activity.

2. *Word families.* Many students develop excellent word-attack skills quickly through the use of word families and initial-consonant substitution. After some instruction on the initial sounds, words can be built quickly.

You know the initial sounds that the letters *t, s, f,* and *p* represent. This word ending is *-at.* Put your consonant in front and see how many make real words:

t-at   *s-at*   *f-at*   *p-at*

Attention is placed on two aspects of reading in these activities: initial-consonant substitution is easy and quick; and when students pronounce words they should always make a check to be sure the word has meaning for them. Then use other word families such as *-in, -and, -et.* Control the pace so that your students are not overwhelmed, but keep it moving in a snappy, interesting way.

3. *Speech-to-Print Phonics.* A commercially prepared program that uses some of all of the above, *Speech to Print Phonics* has been used with handicapped readers with success. The program features learning several sounds, applying them through substitution, checking for meaning, and using repetition. These materials can be used with groups or individually.

4. *Cloze.* Cloze techniques, which were discussed in the diagnosis chapters, can also be used for phonics instruction. Students can be given sentences with parts of words left out and they can attempt to insert the correct part so that the sentence will make sense.

> The __oy hit the __all.
> The dog __ it the man.
> We had __ean soup for dinner.

In a teacher-directed activity, the teacher can ask the group for the letter that goes in the blank for the sentence to make sense. The teacher then inserts the correct letter. For individual practice a similar set of sentences can be developed and the students insert the correct letters themselves. This adds the element of writing the letters, which is reinforcing.

As skill with one sound is developed, other sounds are added, making the activity one that requires more discrimination.

> The __oy baked a __ake.
> Mary __aught the ball.

These activities can be started as teacher-directed and lead to individual performance.

5. *Word-bank words.* Using the reading sight vocabulary of the students, one can develop phonics lessons. Use word bank words to:

> Collect all words that begin or end with the same sound
> Collect rhyming words
> Collect words with the same vowel sound and place them in long sound and short sound groups

Once these collections are made, help the students to draw generalizations about the sounds represented by the letter under investigation. Students will find words with letters that do not fit the generalizations. Use these to discuss the exceptions to generalizations.

> *City, cell,* and *cycle* are exceptions to the *K* (hard) sound of *c* because they are followed by *i, e,* and *y.* Have the students find other words using the letter *c* followed by either *i, e,* or *y.* Do they fit this exception to the *K* (hard sound) generalization?

If none of the above instructional techniques is effective, the teacher is encouraged to employ task analysis techniques (see chapter 7.) Since all learners respond in

Practice sessions allow students to work with what they have learned.

terms of their uniqueness, it may be that some logical explanation exists for a reading difficulty. We may ask what can the students do?

1. Respond to first sounds, final, medial?
2. Recognize familiar parts in unknown words?
3. Know the meaning of the word when it is read? to them?
4. Find the word in a dictionary?
5. Distinguish sounds when words are read to them?
6. Respond to word when it is placed in context?

From such a list of questions, strengths and instructional needs can be recorded.

Practicing learned skills.   Practice sessions allow students to work with what they have learned so that they can gain a degree of comfort with the skill. The following are suggestions for practicing learned skills.

1. *Games.* Teacher-made or commercially developed games can be used to let students practice what they have learned.

SRA Word Games, Phonics We Use Learning Games, Vowel and *Consonant Lotto* are examples of packaged kits that are available. After instruction, students play those games that contain the skills they have learned. Teacher-made games, although time-consuming to construct, can be made to relate directly to the skills of a given lesson.

2. *Learning centers.* Self-directed activities that relate to skills learned can be made available. Small groups or individual students can work through centers, practicing their new skills. Centers can be either self-correcting or they can be checked by the teacher. They are generally on topics of interest to the students and add the dimension of attention getting.

> Look at the picture. Say the word to yourself. Think of the first sound in the word. Find a clothespin that has the consonant that represents that first sound. Clip it to the picture. You can turn it over to see if you are correct.

> A learning center using clothespins and a pizza or cake cardboard plate provides manipulative activities. Note that the center is self-correcting by turning the plate over.

3. *Tutoring.* As soon as a skill is determined to be mastered, it is useful for the students to teach the skill to someone else. It does not matter if the other person knows the skill or not. By practicing the teaching of a skill that has been recently learned, the student is going through the process in the teacher's seat. Students love it and they learn from it.

4. *Work sheets.* Some workbooks contain highly useful activities that can be used for follow-up practice. *Phonics Skilltests, Phonics We Use,* and *Working with Sounds* are a few of the many commercial materials available for practice sessions. It is better to pull the pages needed rather than to overwhelm the students with the workbook.

Try to make practice sessions short in duration and interesting. By paying attention to the students as they practice, teachers can prevent student frustration. If the practice activity is too difficult, it should be adjusted so that the students experience success. We do not want the students to be practicing mistakes.

Using learned skills. After instruction and practice, students should have opportunities to use their new skills in reading. Each remedial session generally should end with a period of silent reading, in order to communicate to the students that the reason for their effort is to make it possible for them to read on their own. Once they get the idea, these reading periods are valued by the students.

Attacking small and large words. Many students can use phonics for word attack with small words but have difficulty using it with large words. This is, in part, because small words tend to be more consistent. However, many students do not have useful ways to get large words into smaller parts. Instructional strategies, practice ideas, and procedures for use must be considered.

Instructional strategies. It is imperative to remember that students will need to use *syllabication* when they come to words of two or more syllables that they cannot pronounce at sight or through the use of other word-attack techniques. An illustration of the difficulty of this task may

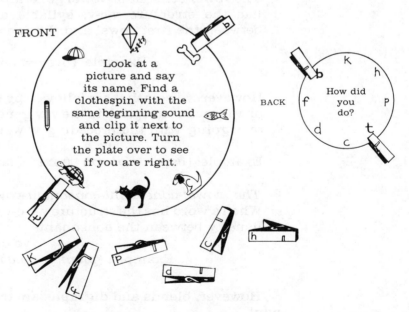

FRONT

Look at a picture and say its name. Find a clothespin with the same beginning sound and clip it next to the picture. Turn the plate over to see if you are right.

BACK

How did you do?

A learning center using clothespins and a pizza or cake cardboard plate provides manipulative activities. Note that the center is self-correcting by turning the plate over.

be seen when an adult looks at the following nonsense words and attempts to pronounce them:

sogtel   *sog-tel*
akot   *a-kot*
sognochest   *sog-no-chest*

It should be realized that when students attack words that they do not know at sight, their procedure is likely to be to divide the word into syllables and to pronounce the syllable without intensive phonic analysis. A highly valuable word-attack technique, syllabication is of particular value to older students. The teaching of the generalizations necessary for accurate syllabication is important. For students who have had this instruction in their normal classroom situations and have failed to respond to it, use discovery techniques.

The number of generalizations necessary may vary with the needs of the students in relation to the types of words they meet at their instructional level. The following three generalizations are essential for all students in learning the syllabication of words.

1. *The vowel-consonant-vowel generalization.* When a word has the structure v-c-v, syllable division is usually between the first vowel and the consonant.

    v cv
    Example: (*over* = *o/ver*)

    However, vowels that are followed by the consonants *r, x,* or *v* form an exception to the vcv generalization, the *r, x,* or *v* going with the preceding vowel.

    vc v   vcv   vcv
    Example: (*carol* = *car/ol*) (taxi = tax/i) (river = riv/er)

2. *The vowel-consonant-consonant-vowel generalization.* When a word has the structure v-c-c-v, syllable division is usually between the consonants.

    vc cv
    Example: (*picnic* = *pic/nic*)

    However, blends and digraphs are treated as one consonant.

    v c v
    Example: (*achieve* = *a/chieve*)

3. *The consonant le generalization.* When a word ends in the structure consonant plus *le,* those three letters form the last syllable.

$$c = le$$
Example: (*ankle = an/kle*)

For students who fail to understand syllabication at this point, the Fernald[7] technique with a modification for emphasis on the syllables of words may be used to direct them to substitute the pronunciation of *syllables* in all steps that require them to pronounce the *word.* Although this technique will not teach the student how to divide words into syllables, its value is in assisting them to grasp the concept of syllabication.

Once the word has been dissected, either through syllabication or through the actual sounding of each letter of the syllable, the students must be able to blend these sounds and to obtain a pronunciation with which they can associate a meaning. Classroom and clinical techniques are similar.

When difficulty with blending arises, the student must be given ample opportunity to divide known words into syllables and then to blend these sounds in order to obtain a feeling for blending. It is clear that the blending of sounds and syllables is an inherent part of each lesson in which the student learns the sound or divides the word into syllables.

There are several phonics approaches that simplify the problem of blending and pronunciation by teaching the sounds as units rather than in isolated pronunciation. In the following case, for example, the sound of *b* will be taught in the initial position as it relates to the various vowels: *ba, be, bi, bo, bu.* This then is immediately substituted in word-building exercises:

bad	*bit*	*but*
beg	*boss*	

Cordts presents in detail the techniques and philosophy of a blending approach to the teaching of phonics.[8]

Student knows sound-symbol relationships but seems unable to use them during reading.   This is a common difficulty and has often led to more isolated skill practice. But, more practice is not what is needed. The emphasis should be on application of learned skills in contextual reading.

One difficulty may be that the students have learned a lot of phonics subskills and are confused about which ones to use. Of course, different skills should be used in different situations. For example, rhyming elements are useful when they are recognized. When they are not, available attention to the initial sound may be most helpful. If phonics instruction is taught with techniques for use, then application may occur. For example, the Speech-to-Print program, previously mentioned, does just that. Once the sound-symbol relationship is learned the students are asked to use their new skill in a substitution activity that focuses upon the use of context as well as the new phonics skill.

Another difficulty is that many students learn far too many phonics subskills. Lesson after lesson on the many variations of the vowel sound-symbol relationships can lead to confusion. Smith states that there are far too many rules for the vowel-sound-symbol relationships for most young students to master.[9] In one count he came up with 106 vowel rules. Excessive instruction in subskills can lead to a distorted view of reading and a confused reader.

Still another explanation may be that initial failure with phonics instruction has created a no–risk taking set while reading. Botel suggests that sound-symbol relationships be taught through the syllable approach.[10] It is easier to learn and easier to blend and it is closer to meaning. This approach involves the teaching of high-frequency syllables (-at/-ate, -an/-ane, -ad/-ade, etc.). He lists all possible combinations.[11] Then the reader substitutes initial consonants and consonant blends to develop a word-attack system.

Structural Clues

Deficiencies in the ability to attack compound words are generally not too serious, for students easily can be taught to pronounce words if they know the parts. If they do not know the parts, the problem is probably inadequate sight vocabulary. Although prefixes cause more difficulty than compound words, the fact that they are (1) at the beginning of the word; (2) usually a separate, easily pronounceable syllable; and (3) concerned with a meaning that directly alters the base word makes them easier to learn and causes less difficulty in remedial reading. However, in the case of suffixes, where the above three factors are often missing, many students experience difficulty. It is with suffixes that the service of the base word is most likely to change, even though a precise difference in meaning is not evident. Note that in the following words when the suffix is removed, the spelling and configuration of the base word is distorted, causing an additional complication in the study of suffixes:

run	*running*	*runn-ing*
hope	*hoping*	*hop-ing*

The discovery technique is again suggested for its advantage in making students generalize structural patterns from known words.[12] This technique is equally applicable to difficulties with prefixes, suffixes, or compound words. In teaching the decoding and interpretations of the prefix *un,* for example, it may be best to follow a procedure similar to this:

1. Present the word *happy* in a sentence. *John is happy.*
2. Change the word to *unhappy.* *John is unhappy.*
3. Have the students generalize the difference in meaning.
4. Present several other words in a similar manner.
5. Have the students generalize by answering the question, "What does *un* generally do to the meaning of a word to which it is prefixed?"
6. Collect word patterns of this type and see if they apply to the generalization.
7. Note that *un* has a sound that is consistent and that it changes the meaning of the words to which it is attached.
8. As the students read, their attention should be called to words prefixed by *un.* They should determine if these words fit the generalization.

Word wheels that contain the base word can be made easily: as they move the wheel, the students add either the prefix or the suffix to the base word. Suggestions for these can be found in Russell and Karp's *Reading Aids Through the Grades.*[13] The teacher is cautioned in the construction of such reinforcement devices to be certain that the problem is not one of the student's not knowing the base word and to be alert to the spelling changes that occur when the suffix is added. Prepared exercises of this type are found in materials such as the *Classroom Reading Clinic.* In this kit, word wheels, upon which base words are altered by prefixes and suffixes, provide ready-made reinforcement exercises.

Practice.   Practice activities for structural skills do not differ from those that follow phonics instruction. Games, learning centers, tutoring, and practice sheets are appropriate here also. For older students *Tactics in Reading* and *Basic Reading Skills* provide mature activities for practice.

Using learned skills.   The reading time provided at the end of practice sessions is important for the students to develop the understanding that all of these activities have but one purpose—to make reading a more enjoyable and successful experience.

Context Clues

Authors provide context clues by the redundancy in their writing and through deliberate attempts to help the reader. Readers pick up on those clues through the use of their knowledge of syntax, semantics, and pronunciation. Just how does a reader gain these skills for use in reading? Probably the best way is to read a great deal. Read all types of material: fiction, content, newspapers, poetry, and magazines. Obviously seriously handicapped readers run into difficulty because there is very little for them to read for practice. However, reading a variety of materials is the best way to learn to use context clues. Questions to ask to determine problems with context clues include:

1. Does the student appear to ignore syntactic cues?
2. Does the student appear to ignore semantic cues?
3. Does the student appear to ignore punctuation cues?

Ignoring syntactic cues.   Students who make substitutions but use the correct part of speech in the substitution are telling us that they understand the language but are missing the exact word. Those who substitute the incorrect part of speech are telling us the material is so strange to them that they cannot even see it as their language. The very first task is to make adjustments in material to determine if the students continue to misuse syntactic cues on easier material or material that is of higher interest to them. If adjustment of materials eliminates the problem, practice in reading should be provided in that type of material.

If students continue to substitute incorrect parts of speech, direct instruction in simple closure activities is appropriate. Students may be asked to discuss which word may fit in this blank:

Mary has a ——————— baseball bat.

Answers such as *new, big, large, small, green, yellow,* and *nice* can be accepted and discussed as to why they fit. Then other parts of speech can be eliminated, and the practice can continue. Students enjoy the open-ended type of response and can quickly become aware of the syntactic cues that our language offers.

Ignoring semantic cues.   If readers substitute with words that do not distort meaning, they are on their way to reading success. However, if they distort meaning with their substitutions, they are missing the ideas of the author. The first adjustment must be with the materials to see if easier materials and materials of more interest can correct the errors. Such adjustments almost always work. If the readers are over their heads in concepts or technical vocabulary, there is little chance of using context effectively. Smith talks of readers using prediction as a technique to develop awareness of meaning.[14] For example, read these sentences to the students:

The team had their high scorer under the basket. The score was 96–94 with three seconds left. Jim thought, "Wow, what a   game."

Then ask, "What words would fit and what words would be wrong? Why?"

The same types of activities can be used in silent reading. Let groups of students work together to determine which word can be used and why. Authors provide semantic cues in all types of reading.

Some commercial materials may assist the teacher in providing many experiences of this type. *Using the Context* provides numerous activities at various grade levels.

For mature readers use newspaper articles and words that can be supplied if the context is understood. Students are excited about such adultlike reading and quickly understand how the use of context clues is more than a guessing game.

Ignoring punctuation cues.   Punctuation errors are often due to the frustration level of the material rather than failure to observe punctuation. If this is true, direct activity to observe the markings will be useless, and time may be spent more wisely on other skill areas with materials of the proper level. However, if the error is due to lack of knowledge about the use of punctuation marks, instruction is needed.

Choral reading is an effective, subtle way for students to obtain a feeling for the function of punctuation marks. Following group oral reading, the students' attention should be called to the fact that punctuation marks have different functions and call for different inflections. Listening to good oral reading on a tape recorder will also assist readers to become aware of the need to observe punctuation marks in their reading materials.

Opportunities for students to follow the teacher's reading to determine observance of correct punctuation also may be used effectively. Intentionally distorting the punctuation, the teacher can ask students to explain what this does to the ideas of the author. When used sparingly, this technique works well with those having trouble hearing their own punctuation errors.

Activities such as the following are interesting for students and create an awareness for observation of punctuation marks.

Read the following sentences:

Nancy is bright.   Jim is in love.
Nancy is bright?   Jim is in love?

One of the difficulties with English is that punctuation marks may be far removed from where the student must make the proper inflection. Wouldn't it be easier if we could write it:

? Nancy is bright

Then the reader would know the statement was to be a question.

When readers have difficulty using punctuation it is almost always because the materials are too strange or too difficult. Teachers should make certain that practice activities always involve appropriate materials that reduce frustration.

Use of Dictionaries

Dictionary skills are excellent, indispensable word-attack techniques. Students with reading problems may benefit from dictionary instruction; however, special help for problem readers usually does not result from a limitation of dictionary skills alone. Work in programming has produced two publications that may be of use in remediation, *Lessons for Self-Instruction in Basic Skills* and *David Discovers the Dictionary*. The appeal of these programs to remediation is their individualized approach, which requires a minimum of teacher supervision to assist the student in acquiring the skills necessary to use the dictionary.

Provide a dictionary for every reader. When word-attack problems occur, let students use the dictionaries. The habit and the skills needed are quickly formed and lead the readers to independence. Of course dictionaries require the use of alphabetizing skills and locating skills. But these can easily be taught and readers can gain self-esteem from the independence that results.

PUTTING IT ALL TOGETHER

As we discussed in the phonics section of this chapter, some students seem to know their subskills but have difficulty using them. More instruction with subskills is obviously not the answer. We must look for other explanations.

One possible explanation is that instruction was not followed by opportunities for the use of the newly learned skill. Through disuse, the skill gradually becomes weakened and then lost. Each lesson must be followed by reading practice, and in some cases it may be well for that practice to be monitored by the teacher so that the transfer of the skill to reading can be verified.

Another explanation may be that the students have received conflicting advice about how to use their new skills. One teacher may suggest starting with the initial consonant, another may suggest using a dictionary, and parents may tell them to spell the unknown word. While many readers weather such conflicting advice, the handicapped reader can become thoroughly confused.

It is useful to establish a minimal strategy for attacking an unknown word. All teachers working with a group of students agree to the strategy and use it with the students. Parents and librarians are also informed of it and use it. In this way, the student is seeing that what is learned in reading classes is important throughout the school and even at home. The strategy that any group of teachers would

Student and teacher record sheets and sample cards from NFL Reading Kit, Bowmar.

Teacher Record Sheet

Teacher's name

School

STUDENT/STARTING LEVEL	SKILL/DATE MASTERED	Details	Context Clues	Main Idea	Sequence	Generalization	Inference	Fact/Opinion

Student Record Sheet

THE NFL READING KIT from BOWMAR

D = Details M = Main idea G = Generalization F/O = Fact/Opinion
C = Context clues S = Sequence I = Inference

CARD No.	1	2	3	4	5	6	7	8	9	10
1. The Man Who Surprised the Cardinals	D	D	D	C	M					
2. The Great O. J. Simpson	D	D	D	C	M					
3. The Quiet Winner	D	D	D	C	M					
4. George Who?	D	D	D	C	M					
5. Superstar Who Never Played Pro Football	D	D	D	C	M					
6. The Man Who Painted the Helmet	D	D	D	C	M					
7. The Man Called Bronko	D	D	D	C	M					
8. The Greatest Pass Catcher	D	D	D	C	M					
9. The Growth of Pro Football	D	D	D	C	M					
10. The Men in the Striped Shirts	D	D	D	C	M					
11. The Player Who Followed His Father	D	D	D	C	M	S				
12. The Player Who Went for the Top	D	D	D	C	M	S				
13. The Runner Who Became a Receiver	D	D	D	C	M	S				
14. Frank Gifford: Announcer and Player	D	D	D	C	M	S				
15. Roger Staubach: Still a Winner	D	D	D	C	M	S				
16. Joe Namath in Super Bowl III	D	D	D	C	M	S				
17. The President Who Helped Save Football	D	D	D	C	M	S				
18. The Great Passer	D	D	D	C	M	S				
19. The Grand Old Man of Football	D	D	D	C	M	S				
20. The Quarterback Who Was Not Too Old	D	D	D	C	M	S				
21. The Player Who Showed He Belonged	D	D	D	C	M	S	G			
22. The Scrambling Quarterback	D	D	D	C	M	S	G			
23. The Player No One Wanted	D	D	D	C	M	S	G			
24. Coach Who Built Something Out of Nothing	D	D	D	C	M	S	G			
25. The Last-Minute Victory	D	D	D	C	M	S	G			

QUESTION NUMBER

1

Comprehension Check
The Man Who Surprised the Cardinals

REMEMBERING DETAILS

1. Terry Metcalf was ___C___ tall.
   a. 6 feet 2 inches
   b. 5 feet 6 inches
   c. 5 feet 10 inches
   d. 7 feet

2. In Terry's first year he went over ___b___ yards on offense.
   a. 2,000
   b. 1,000
   c. 2,058
   d. 500

3. The man from the Cardinals had seen Terry play ___d___.
   a. in high school
   b. for the Chicago Bears
   c. in a baseball game
   d. in college

USING CONTEXT CLUES TO GET WORD MEANINGS

4. "He even got 23 yards when he picked up a loose ball." In this sentence, *loose ball* means ___b___.
   a. ball that fell apart
   b. ball that had been dropped
   c. ball that he found at home
   d. ball with the players' names on it

FINDING THE MAIN IDEA

5. The main idea of this story is that ___c___.
   a. the Cardinals made their players work hard
   b. Terry Metcalf was a poor runner
   c. Terry Metcalf turned out to be a fine player
   d. Terry Metcalf was not strong

SPECIAL WORD MEANINGS

college: a school that people can go to after high school, usually for four years

defense: the players on a football team who are on the field when the other team has the ball

pro: a person who gets paid for doing something (in this case, for playing football); pro is short for professional

offense: the players on a football team who are on the field when their own team has the ball

NFL: the National Football League, a group of teams that play each other in pro football

2

Comprehension Check
The Great O. J. Simpson

REMEMBERING DETAILS

1. O.J. Simpson talked to Jim Brown at ___b___.
   a. a football game
   b. an ice cream store
   c. a park
   d. a baseball game

2. O.J. broke Jim Brown's record in ___d___.
   a. 1961
   b. 1963
   c. 1971
   d. 1973

3. When O. J. broke the record, the officials stopped the game ___a___.
   a. for a moment
   b. for 30 minutes
   c. for 45 minutes
   d. for an hour

USING CONTEXT CLUES TO GET WORD MEANINGS

4. "In 10 years no one had come close to that mark." In this sentence, *mark* means ___b___.
   a. write
   b. record
   c. time
   d. football

FINDING THE MAIN IDEA

5. Another good title for this story would be ___d___.
   a. Jim Brown Loves Ice Cream
   b. The Long Season
   c. O.J. and the Frozen Field
   d. The 2,003-Yard Season of O.J. Simpson

SPECIAL WORD MEANINGS

rush: to run with the football and try to gain yards

officials: the people on the field who make sure that players follow the rules and play fairly

quarterback: the player who stands behind the offensive line and starts each play by taking the ball from the center

snap: the pass from the center to the quarterback

index finger: the finger next to the thumb

develop should relate to what they stress during instruction. The following is an example of such a strategy:

When you come to a word you do not know, use this technique:

1. Read on and look for clues.
2. Frame the word.
3. Try the first sound.
4. Divide the word into smaller parts.
5. Consult.

Here the students are asked to use context clues first, configuration clues second, phonics third, syllabication fourth, and then either use a dictionary or ask someone for help. Teachers should then teach each of these strategies. Students have cards they can refer to with the strategies written on them. They can use these for bookmarks. Teachers post the strategies in each room and the media center, send a copy home, and emphasize the strategy in every lesson. The students get the idea that what they have worked so hard to learn has application for reading.

Using a minimal strategy does not limit those students who have more skills that they can use. It simply gets the readers started on the road to independence in reading using word-attack skills.

Motivation

By far the strongest motivation for students in the study of word-attack skills is being able to see how this knowledge and skill enable them to become more independent in their reading. It is essential, therefore, for students to be put in the situation of transferring learned skills to context in every lesson if possible. Game-type activities, as suggested, make the reinforcement of these skills more informal and pleasurable.

The discovery technique has motivational appeal, especially to some of the older students who need work in word attack. The idea of generalizing the concepts of word attack with a minimum of teacher supervision usually becomes a highly motivating situation.

Graphic illustrations of progress usually help to motivate. Teacher-made materials designed to illustrate established goals and the students' achievement within their scope and capabilities are effective motivating devices too.

Programmed materials with immediate feedback contain inherent motivational appeal. These materials, designed to reinforce, correct, and alter incorrect responses, establish situations in which the reader eventually will be successful—a desirable outcome in all types of remedial programs. See sample materials on pages 298 and 299.

SUMMARY

The remedial techniques to be used in the area of vocabulary deficiencies, whether sight-vocabulary or word-attack, are based on diagnostic findings. Once these deficiencies are determined, educators have a variety of approaches in remediation from which to choose. Starting with those that they believe will serve most adequately, educators remain alert during instruction to the possibility that the original approach may need to be modified as instruction continues.

Constant awareness of the value of incorporating skill activities into contextual situations is the responsibility of both the teacher and the reading specialist. Continued drill, without well-developed transfer opportunities, is of little value.

NOTES

1. Morton Botel, *Forming and Re-Forming the Reading Language Arts Curriculum* (Washington, D.C.: Curriculum Development Associates, 1975).
2. Arthur W. Heilman, *Smuggling Language into the Teaching of Reading*, 2d. ed. (Columbus, O.: Charles E. Merrill, 1978).
3. Edgar Dale and Joseph O'Rourke, *Techniques of Teaching Vocabularies* (Palo Alto, Calif.: Field Educational Publications, 1971).
4. Marie Clay, *Reading: The Patterning of Complex Behaviour,* (London: Heinemann Educational Books, 1972), Chapter 6.
5. Arthur W. Heilman, *Phonics in Proper Perspective*, 4th ed. (Columbus, O.: Charles E. Merrill, 1981), p. 22.
6. Morton Botel, *How to Teach Reading* (Chicago: Follett Publishing Co., 1968), p. 64.
7. Grace Fernald, *Remedial Techniques in Basic School Subjects* (New York: McGraw-Hill Book Co., 1943). Part II.
8. See Suggested Readings and Appendix B.
9. Frank Smith, *Understanding Reading* (New York: Holt, Rinehart & Winston, 1978), p. 140.

10. Morton Botel, *Forming and Re-forming the Reading/Language Arts Curriculum* (Washington, D.C.: Curriculum Development Associates, 1975).
11. Ibid., pp. 36–42.
12. Botel, *How to Teach Reading*, p. 40.
13. David H. Russell and Etta E. Karp, *Reading Aids Through the Grades* (New York: Columbia University Press, 1951).
14. Frank Smith, "The Role of Prediction in Reading," *Elementary English* 52, no. 3 (March 1975): 305–11.

SUGGESTED READINGS

Botel, Morton, *How to Teach Reading*. Chicago: Follett Publishing Co., 1968. In chapters 3 and 5 of this well-written book, Botel presents the "discovery" and "spelling" mastery techniques for use in sight vocabulary and word-attack lessons. The reader will find this a practical guide to developmental as well as remedial activities.

Burmeister, Lou E. "Usefulness of Phonic Generalizations," *The Reading Teacher* 21 (1968): 349–59. This article reviews the research on phonics generalizations. A reading of this review is essential prior to work with children in a program that concentrates on phonics and the use of phonics.

Clymer, Theodore. "The Utility of Phonics Generalizations in the Primary Grades," *The Reading Teacher* 17 (1963): 252–58. This article discusses how functional the generalizations commonly taught to children are in terms of the number of times the generalizations hold true and the number of words to which they apply.

Coley, Joan, and Gambrell, Linda. *Programmed Reading Vocabulary for Teachers*. Columbus, O.: Charles E. Merrill Publishing Co., 1977. This book presents the basic knowledge a teacher must have to work with students in the area of sight vocabulary. The material is presented in programmed format.

Cordts, Anna D. *Phonics for the Reading Teacher*. New York: Holt, Rinehart and Winston, 1965. This entire book is devoted to a description and explanation of a method of teaching phonics that reduces the necessity for extra blending of isolated sounds. The reader will find this technique valuable in working with many problem readers.

Forte, Imogene; Pangle, Mary Ann; and Tupa, Robbie. *Center Stuff*. Nashville, Tenn: Incentive Publication, 1973. A useful collection of ideas for developing centers on many topics.

Fries, Charles C. *Linguistics and Reading*. New York: Holt, Rinehart and Winston, 1963. One explanation for the linguistic involvement in the teaching of reading can be found in this book. For those who have difficulty understanding the linguist, this book is a good introduction. Teachers of problem readers must acquaint themselves with the works of the linguists.

Hall, MaryAnne. *Teaching Reading as a Language Experience*. 3d ed. Columbus, O.: Charles E. Merrill Publishing Co., 1981. This book presents basic information for teachers concerning the nature and uses of language experience as an approach to reading instruction.

Heilman, Arthur W. *Phonics in Proper Perspective*. 4th ed. Columbus, O.: Charles E. Merrill Publishing Co., 1981. Heilman has combined an assessment of the place of phonics with a survey of the skills to be taught and has included examples and appropriate word lists. The educator who works with problem readers will find this book or one like it indispensable in working with phonics.

Herrick, Virgil E., and Nerbovig, Marcella. *Using Experience Charts with Children*. Columbus, O.: Charles E. Merrill Publishing Co., 1964. This booklet will provide the reader with many suggestions concerning the construction and use of experience charts. The classroom teacher should find these suggestions easily applicable to this group.

Lee, Dorris M., and Allen, R.V. *Learning to Read Through Experience*. New York: Appleton-Century-Crofts, 1963. A combination of philosophy and techniques, this book is a must for those who plan to work with seriously handicapped children. As indicated, this approach will be of particular value with many children, and the book will provide the educator with a thorough background from which to work.

Stauffer, Russell. *The Language-Experience Approach to the Teaching of Reading*. New York: Harper & Row, 1970. Chapters 1, 2, and 3 discuss the theory and uses of language-experience approaches. Chapter 10 discusses special uses of language experience including clinical cases.

Waynant, Louise R., and Wilson, Robert M. *Learning Centers . . . A Guide to Effective Use*. Paoli, Pa.: Instructo, 1974. Provides numerous ideas about the construction and use of learning centers. Those who want to use learning centers in remedial programs will find this book useful.

Wilson, Robert M., and Hall, MaryAnne. *Programmed Word Attack for Teachers*. 3d ed. Columbus, O.: Charles E. Merrill Publishing Co., 1979. This book presents the basic knowledge about word attack needed by teachers for instruction. The material is presented in a programmed format followed by tests that enable teachers to demonstrate their knowledge of word-attack skills.

10

Comprehension Development

Chapter Emphasis

- Comprehension should be taught as a personal process.

- Instructional approaches should reflect what we know about comprehension.

- Instructional strategies can be used with any approach.

- Materials for instruction should be picked for interest and relevancy.

  Note: All materials mentioned in this chapter are listed in Appendix B with characteristics specified.

As we address the area of reading comprehension, it may be useful to start with a discussion of the skills needed for successful comprehension. The area of reading comprehension, however, is highly complex and a simple discussion of a set of selected subskills will not suffice. In this chapter there will be a discussion of some of the aspects of comprehension that are important to understand in order to provide effective instruction. This will be followed by a set of instructional approaches that will be followed by some specific instructional strategies. Then each question raised in diagnosis will be treated with instructional suggestions.

ABOUT COMPREHENSION

The process is so complex that we really know very little about how each student processes information. In recent years many scholars have been developing theories about how the process seems to work and researchers are busy attempting to evaluate those theories. The following points about comprehension seem reasonable and have implications for instruction.

It's personal. Smith reminds us of the personal nature of reading comprehension.[1] What the reader understands from reading a passage is related to the knowledge the reader brings to the passage. Prior knowledge on the assasssination of President Kennedy will have a large effect upon how accurately a reader can process a passage on that subject.

Comprehension requires predicting. It is through the active process of predicting that students participate in comprehension. Students must anticipate what is coming and then check to see if their prediction is correct or not. Risk taking is obviously involved with predicting. Frequent inaccurate predictions make predicting risky. This, in part, explains why we enjoy reading about matter in which we have considerable prior information and why we shy away from matter in which we are ignorant. Our prior knowledge helps us make accurate predictions so there is less risk involved in the activity.

It must be practiced. Allington suggests that wide reading for all students is necessary for successful comprehension.[2] However, data exist that indicate that readers experiencing difficulty in reading often have less time to practice reading, spending more time in skills-development activities.[3]

It involves more than answering questions. Durkin reports that the assessment of comprehension prevails in most classrooms and that there is little time spent in activities that could be called instructional.[4] The question-asking mode of instruction uses the technique of assessment. Students either know the answers or they do not. Of course, questioning strategies can be used to facilitate understanding when used for purposes other than assessment.

Organization helps comprehension. How students are helped to organize or reorganize the passage seems to have an effect upon their comprehension. If lessons are constructed so that students are expected to respond to questions on unrelated bits of information, then comprehension is negatively affected.

Comprehension requires attention to task. If for any reason readers are inattentive, comprehension cannot take place. Boredom, difficult material, student expectation, and distractions can take students off task, creating an impossible setting for comprehension. Can you remember "reading" a page only to realize you were attending to tonight's dinner or last night's date? Result—no comprehension.

Product versus process. It is entirely possible that the comprehension products that students produce may fail to provide us with any useful insight into the processes that they used. It is therefore not possible to evaluate the comprehension process solely by examining the product. For example, fluent, accurate oral reading does not necessarily indicate good comprehension. Answering all of a teacher's questions does not necessarily indicate good comprehension. While these types of products are encouraging indicators that something profitable has been going on, they do not give us full information about the readers' processes.

INSTRUCTIONAL APPROACHES

The selection of instructional approaches should reflect the information we have about reading comprehension. Instructional approaches that seem to fit our knowledge about reading comprehension include the directed reading-thinking activity, the problem approach, the language-experience approach, and nonquestioning approaches.

The Directed Reading-Thinking Activity (D-R-T-A)

Stauffer has developed an instructional strategy that focuses on the teacher's role in directing reading as a thinking activity.[5] This strategy can be used with a large group of students or can be adapted to individualized instruction. The steps include the following:

1. Identifying purposes for reading
2. Guiding the adjustment of rate to purposes and materials
3. Observing the reading
4. Developing comprehension
5. Providing fundamental skill-training activities[6]

These steps must be understood by the teacher of readers who have difficulty with comprehension. If this brief discussion does not adequately inform you, review Stauffer's work.

Stauffer's D-R-T-A emphasizes the place of the student in the learning process. His rationale includes a list of assumptions about what students can do. The student then is personally involved in each step of the lesson; the teacher is seen as a member of the group but not the authoritarian figure. For example, in setting purposes, the students are taught to make observations about the materials, set their purposes, then read to satisfy those purposes. The teacher is on hand to guide and assist, but not to dominate. When the students' purposes do not fit the information in the passages they are reading, they are helped to reset their purposes using what they have already read.

This approach is a personal one; it draws upon the prior knowledge of the students, it involves the act of reading, and it encourages attention to task. The students are continuously organizing and reorganizing new information so that it fits with their prior knowledge. Prediction and hypothesis setting take the place of direct teacher questions.

The Problem Approach

Setting the scene for the students to be responsible for the direction of their learning, the *problem approach* encourages student task-oriented behavior. Brigham lists seven essential steps to this approach. They follow.[7]

1. Talk informally with client to put him/her at ease. Listen to concerns and interests of client. Establish relaxed atmosphere with client.
2. Ask client what s/he would most like to learn about—develop as many specific topics as possible. Print responses as client watches on chalkboard or chart.
3. Ask client to group similar to related topics together. Ask which ideas seem to go together, which ones are different from the rest—gradually develop a set of general topics, some with subtopics and questions—record organization.
4. Ask client to decide on which ones s/he wishes to learn about first, second, etc. Help client to develop appropriate sequence.
5. Ask client where, how and from whom s/he may find answers. Develop with client a list of suggested re-

sources from each subtopic and/or question. Record client's responses. Decide together which approach could be used.

6. The general plan developed with the client is typed and then critically reviewed and revised. It then becomes the material for reading, asking such questions as: "Is this just what you decided to do? Is this the best way to do it? Are there ways in which you may wish to change it?"

7. Eventually the client is helped to prepare a summary of what s/he has learned, which may take the form of a brief written report, a construction project, a role-playing skit, or whatever.

In all of these steps, students are being asked to use and develop a wide range of thinking—language skills in an oral situation—as a basis for their application in reading and writing activities. They are required to be active, responsible participants in the instructional situation.

With the problem approach the student is involved in a personal discovery of meaning. The student is the discussion maker, an active learner, and an organizer of information. The teacher is a resource for the students.

The Language-Experience Approach

A natural approach for students having difficulty with comprehension is the language-experience approach. After a common experience (field trip, film strip, science experiment, etc.) the students develop a story that the teacher records. Meaning is assured, since the story is in students' words concerning a recent experience. Stories can be collected and saved for future reading, and comprehension skill extension. Some skill extension activities may include the following:

1. Developing suitable titles for the story
2. Discussing the feelings of various persons in the story
3. Adding to the story a creative ending
4. Changing part of the story to alter the outcomes
5. Checking to determine if the events as given by the students are in sequential order in terms of what actually happened

As with the D-R-T-A and the program approach, the language-experience approach is a personal approach to comprehension. It directly involves the students' prior

Andy, Bruce, Charlie, Danny, David, and Dwight were twelve year old seventh graders who were having difficulty reading material intended for their grade level. These students were very reluctant to engage in any type of reading activity. They possessed strengths in the areas of decoding, literal comprehension, and group participation. They exhibited weaknesses in the areas of higher-level comprehension skills, organizational skills, and study skills, as well as on-task behavior and self-concept as readers.

After examining and taking into consideration the strengths and weaknesses of the group, it was decided to employ the Problem Approach in order to involve the students actively in an instructional situation. The group decided they wanted to learn first about the various jobs and responsibilities involved in running a fast-food restaurant. Next it was decided that the best way to obtain the information was to contact a fast-food restaurant and arrange for a tour and a question and answer session with the manager. After the visit to the restaurant, the students summarized and demonstrated what they had learned by setting up their own fast-food restaurant. Various jobs with corresponding responsibilities were undertaken by each member of the group. Students from other classes were invited to visit the "restaurant," "purchase" food items and ask questions pertaining to jobs, responsibilities, etc.

The students experienced successful instructional situations using this approach, in that they were able to bring their experiential background and prior knowledge to the task in order to provide a resource of information. By being active participants involved in directing their learning, the group of originally very reluctant readers gained a new enthusiasm for reading through the Problem Approach. Their self-concepts as readers, on-task behavior, higher level comprehension skills, organizational skills, and study skills continually improved with each successive use of the approach.

Loretta Palkovitz-Dayhoff

knowledge and it provides a resource of materials for successful reading practice.

Since teacher questioning contains the aspect of assessment in that students are expected to come up with "right" answers, several approaches should be considered that do not rely upon teacher questions. Note that teacher questions need not be of the "come up with the right answer" nature as will be discussed later in this chapter.

Communication with the author.   Write to the author of a story to obtain information about why he/she wrote the book, research that was done to write the book, or personal questions about the author's life.

Add or change endings.   Stories may have surprise endings or expected endings. Students can write or dictate new endings and have enjoyable times sharing them.

Discussion or debate.   Controversial issues in a story or book can be discussed or debated. Students can attempt to determine the validity of a given action based upon their prior knowledge or upon their research of the topic involved.

Communication with a story character.   Various students can take the part of the characters in the story. Other students can interview them, write them letters, question their activities in the story, or ask them to act out their part. These and other nonquestioning activities facilitate the development of comprehension without questioning. You will note that the students respond in a personal manner through a variety of organizational strategies.

What we know about comprehension can be incorporated in each of the four approaches discussed. The teacher or reading specialist can pick one approach and follow it or combine approaches. This decision will probably be based upon age and interest of the students, comfort with a given approach, and the materials available for instruction.

INSTRUCTIONAL STRATEGIES

Within each approach there are instructional strategies that may be selected for comprehension development. These may be used with any approach, used some days and not others, and used with some students and not others. We present these to help provide variety in instructional lessons.

The instructional strategies to be discussed are developing a setting for questioning, adjusting materials, providing wait time, utilizing task analysis, utilizing student questions, developing personal outlines, developing think-links, and encouraging retelling.

Developing a Setting for Questioning

Two situations exist for the students to answer questions. One is a recall situation in which the reading materials are not available to the students. The other is a locate situation in which students can use the reading materials to locate answers to questions. Many regular classroom activities have stressed the recall situation, which involves not only reading comprehension but memory abilities as well.

However, remedial lessons should focus on locating skills. What the students need to be able to do is use the reading material either to find or verify their answers. Students can answer about 30 percent more questions when locating than when recalling. Since remedial lessons should focus on strengths, locating is desirable.

In working with adults discussing the advantages and limitations of recall and locate situations, I often give them some material to read. Their responses are considerably improved when they are allowed to keep the material during questioning. Students have probably read the materials if they can locate the answers. If teachers want to test how well students remember what they have read, they should call it a memory-training activity and not reading comprehension. By stressing locating instead of recalling, students are encouraged to learn how to use reading materials. They begin to see books as resource materials that can be reexamined, and, consequently, they develop mature reading skills.

We all maintain some type of professional and personal library in our homes. We maintain these libraries because we enjoy the privilege of rereading something that was of interest or because we need to locate information that has slipped our memory. After reading an interesting story in a book or the newspaper, we do not want to be expected to remember details. Similarly, in the establishment of mental set, recall demands that the student remember as much as possible during the questioning period; locate calls for the student to be able to use the reading material during questioning.

Adjusting of Materials

Except for periods of self-selection, materials for instruction are chosen by the teacher. If the materials are too difficult or lacking in interest, it is essential to change them. Instead of trying to force students through such materials, the teacher needs to be aware of means of either adjusting the materials or getting different ones. Many students who are experiencing difficulty in comprehension are working in materials far too difficult for success. By expecting them to practice their reading in difficult materials we are creating a situation in which poor reading skills are being encouraged. Halting, inaccurate, slow, nonfluent reading can be learned and reinforced when materials are too difficult. We found good readers reading in materials with 97 percent word recognition accuracy and poor readers in the same classrooms reading materials with which they were 89 percent accurate. Nobody had to point out the poor readers; all one needed to do was listen to their oral reading. In such situations there is no chance for attention to meaning because too much attention needs to be given to figuring out words.

Read-along books, wordless books, and high interest-low vocabulary books need to be acquired for these students.

A materials section is included in Appendix B. Teachers should become familiar with these and other materials so that selections can be made for various students. Other materials may need to be rewritten to reduce either concept load or vocabulary difficulty. See pages 333–342 for a discussion of the use of survival and functional reading materials during remediation.

Providing Wait Time

The work of Rowe on the topic of wait time should be considered by all teachers but particularly by those working with handicapped readers.[8] Rowe found that teachers tend to give very little wait time, that is, the time between asking a question and calling for an answer. One second was the average wait time. By training teachers to wait for three seconds or longer, Rowe found that student responses increased and were more complete.

Rowe also found that the amount of time between the student's answering a question and the teacher's responding to the answer was very short. When teachers waited after a student responded, the student tended to expand the first response, and other students tended to interact without teacher interruption. By providing wait time after asking questions and before responding to answers, students are allowed time to think and form their responses as well as to elaborate upon them.

Most of us have a difficult time applying wait time in our classes. Many of us are so used to constant discussion and to asking questions and responding to answers at a fast clip that it seems unnatural for silence to prevail in the classroom. Yet it can be learned, with practice. Let your students know that you are going to give them more time than usual. Count to yourself for the three to five seconds that you are going to allow. Then take note of the increased quantity and quality of the responses of your students.

Utilizing Task Analysis

Task analysis, as discussed in chapter 7, has special application to reading comprehension. It can lead teachers to make appropriate adjustments when students become overwhelmed in a comprehension lesson and are unable to respond. Briefly, what can the students do and what seems to be the difficulty? Hypothesize several adjustments that you expect to improve the learning situation. Check out each one through diagnostic teaching, and then alter your instructional plan.

Of all of the areas in which task analysis has been useful, it is most useful when severe comprehension problems are encountered.

The following example may be helpful.

Problem:
Warren cannot recall literal details when reading in text material at an eighth-grade readability level.

Strengths and Weaknesses:
Student can read orally with relative accuracy at eighth-grade level (IRI).

Student can respond to about 20 percent of literal questions at eighth-grade level after silent reading (IRI).

Student can respond to 90 percent of literal questions at sixth grade level (IRI).

Student really seems to try.

Hypotheses:

1. Student will respond if material is more interesting.
2. Student will respond if permitted to locate the answers to literal questions at eighth-grade level.
3. Student will respond if passages are shorter.
4. Student will respond if made aware of purposes for reading.

Hypothesis Testing: (See hypotheses above for reference.)

H1. Obtain materials at the eighth-grade level with a variety of interests, let the student pick one to read, then check comprehension.
H2. Pick a passage that the student can read aloud accurately and ask literal questions in a locate situation.
H3. Divide a passage into three parts, asking questions between each part.
H4. Prior to reading, have discussion with student about purposes for reading.

Results:

   Your hypothesis testing indicates that Warren responds successfully to situations 1 and 2, but that 3 and 4 seems to make no difference. Draft an instructional plan.

Instructional Plan:

   You now adjust your instruction by either allowing for self-selection or by encouraging the locating of answers, or both. If Warren responds successfully over time, then task analysis was useful in this setting. If he continues to have difficulties, you repeat the task analysis and develop new hypotheses.

Utilizing Pupil Questions

When utilizing questioning strategies we have often noted that the teachers do all of the work. They decide what is important, form a question, and make sure they have an answer. By utilizing student questions, they involve students in those important steps. Students come to the comprehension session prepared to ask, not answer questions. They can ask questions of the teacher or of other students. They should be able to justify their answers and locate them in the passage from which the questions are derived.

Our observation of students in the question-asking role is that their attentiveness is increased, their enthusiasm grows, and they demonstrate that they have comprehended the passage.

Interestingly, students tend to ask the types of questions that they hear from their teachers. And they tend to respond to the answers to their questions in the same manner in which their teachers respond when they ask questions. Should you not like what you are hearing, it may be time for a reevaluation of your question-asking and answer-responding techniques.

Developing Personal Outlines

Outlining is an effective way to organize the important matter from a passage. All too often, however, outlining activities are another of those "right" or "wrong" experiences that are so frustrating to students who are already having difficulty being "right." Personal outlining for a reading-comprehension lesson could go something like the following. Start by eliciting from the students which ideas they think are important or interesting. Such a start on a comprehension lesson tends to create a thinking atmosphere instead of a testing one. The teacher is encouraged to accept all suggestions, noting them on the chalk board. Some may be quite divergent from the message in the passage, but it is important to know what the various students gather as the important message. Each idea is recorded without comment. After several ideas have been suggested, the students are encouraged to pick the one they really think is most important. The opportunity to change one's mind is likely to enhance the thinking process.

Next, pairs of students are formed according to agreement about the important idea. Their task is to go back through the passage to find support statements or proof for the idea selected. It is useful to provide a format sheet such as the following:

1.   (Important idea)
    a.   Support
    b.   Support
    c.   Support

This procedure can be repeated in long passages of several paragraphs, since there may be several important ideas. Students can then discuss or otherwise share their efforts. Aside from giving students practice in the impor-

Personal outlining helps the students elicit which ideas they think are important or interesting.

tant skill of outlining, this approach has several advantages:

1. The locating of literal facts has a purpose, the purpose selected by the students.
2. Students learn to locate swiftly and accurately, since the location is specified.
3. On-task behavior is promoted, since students are working in areas of their choice.
4. Poor choices for what is important are clearly illustrated to students, since they have difficulty finding support for them.
5. Students accustomed to this approach perform well in literal comprehension activities that may follow.

Throughout this activity students are encouraged to paraphrase instead of using the exact words of the author. Those reading above the second-grade level can work effectively in this manner and learn to direct themselves after four or five lessons.

Personal outlining combines the notion that reading

comprehension should be personal and that it should result in some type of organization of the material.

The transfer of this type of comprehension demonstration to a system of report development is clear. Now the students go to the library seeking certain information for a report. They read the materials, decide what is most important, go back to the material and seek support for their important ideas. When they come back to their classroom they can read their report, talk about it, and write paragraphs about each important idea.

Developing Think-Links

Another organization instructional strategy involves the use of *think-links*.[9] After reading a story, the teacher asks the students to think about what they have read. The teacher then uses the following strategy:

1. Write the name of a character in the story with some words about how the character may have felt during certain parts of the story:

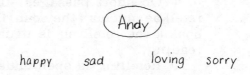

2. Ask students when Roy was happy in the story. Various students will identify happy events and the teacher will record them:

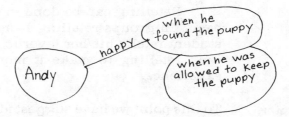

3. Step 2 is repeated using other feeling words.

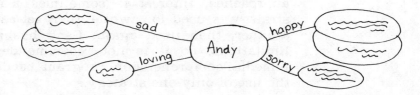

4. When all of the words have been used, the students see a reconstruction of the story they have read.

They can talk about the new organization, they can write about it, and it encourages them to think about it. Think-links are not limited to character feelings. They may take any form and any content. For example, they could have a cause in the middle and events that relate to that cause on the outside. They could be used to summarize a science experiment or a geography unit. Once students have worked with their teacher developing several think-links, they can start to develop them independently.

Encouraging Retelling

The final strategy to be discussed in this section is the one of retelling stories or portions of stories. *Retelling* is a personal reorganization of the parts of the story that made an impact on the students. One may ask students to retell parts of the story that were most interesting, parts that were most important, funny parts, or sad parts.

On short passages students may be encouraged to retell as much as they can. On long passages, chapters, or books, the retelling is usually centered on a part of the reading.

Retelling is open ended. The students do what they can do. Prompting can aid retelling. Such comments as "Who else was at the scene of the accident?" or "Why do you think she did that?" can jog the memory to facilitate the complete incident.

Retelling can be done in groups or on an individual basis. In groups retelling has a sharing effect when each student retells his/her favorite part. Discussion can follow each retelling to make it more like a real-life sharing experience.

Mid Chapter Summary

To this point we have suggested four approaches that can be used individually or in combination, each of which reflects what we know about comprehension. Then eight instructional strategies were suggested to be used with any of the approaches. Interest is sometimes maintained when a strategy is used for awhile, then set aside for the use of another, then used again. Each has its strengths and limitations, so it is not recommended that an entire remedial-comprehension program be developed through the use of only one strategy.

SPECIFIC REMEDIAL ACTIVITIES IN COMPREHENSION

As in other skill areas, specific remedial efforts in reading comprehension will be discussed in terms of the questions asked as a result of diagnosis:

1. Do large units of material seem to interfere with comprehension?
2. Do comprehension difficulties occur with some types of comprehension and not others?
3. Does the student have difficulty using locating skills?
4. Does the student have difficulty reading content material? Why?
5. Does the student fail to comprehend most of what is read?

It is most likely that if a comprehension difficulty exists there will be no one answer. For example, the student having difficulty with locating skills will likely have difficulty in reading content materials also. By continuing to look at reading as a complex process, teachers realize that single solutions are unlikely.

Large Units of Materials

The improvement of reading skills depends on the student's ability to respond to units of print of increasing length. In diagnosis it is easy to note whether the reader's comprehension is limited basically to sentences, paragraphs, or to larger units. In these cases the problem is one of not being able to recognize the relationship between units of varying sizes and the flow of ideas created by the author.

All remedial approaches must start at the instructional or independent level. When the difficulty is related to the size of the unit, the instructional level should be the largest unit each student can handle effectively. Using the D-R-T-A, teachers can help students set objectives for reasonable amounts of material. Students quickly become aware of the amounts of materials they can handle and learn to set objectives accordingly.

The paragraph appears to be a reasonable starting place, usually containing one major idea and some supporting details. Helping students to understand paragraph structure through identification of the topic sentence is also useful.

Materials such as *SRA Reading Laboratories* provide smaller units of material at lower levels but manage to maintain interest. Students can set purposes for such reading and read to answer their purposes, not just to answer the questions on the card. Some materials have numbered paragraphs at easier levels. Locating skills can be taught by asking questions in relation to the paragraph number. In this manner, the students are helped to locate the area in which the answer can be found—a real time saver for beginning instruction.

Teachers can also adjust the amount of material included in experience stories. If a long story is dictated, the teacher can place it on two or three sheets, making parts 1, 2, and 3. Students can respond to each section and finally to the entire story.

Highly motivating teacher-made materials can be developed easily to help students handle large quantities of material. For example, a tv guide from the Sunday newspaper can be used to help students handle varying amounts of printed material and to respond to tasks of varying difficulty. Students can be asked questions such as these:

1. What show is offered on Channel 4 at seven o'clock on Tuesday evening?
2. What sports events are offered on Saturday?
3. Select four movies you would like to watch during the week.
4. What shows are featured at eight o'clock each day?
5. Take one and one half hours per night and schedule your own television watching for the week.

The use of newspaper articles, want ads, telephone yellow pages, cookbooks, shop manuals, catalogues, encyclopedias, and dictionaries can be developed similarly by starting with a specific activity requiring a minimum of reading and moving toward extended activities requiring considerable reading. Students in remedial programs can relate easily and enthusiastically to materials such as these, even though they may tend to be uninterested in reading. Some of these types of materials, contain very small quantities of print and are, therefore, ideally suited for students who have difficulties with larger units.

Difficulties with Some Types of Comprehension

Teachers use questions to determine the ability of students to respond to various types of comprehension activities. When responding to teacher questioning, students may indicate strengths and needs by the type of questions being asked. The type of question and the type of response need careful consideration prior to discussion of remedial activities. All too often, the type of question asked in commercially prepared materials is designed to obtain specific facts from the story (literal understanding). When working with groups of students, questions at the literal level can be asked of the entire group at one time. Using Durrell's idea of every-pupil-response cards, all can quickly respond to literal questions. Each reader, for example, has a card stating *yes* and one stating *no*. The teacher can select five or ten important details from the story and ask questions calling for a yes or no answer. Cards with names of story characters, dates, and numbers to indicate choices in multiple-choice questions also can be used. The teacher notes all of the responses and directs rereading, or reformulates questions when responses are inaccurate. Literal understanding can be checked in a short period of time, leaving more time for questions and activities of the interpretive and problem-solving types. While literal comprehension is extremely important, the time normally allocated for it is out of proportion.

When interpretive questions are asked, the reader is expected to respond by paraphrasing the ideas of the author. Such questions as the following may be asked:

1. In your own words state the most important idea of the story.
2. How would you summarize the author's major point?
3. Why did the major character lose his temper?

Questioning at the interpretation level requires that the readers draw upon their fields of experience to interpret the author's words. Although interested in accurate interpretation, the teacher MUST NOT have a preconceived statement of the answer. Readers interpret in the best way they can and their efforts must be accepted. If answers contain inaccuracies, there is the possibility of inaccurate reading or of an inappropriate background of experiences. In either case, inaccuracy calls for reteaching rather than criticism.

When questioned at the problem-solving level, students are expected to think beyond the content of the story, applying either critical- or creative-thinking skills to the author's ideas through such questions as the following:

1. What would you have done if you were Jim? (creative)
2. Did Jim make good decision? Why? (critical)
3. Can you think of a better ending for the story? (creative)
4. What reasons can you give for Father's actions? (critical)

Obviously, questioning at the critical- and creative-thinking levels calls for even more openness on the part of the teacher. When the teacher asks critical questions, the students must understand the author, must be able to interpret the author, and must apply their experiences in order to analyze what has happened. The students' answers may differ from the one that the teacher has in mind and still may be accurate. If reasoning is not clear, probing questions assist students to seek alternatives.

In creative thinking, any answer given is acceptable and correct. Students are being asked to create, and what they create is good. Students tend to enjoy creative activities and, when their answers are accepted, tend to become more creative. For example, ask a group of students to think of a new title for a story with the idea of making the story into a television show. Tell them the title should attract attention. They usually start with rather traditional titles but soon open up as they see the teacher accepting all of their responses.

Questions asked by the teacher are important, but even more important, perhaps, are the teacher's responses to the students' efforts. Accepting, probing, reteaching, and making reading activities exciting for students depend upon the teacher's attitude toward the responses of those students. Students also will learn to accept and to value a variety of peer responses as they see the teacher accepting them. For those in need of further explanation of the types of comprehension, *Programmed Comprehension for Teachers* may be a useful source of information.[10]

The discussion of the three types of comprehension in terms of remediation, will treat interpretive comprehension, literal comprehension, and problem solving.

Interpretive.   The importance of interpretive comprehension is the key to success with literal comprehension. Strategies for developing skills can be developed through some of the following suggestions. Closure activities are excellent means of helping students develop awareness of interpretation. Given the cloze activity:

Mike is a _____ football player.

groups of students can see how many words they can fit into the blank and still have the sentence make sense. To do so calls for awareness of the meaning of the rest of the sentence. Later, a full sentence can be provided, and students can add words that do not necessarily change the meaning, for example:

Pat is a tennis player.
Pat is a *tremendous* tennis player.

Using brainstorming, glossaries, or dictionaries, students can build many sentences without significantly changing the meaning of the sample sentence.

After experience stories are written, the teacher can write the same story while paraphrasing the students' stories. Students match the specific section of the teacher's story with their own. Once that skill is developed students can work in teams, paraphrasing their own stories.

Since interpretation involves the ability to relate one's thinking to that of the author, the first step of the D-R-T-A will need emphasis. Reading purposes will stress such activities as summarizing, reading between the lines, and determining the main idea instead of reading for details or facts. The first step of the D-R-T-A is also the place for building a background for the story. Pictures, discussions, film strips, and motion pictures may be used to assure that the students have experiences with the story's concepts. At other times, the simple procedure of using several of the terms in the story and of discussing situations using those terms assists the students when they meet the terms in the story.

Building a story into a motion picture by identifying the three most important scenes and then formulating a selling title for the movie is motivating and is a subtle way of stressing main idea. If interest is high, several students may develop a play or a movie from the story. When stressing interpretation, students perform their roles without reading lines from their books. Paraphrasing, inferring, and selecting the main idea will be essential. Many students demonstrate such skills in highly unique ways; for example, they may make a comic strip from a favorite story by creating both comic pictures and captions. Of course, acceptance of such efforts is the key to encouraging students to continue trying.

Analysis of the topic sentence in a paragraph can also develop interpretation skills. The topic sentence contains the main idea. By stating the topic sentence in their own words, the students are studying both main idea and paraphrasing. An independent activity can involve matching cut-out topic sentences with appropriate paragraphs.

Open-ended questions that call for summarizing can be developed and can result in performances acceptable at many levels of refinement. For example, a summary can be a word, a phrase, a sentence, a paragraph, or several paragraphs. Summaries can be either written or oral and can be either drawn or acted out. By changing the activity, teachers can maintain student interest while continuing to develop the same skill.

Students can learn from their peers if they are grouped so that readers having difficulty paraphrasing can work with those who are quite good at it. They can work in teams of two or three to come up with an answer to a teacher's posed question. By teaming students carefully, all will be able to make contributions to the final product. Pairing of students does not necessarily teach independence, but it often helps students overcome the feeling of frustration, of giving up, or of simply not understanding what is going on. It also assists in making them active rather than passive learners.

With older students, questions can be written (e.g., multiple-choice questions) relating to the content of the story but changing the author's wording. In such cases, teachers do the paraphrasing by means of the way in which they ask questions. The student's task is to match the paraphrased idea to the author's idea. Thus, they see that the same idea may be expressed in several different ways.

Sometimes a simple probing question can be helpful. For example, if a student answers with the precise words of the author, the teacher can respond, "Yes, that is correct. Now let's try to think of other ways to say the same thing." So, if the author has written, "The general led a successful charge," the teacher may suggest that the students attempt to say the same thing using another word for *successful.*

When inferences are stressed as an interpretation skill, the teacher must be aware of two types of inferences. One the author provides intentionally; the other is developed by the reader. For example, some authors lead the reader to a conclusion without actually stating it. Since inferring involves reading between the lines, the teacher should talk with students about it in exactly those terms.

Ideas such as mood, time, danger, and happiness are often only implied by the author. Questions such as "How do you think the player felt after the game?"; "When in history did the story take place?"; and "Would you consider the people to be in danger?" are examples of questions that stimulate students to infer. Each question can be followed by probing, "What did the author say to make you think that?" The probing activity helps students to clarify their own thinking and understanding of how others have reacted to the same story they have read.

Cartoons can be used in activities for paraphrasing, obtaining the main ideas, and developing inference skills. For example, using three or four cartoons on the same subject, the teacher can have groups of students write captions for the cartoons and then let other groups try to match the captions with the pictures. Such an activity can be developed at many levels, all of which can be highly motivating.

When students have severe difficulty with interpretation of written material, the teacher should start with picture interpretation, help the students look at pictures that have story possibilities in terms of what they can see in the picture, then move to interpretation. For example, the teacher can ask, "How do you think the children feel?"; "How is that street different from the street you live on?"; and "Make up a title for the picture." Once students have skills in picture interpretation, these responses should be developed into experience stories.

When a reading specialist draws experience stories from pictures, both literal understanding and interpretation responses should be developed. To modify the language-experience approach in order to develop interpretation, students can be asked to change a sentence without changing the meaning, change a word without changing the meaning, identify the sentences that describe the picture and those that interpret the picture, and discuss the main ideas. By moving from pictures to language-experience stories, reading specialists can make a natural transition from vicarious experiences to reading. The next step is to move to stories written by others.

Perhaps groups of students can write stories about the same picture. These stories can be compared using the above questions. When students are successful with the stories of others, they are indicating that they are ready to start with other printed material.

Literal. Literal comprehension calls for the student to locate or recall specific facts or sequences from the passage read. Again, it is encouraged that all literal comprehension occur in the locate situation. Since a fact or sequence question has a right or wrong answer, the students have no resource in a recall situation but to know or not to know the answer. However, when permitted to locate, if they do not remember the answer they have a way to find it. The comprehension strategy suggested at the beginning of the interpretive section is also very useful in helping students become aware of how to find important facts in a story.

Pointing out the important information via italicized print, boldface type, information repeated for stress, and illustrated information highlights clues to important details to be remembered. Perhaps more subtle but equally useful are clues that words contain. Descriptive adjectives, proper nouns, action verbs, and the like all call attention to those types of details that should receive more careful attention. For example:

The *large house burned* in the middle of the *night*.

Most basal material is well designed to develop understanding skills. The classroom teacher using basal materials first must be certain that the student is working at the appropriate level and then select those lessons that appear to be most useful.

Understanding sequences causes considerable difficulty for many students. When this skill is deficient, students are limited in their ability to handle content-type materials and to fully appreciate reading of longer units. The thought processes needed involve perceiving groups of items that are related in time (i.e., one comes first, then the next, and so on). Initially, students must obtain sequencing practice from such activities as following oral directions, doing independent work from oral and written instruction, or discussing events from a story that has been read to them by another.

To aid development of sequencing, it is normal to start with a sequence of two events and to advance to more involved sequences after that is understood. For example, begin with two events that are clearly representative of the beginning and ending of the story. When the students can perform with two events (i.e., when they can tell which one came first), add a third event, then a fourth, and so on. Starting with many events to place in sequence tends to smother readers with choices and does not lead to effective sequencing.

Placing comics taken from the Sunday newspaper in sequence is a motivating technique for teaching sequences. Start with obvious sequences and move toward more subtle ones. If they are cut apart and pasted to cards, the comics are quite durable. Numbers on the backs of the cards to indicate the sequence make the activity self-correcting. Obviously, a teacher can build many sequence activities from comics in a short time and with little expenditure of school funds. Teachers can also develop sequence activities from newspaper headlines. Students can read the headlines and place the events (recent to their experiences) in order. They can also match the headlines with newspaper pictures that they have placed in sequence.

Some experience stories can be cut into parts. When experience stories are stimulated by photographs taken during a trip, the photos can be arranged in sequence, topics can be written for each picture, and then topics can be arranged in order. Students can thus arrange the parts to make a sequential story.

Directing the students' attention to sequencing clues used by authors for emphasis is usually of some value. Items that are numbered, steps in a process, dates, the mention of time, and the use of sequence words (e.g., *afterwards, before, during*) are all indications that the author feels the sequence of events is of particular importance.

The development of consciousness of sequence often is done best by more subtle means. We may attempt to direct the student to the idea of making a movie in which three or four scenes are to be produced by asking, "What is the order of scenes so that the audience will understand the story?" Many teachers have used the technique of asking the students to retell the story successfully. However, it is important to realize that the reader who is deficient in the sequencing skill may experience considerable difficulty in telling the story in sequence and may merely relate the details indiscriminately instead. In such cases locating sequential events is preferred.

Although initial instruction in this area should be conducted at easy reading levels, it is necessary to move to the instructional level, for it is at this level that the student is most likely to see the necessity for concentration in order to reach desired goals.

The *Reading Skilltexts, Reading for Meaning, SRA Reading Laboratories, Working with Sounds, Reader's Digest Skill Builders, Standard Test Lessons in Reading*, and the *BFA Comprehension Kit* are examples of the types of readily available materials assigned for literal understanding. It is a mistake to drill students in materials without immediate teacher follow up to evaluate and redirect, since in the case of continued failure, materials can soon become burdensome and uninteresting. By correcting errors immediately, one enhances the likelihood of reinforcing correct responses. Of course, it is usually better to provide answer keys so that students can check their own work. When they check their own answers, reinforcement possibilities increase. They are more involved in the appropriateness of their work; their responses are reinforced immediately; and they can look for the correct answer when they cannot figure it out from the question asked. Self-correction is a highly desirable activity for students and saves teachers considerable time. It is important to remember that when a check exists in a practice situation (not a testing situation), students can use several routes to answers. They can figure out the answer themselves; they can ask someone else; or they can self-check with an answer sheet.

We often start with experience stories in which the student is asked to explain how to do something, such as build a model airplane, and then is directed to sequence the steps. When possible, the teacher can obtain funds to purchase car, ship, or airplane models and help students to see the importance of sequences by working with them to construct models using the sequential directions on the box.

Problem solving.   Students usually are not classified as being in need of remedial assistance if their only difficulty is in the area of problem solving. However, problem-solving activities ought to be considered necessary and valuable in remedial situations. Such activities involve the reader in a reaction to the message of the author. The reaction takes on one of two forms, critical or creative. A critical reaction calls for convergent-thinking activities. The author's ideas are challenged, defended, and evaluated. Creative reactions call for divergent-thinking activities. The ideas of the author form a base from which new ideas can be developed.

When students set their own purposes, their choices are frequently at the problem-solving level. They want to know how to use a piece of equipment, or they want to challenge the ideas of the author. When they make such choices they should be encouraged and also made aware that they are illustrating mature thinking.

Newspaper reading is a natural activity for problem-solving lessons. Generally, the headlines are stated in such a way that the students either wonder what the problem is or what the solution is. The articles also lend themselves to scanning, since they are generally written from the most important to the least important facts. Students can be encouraged to take sides on issues and find support for their sides in news articles and editorials. Students' questions can be developed with teacher assistance. Do you agree with the author's position? Is the story true? Were the people justified in doing what they did? Each of these questions can be backed by other questions such as, "Why?" or "Why not?"

Problem solving can also be stimulated by working in pairs or small groups. In groups, students get a chance to try out their thinking without committing themselves to a specific point of view. It if often through give-and-take discussions that problem-solving skills are refined.

Students often see problem-solving activities that are related to content subjects, such as history, as highly relevant. This gives the classroom teacher an opportunity to use content materials as reading instructional materials. Thus, the students are helped in two school subjects at once. It is also a technique to prepare students for lessons focusing on materials that they have difficulty reading.

Myers and Torrance have developed a series of critical and creative activities for use at various classroom levels. Students enjoy working with these materials. For example, one activity involves asking, "What would happen it it always rained on Saturday?"[11]

With picture interpretation, problem-solving questions are asked about action pictures (e.g., "How would you feel if you were there? " or "What do you think will happen next?"). As students develop skill in responding to problem-solving questions concerning pictures, they can create the language-experience stories. Once several groups of students have worked on the same picture, stories can be compared, read, and discussed. The use of materials such as *Tweedy* transparencies bring action and life to pictures. Even very young readers find these transparencies stimulating and thought provoking. Older students respond to them equally well, and the teacher can move from discussion to writing activities using the transparencies as a basis for instruction. Moving to very easy reading material, the teacher can help the students develop problem-solving skills by using the writings of others. With older students, newspaper advertisements and television commercials are helpful to stimulate problem solving–type thinking. The teacher can ask students what this written material is really saying. What words are used to influence? Is the ad truthful? Why or why not? How would a competitor rewrite the ad? Basic to all of the above steps should be the teacher's reading to the students. Students can watch the book, looking at words and pictures.

Role playing is also useful for students who have difficulty reacting to reading creatively. They can be helped to respond creatively through materials such as *Teaching Reading Through Creative Movement,* which consists of records with voice, music, and stories, permitting a considerable amount of action. As students become freer in creative expression, they can react to many things that they read. After the creative expression, discussions about why they feel the way they do make a logical transition to creative discussions.

Difficulty Using Locating Skills

Locating information is a learned skill. It does not help handicapped readers much simply to allow them to use the book to answer questions. Instead, some systematic instruction is necessary, coupled with large amounts of practice.

By starting with materials of high interest and with the objective of trying to obtain literal information, the chances of success are enhanced. Record club memberships, cooking instructions, and local map reading are the kinds of material that can get students accustomed to locating information. Then paragraph-size passages can be introduced.

In longer passages, encourage students to think first about whether the information needed is in the front, toward the middle, or at the end of the passage. Considerable time can be saved if students do not have to start searching in the beginning for information that occurs toward the end of the passage. Obviously the mental set for locating can be developed. Instead of trying to recall details, the student tries to get the flow and direction of the passage. Then it is easier to locate specific information.

The best way I have found to teach locating skills is through the strategy of personal outlining (See page 317.) With this strategy, students will be locating information that has already been determined to be important. They can locate information for topics of interest in the library and in other types of resource materials.

Real Life Reading File Folder materials have been developed to help students locate information using the types of materials they are likely to encounter in their daily lives. These materials stress the importance of using prediction strategies, careful, critical reading, and vocabulary development, as well as locating strategies. Materials are classified according to following directions, obtaining information, and reading labels and forms. They are suited to students reading on the third-, fourth-, fifth-, and sixth-grade levels. See sample on pages 334 and 335.

Newspaper activities are also useful in developing locating skills. Take a sports article about an important baseball game and have students locate the reason for the high score in a Pirate game. Obviously, every word in the article is not important to accomplish this objective. Students can be taught to skim through the article to get to the important section or can locate the box score and determine which players were responsible for the scoring. In fact, all sections of the newspaper *require* skimming to locate important information. The American Newspaper Publishers Association publishes and distributes, free of charge, a bibliography of the best materials available for using newspapers in an educational setting.[12] Wilson and Barnes present ideas for teachers to use local newspapers for the development of a variety of comprehension skills including the locating of information.[13]

BIKE SHOP

Sometimes, when we can't repair things ourselves, we must take them to a repair shop. Most repair shops present the customer with an invoice when the work is done. An invoice is an itemized bill for goods and services.

Look at this invoice from Bill's Bicycle Shop.

INVOICE 5386
BILL'S BICYCLE SHOP
101 Main Street
Anderson, South Carolina
385-9360
Sales and Service

Name: *Shirley Carter*　　　　Date: *1/3/80*

Address: *109 Edner Road.*　　　Phone: *389-4290*

Anderson, S.C.

Services Requested: *Repair back fender and replace chain.*

QUANTITY	MATERIALS USED	PRICE	AMOUNT
1	chain	3.50	3.50
1 sm. can	red paint - #303	2.50	2.50

DATE	WORK PERFORMED	HOURS	RATE	AMOUNT
1/5/80	Straighten fender & paint.	2	3.80/hr.	7.60
	Replace chain.	1/2 hr.	3.80/hr.	1.90

Work performed by:

David Caley

X _____
Signature — The above work completed satisfactorily
All services guaranteed for 30 days after completion.

Sales Tax	.18
Total	15.68

Use this page with duplicating pages Bike Shop 1 and Bike Shop 2

Published by Instructo/McGraw-Hill, Paoli, Pennsylvania 19301 Copyright © 1980 Instructo/McGraw-Hill, Inc.　No. 8511

Sample of locating skills from McGraw-Hill's Real-Life Reading, Grade 6, Reading Forms and Labels.

It looks like this bicycle needs some repair work. If you read and answer the following questions carefully, you will learn about invoices and repair expenses.

Write your answer in the space provided.

P 1. How do you think the bicycle might have been damaged?

Any reasonable answer is acceptable.

P 2. Can you list two advantages of taking a damaged bike to a shop instead of trying to fix it yourself?

It might look better afterwards.

It might last longer.

It might be safer to ride.

Or any reasonable answer.

L 3. Bill's Bicycle Shop is located at _____

101 Main St., Anderson, S.C.

L 4. The telephone number for Bill's Bicycle Shop is _____ 385-9360 _____.

L 5. Where was the bicycle taken for repairs?

Bill's Bicycle Shop

L 6. What services were requested?

Repair back fender and replace chain.

L 7. Who requested the repairs?

Shirley Carter

L 8. On what date were the repairs requested? _____ 1/3/80 _____

L 9. On what date were the repairs made?

1/5/80

C 10. Who made the repairs? _____ David Caley _____

C 11. How much did it cost for 1 hour of labor?

$3.80

Published by Instructo/McGraw-Hill, Paoli, Pennsylvania 19301 Copyright © 1980 Instructo/McGraw-Hill, Inc.   No. 8511

Bike Shop 1

Difficulty Reading Content Material

Many students seem to read satisfactorily in reading classes but are not able to read content materials. One problem may be the content and readability of the materials, since we know the student can read. Another may be that students find success when working under teacher direction and difficulty when working alone.

The first consideration in such instances must be the readability of the material upon which students cannot perform. Often there are extreme differences in readability between the books used in reading class and the books used in content areas. Content-area books often are written at a level much higher than the graded reading books. On an informal basis, the teacher should note the differences in the size of the print, the length of sentences, the vocabulary load in terms of difficult words, and the difficulty of the concepts. If any of these factors varies noticeably from the reading class materials, the problem is probably one of material difficulty. Yoakham,[14] Gunning,[15] Spache,[16] and Fry[17] present readability formulas that may be used to obtain a grade level of readability, although they do not evaluate the concept load of the material. The "cloze procedure" also has been developed to enable teachers to determine the ability of the student to handle materials; it will also indicate the ability to handle concepts, as well as word and sentence structures. Taylor claims it is of value in determining readability.[18] This technique has been used at the University of Maryland clinic with the materials students are expected to read and has been found to be helpful. It involves these steps:

1. Selecting at random several passages containing samplings of about 100 words each.
2. Retyping this passage, leaving out every fifth word. (Authorities differ on which word to omit, but I have found the fifth to be effective.) As a rule, neither the first word in a sentence nor proper nouns should be omitted. An example of a clozure test on easy material would appear as follows:

Nancy was anxious to _____ her birthday party this _____. She had invited some _____ to her room at school. She _____ that they would all _____ able to attend.

Have the reader read the incomplete sentences, filling in

the missing words. To "cloze" properly, the student must know the words and understand the concepts, thereby anticipating the author's ideas.

As teachers gain familiarity with the clozure technique, they will find it a valuable aid in determining whether the book is appropriate for a given student.

Bormuth has found that a *clozure* test score of 38 percent right is approximately equal to a *regular* test score of 75 percent right.[19] Therefore, as a rule of thumb, clozure scores below 40 percent right should be regarded as danger signs for that student with that material. Either instructional adjustments are needed or easier material must be used for instruction. (For limitations of the 40 percent criteria, see chapter 4.)

Reading problems in understanding content materials usually do not become pronounced until the student has reached the fourth grade. It is at this point that content reading becomes a regular part of the school program and the student with study skill problems is clearly handicapped.

Strategies to assist students in reading content material.
The teacher should use the D-R-T-A with materials in content areas. Students who fail to see the need for attacking unfamiliar materials must be directed in the same manner that was used in reading class. Each step of the D-R-T-A must be used carefully in the development of skill in reading content materials, gradually permitting students to guide themselves through the steps.

Older students may find it beneficial to follow a specific study technique in their reading of content materials. Several of these are available, the most prominent being SQ3R (survey, question, read, recite, review)[20]. The effect of this type of technique is the same as a D-R-T-A except that students are to apply it to their studies without supervision. Independence in reading content material is the desired objective of this system.

Activities in which the students organize and classify ideas are useful in remediation. Students who cannot read in the content areas usually have difficulty with outlining skills. Beginning with completed outlines of material recently read, the teacher illustrates the method of following the author's train of thought. An outline format is then presented for students to complete, followed by simple outlining of clearly organized material with little or no direction from the teacher. The *Reading For Meaning* workbooks, designed for the intermediate and secondary grades, have practice exercises to develop students' abilities to organize material through a gradual exposure to outlining techniques. The *SRA Organizing and Reporting Skills Kit* has individualized exercises that gradually introduce the concepts of note taking, reporting, and outlining.

The ability to follow directions has a direct relationship to the ability to perform in study situations. Composite in nature, this skill depends upon students' abilities to follow the sequence and organization of the author's thoughts, as well as their abilities to obtain the main idea. The *Specific Skills Series* (e.g., *Using the Context, Locating the Answer*) includes sets of intensive exercises in following directions at the various grade levels. Once the ability to follow directions is mastered, remedial sessions should provide additional experiences with this concept at regular intervals.

These examples of activities for following directions have been useful in helping students develop mastery of that skill. As has been suggested, the use of model cars, ships, and airplanes helps a reader to realize the importance of following directions carefully. Reading the directions on the box and following them step by step to completion can be a highly useful reading and learning experience. If students cannot read all of the instructions, they should work in pairs, helping each other. Learning centers can be developed to help students follow directions. Using pages from telephone books or newspapers, students can be instructed to follow directions ranging from the simple to the complex (e.g., find a phone number, find a phone number and address, find the phone numbers of three dentists—give their names, get their addresses, and determine which lives closest to your home).

Another SRA study aid is the *Graph and Picture Study Skills Kit.* Designed to be adapted to any subject area, these materials are useful in developing a type of reading often overlooked in remedial programs. The *Be a Better Reader* books provide specific suggestions for study in the major content areas, particularly for older students. The *Study Skills Library,* which provides specialized instruction in developing the same type of concepts, is useful with

Using newspapers, students can be instructed to follow directions ranging from simple to complex.

younger students. Individualized for clinical use, these materials can serve a highly useful function with students who are deficient in these skills.

Adaptation of the language-experience approach to content subjects has been very effective.[21] Four teachers agreed to work with students in the seventh grade who had serious reading problems. They taught mathematics, science, social studies, and English through the language-experience approach and were pleased to find that these students could learn the content when the materials were presented in a personalized, readable manner. Reading specialists can work with classroom teachers to develop skill in presenting material and information to the students without using texts (e.g., lecture, discussion, tapes, films, pictures, demonstrations, experiments); in drawing students' verbal expressions of what they have learned; in writing language-experience stories based on the students' contributions; and in developing reading and content skills from the written stories.

Reading specialists also can help content teachers rewrite materials that are too difficult. Basically the rewrit-

ing involves cutting sentence length, eliminating complicated sentence structures, and reducing word difficulty
through the use of synonyms.

Herber suggests several teaching strategies that are
useful in helping students in the content areas.[22] He
suggests that teachers use study guides to assist students
in content reading. Study guides assist students to understand content objectives; guide students to use specific text
materials to understand the organization of that material;
and guide them to use that material to meet the stated
objectives. He suggests the use of small-group instruction
to encourge risk taking behavior, and he suggests that such
groups contain a range of achievement levels so that
students can learn from one another.

Bruner and Campbell recommend the study of book
parts so that students can utilize the book organization to
their advantage.[23] Lessons on the use of the table of
contents, the index, the glossary, and the appendices are
recommended. They also recommend lessons that help
students utilize maps, graphs, pictures and cartoons to
assist comprehension.

When students have great difficulty with content
reading, paired learning is recommended. Two students
work together to accomplish the content objectives. In our
clinic we have pairs or small groups of children working
together most of the time. It has a double effect. First, the
student having the most difficulty feels that learning is
possible and that help is available. Second, the helping
student experiences the satisfaction of being able to help
someone else and learns more in the process. It is often
through teaching that one gains a more thorough understanding of the material to be learned.

**Failure to
Comprehend
Most Reading**

For the student who does not respond to any type of
comprehension check, even at relatively easy levels of
performance, remedial techniques are difficult to apply
because starting places are difficult to determine. The
continued use of materials previously used with the students is difficult to defend. For these students, the level of
the material must be easy, the interest of the material must
be high, and the quantity small.

Intensified use of experience stories permits a start
with relatively easy, interesting material of as small a
quantity as desired. Again, students are directed to demon-

strate an understanding of the experience stories, which, because they contain their concepts, can usually be done without difficulty. Once a feeling for this type of activity is developed, the student is exposed through the D-R-T-A or the problem approach to easy, interesting printed material.

Placing the student in reading situations that call for action and reaction is often successful too. Signs, posters, and flash cards calling for reaction are developed from the opportunities that appear daily in and out of the classroom. One type of action material (involving a reaction from students at each step) has been produced under the name of *Programmed Reading*. As students read through the programmed books, they are expected to react to every sentence. Their reactions are immediately reinforced by the correct response (See chapter 9). These materials place students in situations that demand thought about what they are reading.

Vocabulary exercises that involve the students in nonverbal responses to printed symbols have considerable usefulness here. The *Nichols Slides* or their equivalent can be used by starting with very simple, direct commands and progressing as students develop the skill (e.g., start with words such as *sit, stand,* and *jump,* and go to more complicated combinations of words such as *stand and sing now* or *jump three times*). With these students, drill activities without contextual emphasis certainly should be discontinued.

Several techniques have been developed to encourage students to respond to reading in rather nontraditional ways. One involves the use of creative movement to display understanding of a story that has been read to the students or read by them. Materials entitled *Teaching Reading Through Creative Movement* have been successful with seriously handicapped readers.

Another approach is through popular music. With a phonograph, records, and lyrics the stage is set. Students listen to the music and sing along. When the music is over, the meaning of the lyrics is discussed. Rereading is done to verify opinions. Older students seem to respond well to remediation involving music as the motivator.

Reading, which involves essential information for getting along in our society, has also been used effectively. For example, students use driver's manuals and job applications. *Real Life Reading* materials are particularly useful because they are written at low readability levels but they contain highly motivating content such as understanding skateboard rules, how to earn money, and using the tv guide. These materials can be used in teacher-directed lessons until the students feel comfortable enough to work on them independently or in pairs.

EXTENDED REMEDIATION

The problems students encounter related to speed of reading and distractability can become instructional concerns.

Reading Speed

It is not unusual to find that the inappropriate responses of students are due to slow speed. In these cases, students have been asked to read a selection (ample time must be allotted) and to answer several questions. Not having completed the material, their comprehension responses appear to be unsatisfactory. Upon careful examination, it is often found that they have responded properly to those questions related to the material that was read by them and have missed those concerned with material not read. Teachers must question why the students are reading slowly. If they are having difficulty with breaking the written code, activities designed to increase speed of reading are useless. The same is true if they are struggling with unfamiliar concepts. However, some students read slowly because they have applied oral reading speeds to silent reading, lack concentration, or do not know how to vary their reading speed. In these cases, some remedial instruction may be helpful.

For readers who have developed slow reading speeds, the first step is to be certain that they are reading in material that is both easy and interesting. Unknown words should not be introduced, because they slow or stop the readers. The second step is to be certain that the students are reading for personally set purposes. Purposeless reading is bound to be slow. Use the first step in the D-R-T-A for purpose setting. Then help readers to read for those purposes using skimming techniques. We have found the newspaper an excellent material to teach skimming skills. Purposes are set according to what is known from the headlines, pictures, or prior information. Students will find the time needed for reading will vary with the type of purpose set. At times it will be useful for the teacher to set the purposes and permit a limited amount of time to find the answer. This is often best done after the material has been read silently. Readers can be asked a question and then asked where they remember seeing the answer in the passage. They quickly get the idea that one need not read all of the words in the passage to obtain a specific answer. As flexible rates are developed, students can begin to utilize those various rates in specific settings.

Prepared materials are available for students to use for practice exercises in reading within certain time limits. The *SRA Laboratories* have rate-building exercises in which the student must read and answer the question in three minutes. The student should be started with rate-building exercises at very easy levels. The emphasis here is on efficiency in relatively easy material of high interest. The *Standard Test Lessons in Reading* also have the three-minute time limitation. In the remedial session, the three-minute time limit will often need to be adjusted. Since there is no magic formula warranting the three-minute limit, teachers should allow more time for those students who need it. Time should be controlled, however, and the students should be encouraged to complete the work accurately as swiftly as possible.

Other available exercises are designed to motivate improved time performance by emphasizing such measures of reading rate as number of words read per minute. In remediation none of this emphasis should be stressed without equal or greater emphasis on the quality of comprehension that accompanies the rate. The *Better Reading Books* are an example of this type of material to be used with older students, providing personalized charts for easy motivation to better speed and comprehension.

Charts and graphs that illustrate the students' progress are always helpful. These should be constructed so that each student can note small gains in improved rate, so that the aspect of comprehension is charted as well as the reading rate, and so that the goals are realistically within reach. If students reach the graph's goal quickly, the teacher simply makes a new graph, again with easily reached goals. All such charts are maintained as private information.

Distractibility

One must question why the student is distracted. One reason may be that the material is boring—everything else is of more interest than the material. In these cases, the purposes for reading may be adjusted or different materials can be used. However, some students are distracted by the attractiveness of the classroom. Everything is asking for their attention—other students, learning centers, bulletin boards, art work, and sometimes the teacher. In these cases, several suggestions are offered:

1. Distractible students should be placed so that the actions of the others are no more distracting than necessary. In the classroom, this would normally involve a front corner seat.

2. Remediation with distractible students should not be conducted in physical surroundings in which pictures and other distracting objects are prominent. In clinical situations, a plain room where a student's total efforts can be directed to the book should be used initially. In the classroom, distractible students should take their reading instruction in an area of the room that lacks extensive decoration.

3. When distractibility is recognized as a serious limitation, it is often helpful to use books that contain a minimum of pictures, thus permitting students to focus attention upon the print and the skills necessary to read it.

4. Distractible students will need to have skill exercises in periods of shorter duration. They should understand that their entire attention will be expected for a short period of time, after which they may move to another activity and return to reading skill activities later. In the clinic, we have found it helpful to vary activity as much as possible. Unfortunately, such adjustments are difficult and at times impossible in the classroom, for they disrupt the activities of the other students. The classroom teacher, however, should provide a variety of activities and at least refrain from punishing students for distractibility over which they have no obvious control. In the more extreme cases, students should run, jump, and play actively in other ways between their periods of skill activities in reading. Opportunities should be used to get them to be active in class as well as out. For example, the teacher could have them come to the board for some of

their work and let them pass out materials to others, thus providing them with opportunities to release some of their energy. In this way, their tensions are released, and they become more receptive to the required silent work at their seats.

5. Students who are easily distracted generally enjoy a program that has as much consistency as possible. When they can anticipate an interesting routine, they are more likely to be able to concentrate on it to its completion. In rare instances, continued distractible behavior, even after adjustments have been made, calls for medical referral. These students may be demonstrating symptoms of behavior that needs medical attention.

The Reluctant Reader

Most students experiencing difficulty with reading are reluctant to engage in reading activities. However, the term *reluctant reader* as used in this section has to do with those students who have the necessary skills for reading but are reluctant to use them. The need exists for these students to see reading as a rewarding experience. In every lesson, they should be reading for purposes that they feel are important. Drill-type activities should be held to a minimum, and purposeful reading should be increased.

First of all, it is important for these students to develop the attitude that free reading is an activity that the teacher feels is worthwhile. Therefore, free-reading opportunities should occur periodically in all classrooms. *Free reading* in this case implies reading that is not followed by question-and-answer periods, and reading in which the students choose the desired materials. As students develop the understanding that free reading can be fun and is important enough to take school time, gradual changes of attitude are likely to be noted.

The development of an attitude of willingness to read obviously involves the availability of books. The reluctant reader must have books available for free reading in the classroom library, in the school library, and at home. There is little chance to develop attitudes and habits that favor reading when books are difficult or impossible to obtain. School administrators should note that attempts to be thrifty by cutting appropriations for classroom and school libraries place teachers in the position of being unable to encourage the reading habit.

Learning centers that provide students with opportunities for selecting the materials they are going to use, for pacing themselves, and for correcting their own work have been used with considerable success.

Every opportunity should be utilized to promote free reading through the use of peer group recommendations. Students who have read interesting books and want to share them with others can often create more interest than can the teacher. Sharing may be done through brief, voluntary, oral reports; through a classroom card file including the name of the book and the reasons that the student enjoyed it; or through a school book fair where interesting books are displayed.

The teacher can develop interest by reading to the students from books that would be too difficult for them to read themselves but contain stories and ideas of interest. Teachers who read children's books are able to provide book summaries to develop interest in new books as they appear in the library. They also subtly develop attitude by showing enthusiastic interest in their own personal reading.

Teachers may find it useful to consult book lists prepared by authorities to facilitate the guidance of students and the recommendations they are expected to make. *A Teacher's Guide to Children's Books,*[24] *Children and Books,*[25] *Your Children Want to Read,*[26] *Good Reading for Poor Readers,*[27] *Creative Growth through Literature for Children and Adolescents,*[28] *Easy Reading,*[29] and are six examples. Through the use of such resources, the teacher can also recommend to parents books that would be appropriate gifts. Teachers should encourage parents to consider a book a valued, highly desirable gift.

Often reluctant readers are hesistant to select a book that is threatening in terms of volume alone. Perhaps due to pressure from adults, the readers have developed an attitude that taking a book from the library commits them to read the book from cover to cover. The teacher, of course, must discourage this attitude, for we all have been in situations where, after starting a book, we feel no desire to finish it. Nevertheless, too many false starts tend to discourage students from sampling brief portions of books prior to selecting the books from the library. Two materials that let students sample books are *The Literature Sampler* and the *Pilot Library.* Both of these provide the teacher with a guide to the readability of the book and the interest factors involved.

Extensive use is made of book series that, while maintaining high interest, have low vocabulary levels and facilitate interesting reading. Without books to reinforce the skills that are being developed in remediation, the chance for transfer of these skills is seriously limited. The following high-interest, low-vocabulary books have been used effectively in classrooms and clinics:

Series	Vocabulary level	Publisher
About Books	2–4	Children's Press
All About Books	3–6	Random House
American Adventure Series	2–6	Wheeler
Bucky Buttons	1–3	Benefic Press
Cowboy Sam	1–3	Benefic Press
Dan Frontier	1–3	Benefic Press
Deep Sea Adventure Stories	1–3	Harr Wagner
Dolch First Readers	1–2	Garrard
Interesting Reading Series	2–3	Follett
I Want to be Books	1–3	Children's Press
Sailor Jack	1–3	Benefic Press
The Monster Books	2–4	Bowmar

Books such as these are inexpensive and readily available.

Free reading may be permitted in materials such as the *SRA Reading Laboratories* and *The Reading Skill Builders.* When they are used for free reading, students should not be required to answer questions or to do the vocabulary exercises. Of course, selections should be at the recreational reading level.

Other types of material that can be used with reluctant readers are those classified as survival or functional reading materials. Throughout the discussions on remediation, attention has been called to the types of materials that students need to read in order to function and survive in our society. These materials have strong appeal, are relevant, and are essential.

Survival materials include such items as medicine labels, danger signs, road signs, and warning notices. Students who cannot read these types of materials are in danger. Their chances of survival in our society are enhanced when remedial instruction includes these types of materials and the skills needed to read them. Functional reading materials include such items as newspapers, menus, employment forms, and phone books. If students are unable to read such materials, their ability to function in our society is seriously limited.

Originally, survival and functional reading programs were being recommended for only the seriously handicapped reader. Today, however, these programs are recommended for all readers as an important part of the reading program. In many schools, they are developed in learning-center format, and students use them throughout the year.

In remedial programs, survival and functional reading materials are especially important. For seriously handicapped readers, the entire remedial program is developed around such materials. Older students with serious reading problems especially profit from survival and functional reading programs. Sight vocabulary, word attack, and comprehension activities are drawn from the materials. Experience stories supplement the materials. Lists of words such as The Essential Driver's List and The Essential Vocabulary List are utilized.[31] Such programs tend to encourage the readers, and they often ask for instruction beyond the survival and functional programs.

Students' interest and reading needs are surveyed. For example, a group of students may be about to obtain learners' permits for driving a car. All types of materials related to driving can be collected. The students can bring their driver's manuals and car maintenance manuals to the lessons, and instruction can be directed toward the understanding of such materials. Actual auto trips can be planned during which students utilize their learned skills.

One elementary school developed boxes of actual materials needed to function or survive in society. One box included medicine bottles; another contained boxes, cans, and bottles from the grocery shelf; another contained all types of maps. Students picked the area of concentration they wished to pursue and immersed themselves in the activities. A source of ideas about survival and functional reading activities can be found in the suggested readings at the end of this chapter.

REMEDIATION FOR THE CULTURALLY DIFFERENT

From diagnosis, the reader will recall that certain groups of students with experiential backgrounds that are quite different from those of the average student do not make normal progress in reading. Remediation for these students must be designed to permit development of experiential background, success in decoding activities, and personal success in the total reading act.

Teachers must take every opportunity to develop language experiences throughout all remedial sessions. For example, if the student who is reading about the zoo has never been to the zoo, a trip to the zoo, a film, or pictures must precede a reading lesson that has to do with those types of animals that one finds in a zoo. It can be assumed that students have experienced considerable frustration by being placed in reading situations for which they have not had sufficient experiential background. For those who desire a systematic program of language experiences, the *Peabody Language Development Kit,* the *Visual-Lingual Reading Program,* and *Building Prereading Skills Kit-A-Language* mentioned previously can serve as guides.

Decoding activities for these students should always be in terms of language involving concepts that they possess. The use of such auditory reinforcement aids as the *Language Master* are particularly useful in developing sight vocabulary. Written words and a picture representing those words can be placed on the cards. The teacher then orally records the word on the tape that appears on the bottom of the card. The students run these cards through the machine, seeing the word and the picture while hearing the word read.

Although motivation is an important part in all remediation, for these students it is extremely important. Remedial sessions should have an aura of excitement about them, and the values of reading should be subtly stressed.

Selection of books for students from different cultures also should be of prime importance. Attempts to match books used in remediation with the culture of the students proves to be most worthwhile. Spache's book *Good Reading for the Disadvantaged Reader* can serve as a useful reference.[32]

A student working on his sight-word vocabulary by using the Language Master, a device that "reads" words prerecorded by his teacher.

twin   twig

5-9 Card 10

The Reading Game Sound System, Developed by American Learning Corporation for Bell & Howell • ©®ALC 1974

An example of a Language Master Card.

PITFALLS OF REMEDIATION

In concluding the discussion of remedial techniques, the classroom teacher and the reading specialist should consider the following pitfalls that, when not avoided, disrupt the efficiency of many remedial programs.

Fragmented Programs

Remedial programs that focus on the development of skills without the elements of practice and utilization of the skills are generally ineffective. Students in such programs often develop faulty concepts about the purposes for reading. Similarly, programs that fail to provide balance between materials at the independent and instructional levels of the students and materials involving reading content materials are limited in their effectiveness. Many packaged remedial programs are seriously fragmented and should only be used if supplements for balance can be provided.

Compulsion to Teach

Many well-designed programs are ineffective, due to the teacher's compulsion to teach. Involving students in planning, materials selection, purpose setting, and follow up activities really works. By using contracting, the D-R-T-A, survival reading, and other strategies that involve students, remedial programs have excellent opportunities for being successful.

Teaching to Needs

Constant attention to needs or weaknesses tends to overwhelm students. Every remedial program should be designed to focus on strengths of students a large portion of the time.

Oral Reading

Many programs stress oral reading and often oral reading at sight. Although students should develop fluency in oral reading, and oral reading gives teachers useful diagnostic information, there is no justification for its being the major emphasis of the program. Oral reading stresses word pronunciation, an important part of the reading process, but not the ultimate objective. In this chapter, silent reading comprehension has been stressed. Teachers should be certain that silent reading is a part of every lesson.

Oral reading at sight has no place in a remedial program. Students should always be permitted to prepare for oral reading by (1) practicing silently or (2) practicing orally by themselves. By such preparation, students will be able to produce their best, most fluent oral reading.

Illustrating Progress

While often delighted with the progress of their students, many teachers fail to relate this to them. Through contracting, students can understand their progress as each contract is evaluated. Personal charts of progress in sight vocabulary development, books read, and skills mastered are effective. Without recognition of success, the students often become discouraged and quit trying.

Sharing Information

When more than one educator is working with a student, a communication system needs to be developed. Each person should know what the other is doing. Without communication, the student is likely to be exposed to conflicting strategies that serve to confuse rather than enlighten. This pitfall becomes very complicated when the student is being tutored outside of the school. In such cases, communication from one educator to another after each lesson is necessary.

SUMMARY

By selecting approaches for teaching comprehension that reflect what we know about comprehension, one can enhance the chances of a successful program. With these approaches, a variety of instructional techniques can be developed that will make the lessons interesting. Specific activities that are based upon information that was obtained during the diagnosis are often needed. By using high interest materials with all instructional strategies, we can keep interest high and success coming in large quantities and we can assure positive student attitudes.

NOTES

1. Frank Smith, *Understanding Reading* (New York: Holt, Rinehart & Winston, 1978), p. 67.
2. Richard Allington, "If they don't read much how they ever gonna get good?" *Journal of Reading* 21, no. 1 (October 1977): 57–61.
3. Linda Gambrell, Robert M. Wilson and Walter N. Gantt, "An Analysis of Task Attending Behaviors of Good and Poor Readers," unpublished.
4. Dolores Durkin, "What Classroom Observations Reveal about Reading Comprehension Instruction," *Reading Research Quarterly* 14, no. 4 (1978–79): 481–522.
5. Russell G. Stauffer, *Teaching Reading As A Thinking Process* (New York: Harper & Row, 1969).
6. Ibid., p. 12.
7. Betty S. Heathington, Patricia S. Koskinen, and Bruce W. Brigham, "The Problem Approach," *Adult Reading Academy Tutor Handbook*, (College Park, Md.: Adult Reading Academy

Program, University of Maryland, Right to Read Federal Grant, 1979), p. 4.

8. Mary Budd Rowe, *Teaching Science as Continuous Inquiry* (New York: McGraw-Hill, 1973), pp. 242–66.

9. Frank Lyman, Chlene Lopez, and Arlene Mindus, *Elementary Language Arts Guide* (Clarksville, Md.: Howard County Board of Education, 1977), pp. 47–69.

10. Robert M. Wilson and Linda B. Gambrell, *Programmed Comprehension for Teachers,* 2d ed. (Columbus, O.: Charles E. Merrill, 1980), chapters 3 and 4.

11. R. E. Myers and E. Paul Torrance, *For Those Who Wonder* (Boston: Ginn and Co. 1966), p. 1.

12. Bibliography, Newspapers in Education, ed. Merrill F. Hartsorn (Reston, Va.: American Newspaper Publishers Association, 1977).

13. Robert M. Wilson and Marcia M. Barnes, *Using Newspapers to Teach Reading Skills* (Reston, Va.: American Newspaper Publishers Association, 1975).

14. Gerald A. Yoakham, *Basal Reading Instruction* (New York: Prentice-Hall, 1955). Appendix I.

15. William A. Jenkins, ed., "The Educational Scene," *Elementary English* 37, no. 6 (October 1960): 411.

16. George Spache, *Good Reading for Poor Readers* (Champaign, Ill.: Garrard Press, 1968). Chapter 4.

17. Edward B. Fry, "Fry's Readability Graph: Clarifications, Validity and Extensions to Level 17," *Journal of Reading* 21, no. 3 (November 1977): 242–51.

18. W. L. Taylor, "Cloze Procedure—A New Tool for Measuring Readability," *Journalism Quarterly* 30 (Fall 1953): 415–33.

19. John R. Bormuth. "Comparable Cloze and Multiple-Choice Test Comprehension Scores," *Journal of Reading* (February 1967): 295.

20. Francis P. Robinson, *Effective Study* (New York: Harper & Row, 1961).

21. Robert M. Wilson and Nancy Parkey, "A Modified Reading Program in a Middle School," *Journal of Reading* (March 1970): 447–52.

22. Harold L. Herber, *Teaching Reading in the Content Areas,* 2d ed. (Englewood Cliffs, N.J.: Prentice-Hall, 1978). Chapter 4.

23. Joseph F. Bruner and John J. Campbell, *Participating in Secondary Reading* (Englewood Cliffs, N.J.: Prentice-Hall, 1978), pp. 53–62.

24. Nancy Larrick, *A Teacher's Guide to Children's Books* (Columbus, O.: Charles E. Merrill, 1969).

25. May Hill Arbuthnot and Zena Sutherland, *Children and Books* (Chicago: Scott, Foresman & Co., 1977).

26. Ruth Tooze, *Your Children Want to Read* (Englewood Cliffs, N.J.: Prentice-Hall, 1957).

27. George D. Spache, *Good Reading for Poor Readers* (Champaign, Ill.: Garrard Press, 1968).

28. Margaret Gillespie and John Conner, *Creative Growth through Literature for Children and Adolescents* (Columbus, O.: Charles E. Merrill, 1975).

29. Michael F. Graves, Judith A. Boettcher, and Randall A. Ryder, *Easy Reading* (Newark, Del.: IRA, 1979).

30. Marian White, *High Interest Easy Reading for Junior and Senior High School Students* (Urbana, Ill.: National Council of Teachers of English, 1979).

31. Corlett T. Wilson, "An Essential Vocabulary," *The Reading Teacher* 17 (November 1963): 94–96.

32. George D. Spache, *Good Reading for the Disadvantaged Reader* (Champaign, Ill.: Garrard Press, 1970).

SUGGESTED READINGS

Carin, Arthur A., and Sund, Robert B. *Creative Questioning and Sensitive Listening Techniques,* 2d ed. Columbus, O.: Charles E. Merrill Publishing Co. 1978. The treatment that Carin and Sund give questioning is important. They illustrate how our questions help and hinder learning and learners. This is a book for all teachers.

Cook, Jimmie E. and Earlley, Elsie C. *Remediating Reading Disabilities.* Germantown, Md.: Aspen Systems Corp., 1979. This book presents thousands of ideas for enriching instruction beyond the basal series. Chapter 9 focuses on numerous suggestions for making comprehension meaningful and interesting.

————. *Functional Reading.* Volumes 1 and 2. Baltimore, Md.: Maryland State Department of Education, 1975.

Robinson, Francis P. *Effective Study.* New York: Harper & Row, 1961. The teacher of older students who desires to stress study skills in remedial sessions will find the SQ3R technique well defined and explained in this book.

Rowe, Mary Budd. *Teaching Science as Continuous Inquiry.* New York: McGraw-Hill Book Co., 1973. Wait time is presented in detail. Every teacher working with handicapped readers should be familiar with the research and recommendations of Rowe in relation to wait time.

Stauffer, Russell G. *Teaching Reading as a Thinking Process.* New York: Harper & Row, 1969. Stauffer provides rationales and procedures for use of the D-R-T-A. Any student not familiar with the D-R-T-A is referred to this source.

Wilson, Robert M., and Barnes, Marcia M. *Survival Learning Materials.* York, Pa.: College Reading Association, 1974. This book presents a rationale and many ideas for developing survival and functional learning materials.

Wilson, Robert M., and Gambrell, Linda B. *Programmed Comprehension for Teachers,* 2d. ed. Columbus, O.: Charles E. Merrill, 1980. For those in need of fundamental information in the area of reading comprehension, this book will provide a quick overview of the process.

11

Evaluation of Diagnostic, Remedial, and Resource Programs

Effective Evaluation

Change in Student Behavior

Ways to Manipulate Gain Scores

Educator Efficiency

Chapter Emphasis

- Student self-evaluation is encouraged.

- Evaluation is the final step in continuous diagnosis.

- Pretest-posttest evaluation is of questionable value.

- Educator efficiency should be included in evaluation of diagnostic and remedial programs.

EFFECTIVE EVALUATION

Instruction that has been determined by effective diagnosis to meet the strengths and needs of students stands a good chance of succeeding. Upon completion of the remedial program students are likely to show signs of being improved readers. The problem for the educator is to determine what changes have taken place and how strong those changes are.

Many questions need answers if a remedial program is to be effectively evaluated. A few of those questions may be these:

1. Has performance in reading improved?
2. Has attitude toward reading changed?
3. Has reading become a free-time activity of choice?
4. Could more have been accomplished with better diagnosis—or less diagnosis?
5. Was noted progress attributable to the remedial program?
6. Do parents notice behavior changes?
7. Were noted changes in areas stressed in the remedial program?
8. If the program was conducted outside of the classroom, has the classroom teacher been able to build upon progress noted?

These and other questions are to be answered. Naturally, not all of them apply to every situation. And some are more difficult to answer than others. For example, if a student made great gains during a remedial program that was designed to supplement what the teacher was doing in the classroom, to what does one attribute the progress? Maybe the teacher made important adjustments in instruction and is responsible for the student's improvement. Or maybe it was the remedial program. Probably it was some combination of the two.

Guidelines for Evaluation

The following guidelines, applicable to all of education, have particular application when evaluating the effectiveness of remedial reading programs.

Evaluation should be broad in base. Ample allowance must be made for factors such as improved medical attention, relaxation of home pressures, and reaction to both negative and positive diagnosis. If a student has been provided with glasses as a result of physical screening, a proper evaluation of the tutoring program must give consideration to the effect of the glasses as well as to the instruction. In an examination of clinic cases at the University of Maryland, for example, it was found that students referred for inadequate visual screening performance made better progress (as a group) if the parents followed the referral advice than did students whose parents did not follow referral advice. Apparently, attention to the visual needs of these students had an effect upon the progress they made. The appropriate importance to be applied to each factor in evaluation is extremely difficult and, at times, impossible to determine.

Evaluation should be continuous. Actually, evaluation is the final act of continual diagnosis. It involves many of the same processes as diagnosis (i.e., an evaluation of the student's skill development and reading effectiveness). Evaluation of past performance should be considered diagnosis for future instruction; therefore, evaluation is continuous.

Evaluation should be objective. Objective measures of performance should be used as an effort to control bias. One often reads evaluation reports that state that the teachers and students were enthusiastic about the progress that had been made. Although enthusiasm is a highly desirable factor, it cannot be the sole basis for evaluation of program effectiveness. However, nonobjective evaluation techniques are certainly valuable and are not to be precluded by this guideline.

Evaluation should be in terms of established goals. It is sometimes desirable and natural for considerable progress to be noticed in areas for which instruction had not been planned. Such progress, however desirable, must be considered secondary to the goals of the program. We should be cautious about claiming credit for attitude change, for example, unless the program included attitude change in its objectives.

Student Self-evaluation

Student evaluation of remedial progress and of remedial programs should not be overlooked. Students often render insights toward remediation that elude educators. Teachers should seek student self-evaluation and program evaluation, and they should use those in their evaluation of remedial programs.

Pupil-teacher conferences can be used for self-evaluation. If they feel that they will not be penalized for their honesty, many students can provide accurate, useful statements concerning their feelings about how they have done, about their remedial sessions, or about their reactions to specific materials and techniques. Questionnaires also can be used in student evaluation. Questions concerning how they feel they have performed in terms of specific objectives, the portions of the program they enjoyed most and least, and the changes they would recommend may be included. Finally, contract evaluation can be used for self-evaluation. Such evaluation occurs immediately after the contract is completed when students can evaluate their own work honestly.

CHANGE IN STUDENT BEHAVIOR

Of first concern is the effect of the program on student behavior. Basically, four avenues are open for observation of change in student behavior.

Attitude Changes

Discussed first because of importance, attitude changes can be observed. If students enter remedial programs with poor attitudes toward reading, school, and themselves, a major

A major goal of the remedial program is to strengthen good attitudes toward reading, school, and self, including play experiences.

goal of the remedial program would be to improve those attitudes. Data for justification of attitude change are readily available. Behavior in class, willingness to attend to reading tasks, choice of reading for free-time activities, willingness to discuss ideas obtained from reading, and willingness to be helpful to others—perhaps as a tutor—are all examples of useful indicators of attitude changes.

Following remedial sessions at the University of Maryland clinic, parents are petitioned for information on changes they have noticed. The most frequent change noted is that the student is now reading. "He picks up the newspaper and actually reads it." "She reads road signs and bill boards now as we drive down the road." Such comments show that the students are happy to display their reading skills and see themselves as readers. Information can be obtained from students as well as parents to assure the reliability of the responses. The inherent danger of interviews and questionnaires is the tendency for respondents to maintain a "halo" effect. Therefore, it is important that the interview or questionnaire be structured to avoid pointing to obviously expected responses.

Mager suggests that attitude behavior can be objectively observed.[1] He classifies attitude responses as either *approach* or *avoidance*. Approach responses may include such behavior as coming to remedial sessions on time or early, being ready and eager to work, bringing books to class to share, and asking for help with certain skills. Avoidance responses include such behavior as skipping remedial sessions, refusing to work unless directed, forgetting to bring books to class, and disrupting the learning of others. If teachers were to record both types of responses at the beginning, during, and at the conclusion of a remedial program, objectivity could be added to the measurement and evaluation of attitude changes. Attitude changes may be observed easily by parents and by teachers.

Reading Behavior Changes

During remedial activities teachers should keep records of reading behavior changes. What skills in reading can the students display that they could not display when the program started? These data will be available if teachers collect it as instruction proceeds. Evaluated contracts can be a source of such data. Informal, teacher-made check tests can be administered when the teacher feels that some students have developed a new skill. Teachers are more receptive to a discussion of reading behavior changes of their students than to a discussion of test score improvement. The changes in reading behavior can be readily utilized in the daily classroom reading program.

Behavior changes can be noted and recorded best through some type of systematic observation procedure. By establishing a list of kinds of behavior desired and by observing students periodically with the use of a check list, the frequency of that behavior can be recorded. If such behavior were observed two times in twenty observations at the beginning of a program and eighteen times out of twenty observations later in the program, then one can start to talk specifically about that behavior change. Casual observations, however, are very difficult to quantify.

Test Results

Using entry diagnosis as a starting point, posttesting can provide some information about student progress in a remedial program. But the problems are almost great enough to discourage much reliance upon pre-posttest results.

First, the results that report gains in reading levels are impossible to interpret in terms of reading behavior. For example, a report indicating that a student gained four years in reading comprehension tells nothing about the student's reading behavior.

Second, gain scores are notoriously unreliable. On many tests, a difference of one or two items can make a large gain score.

Third, it is difficult to obtain two forms that are truly equivalent of any test. When different forms are used, it is difficult to say whether noticed gains are the result of the remedial program or the test form that was used.

When educators need test results for evaluation of remedial programs, teacher-made criterion-referenced tests (CRTs) containing numerous items for each objective to assure maximum reliability should be used. For example:

1. Word lists taken from reading materials at various levels can be used to measure gains in word recognition.
2. Paragraphs followed by carefully constructed questions taken from materials of varying reading levels can assist in measuring gains in reading accuracy (when reading orally) and in comprehension (when reading silently).
3. Skill quizzes constructed by teachers to assess students' abilities to perform in the areas upon which instruction is given can be used to measure skill development. Such information is useful for those who will work with the students next. The information is reported in terms of reading behavior and can be interpreted further if desirable.

Table 11–1   **Using CRT for Pre-Post Evaluation Comprehension**

	Response to Interpretive Questions Passage Level			
	Grade 5		Grade 6	
	Pre	Post	Pre	Post
Brook	70%	100%	50%	80%
Jennifer	80%	100%	60%	90%
Molly	60%	90%	40%	70%

Table 11–1 illustrates how CRT pre-post evaluation can be used to evaluate comprehension performance. Each student made impressive gains.

Performance in School

For those students who have been removed from the classroom for remedial assistance, the ultimate evaluation of the success of the program is in terms of how well they do when they return to the classroom. Feedback from the classroom teacher is one source of information; grades earned are another.

Teachers can be interviewed or polled through a questionnaire to discuss observed changes in classroom behavior. If the students improve behavior in small groups out of the classroom, we must be certain that those changes carry over into the classroom setting. If not, then the program should be adjusted either in the classroom or for more extended remediation out of the classroom.

Grades are another way of looking at classroom performance; however, there are so many variables that it would not be justified to rely very heavily upon their meaning. Over a long period of time, the grades in Table 11–2 seem to tell us that Nancy was doing poorly prior to remediation and has done much better since remediation.

Table 11–2

Earned Grade Record Over Time

Nancy	Grade 2	Grade 3	Remediation in Grade 4	Grade 5	Grade 6
Reading	D	D	C	B	B
Language	C	C	C	B	B
Spelling	D	F	D	C	C

These changes cannot necessarily be attributed to the remedial program. Maybe Nancy got turned on to learning in fourth grade. However, if most students showed these kinds of improvements after remediation, a bit more confidence could be placed on the remedial program as having some effect.

WAYS TO MANIPULATE GAIN SCORES

The work of Bleismer is included for those who are interested in using gain scores regardless of the severe limitations they have for interpretation.[2] These manipulations of gain scores create some interesting problems when one is attempting to evaluate a remedial program through gain scores.

Grade-Level Improvement

Bleismer, in citing three basic postremediation evaluation techniques, calls this a simple pre- and post-test comparison. If a student enters a remedial program reading at 4.5 grade level and leaves the reading program at 5.5 grade level, it can be concluded that he has gained 1.0 years in grade level. Obviously, the adequacy of the test instrument used to determine grade-level performance limits this aspect of evaluation. It does not account for the student's chronological or mental age increase or for changes that would have occurred without remediation.

Reading-skill performance as compared to grade level is of particular interest to both the classroom teacher and the principal, for it has much to do with the placement of the student in a particular room and within a class.

Reading Potential

Evaluation in this area attempts to determine whether students are working up to their potentials. Bleismer calls attention to the fact that potential (mental age) will change with age and that estimates must be adjusted for effective evaluation.[3] Regardless of a student's grade-level performance and ability to perform in an assigned classroom, growth up to potential is generally considered a desirable goal of remediation. In Table 11–3, if Jim has an estimated potential of 5.0 and a reading level of 3.0, his working development is lagging behind his mental development by 2.0 years. If, after a semester of work, his reading level rises to 4.2, his potential will have to be reestimated before growth can be measured.

Table 11–3   **Comparison of Potential and Achievement**

Jim	January	May
Potential	5.0	5.8
Reading	3.0	4.2
Difference	2.0	1.6

Note that in Table 11–3 Jim's reading potential increased as he grew older, thereby lessening the apparent effect of the difference in reading grade-level changes.

Remedial sessions accelerated his growth over his potential by .4 years (found by subtracting the differences). Reading potential techniques will be of more interest to the reading specialist than to the classroom teacher or the parent. One major problem with using potential as a standard occurs when remedial efforts are being made to improve skills related to these measures of potential. In those cases, potential is not a standard. For example, if a remedial program includes opportunities for language development, opportunities of potential improvement are also included. Such programs actually have resulted in considerable improvement on tests of intelligence.

Past Performance

Evaluation of skill improvement in terms of students' previous performance rates is of some advantage with older students. Bleismer is asking that the identifiable variables be controlled.[4] Suppose that Judy (Table 11–4) has completed six years of school and has scored at grade level 4.6 before remediation is begun. This indicates an average growth of .6 years of reading skill for each year in school

Evaluation of the student's previous performance rates is of some advantage with an older student.

$(4.6 - 1.0 \div 6)$. Note that 1.0 must be subtracted, as all children start with a reading level of 1.0 (the zero month of first grade). If she obtained a reading level of 5.5 by the end of one year in remediation, she would have gained .9 years of skill in one year $(5.5 - 4.6 = .9)$. Yet she is not reading up to grade level and may not be reading up to expectations. She has not progressed even one full year under intensive remediation. But her improvement is greater than it has been in the past, thus indicating that she is profiting from the remedial program.

Table 11-4

Comparison of Current Achievement with Past Achievement

	Years in School	Average Yearly Gain Before Tutoring	Gain During Year of Tutoring	Growth Attributed to Tutoring
Judy	6	.6 $(4.6 - 1.0 \div 6)$	.9	.3

Note that the gain of .9 years is greater by .3 years than could have been expected from the average of previous efforts. While of interest to the reading specialist and the classroom teacher, the rate of improvement during remediation is of little interest to the student or the parent, especially if the student remains limited in ability to perform in the classroom.

Evaluation of past performance is limited by the unlikely assumption that the past performance was evenly distributed. However, older students who are seriously handicapped in reading are less likely to score effectively in the other aspects of evaluation even though they are making significant progress.

Limitations

All of the evaluation techniques suggested above are limited by the instruments being used to make comparisons. Standardized tests are inherently unreliable and cause notable gains to be suspect, due to the error on the measuring instrument. Grade-equivalent scores on these tests are not equal units for measuring gains. If such tests are used at all, standard scores should be used. In addition, the test selected may not measure the skills that were the

As a reading resource teacher, I have had numerous opportunities to assist many classroom teachers with the arduous responsibility of meaningfully interpreting group standardized test data for the purposes of instructional planning and parent communication.

In an effort to respond to the ramifications of Public Law 94-142, as well as additional state and local school district accountability demands, many teachers are confronted with the chore of trying to sensibly explain such concerns as why a student achieved a score of 2.4 on a pre-test in the fall, and then received a score of 1.9 as a post-test score in the spring!

Some schools have found it easier to eliminate the grade equivalent discussion and focus their efforts on interpretations of stanine and percentile scores. They have been assured by people like me that while the term *stanine* may appear more difficult to understand than the term *grade equivalent,* that it is a more reliable score to use when evaluating the scores of individuals. Given this assurance, how then do you help the classroom teacher provide meaningful instructional goals or communicate useful information to parents when a raw score of 43 on one subtest yields a stanine of 9 and a raw score of 42 (on the same subtest) yields a stanine of 6!

While we still appear wedded to the use of group standardized tests, examples such as the two above helped convince me that group standardized testing cannot help classroom teachers provide for appropriate individual instructional objectives, nor can it help us interpret individual students' achievement and progress.

In an effort to obtain some meaningful data on individual students, sixteen classroom teachers worked with me on a self-evaluation project. Following specific evaluation of selected comprehension skills, through the use of a teacher-made IRI, a survey of selected phonetic skills, and a vocabulary meaning test, students were grouped for instruction relevant to their strengths in each of the three areas. Each teacher met, with each instructional group, three times per week in order to provide students the opportunity to self-evaluate their progress. Students were asked two questions: (1) How do you feel about the activity? and (2) How do

you think you did? Before their discussion with the teacher, students filled out their record keeping sheet using a ☺ , ☺ , or ☹ to indicate whether they felt good, indifferent, or poor about the activity, and whether they felt they had accomplished the objective to their satisfaction.

In addition to these individual student records, teachers were asked to keep anecdotal records of students' comments made during the self-evaluation sessions, as well as samples of the work the students evaluated. Records were kept over the course of a six week period. Following the six weeks I met with all sixteen teachers. Several interesting, notable observations surfaced during our discussion.

All teachers involved volunteered that one of the chief advantages of this experience was that it helped them focus their attention onto an exact instructional objective, with a specified number of activities designed to help students master the objective.

All teachers noticed that there was a definite need for continuous diagnostic assessment of students' specific skills, as many differences appeared between the students' original scores and their ability to participate in an activity once they were actually placed in a teaching situation.

Most teachers observed that through discussion of individual students' self-evaluation they became aware of which students did poorly due to misinterpretation of the assignment and which students did poorly because they did not understand the concept involved in the objective.

Most teachers also agreed that by participating in this experience their awareness of skills students needed as well as appropriate materials and experiences for increasing these skills was improved.

Finally, all teachers unequivocally agreed that they felt more certain that they were providing the most suitable instructional experiences for their students. They also felt confident about their ability to communicate their students' growth in terms of concrete goals directly related to their instructional program.

Marcia M. Wilson

objectives of the remediation, and the standardization population may be mismatched with the remedial group. It is recommended that standardized tests be used to indicate gains with groups of students and that informal tests be used to measure the gains of individual students.

Two other problems occur when evaluating in terms of standardized tests. First, all standardized tests contain error in their measurement; the amount of error makes score changes possible by chance. Therefore, small gains over short periods of time cannot be measured by standardized tests. Second is the problem of the phenomenon referred to as *regression*. Stated simply, if a group of students were given a standardized test today and then the same test were readministered a week later, low-scoring students would tend to improve their scores (scores would move toward the mean), while high-scoring students would decrease their scores (scores would move toward the mean).

EDUCATOR EFFICIENCY

The efficiency of an educator is more difficult to evaluate and is, therefore, less likely to receive the evaluation efforts that student growth receives. Educator efficiency in programs should be evaluated in the following areas.

Adequacy of Diagnosis

Because of emphasis placed upon the proper use of diagnosis and the time spent in accomplishing it, there is valid reason for its inclusion in evaluation. Educators must determine whether diagnosis has uncovered the remedial strengths and needs of the student effectively and precisely. Furthermore, they must decide that the diagnosis, while not overextended, is complete enough to cover the areas of the students' skill development. When there is a failure to evaluate in all areas, there is a likelihood that inefficiency will develop in remedial sessions. At times, teachers use tests that, for them, appear to supply essential information for a diagnosis; however, upon closer examination, these tests do not provide any information that could not be determined more easily by other diagnostic techniques.

Adequacy of Remedial Approach

As educators become accustomed to working in remediation, specific approaches often develop into standard procedures with all students. The error resulting here, unless there are constant attempts at evaluation, is that diagnosis is disregarded, since a given remedial approach is used with all students. For example, if all students were to be tutored through the use of the language-experience approach, diagnostic conclusions are not used to determine the remedial approach. It is through evaluation of remedial approaches that the educator is led to develop the variety of effective approaches prescribed by the diagnostic strengths and needs of the students.

Adequacy of Remedial Techniques

Similar to the difficulty of adequate remedial approaches, a prescribed technique used with all students regardless of the remedial approach is equally limiting and should be avoided through careful evaluation of remedial techniques. For example, a graph to illustrate progress will not motivate all students in all remedial techniques. The evaluation of techniques will save time in remediation and lead the educator to those techniques best suited to the strengths and needs of students.

Adequacy of Remedial Materials

As educators become familiar with the manuals and contents of the variety of materials available in remediation, they are likely to select and use those that appeal most to them. This action is proper when these materials are selected after an evaluation of their effectiveness; however, if they are selected on the basis of familiarity alone, their adequacy should be evaluated. As the flood of materials continues, the educator will need to be involved with more material evaluation.

A variety of techniques is available to assist the educator in the various aspects of evaluation discussed above. The teacher can and should consult with other teachers; ask for help from a reading resource person in the school or district; read evaluations of materials in the professional literature; talk with students about books they like and dislike; conduct studies using certain materials with one group of students and other materials with another group; examine the activities required by the materials and compare them to objectives for the remedial program; and give students choices of materials to use, observing their consistent selection of one over another.

Adequacy of Total School Efforts

If requested, the reading specialist should be able to conduct an evaluation of the total school efforts in the area of diagnostic and remedial reading. Assuming that the reading specialist is acquainted with research design and controlled experimentation techniques and has the ability to interpret research data, there is little reason for not using such techniques. Austin, Bush, and Heubner discuss the school survey in detail with specific suggestions for its implementation.[5] If many teachers are unprepared for this type of evaluation, it will be necessary to call upon others, for example, school or university personnel, to assist. Such a course of action has an added advantage in many cases, because evaluation conducted by persons not directly involved in the program lessens the role of bias.

Adequacy of the Resource Role

If the reading specialist functions in a resource role, that role deserves careful evaluation also. How one functions on screening committees, in teaming situations, in helping teachers try new ideas or materials, and when conducting staff development sessions are examples of areas that may be included.

Reading specialist self-evaluation, teacher evaluation, and supervisor evaluation can all be included. Questionnaires, observations, and teacher requests for assistance can be used to compile an evaluation report.

The resource role is of major importance (see chapter 12) and therefore should receive a most objective and careful evaluation. If ignored, there is a real possibility that one may go on performing functions that are not valued by others and are thereby ineffective. For example, a reading specialist may develop a newsletter each month that highlights new materials that have arrived in the school. If, upon evaluation, the reading specialist finds that no one reads the newsletter, then another form of communication about new materials needs to be developed. To continue with the newsletter would be a waste of effort and the continuation of an ineffective way for informing teachers of new materials.

If it is discovered that teachers do not value the resource role and would prefer that the reading specialist work more with students, a reevaluation of the activities in that resource role needs to be undertaken. Discussions with staff and supervisors may facilitate a better use of the specialist's time and efforts. For example, one may find that teachers really appreciate the efforts to facilitate the use of new materials by way of demonstrations but they do not value the one-half hour per week staff development sessions on classroom management. A reevaluation of the staff development sessions would then be in order and a possible increase in the demonstration of new materials may be useful.

SUMMARY

Evaluation should be carefully planned for all remedial sessions. To make valid comparisons, pretesting and noting of behavior prior to remediation are essential. To evaluate the successes of students in a remedial program, teachers should be expected to use assessments of attitudes, reading skills demonstrated, test performance, and classroom performance. To assure this professional growth, teachers should continuously evaluate their own effectiveness in both diagnosis and remediation.

NOTES

1. Robert F. Mager, *Developing Attitude toward Learning* (Belmont, Calif: Fearon Publishers, 1968), pp. 21–29.
2. Emery P. Bleismer, "Evaluating Progress in Remedial Reading Programs," *The Reading Teacher*, March 1962, pp. 344–50.
3. Ibid.
4. Ibid.
5. Mary Austin, Clifford L. Bush, and Mildred Huebner, *Reading Evaluation* (New York: The Ronald Press, 1961).

SUGGESTED READINGS

Ahmann, J. Stanley, and Glock, Marvin D. *Evaluating Pupil Growth.* Boston: Allyn & Bacon, 1959. In Chapter 14, the authors discuss the aspects of evaluating personal-social adjustment. Chapter 16 is devoted to diagnosis and remediation. The entire book will provide the reader with an effective basis for evaluation.

Austin, Mary C.; Bush, Clifford L.; and Huebner, Mildred H. *Reading Evaluation.* New York: The Ronald Press, 1961. This entire book is devoted to the subject of evaluation in reading. Without restricting themselves to remedial evaluation, the authors have provided specific evaluation techniques and tests. The reading specialist will find this book to have particular value when he is considering an all-school survey.

Bleismer, Emery P. "Evaluating Progress in Remedial Reading Programs." *The Reading Teacher,* March 1962, pp. 344–50. A detailed explanation of three basic techniques for evaluating remedial programs is provided in this article. Reviewed in this chapter, these techniques can be studied more thoroughly by a quick review of this excellent article.

Farr, Roger. *Reading: What Can Be Measured?* Newark, Del.: International Reading Association, 1969. Farr takes an objective but critical look at evaluation instruments used by reading personnel in the schools and clinics. He provides guidelines for the application of research to work in reading. Farr has made a significant contribution that should be considered required reading.

Mager, Robert F. *Developing Attitude Toward Learning.* Belmont, Calif.: Fearon Publishers, 1968. This is a highly valuable book that stresses the need for teachers to observe objectively children's attitudinal responses to their instruction.

Mager, Robert F. *Preparing Instructional Objectives.* Belmont, Calif.: Fearon Publishers, 1962. This is an extremely well-written, short paperback designed to help teachers gain skills in developing behavioral objectives. For those unfamiliar with behavioral objectives, Mager's book is required reading.

Maginnis, George. "Evaluating Remedial Reading Gains." *Journal of Reading,* April 1970, pp. 523–28. This article discusses several of the inherent problems involved in evaluation of remedial reading. Maginnis leaves the reader with several positive suggestions for avoiding those problems.

Strang, Ruth, and Linguist, Donald M. *The Administrator and the Improvement of Reading.* New York: Appleton-Century-Crofts, 1960. This booklet, designed for the administrator, has evaluation clues built into each chapter. Chapter 4 addresses itself to the evaluation of suitable reading programs. Appendix B is a guide for teacher self-appraisal. These two references will be of interest to the reader who desires more information on teacher effectiveness evaluation.

Wilhelms, Fred T. *Evaluation as Feedback and Guide.* Washington, D.C.: ASCD, 1967. This important book concerns the uses of evaluation for decision making—a "must" reading for those planning evaluation programs.

12

Parental Roles

Parents Can Help

Chapter Emphasis

- Parents can help.

- Parent involvement is increasing.

- Parent training programs are helpful.

"Let your child alone!" or "Don't worry, we'll handle it" are quite often the only suggestions that some teachers have to offer parents who are seeking ways to help their children with reading difficulties. Today, such advice is inappropriate and will likely fall upon deaf ears, for parents want to help their children, can help their children, and will help their children! As the educational level of our adult population rises, as the emphasis upon education for success in life continues, as education continues to be examined in the public press, and as commercial exploitations of parental concerns expand, it is no longer defensible to keep parents from assisting their children with reading. It is imperative that educators realize this fact and seek ways for parents to be most helpful in terms of the educational goals that have been established.

On the other hand, left without guidance, parents may do things to "help" their children that may be inappropriate and often harmful. For example, it is not uncommon for uninformed parents to attempt to motivate a child through comparisons with brothers and sisters or playmates. More often than not, undirected parental activity merely compounds the child's aversion to reading and actually interferes with progress in a remedial program. So, again, it behooves us to direct parents to that role which will fulfill most effectively the educational goals that have been established.

Although not a hard and fast rule, parental anxiety is likely to mount as a child's progress in reading declines.[1] There comes a point where parental anxiety is felt by the child to such a degree that it complicates the reading problem. These parents, too, must have their concern and anxiety channeled into useful, helpful educational activities. It does not help to tell the parents not to worry. The answer is to establish for them a role through which they can be most helpful.

Clinical and classroom diagnostic and remediation situations inherently demand that the parental role vary.

The difference in roles is generally one of degree, since by the very nature of clinical situations the parents are more actively engaged in what their child is doing. In this chapter, as the role of the parent is discussed in diagnosis, remediation, and prevention of reading problems, suggestions are termed in reference to the classroom teacher and the reading specialist so that they may direct the parent toward useful activities. It certainly is not to be assumed that all parents can perform all of the roles to be discussed.

PARENTS CAN HELP!

Parents teach their children to walk, to talk, and to do numerous other useful activities required in our society. Educators rely heavily upon the ability of the parents to do these jobs well. When they do not fulfill this responsibility, parents leave their children ill-equipped for progress in school. As the children develop difficulties in reading, it is logical to call upon their first teachers, their parents, to assist the educator in any way that will be useful. The suggestions that follow, then, are based upon the following beliefs:

1. Parents can help.
2. Parents often know what makes their children react most effectively.
3. Children want parental support and assistance and strive to please their parents through school success.
4. Without parent-teacher teamwork, success with severely handicapped readers will be unnecessarily limited.
5. When directed toward useful roles, parents are usually willing to follow the advice of educators.

Parental Roles in Diagnosis

Except for the classroom teacher, parents most likely will be the first to recognize that their children are not making satisfactory progress in the development of reading skills. When the classroom teacher fails to observe the signs of frustration in a child, one can be certain that such awareness will not escape the parents for long. The responsibility for the initial identification of the reader's difficulties, in such cases, often falls to the parents. Parents properly may be directed to observe their children in reading and to call any of the following symptoms of frustrated reading to the attention of the classroom teacher or the reading specialist.

1. Avoidance of reading
2. Inability to complete classroom assignments or homework
3. Inability to discuss with parents material that the child has just read
4. Habitual difficulty in attacking unknown words, especially if the problem is noticed after two or three years of schooling
5. Word-by-word, nonfluent oral reading, especially when the child has practiced this reading silently before reading it orally
6. Complaints from the child of visual discomfort in reading periods of fifteen minutes or more

By directing the educator's attention to specific symptoms such as these, parents may identify reading problems before they become serious enough to necessitate the more formal types of reading diagnosis and remediation. Upon receiving observations such as these from parents, the educator should conduct as much diagnosis as is necessary to find the nature of the problem.

That many parents will become overly anxious while observing their children for these symptoms must also be considered. It is just as important for anxious parents to know that their children do not have reading problems, when this is the case, as it is for other parents to know the nature of their children's reading problems. In this way, needless anxieties can be relaxed, thus creating better learning situations.

Many schools involve parents in each step of the diagnosis. Permission is requested to assess the student's reading achievement. Results are discussed with parents. And parents are involved with screening committees that are seeking the most appropriate resource assistance for the student. In cases involving "handicapped" students, parent signatures must be obtained to place the student in an optimum learning environment. Public Law 94-142 requires that parent signature and provides for parental appeals when they disagree with the placement of their "handicapped" child.

Another important role of parents in diagnosis is the supplying of information in support of or in conflict with the tentative hypotheses that have been established in classroom diagnosis or initial screening techniques. The parents' role in clinical diagnosis, then, is to supply supporting observations concerning their children's work in school, attitudes toward reading, and physical well being. See pages 149–151 for a sample parent questionnaire. Without this information, which is frequently obtainable through either questionnaires or interviews, the reading specialist is likely to err in making judgments based on relatively short exposure to the children. It is generally more effective to obtain information from parents after tentative hypotheses have been reached, lest the feelings of the parents tend to bias the examiner.

Parents have complete responsibility for the followup in areas in which referral has been made. It is the right and the responsibility of parents to attend to the physical and emotional needs of their children, and it is the parents to whom we most often look for assistance in taking children to vision specialists, neurologists, psychiatrists, and other specialists.

As parents become involved in the diagnosis, it is important that they also be consulted concerning the findings. Perhaps nothing is more frustrating to parents than to know that their child has undergone extensive study, yet they have not been consulted about the findings. However, making diagnostic conclusions available to parents is far more than a courtesy, for quite often it is the parents to whom the suggestions alleviating the problem most appropriately apply. At times, parents are consulted concerning their child's problem; from that point on, the child improves and no longer needs remedial help.

Any time a diagnosis has been conducted on a student, the parents should be informed, in detail, of the results. In the past, it was suggested that parents should not receive a full report with test scores because it was thought they could not interpret those scores and might misuse them. Consequently, parents were making inferences from vague descriptions, inferences that were far more serious than the case called for. Today the position has changed. Educators now suggest that parents get a full report of any diagnosis, including test scores. In this way, parents are not left with vague descriptions of their child's performance. The policy today is to give the parents the same report sent to the schools, discussing every aspect of it with the parents, including test scores, their interpretations, and the recommendations.

Parents appreciate this openness. They feel fully informed, and they know what information is going to the school. They can follow up the report through a conference with the teacher. Naturally, instances will occur when a parent may abuse such information and go to the school with an "I told you so" type of comment. In general, however, far less abuse occurs when parents are fully informed than when they are partially informed.

Parental Roles in Remediation

For parents to have any role at all in remediation, there must be a general understanding of the educational goals set by the person conducting the remediation. It is not only ethically appropriate for the educator to inform the parents of such goals, but reaching the goal is far more feasible when the parents are effectively involved. The first task, therefore, is to inform parents of realistic goals and of the general approaches to be used in attaining these goals. It is extremely helpful if these goals are short range and easily attainable so that the child, the parent, and the educator all can see clearly that progress is being made. Of course, this will necessitate contacting the parent as the goals are readjusted and as progress in reading skills is made. Again, contacts with parents are most effective when they occur in consultation sessions.

The most appropriate role for the parent, after an understanding of the program has been made available, is to provide situations in the home whereby the skills learned in remediation can be reinforced. Although reinforcement activities may be time consuming, parents should recognize the necessity for providing reinforcement opportunities. Specifically, this work involves parents in the following actions:

1. Providing a quiet, comfortable, and relaxing place for reading in the home
2. Providing a planned time during the day when the household becomes suitable for reading: the television is turned off; other members of the family pursue reading

interests; and a pleasant attitude regarding this time is created

3. Assisting the child with material that is difficult in either word pronunciation or sentence and paragraph meaning. This work, of course, involves the availability of one of the parents but should not be construed to imply that the parent must be "breathing down the child's neck." On the contrary, the parent (while reading something of interest to himself) simply may be in the same room and available to the child, if needed.

4. Assisting the child with follow up exercises that are sent home after a remedial session. The parent must understand that the child is learning a skill and will probably not be letter-perfect in these attempts. Neither the classroom teacher nor the reading specialist will send material home for practice unless there is relative assurance that it can be completed with some satisfaction. However, there will be instances when, regardless of the care taken, the child will take home materials that are too difficult to read without assistance.

5. Being available when an audience is needed or when discussion is desirable following either oral or silent reading. Parents should display interest in what the child has read, thus permitting a sense of having done something that pleases the parents.

6. Providing the praise and reward for demonstrations of skill development. Since the materials sent home for practice should allow the child to demonstrate reading strengths, positive reactions from parents can do much to help the child feel good about being a reader.

These activities should be conducted in cooperation with the reading specialist or the classroom teacher; specific activities should be originated by these educators in terms of the goals that already have been explained to the parent. Furthermore, it is helpful to demonstrate these techniques to parents. Illustrating how effectively the recommended suggestions actually work with their child builds the parents' confidence in the recommendations.

On the negative side, parents should understand what not to do as well as what to do. Depending upon the educational goals, the educator should anticipate the types of problems likely to arise and direct the parents away from them. For example, it is far better to have the parents in the role of reinforcing skills learned in remedial sessions than it is to have them attempt to teach these skills themselves. If the parents feel that there is a great deficiency in phonics skills, for example, the educator should be informed and the parents provided with an explanation of when that skill will become a part of the program. Furthermore, it should be made clear that no matter how great the temptation to have the child "sound out the word," it is the parents' job to tell the child unknown words until the sounding skill is approached remedially. Note that these examples relate to phonics. Although it is in this area that most parents feel most anxious, it is the area in which they do the poorest job of assisting the educators. As a general rule, therefore, parental attention should be directed away from instruction in phonics, while opportunities are provided for the parents to notice their child's development in reading through carefully prepared home assignments. Once again, children demonstrate their strengths to parents through such activities as reading orally an experience story that they have mastered, drilling for five minutes on the word cards, they have mastered, and discussing exciting problem-solving activities that they worked on in school.

Another parental role in remediation is obtaining books for the children to read. Normally, the educator will supply the first books from materials available in the remedial program; however, since the supply of books is often limited, parents can be encouraged to assume responsibility for obtaining books. The educator, in this case, will supply the parent with a list of appropriate books for the child to read at home, asking the parents to obtain these books from libraries, friends, book stores, and the like. Consideration for the level and the interest factors of available books should be evaluated in the recommendations made to parents. It is particularly worthwhile to recommend books to parents near the child's birthday or at holidays so that books can be included on gift lists. More than simply supplying the child with a book, such activity develops the attitude that a book is something of considerable worth, for it is given as a special gift. Parents should also take the responsibility for taking their children to the library on a regular basis. There the children experience self-selection of books and develop the library habit.

Parents commonly desire to supplement the efforts of the remedial program with commercially available materials. Unless these materials are in accordance with the educational goals that have been established and unless the educator knows of the materials and can recommend their appropriateness for this child, they should be avoided. By placing parents in the teacher's role, unsuitable commercial materials involve the parents to a degree that is unprofitable for them, the child, and the educational goals for which they are all striving.

In our clinic we involve parents in two more ways. First we conduct seminars that are designed to help parents understand the nature of their child's reading difficulties and to help them understand our approach in remediation. These seminars often include the involvement of public school personnel such as principals, reading specialists, and supervisors, so that parents can obtain answers to their concerns about their child's schooling. The seminars are quite popular and we believe that they reduce a lot of unnecessary anxiety.

We further involve parents as instructional materials constructors. We noticed that many parents bring their

Next to the classroom teacher, parents can do more to prevent difficulties from arising than anyone else.

children to the clinic and wait for them instead of going home and coming back. We asked them if they would like to help. All volunteered. Clinicians would leave plans and materials for the construction of games, centers, or posters. The parents would develop the materials. We always had the parents personally deliver the materials to the clinician and stay to observe them in use. This process increased parental understanding of our remedial program.

Parental Roles in Prevention

It is well to discuss the role of parents once children have developed reading problems, but it is far more important to reach parents before children develop such problems. Next to the classroom teacher, parents can do more to prevent the development of difficulties than anyone else. But part of the problem here is to communicate effectively with parents who are not anxious about their children's lack of success in reading. When unconcerned, parents are less likely to seek assistance even if it becomes necessary, thus implying to the children that they do not care. Each school and each teacher should take every opportunity to present preventive information to parents. Programs during Education Week, PTA meetings, individual conferences with parents, and notes sent to the home may be used to help parents prevent the occurrence of reading problems.

The following suggestions are designed to inform parents of activities that diminish the possibility of reading problems' developing. They should be recommended by educators with discretion and for application when appropriate. No attempt is made here to supply a formula that will work with equal effectiveness with all parents.

Physical care.   Parents who desire to avoid the complications involved with failure in school (in reading, particularly) should reflect upon their children's physical needs. A visual examination prior to school entrance and at least every other year thereafter is excellent insurance. An annual physical examination with follow ups that are recommended by the family doctor eliminates the necessity of waiting until symptoms of physical disability become so apparent that they interfere with success in school. Many physical difficulties go unnoticed until failure in school is so acute that remedial programs are inadequate to handle them. For example, if children have refused to read for years because of visual discomfort, they have a void of reading experiences for which, at times, it is impossible to compensate.

From the number of children who come to school too tired to accomplish the expected assignments during a given day, it seems that parents may well require ample amounts of sleep for their children. Since most teachers' consider the first period of the morning the most effective instructional time, it is imperative that children be awake and alert. Parents who need suggestions concerning the amount of sleep their children require should consult the family doctor.

Hand in hand with alertness is the need for a substantial breakfast to replace an inadequate breakfast or none at all. Children who go without breakfast, fighting hunger long before the noon hour, are incapable of efficient use of school time. Recommendations for minimum breakfast requirements are readily available; however, when in doubt, parents should consult the family doctor. If parents send children who are physically sound to school, the educational program has a greater chance for success.

Emotional climate. When the school receives children who are secure, loved at home, and understood, interference with success in school is further reduced. Parents can implant an attitude that learning will be fun and, though difficult at times, always worthwhile. They can develop an attitude by incorporating (1) no threats for failures in school (e.g., withdrawing television privileges), (2) no promises for success in school (e.g., paying for good grades), (3) respect and confidence in the teachers, and (4) interest and enthusiasm for what is being accomplished in school. Parents should avoid criticism of the school and the teachers in front of their children. As parents, they have a right to voice their objections, but they should do so to the school authorities and the teachers rather than to the children. When children have the attitude that the school is weak and the teachers are incompetent, learning difficulties are compounded. Furthermore, parents can be directed to avoid as much as possible the direct and/or subtle comparison of their children to peers and siblings. The reaction of a child who is striving to do as well as a sister is seldom positive or desirable. More concern should be demonstrated over each child's ability to perform as well as

Parents want to help their children learn to read. In our elementary school we feel very strongly that parents should be actively involved in their child's reading program.

In our Corrective-Remedial Reading Program, we use games to teach reading, because they're individualized and adaptable. They give the necessary practice and repetition without the dullness and monotony characteristic of drills, worksheets, or workbooks. Children like games and coaxing is rarely, if ever, needed. By basing each game on a popular format such as Bingo, directions are kept to a minimum. Children know these game formats and can even play many of them independently once they have been explained.

We discovered that reading games were very effective in improving specific reading skills, but we also noticed a slight problem. Children were highly motivated to play them and often wished to continue playing even when we had run out of time. To solve this problem, we decided to talk to the parents at PTA about continuing games at home.

When the parents arrived, we explained how games were being used to reinforce reading skills. We described some games being used and mentioned some of the reading skills that were featured.

Parents were then invited to the reading room, where their own children taught them how to play the games. Having the children teach their parents how to play the games did much to enhance the self-concepts of the children. Proud parents thoroughly enjoyed themselves.

We distributed a booklet to the parents containing complete directions for constructing reading games using inexpensive and easily available materials (magic markers, index cards, file folders, etc.). At the request of several parents, we scheduled a time each week when able and interested parents could come to school to construct reading games along with us. We later arranged a loan system so that the teacher-constructed games in the reading room could be signed out by the parents and used at home at the suggestion of the child's classroom teacher.

The enthusiasm, response, and follow-through of the parents was tremendous. One dad commented several weeks later, "This sure beats the two-hour battles I used to have trying to get my son to practice reading at home. It's fun. And it really works!"

Communication between home and school has improved as a result of this game sharing. We have witnessed considerable improvement in reading for many of the children who have been using the reading games at home with their parents. Probably the best thing that has happened has been the strengthening of the bond between parent and teacher and the cooperative efforts of both to help children achieve their educational goals. Parents truly feel a part of their child's educational program and this positive parent-teacher relationship is clearly evident to the child.

Pat Russavoge

possible; performance that matches a sibling's should not be the goal adopted to satisfy parents.

Setting an example. Probably all parents have heard that it is good for them to set an example for their children. In reading, that example can be one of reading for enjoyment. Children who from their earliest years notice that both parents seem to enjoy spending portions of their leisure time reading can develop a favorable attitude toward reading before entering school. Some leisure reading may be done orally for the children or for the family. Note that all oral reading should be accomplished with as much skill as possible; therefore, parents should first read silently all materials that they plan to read orally. Often parents are inclined to discontinue oral reading as soon as their children develop skills in reading; however, oral reading by parents should continue. Parents should take every opportunity to read to children the books that are of interest to the children but that are too difficult for their developed reading skills. Children who come to school with family leisure reading experiences have definite advantages in learning to read, for they realize the wonders that reading can unlock for them.

Some parents have found success with a daily silent reading time. All family members read for ten to twenty minutes. They read materials of their choice for their own enjoyment. Such sessions provide additional models of reading for fun.

Providing language experiences. Parents are to be encouraged to use every opportunity to widen their children's language experiences. Through such activities as reading to children, taking them on trips, and discussing events with them, situations are created in which language can be developed through experiences. Parents should be encouraged to lead children into discussions that will add listening and speaking vocabulary words to the experiences. It is, of course, the listening and speaking vocabularies upon which the reading vocabularies hinge. Parents miss opportunities to help their children by failing to discuss trips and experiences with them. Trips about which little is said are not necessarily useless, but all parents should be encouraged to reinforce experiences with language experiences relating to them. For example, during a trip, parents can let children help read maps, menus, and road signs; they can take photographs and discuss them later; they can help children write captions for photographs to be placed on the backs of pictures. Alerted to the potential of structuring language experiences, parents can learn to use them more effectively.

Regulation of out-of-school activities. Parents who permit their children to do as they wish with all out-of-school time indicate their lack of concern about what the children do. First, parents must understand that a full school day takes a good bit of concentration and is mentally fatiguing. Therefore, children should be exposed to opportunities after school for active, expressive free play. Outdoor play, which physically releases children, is desirable when possible. Secondly, the school program relies upon the interest and excitement that can be developed by the teacher and the materials from which the children are learning. Therefore, unusually large amounts of television viewing may interfere with the school program. After five hours of murder, passionate love, dancing girls, and the funniest of comedies, it is difficult to imagine that children are going to appreciate fully a program that features the elementary school band or a story in the first-grade reader that must be geared to a limited reading vocabulary. Although no formula is prescribed, limiting children to an hour of television viewing an evening is not unreasonable. Of course, parents cannot expect children to sit in the living room and not watch the shows that the parents are watching. This suggestion, then, implies that television viewing for the family should be restricted, especially during school days. Consideration can also be given by parents to the need for children to accomplish home assignments and have some quiet time. Quiet time, of necessity, involves the entire family.

Following advice. Parents must be encouraged to follow the suggestions of school personnel in matters concerning the education of their children. The most difficulty in this respect is experienced in considering the age at which children should enter first grade and the decision to retain children in a given grade. Each school system has its own method for determining whether children are ready to profit from first-grade instruction. When, after careful consideration, the school advises parents to withhold a child from first grade for one year, the parents much understand that it is foolhardy to insist upon entrance. Scenes create needless anxiety for children, antagonize everyone, and generally result in the entrance of children into programs in which they will not be successful. Scores of children with reading difficulties are victims of early entrance against school advice.

School advice in connection with the retention of children generally receives parental concern that is passed directly to the children. Educators not only want the parents to comply with this advice but to embrace it with enthusiasm, so that children feel they have not let their parents down. Unfortunately, in our pass or fail system, other children pick up the connotation of failure that will, unwittingly, create some disturbance within the children. Failure need not be compounded in the home by parental anxiety. To start with, parents can refer to repeating a year instead of failing a year. Perhaps, the time is near when retention in school will not be marked by failure to be promoted at the end of the year. All children should be on a program of continuous progress, making it realistically impossible for each failure to occur. Continuous progress involves an educational program in which each learner starts each year in terms of the points that instruction ended the preceding year. In the final analysis, it is our present system, not the children, that creates the failures. Many schools have instituted continuous progress programs, much to the satisfaction of parents, children, and teachers.

Reinforcement of learned skills. As discussed under "Parental Roles in Remediation," skills learned in school can be reinforced by understanding parents in the home. The suggestions made in the previous discussion apply equally well here but with special emphasis on the fact that home reading situations should always end pleasantly with children's feelings of satisfaction. Parents who cannot control their anxieties and tempers should avoid working with their children at home. When children read orally to anxious parents, difficulty frequently arises regardless of the care teachers have taken to make sure that the children can read the books that have been sent home.

In practical terms, when children come to unknown words, what should the parents do? In order to make the reading pleasant and meaningful, parents should tell the children the words. If they miss them again, they should be told again and again. Words missed with regularity should be noted and sent to the teacher for analysis of the type of error and the necessary instruction. However, parents are seldom satisfied with this limited role; thus, the following course of action is suggested. When children miss words again and again, it is helpful if the parent print the words carefully on cards. When the reading is finished and the story has been discussed, a few minutes can be spent glancing over these cards. As the words are pronounced, the children should be asked to use them in sentences, which should be written on the back of the cards with the unknown words underlined. Preceding the next reading session at home, a little game-like drill can take place in which the children read the sentences and the unknown words.

Pitfalls in Parental Cooperation

Obviously, there are numerous opportunities for parental cooperation to go astray, creating more harm than good. Educators must be alert to these pitfalls and, when signs of their appearance occur, use alternate approaches to parental participation.

Lack of contact. Perhaps the worst pitfall is to make no contact with parents. Since parental roles will be assumed, it is best that they be taken in terms of the school's program. Parental contacts should be periodic, calling for follow-up sessions to reinforce parental behavior. All too often, one parental conference is seen as meeting the need for parental involvement. On the contrary, in a six-week summer program, for example, three formal parental conferences and numerous informal conferences are needed to help parents become effective helpers.

Underestimating parental love. Parents, even those parents who appear to be unconcerned, love their children. However, parental love easily can be misdirected. For example, some parents criticize the school in attempts to make their children feel more comfortable. When parental love is ignored by schools, the result can be a lack of cooperation between parents and educators. As has been suggested, sending the children home with activities that will permit them to demonstrate their strengths to the parents gives parents opportunities to demonstrate their love for their children with positive reinforcement.

Numerous informal conferences are needed to help parents become effective helpers.

Needless anxiety. Many parents confront educators with demonstrations of considerable anxiety. They are afraid, frustrated, and upset. For such parents to become useful partners, educators need to work with them to overcome their feelings of anxiety; for overanxious parents find it extremely difficult to work with their own children in any activity. When conversing with parents, the educator should listen to what they have to say. Really listen. Postpone judgments. Extra care should be taken to make activities for such parents as positive in nature as possible. As parents start to relax and gain confidence in the school's program, they can become more helpful partners.

One parent. Educators often are forced to settle for the reactions and opinions of only one of the child's parents. One must avoid this pitfall, for children act to please both parents. Therefore, every opportunity should be made to involve both parents, even if a home visit is required to attain this end. Upon talking with the other parent, teachers have often reversed their opinions of the home and the learning climate.

Failure to follow up. When a remedial program is finished, the parents deserve to be given a summary of the results. Without this follow up, parental activities may continue as the educator has directed following diagnosis, thus creating feelings of discomfort and needless anxiety within the children. The summary, therefore, should include specific recommendations for future parental roles concerning the changing needs of the children.

Assuming the teacher's role. Sending workbooks home so that parents are placed in a teacher's role is seldom useful and often harmul. Educators must clearly see the difference between the parents' role as reinforcer of learned skills and the educator's job of developing new skills. Workbook activities provide too many teaching situations for most parents to handle well. However, if children have worked in a skill activity successfully in school, allowing them to demonstrate that success to their parents is exactly what is desired.

Overreaction to information in the press. Newspapers and magazines often carry articles about some aspect of reading: "Scores are down;" "Be sure your school is using this approach;" "Your child's diet can affect learning." These and other such topics are anxiety building. Parents should be helped to obtain as much information as possible before reacting to such articles. The information in the article may be true but inapplicable to a certain school or to their child. The information in the article may be a distortion that needs clarification. And, at times, the information may be inaccurate, requiring that correct information be supplied.

Training for parents. Today's parents are likely to have training sessions available to them. These sessions are usually designed to inform parents about reading and offer suggestions as to how they can help their children at home.

Many administrators are inviting parents to teacher inservice sessions. Those administrators feel that parents should know what training teachers are getting and what innovations are being suggested. By informing them in this manner, educators avoid misinterpretations.

Some clinics offer classes for parents of children who are attending the clinic. They inform the parents about their objectives, their procedures, and the anticipated outcomes of the clinic experience. They talk about how reading problems get started and how they can be corrected. They offer strategies for parents to use when they need to contact school personnel about their children. And they offer ideas that parents can use at home. Attendance at such classes is excellent, and responses are enthusiastic.

Parents are serving as aides and volunteers in many schools. As such, they get two types of training. They attend workshops and seminars designed to instruct them in their role in the school, and they get on-the-job training from the teacher with whom they are working. Frequently, parents are enrolled in graduate classes, not working for a degree, but simply wanting to be better informed.

We now offer courses designed for parents who are interested in helping their children. Parents are interested in knowing about the reading process, about how reading is taught in school, and about how they can help at home. In every instance they inform us that they have been working with the children and that they intend to continue to do so. It seems that our best action is to provide them with enough information so that what they do at home can be as helpful as possible. We have found that fifteen hours of instruction suit the purpose and parents can either earn a credit or a certificate.

SUMMARY

Parents can help! Educators must evaluate the home situation and make specific recommendations to the parents of problem readers as to which roles are most appropriate to enable parents and educators to work as a team. All parental roles should be in keeping with the educational goals that the remedial program is attemping to accomplish. When parents are not actively involved, needless limitations are placed upon the educator's effectiveness. On the premise that most parents are going to help their children with reading, educators must direct their efforts toward the most useful purposes.

NOTES

1. Robert M. Wilson and Donald W. Pfau, "Parents Can Help!" *Reading Teacher* 21 (May 1968): 758–61.

SUGGESTED READINGS

Artley, A. Sterl. *Your Child Learns to Read.* Chicago: Scott Foresman and Co., 1953. This book is a guide for parents to use with Scott Foresman series. However, it includes many practical suggestions for parents whose children do not happen to use this series in school. Of particular interest may be the graded book list under the title "Guide for Building a Home Library."

Gambrell, Linda B. and Wilson, Robert M. *28 Ways To Help Your Child Be a Better Reader.* Paoli, Pa.: Instructo/McGraw-Hill Book Co., 1980. Practical suggestions are offered to parents so that they can work with their children. Suggestions take little time and do not interfere with school curricular activities.

Landau, Elliott D. *Creative Parent-Teacher Conferences.* Salt Lake City, Ut.: E.D. Landau, 1968. This work presents guidelines for various types of conferences with which educators are confronted. It offers specific suggestions to make conferences effective.

Oliastro, Louis A. *Parents Teach Your Child to Read.* Uniontown, Pa.: LIZ Publications, 1979. This seven-page booklet provides information for parents about how to use photographs of their children's experiences as a basis for language development. As the children talk about the pictures the parents record the story. These personal stories with pictures are then used for reading instruction.

Reading Teacher, May 1970. Through twelve articles featuring the role of parents in reading activities, this entire issue of the *Reading Teacher* focuses on the topic of this chapter.

Smith, Nila B. *Reading Instruction for Today's Children.* Englewood Cliffs, N. J.: Prentice-Hall, 1963. Chapters 19 and 20 provide specific suggestions on how to advise and work with parents. Included are sections on materials, selections, and some critical dos and don'ts.

Wilson, Robert M., and Pfau, Donald W. "Parents Can Help!" *Reading Teacher* (May 1968): 758–61. This article summarizes a study in which parents of children were asked how they helped their children at home. Children were grouped as below-average readers and above-average readers. Those children receiving most parental assistance at home were the below-average readers.

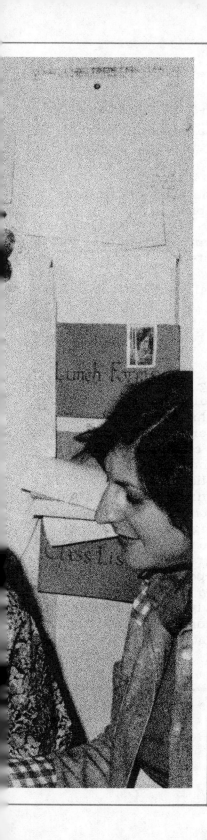

13

Professional Roles

Chapter Emphasis

- Reading specialists should be important partners in decision making regarding reading placements of students.

- Classroom teachers should have important input to decisions regarding reading placement.

- Reading specialists should plan their time to be able to work with all types of students.

- Teachers must know the legal ramifications of their actions.

- Teachers should model the reading habit for their students.

Public concern over school reading programs continues to grow. Newspapers, magazines, radio, and television focus public attention on the strengths and weaknesses of reading programs. Professional concern about reading is reflected in the large number of reading journals being published and the extensive amount of reading research as well as the volumes of books published each year. Public and professional concern combined have resulted in pressures on school systems to produce better readers and to supply more programs of reading support. Unfortunately, such pressures occasionally create more problems than they solve. Hastily developed programs may emerge; inappropriate materials may be incorporated; personnel with questionable qualifications may be hired; too many duties may be placed on personnel already employed. Therefore, consideration of professional responsibilities and roles may help both the teachers and the administrators who are planning reading programs.

PROFESSIONAL RESPONSIBILITIES

"Am I qualified to help students having difficulties with reading?" "How will I be able to start a program in my classroom, in my school?" "To whom should I look for help?" These are questions educators ask when they realize that many students with reading problems could be helped by establishing special reading services. Preceding a discussion of programs, however, must be a clear understanding of the professonal responsibilities of the educators attempting to establish remedial programs.

The Student

Regardless of the type of program or the competency of the person conducting it, consideration first must be given to the student who is to benefit from the program. Educators are professionally responsible for the direction of students toward those programs that seem to be best designed for their needs. Referral need not reflect negatively upon educators if they decide that they cannot assist the student as well as another can; rather, this action is to their credit. Clearly, many educators feel threatened when they become aware that they cannot help certain students. To call for outside help may seem to indicate a lack of competency. However, the diagnosis and correction of many reading problems cannot possibly be handled by any one person. Consequently, to call for assistance when it is needed is a sign of professional maturity.

Cooperation

As mentioned in previous chapters, diagnosis and remediation are programs that cannot be conducted without full cooperation from all persons involved with the student. Programs that are conducted in isolation are limited in their ability to offer the student a complete program. Therefore, programs should not be instituted without thorough communication with the parents and student's classroom teacher, and other resource personnel.

Referral

When possible, all referrals—medical, psychological, and psychiatric—should be made prior to remediation and the formation of program procedures. It is inefficient to start a remedial program without consultation when a student demonstrates symptoms of difficulties in these areas. All conclusions should be considered tentative and verified by appropriate professional assessment. Even then the final effectiveness of a diagnosis is only confirmed during instruction. The educator does not refrain from working with these students; however, the full efficiency of remedial programs normally will not be realized without referral reports.

When considering the role of the reading specialist, the school screening committee becomes important. As discussed previously, the screening committee consists of teachers, administrators, specialists, and sometimes parents or students. The committee works to bring the most appropriate resources of the school to assist the teacher with students who are experiencing difficulty with their learning activities.

Qualification

Since the terms *reading specialist, reading consultant, reading supervisor, reading teacher,* and *reading tutor* appear to be defined differently within various states and school districts, educators clearly are obligated to represent themselves as honestly as possible. The International Reading Association has established suggested requirements for reading specialists, and these requirements may serve as a guide to educators.[1] Many states now have certification in reading. By using the titles connected with the certification, educators can most properly represent themselves.

School Rapport

When remediation is conducted outside the classroom, the educator is professionally responsible for avoiding casting unwarranted reflections of inadequacy upon the school program, particularly to parents. However, if the school program is suspect, the educator is professionally obligated to consult appropriate school personnel in an effort to remedy the deficiency.

Here, the reader's attention is called to the Code of Ethics approved by the International Reading Association as it appears in Appendix D of this book.

Guarantees

Seldom can an educator guarantee specific outcomes as a result of specialized reading services. Many variables may influence a student's performance in reading. To offer guarantees to parents or school officials is clearly unethical. What can be offered, however, are the best services of the personnel who willingly will submit their efforts to carefully conducted evaluations.

THE READING SPECIALIST IN THE SCHOOL PROGRAM

**Program
Suggestions**
The following suggestions are designed to assist reading specialists in assuming the role that will best suit the needs of the schools for which they are responsible and the students within those schools. A reading specialist may assume responsibility for more than one of these program suggestions, for they are frequently related.

Diagnosis. As discussed in Chapters 2, 3, 4, and 5, clinical diagnosis is a major responsibility of most reading specialists. The reading specialist conducts the diagnosis and prepares the recommendations with directions for remediation. Many reading specialists feel that they can be very useful to the classroom teacher through diagnostic services, because it may be difficult for the classroom teacher to find the time that clinical diagnosis requires.

Remediation. Much of the job responsibility for reading specialists usually involves working instructionally with students. Three different strategies have been used effectively:

1. Some specialists find working with students in their classroom to be advantageous. The teacher works with some students and the specialist with others. Communication problems are diminished as both the teacher and the reading specialist have opportunities to learn from one another. By working in the classroom, the specialist has the opportunity to work with all types of readers. Such a strategy can also be a means for training a teacher to use a new technique. For example, one principal places the reading specialist in first grade for an hour every morning. The specialist works with students, referred by the teacher, using the V-A-K-T technique with students having difficulty developing sight vocabulary. Working one to one, the specialist reinforces the words the students select to learn from their language-experience stories.

2. Other specialists prefer to work with the students outside of their regular classrooms. They establish a learning environment that is different from what the students are

used to. Distractions are lessened, and students feel honored by such attention. This strategy usually calls for the specialist to work with small groups of students who have similar strengths and needs. One specialist has set up a rich learning environment and accepts students referred by teachers on a contract basis. The students may come one day for a little reinforcement, or they may come on a regular basis.

3. In order to serve as many students as possible, some reading specialists establish miniclinics. A small group of students comes for a short time period to develop a specific skill. For example, a teacher may have seven third graders who are having difficulty locating information. A miniclinic can be set up for two weeks, one hour a day, for these third graders. At the end of the clinic, the students are evaluated; the evaluations are shared with the teacher; and a new miniclinic can be developed for others.

Most specialists will probably find it useful to use some combination of these three strategies with students in remedial situations. One reading specialist works during the morning with students who have been identified as having serious difficulties with reading. Afternoons are composed of several activities.

1. She conducts miniclinics. All types of readers attend these various miniclinics, including some gifted and talented students.
2. She conducts diagnosis when it is needed.
3. She meets with each team in the school during its planning time at least once a week.
4. She schedules time when she will be available to work in classrooms with teachers. At times she works with students and at other times she works with the teachers.

This type of scheduling of the reading specialist seems to obtain maximum utilization of various skills. It also keeps the reading specialist from getting bogged down with one type of activity all day long. All students view the reading specialist as a helpful person in the school, not just those who are experiencing difficulty with reading.

Planning.   Planning with teachers so that the educational programs of students are coordinated can be an important

When the teachers at my elementary school were surveyed, they indicated a desire to have the reading teacher spend some time working with children in need of specific skill development, rather than spend the entire day working with only the most severe reading problems.

A fifth-grade teacher approached me and explained that several of the slightly below average readers in the class were struggling with a unit on report writing. The complaint was a common one. The children were locating information on their topics and simply copying what they found word for word with little understanding of what they had copied. I suggested that we set up a skills group on note taking, and the teacher agreed to send the six fifth graders to work with me for six half-hour sessions.

During these sessions we learned and practiced a note-taking technique that focuses on the reduction of ideas to key words, followed by expanding the key words into complete thoughts using each child's own words. We were concerned about the transfer of these newly acquired skills from the small skills group to the regular classroom, so I asked the teacher to monitor the progress of each child in the group.

The teacher noticed dramatic improvement in the ability of these students to take notes and paraphrase information with much greater comprehension. She also requested my assistance in teaching this note-taking strategy to the rest of the class.

In our first planning session, we decided to use the six children who were now highly skilled in note taking as tutors, giving them an opportunity to share this strength with the rest of their class. We planned each session carefully and divided the responsibilities so that we were actually team teaching the lessons, rather than having me do a demonstration lesson. Since the teacher planned to have the students continue using this strategy throughout the year, it was essential that the teacher be fully involved in the planning as well as the execution of the lessons.

The children responded enthusiastically to the note-taking lessons and, with the help of their six classmate tutors, learned to apply the new strategy quite well. This cooperative effort had many positive effects. The entire fifth-grade class learned a more efficient and effective way of taking notes. The six tutors reinforced their own skill in note taking and greatly enhanced their self-concepts. The teacher also enjoyed the team-teaching experience and is now aware of more services that can be provided by the reading teacher.

Finally, I had the opportunity to work with a wide variety of students, broadening my perspective, and also reducing the negative feelings of children who prior to this experience saw the reading teacher as one who only worked with the less able children. I also had an excellent team-teaching experience with a dynamic and most cooperative fifth-grade teacher!

Pat Russavage

Teachers and reading specialists should coordinate planning of the educational programs for students.

part of the reading specialist's responsibilities. In schools where teachers work and plan in teams, the reading specialist should make efforts to be a part of every planning session. If a unit on space is being planned, then that unit can be incorporated into the instruction being conducted by the reading specialist. The specialist may also have input to team planning in regard to sound reading instruction.

Clinic Director. In larger school districts, the reading specialist may direct a reading clinic in an attempt to serve severely handicapped readers. Clinics usually are established in buildings to which the students can be brought for help. As director of the clinic, the reading specialist may assume all of the above roles as well as the administrative functions of the clinic, supervision of staff, and the communication between clinic and classroom.

Inservice education. Occasionally, the reading specialist will find it worthwhile to conduct inservice programs with teachers. Through demonstration, discussion, and consultation with authorities, teachers gain insights into effective methods of working with problem readers. In these situations, the specialist's responsibility is supervisory in order to inform teachers who have a common lack of understanding in certain areas. Reading specialists do not need to view inservice programs as formal, day-long types of training sessions. In addition, while having released time for inservice programs is desirable, it is not always necessary. Examples of two successful strategies involving small amounts of time follow.

Reading specialists prepare informational notes on recent developments in reading and pass them on to teachers. Any teacher interested in more details can contact the reading specialist. For example: (1) the specialist has just read an article on wait time and shares the idea in a note to the staff, or (2) the specialist has just received some new information about oral reading diagnosis and shares it with the staff. At times, one little idea has a better chance of being implemented than do ideas that require major changes and considerable training of the teachers.

Some specialists have developed modules for inservice programs, which can be conducted in fifteen minutes. These modules are single concept in nature and include handouts, transparencies, and materials for implementation. The specialist announces which modules are available, and interested teachers sign up for the modules of their choice. At a designated time, the teachers meet and the module is presented. Discussion follows, and the teachers decide whether they want to try the new idea. They also may decide they would like to try it but would need some help from the specialist during the initiation of the idea. Examples of some of these short modules are listed:

1. Helping teachers develop maze tests from one of their books
2. Showing teachers a way to develop note taking skills with their students
3. Discussion of the meaning of test results from a diagnostic session
4. Sharing a new material that has come to the school
5. Discussion of a position taken by a reading authority in a recent article

At times enough interest is generated in one of these short sessions that teachers ask for more information on that topic.

Resources for classroom teachers. Many reading specialists find their training best utilized when they can serve as resource persons to the classroom teacher. Instead of working with students outside the classroom in diagnosis and remedial activities, resource teachers can aid the classroom teachers in various ways:

1. By helping with diagnosis: test administration, scoring, and interpretation can be conducted as a team, thus permitting the classroom teacher to learn diagnostic skills.
2. By helping in the classroom with students who are experiencing difficulty: planning and team teaching special lessons as well as offering continued support to help the teacher better handle students with reading problems allows for teacher development as well as providing service to students.
3. By obtaining materials for the teacher: instead of keeping reading materials in a reading room, the reading specialists can bring needed materials to classroom teachers and help them use them effectively. The resource teacher may obtain materials that the teacher requests and may recommend new materials for certain situations. Resource teachers can also suggest professional materials such as books, pamphlets, and articles.
4. By planning with the teacher to develop effective instructional goals: the teacher, using the knowledge and skills of the reading specialist, can develop better plans for instruction.
5. By evaluating program effectiveness: by applying research and evaluation skills, the resource teacher can assist classroom teachers in looking objectively at their reading programs, modifying portions of the programs that appear to be weak, and assisting them to emphasize portions of the programs that appear to be strong.
6. By interpreting for teachers the reading research that may have application for the classroom: as a result of their own reading, attendance at conferences, formal course work, and discussions with their colleagues, resource teachers should be alert to the most recent trends, research, methods, and materials.

Generally, reading-resource personnel should be assigned duties that will allow them freedom to work effectively with teachers. They should not be assigned to evaluate teachers. They should not set policies that teachers must follow, nor should they force themselves into situations where teachers do not want them. In effect, resource persons should be assigned duties in which they can practice the philosophy of acceptance and challenge with teachers.

Summer school. An increasingly large number of schools are establishing summer programs for students who have not made adequate progress during the school year. Reading specialists probably will be responsible for such programs, with particular emphasis being placed upon the screening and selection of the students who are to be assisted. In addition, they may be responsible for the selection of the teachers who will be involved. The financing of these programs, normally assumed by the school, may to a small extent be supplemented by a nominal fee paid by the parents. Such a fee stimulates a more serious attitude toward the work required in the program. Through summer programs, it may be possible for students to remain in the classroom during the year, thereby providing them the fullest opportunity to benefit from the classroom program. Of course, students with serious reading problems cannot always profit from summer programs alone. To avoid the stigma of failure that is often attached to such programs, summer facilities can be developed for good readers as well. All types of readers can then be involved, making it no disgrace to attend a summer reading program.

Public relations. Public relations duties, which include PTA meetings, conferences with parents, and home visits, may fall to the reading specialist. At such meetings, the school's reading program can be explained, questions answered, the misinterpretations corrected. The reading specialist can take advantage of the suggestions mentioned in chapter 10 when provided with opportunities to meet the public. Public relations opportunities such as conferences with parents and home visits as well as public-speaking engagements may be available to reading specialists.

Supervision of tutoring. Some schools ask qualified teachers to tutor readers after school hours and on weekends under the direction of the reading specialist. It is the reading specialist's responsibility to help select the students, make available appropriate diagnostic and remedial materials, and, again, keep communication open between the tutor, the classroom teacher, the parents, and others.

Training of paraprofessionals.   As paraprofessionals become more available for reading assistance, the job of training those persons will fall upon reading specialists. The better the training, the more useful will be the paraprofessional. A model program for such training has been developed in Prince Georges County, Maryland. Hundreds of paraprofessionals are trained and supervised by reading specialists as they work with classroom teachers to reach individual students.

All schools are being encouraged to consider the maximum use of such personnel to assist overburdened teachers. Reading specialists will need to consider the many duties that paraprofessionals can perform, and develop training programs to make their work as effective as possible.

Pitfalls for Reading Specialists

Programs developed by reading specialists are not without potential difficulties. Especially for those with little experience, there are certan pitfalls involved in establishing reading programs. Anticipation of several possible ones before beginning such a program may relieve reading specialists of frustrating situations that can ultimately cause considerable difficulty.

Overloading.   It is common to find reading specialists assuming responsibilities that overload them to a point of ineffectiveness. First, they should not be expected to assume all the roles that have been suggested in this chapter; rather, they should start where they can be most effective and slowly expand as they see opportunities. Second, in the diagnostic and remedial role, they cannot be expected to carry the student load that a classroom teacher does. They very nature of the clinical situation precludes large groups. When overloaded, the reading specialist's effectiveness will be limited unnecessarily.

Inadequate housing.   Teachers' rooms, damp basements, and even worse locations have been relegated to the reading specialist to conduct diagnostic and remedial programs. Assuming that a program is worth having, the school administrator must make provisions for a well-lighted, comfortable, nondistracting environment for the students and the teacher. To be most effective, housing considerations should be built into the basic plans for the program's development.

Screening.   Final responsibility for determining which students can be helped most effectively must be left to the reading specialist. Without diagnosis, a given classroom teacher is likely to select the dullest student for remedial attention, when dullness alone is not a sufficient criterion for program enrollment. Reading specialists should provide for the screening of all referred students, yet retain the right to reject any student who they feel cannot profit effectively from the established program. They will have to reject temporarily those students who add to the tutoring load, creating class sizes that cannot be taught effectively. Interschool relations may be strained unless clearcut procedures are established concerning the final responsibilities for the identification of students to be accepted in the reading specialist's programs.

One such procedure involves the screening committee that contains all of the resource personnel available in the school as well as the principal. The reading specialist makes recommendations regarding reading placements to the committee. Others provide their input and a decision is made.

The image.   Specific efforts should be made to avoid the image that the reading specialist is the educator who works with failures. As previously suggested, reading specialists should work in the classroom, participating in all types of programs for readers. Such adjustment will help the students assigned to them by relaxing their anxiety about their failures. It will also prevent their getting a distorted opinion of the school's reading program. (This easily occurs when one works hour after hour, day after day with only the problems that a given system has produced.) Working with teachers in the classroom also aids reading specialists in maintaining perspective, especially concerning the difficulties teachers may have working with specific students in large groups.

Another aspect of image is related to the way teachers view reading specialists. Reading specialists should be treated as part of the teaching staff, assuming their share of teacher special chores such as bus duty or playground duty. They should attend all teachers' meetings and, in general, do what teachers do. If the image is developed that the reading specialists get special treatment, rapport with the teaching staff will suffer.

Demonstrations.   Normally, demonstrations are requested when teachers are uncertain of how to use a new technique or material. Traditionally, the demonstrator replaces the teacher and thereby falls into a trap of ineffectiveness. It is suggested that demonstrations be conducted in cooperation with the classroom teacher as a participant. Specifically, the classroom teacher plans the lesson with the reading specialist; the classroom teacher teaches portions of the lesson; the classroom teacher remains in charge of the class; and the reading specialist assists with the planning and execution of the lesson. Immediately upon completion of such lessons, the classroom teacher and the reading specialist discuss what happened and how it can be applied to an everyday situation.

Using techniques such as those described above removes teachers from the passive, observing role and places them in an active, participating role. Teacher behavior is more likely to be modified with such an approach.

This procedure does not rule out the use of a demonstration when it is appropriate. For example, if a new material is provided and no one knows how to use it, it would be appropriate for the reading specialist to prepare a lesson for others to observe.

THE CLASSROOM TEACHER IN THE SCHOOL PROGRAM

Program Participation

With various degrees of competency, classroom teachers participate in school programs with readers in several ways. An understanding of the possibilities may assist each teacher to serve most effectively.

Classroom diagnosis.   As teachers develop skill in the techniques of classroom diagnosis, they are likely to find themselves assigned to students who are in need of this service. The best teachers will perform this type of function as an ongoing part of their teaching program. The administrator is cautioned that overloading excellent teachers is unwise, since excessive numbers of weak students obviously will hamper their efforts with all students assigned to them. Classroom teachers will provide additional input to screening committees when sharing the information from a classroom diagnosis.

Classroom remediation.   Using their remediation skills, teachers should work to develop successful readers. The following strategies are useful for teachers working with handicapped readers in the classroom setting:

1. Flexible skills grouping calls for teachers to establish skills groups for specific purposes: when the purpose is accomplished, the group is disbanded and a new group is formed. If ten students need instruction on the use of initial consonant substitution, then a skill group is formed. As students gain the skill they leave the group.
2. Utilizing small bits of time when all other students are occupied, teachers can provide the reinforcement necessary for practice sessions to be on target. For example, such time can be used to review a lesson taught the day before or to go over the student's sight words.
3. Some administrators arrange for released time for teachers with skill in remediation. This time is set aside so that small-group instruction can take place without distracting the entire class. The benefit of such arrangements on student progress has been well worth the administrative inconvenience.
4. Some teachers find a few moments before and after school useful for that little bit of extra instruction and attention that makes so much difference to students.
5. Most of what has been discussed under remediation can be incorporated into the regular reading lessons being taught. For example, the regular lessons can focus on locating if students need practice locating information.

Classroom teachers will find combinations of these strategies effective ways of conducting classroom remediation.

Tutoring.   Having developed skills in diagnosis and remediation through either inservice or formal course work, many teachers serve as tutors in school-established programs. The teachers' activities in these programs are usually supervised by the reading specialist and are directed toward the instruction of individuals and/or small groups.

Demonstration.   When teachers are particularly skillful in either classroom diagnosis or remediation, other teachers should observe them. Observations may be made during after-school programs or through released time. To create strong feelings about their teaching competencies, teachers should be permitted to evaluate their own strengths and to offer their rooms for observations. Reading specialists can assist teachers in the identification of strengths and urge them to offer their classrooms for the benefit of their colleagues.

Public relations.   All teachers have the responsibility of interpreting the school's program to parents. Those who have studied the program more thoroughly may assist in events such as the PTA in order to illustrate clearly the program's features to parents. Parents may accept the classroom teacher in this role better than they do the reading specialist, for they know that the classroom teacher works with their children each day.

Pitfalls for the Classroom Teacher

Like the reading specialists, the classroom teachers also must be alert to several pitfalls in their roles.

Overloading.   Teachers who are skilled in diagnosis and remediation may become overloaded with poor readers. Ultimately, overloading is a detriment to effectiveness with these children. Even when using free periods, short sessions before and after school, Saturdays, and summers, many good teachers need more time to do an efficient job. In addition, teachers must regulate their time so that relaxation and recreation are also part of their daily schedule. Their major responsibility continues to lie with the whole class and the education of all students assigned to them; so overloading should be avoided.

Shortcutting.   Attempting to diagnose without using the suggestions in chapters 2, 3, 4, and 5 leads to inadequate classroom diagnosis. However, after limited experience, classroom teachers can start to modify and refine these suggestions to their classrooms and the needs of their students. After several diagnostic efforts, teachers will realize that their students are all proficient in some area(s) and that study in those areas is not essential in classroom diagnosis. However, this does not justify excluding major portions of classroom diagnosis.

Cooperation.   Regardless of the feelings teachers may have toward the total school reading programs, they should work as team members. Gross distortions of the school program in an effort to satisfy personal philosophies of reading must be avoided when they interfere with the overall school objectives. By cooperating and attempting to convince the school of the need for basic changes, teachers will better serve their students. Needless to say, discord within the school should remain there and not be topic for community gossip.

Continued study.   As changes occur in the field of reading, teachers must have a system for continued study. Some find that the study of educational periodicals serves this purpose. Specific reference is made to the journals of the International Reading Association,[2] the National Council of Teachers of English,[3] and the College Reading Association.[4] These organizations are striving to keep teachers informed of developments in the field of reading. Other teachers prefer inservice workshops and institutes; still others prefer formal course work in the colleges and universities. Of course, most teachers seek a suitable combination of methods.

OUT-OF-SCHOOL PROGRAMS

Many educators take part in "out-of-school" programs designed to assist problem readers. Some find themselves teaching in these programs; others have parents asking them for their opinions of the programs; and still others find these programs to be interfering with the educational objectives of the school. A brief look at the nature of some of these programs may assist the educator to make decisions concerning them.

Teacher-education clinics. Many teacher-education institutions operate reading clinics to educate teachers. Students who are brought into these clinics for assistance are generally diagnosed and tutored by teachers doing advanced work in the field of reading. Normally the costs for services in teacher-education clinics are small since the programs are not expected to pay for themselves. The effectiveness of these programs is generally related to the effectiveness of the clinical supervision that the teachers receive and the prerequisites for entrance of college students into clinical courses.

Some teacher-education clinics limit themselves to diagnosis, while others include remediation as well. Although the thoroughness of each program varies, they generally follow the lines of clinical diagnosis and remediation presented in this book, and are reliable.

Privately operated clinics. A variety of privately operated clinics are usually available in large population centers. Designed for financial profit, these clinics generally charge fees much higher than do teacher-education clinics. The effectiveness of these clinics is clearly limited by the personnel and materials available for diagnosis and remediation. Referrals to this type of clinic should be made only after acquaintance with the personnel and the attitude of the clinic. Private clinics can accept this as a challenge: work with the schools! Unless cooperation is achieved, the effects of privately operated clinics are limited indeed.

Private tutoring. Ranging from excellent to horrible, programs designed by private tutors are generally restricted by the proficiency of the tutor and by the materials available for precise diagnosis and remediation. These private tutoring programs are most effective with mildly retarded readers. Students with severe problems seldom benefit; however, it should be noted that there are many excellent, well-qualified private tutors performing highly satisfactory services. Unfortunately, there are others who cause more harm than good. Private tutors are obligated to work closely with the school, which has the student in an instructional program every day. There is no justification for programs that do less. Referral should be based only on a personal evaluation of effectiveness.

Commercial programs for parents. Often advertised as panaceas, programs that place parents in teachers' roles assume that all teachers have a common deficiency and that instruction with a given technique can be done without diagnosis. Unless the educator is familiar with the contents of the program and unless a diagnosis has been conducted to pinpoint the remedial area, these programs are not recommended. These programs were mentioned in chapter 12. Not all such programs are inherently bad; on the contrary, some of them are well designed and have been used with considerable success. The educator simply is advised to study them closely. An assessment must also be made in each case of the parent's suitability as a teacher.

Temporary programs. Several private companies have organized crash programs designed to send materials and instructors into schools and industry to improve general reading skills. As crash programs, many of these are well designed and taught excellently; others are not. The long-term gains of such programs properly may be questioned, and these companies should be willing to answer questions and submit to research concerning these claims. The educator will have to evaluate the relative worth of any such program.

Outpatient parental instruction. Several clinics have been established to diagnose children and train parents to conduct remediation. Amazing results have been reported with this technique; however, the long-term gains are in need of evaluation. Outpatient clinics usually handle large numbers of children and usually request periodic return for reevaluation and retraining for the parents. Since the programs are outpatient in nature, their overall costs are not great, although the per-hour cost may be high. Note that these programs are generally designed for children with specific disabilities and usually should follow referral from medical personnel, psychologists, psychiatrists, or reading specialists.

Pitfalls of Out-of-School Programs

The basic limitations of each of these have already been mentioned. Specifically, however, the pitfalls of such programs include the points discussed below.

Goals. Do these programs assist us toward the most desirable educational goals or do they, in reality, interfere?

Once this question is answered, referral may be made more specifically. When it is established that the programs are not in agreement with the school's goals, attempts should be made to reconcile the differences. When reconciliation is not possible, educators should strongly recommend nonparticipation by the parents of the students assigned to them.

Personnel.   The effectiveness of all of these programs is dependent upon the supervisory as well as the instructional personnel. Weakness in personnel means weakness in the program. No compromise can be made by educators in demanding that out-of-school programs meet certain standards of quality.

Intention.   Since each of these programs has other aims beyond simply assisting students, it must be determined if assisting students is even included in their aims. Naturally, they will claim to help problem readers, but do dollar signs or teacher education become so important that the student does not matter? When alternate aims prevail, the worth of the program is suspect.

A diagnostic teaching approach can help each student to learn more successfully.

ACCOUNTABILITY

That educators and commercial companies should be held accountable for their efforts with students is an issue of great interest, for this is, of course, the whole purpose of diagnostic teaching. Teachers should be accountable for providing efficient instruction based upon diagnostic techniques. Lockstepping students through one commercial program and indifference to individual learning styles are not to be tolerated. The teacher who knows the strengths and needs of children and who provides the best possible instruction is truly teaching with accountability.

Accountability has nothing to do with obtaining the same results with all students. It has nothing to do with helping each student to read on some type of mythical grade level. It refers to helping each student to successful learning—a task that can only be done with a diagnostic teaching approach.

Of necessity, accountability requires careful record keeping. Careful record keeping does not need to be a time consuming activity. In some school districts and states, however, mandatory record keeping becomes an interference to quality instructional programs. At times different agencies are requesting the same type of information but are using different forms. There is an urgency today for administrators at all levels to try to consolidate information needed and to minimize record keeping while remaining able to account for the progress of students in their schooling.

LEGAL RESPONSIBILITIES

Teachers have always been responsible to act within the law. Today, however, considerable attention has been given to the rights of students under the law. Many school districts have developed student handbooks that identify particular student rights. Some are understandable as common sense while others involve special procedures to be followed under the law. Every teacher should be well informed about the laws in their state as well as local school district policies.

When working with test results some particular legal responsibilities need attention. McClung discusses them at length.[5] I believe the most important consideration should be to be able to defend the validity and reliability of any tests used for making decisions about the placement of students. If the tests cannot be defended how can the decisions be defended? Yet the practice continues. Students continue to be labeled and grouped by the data obtained from tests of unknown reliability and validity. If such practices continue, educators are asking for legal intervention.

Other matters deserve our attention. Students have the right to privacy, to due process, to fair treatment, and to their personal records. The technical discussion of these rights is beyond the scope of this text, but three suggested readings at the end of this chapter should be studied in order to obtain detailed information on student rights.

BE A READER

In closing, let me urge all teachers to be readers. If we are to nurture students to value reading, we must set the example. How can one develop a love of reading in students when there is no love of reading within the teacher?

Duffey found that 34 percent of the teachers surveyed in his study were not reading a book and that 50 percent had no plans to read a book.[6] Twenty percent reported not to be reading any professional literature. Duffey informs me that the trend he reported is continuing as he collects data on teacher reading habits.

A determined effort can change the sorry picture painted by the Duffey data. Read to your students every day. Go to a book store and pick a good book for your own reading enjoyment. Provide time in school for student reading of personally enjoyable material. As the student reads, so should the teacher. Subscribe to a professional journal of your choice. Talk with students about what you are reading, showing your enjoyment and your enthusiasm.

It is the desire to be a reader that can often make a difference. I urge you not to let the opportunity slip by you.

Teaching to strengths can make learning to read enjoyable and successful.

SUMMARY

Once the professional roles of the classroom teacher and the reading specialist are understood, programs can be developed to incorporate them appropriately. An awareness of the types of programs available within the realms of the school permits educators to strive to develop those that the needs of their community demand. All facilities—local school, county, state, college, and university—should be incorporated when it is felt that they can be helpful.

Out-of-school programs for children must be evaluated, and cooperation should be encouraged when possible. In areas where out-of-school programs proliferate, more concentrated efforts will be needed to assure educational programs of the most effectiveness for students.

Teachers should be aware of the legal ramifications of their actions in decision making. They should also model the reading habit for their students.

NOTES

1. International Reading Association, *Roles, Responsibilities, and Qualifications of Reading Specialists* (Newark, Del.: International Reading Association).

2. *The Reading Teacher* and *Journal of Reading* (Newark, Del.: International Reading Association).
3. *Language Arts* and *The English Journal* (Champaign, Ill.: National Council of Teachers of English).
4. *Reading World* (Shippensburg, Pa.: Shippensburg State College, College Reading Association).
5. Merle S. McClung, "Competency Testing: Potential for Discrimination," *Clearinghouse Review,* Sept. 1977, pp. 439–48.
6. Robert V. Duffey, "What to do?" *Reading Teacher,* 27, no. 2, November 1973, pp. 132–33.

SUGGESTED READINGS

Clague, Monique W. "Competency Testing and Potential Constitutional Challenges of Every Student." *Catholic University Law Review* 28, no. 3, Summer 1979: 469–509. Clague cities court cases relating to competency testing and discusses their implications.

Cohn, Stella M., and Cohn, Jack. *Teaching the Retarded Reader.* New York: Odyssey Press, 1967. The Cohns discuss in detail the roles and responsibilities of reading personnel in establishing and administering reading programs. Based on experience in the city schools of New York, this book offers many practical suggestions.

Combs, Arthur; Avila, Donald L.; and Purkey, William W. *Helping Relationships.* Boston: Allyn & Bacon, 1971. This book provides an interesting discussion of the ways people relate to one another. It also provides specific suggestions for developing successful strategies when working as a resource to others.

Harper, Robert J., and Kilarr, Gary, eds. *Reading and the Law.* Newark, Del.: IRA, 1978. Seven articles regarding the law and the reader are presented. Written for lay persons, this book should be a must reading for all educational decision makers.

McClung, Merle S. "Competency Testing: Potential for Discrimination." *Clearinghouse Review,* September 1977: 439–48. McClung discusses six potential areas of legal difficulty in the use and interpretation of competency testing as a criterion for high school graduation.

Robinson, H. Alan, and Rauch, Sidney J. *Guiding the Reading Program.* Chicago: SRA, 1965. The reader will find this entire book an excellent source of information. Subtitled *A Reading Consultant's Handbook,* the emphasis is on developing reader insights into all aspects of the reading program from the specialist's point of view. This, it would seem, is required reading for the reading specialist.

Spicknall, Stella, and Fischer, Drema, eds. *A Handbook for the Reading Resource Program in Prince Georges County.* Upper Marlboro, Md.: Board of Education, 1969. This handbook describes the various duties of reading personnel in resource roles. The work, done in Prince Georges County, Maryland, is one of leadership in seeing the reading specialist as a resource person.

Glossary

alliteracy
A label to describe a condition in which a student is capable of reading but chooses not to do so.

auditory acuity
The ability to hear different pitches of sound.

auditory discrimination
The ability to hear differences in spoken sounds.

causation
The determination of exactly what factor(s) have contributed to a reading difficulty.

cloze
The elimination of every nth (usually fifth) word from a passage.

concurrent validity
The determination of how accurately a test score matches another variable (usually another test score).

context clues
A strategy for dealing with unknown words, in which students use the text for meaning clues for the unknown word(s).

content validity
The determination of how well a test samples the curriculum.

criterion-referenced tests (CRTs)
Tests upon which the items are matched to specific educational objectives.

dialect transfer
The ability of a person to move from one dialect to another without changing meaning.

directed reading-thinking activity (D-R-T-A)
An approach to teaching reading in which students predict outcomes and read to confirm their predictions.

disadvantaged
A label used to identify students who come from limited or different experiential backgrounds.

dyslexia
A label used to identify students who experience serious difficulty in learning to read.

focus on strengths
An instructional approach designed to assure student success.

graphic cues
Students use the letters and combinations of letters to unlock word pronunciation.

individul education program (IEP)
A plan, required by law, outlining the educational activities of those labeled as handicapped.

informal reading inventory (IRI)
A teacher-made test developed from materials used for instruction.

language disabled
A label used to identify students who have language problems that prevent them from performing fully in school.

language-experience approach
An approach to teaching reading that utilizes the student's experiences as a source of instructional materials.

learning climate
Those variables in a classroom that foster or limit learning.

maze test
An alternative to cloze tests, in which three words are supplied from which the student chooses one.

mental age
A type of potential for learning derived by multiplying one's I.Q. by chronological age.

minimally brain damaged
Students who show no hard signs of brain damage but seem to suffer from some type of mental dysfunction.

nonquestioning approach
An approach to teaching comprehension that uses strategies other than questioning to assess student comprehension.

oral reading behavior (ORB)
The student's oral reading is analyzed according to some predetermined system.

personal outlines
A strategy to develop comprehension skills that utilizes personally important information in outline format.

personal starter questions
A strategy for helping student comprehension in which the teacher asks personal questions about the passage to encourage risk taking.

predictive validity
The ability of a test to predict performance in other areas.

problem approach
An approach to teaching reading that places major responsibilities upon the students for determining objectives, procedures, and evaluation.

readability
A term used to describe the difficulty level of a passage.

regression
Those portions of student scores that are obtained by chance will tend to move toward the mean on subsequent testing.

reliability
A statistical procedure used to determine how consistently a test measures whatever it measures.

reluctant reader
A student who has necessary reading skills but is unwilling to take risks to use them.

retelling
A strategy to assess student comprehension in which the reader tells as much as possible about a passage that has been read.

risk taking
A type of learning behavior in which the student decides that it is worthwhile to attempt to respond.

self-assessment
A diagnostic strategy in which the students are encouraged to describe their own performance(s).

semantic cues
Students use the meaning of the passage to obtain the meaning of unknown words.

standard error of measurement
The amount of possible error between a given score and a true score.

syllabication
A process of dividing words into syllables as an aid to pronunciation of unknown words.

symptoms
Those types of reading behavior that are observed as being different from what they ought to be.

think links
A comprehension strategy that helps students reorganize the author's message.

vision specialist
A person trained and authorized to examine visual functioning.

Appendix A

DIAGNOSTIC INSTRUMENTS

Appendix A, provided for the reader's reference, is based upon the tests that have been cited in this book. No effort has been made to include all known reading tests, nor have evaluations of the tests' merits been included. For that type of information the reader is referred to Buros's *Reading Tests and Review*.

The age range of each test is approximated. We realize, of course, that in diagnosis the use of a test will depend upon instructional level, not the age, of the child. The educator must determine this instructional level and then select the appropriate test.

Administration time for tests often varies with the age of the child. The reader should accept these times as approximate—a factor that may determine the use of a test in a particular situation.

Publishers are coded. The key to the code is in Appendix C. The reader is referred to the publisher for the cost of the tests, the specific directions, and other desired information.

* available in

Designed to Assist in Evaluation of:

Name of Test	No. of Forms	Type	Age Range	Approximate Administration Time, Reading Section	Speed	Comprehension	Vocabulary	Word Attack	Spelling	Auding	Other	Publisher's Code
ACHIEVEMENT												
Botel Reading Inventory Revised	2	Individual and Group	6–18	15–30 min.			X	X	X			FOL
California Achievement Tests	2	Group	6.5–7 7–9 9–11 11–14 14–17	2 hrs. 2 hrs. 2½ hrs. 2½ hrs.		X	X	X	X		Language, Math Reference Skills	CAL
Dolch Basic Sight Words	1	Individual	6–8	15 min.			X					GP
Durrell Listening Reading Series	1 1	Group	Prim. 6–8 Inter. 9–12	80 min.		X	X			X	Compares Listening Ability with Reading Achievement	HBJ
Gates MacGinitie Reading Tests	2*	Group	6–7 7–8 8–9 9–11 11–14 14–17	40 min. 40 min. 50 min. 45 min. 44 min. 44 min.	 X X X			X X X X X X		X X X X X X		TC

Test	No. of Forms	Type	Age/Level	Time	Subject Areas	Publisher
Iowa Test of Basic Skills ✱	2	Group	8–14	70 min.	Language, Work-Study, Arithmetic	HMC
Metropolitan Achievement Tests ✱	4	Group	6–8, 9–12, 12–18	50 min.	Science, Language, Arithmetic, Social Studies	HBJ
Stanford Achievement Tests ✱	4	Group	6–8, 8–9, 10–12, 12–15	45 min.	Arithmetic, Study, Science, Social Studies	HBJ
The Test of Reading Comprehension	1	Group	7–14		Syntactic Similarities, Content Area, Vocabularies, Reading Directions	PE
DIAGNOSTIC						
California Phonics Survey ✱	2	Group	13–20	40 min.		CAL
Diagnostic Reading Scales ✱	1	Individual	6–14	1 hr.		CAL

*There are three forms for age levels 9–11 and 11–14.

Designed to Assist in Evaluation of:

Name of Test	No. of Forms	Type	Age Range	Approximate Administration Time, Reading Section	Speed	Comprehension	Vocabulary	Word Attack	Spelling	Auding	Other	Publisher's Code
Diagnostic Reading Tests	2–4	Group and Individual	5–13	Varies	X	X	X	X				CDRT
Diagnostic Reading Test (Bond-Balow-Hoyt)	1	Group	8–14	90 min.				X		X		LC
Doren Diagnostic Reading Test	1	Group	8–12	3 hrs.			X	X				ETB
Durrell Analysis of Reading Difficulties	1	Individual	6–12	40–60 min.	X	X	X	X	X			HBJ
Gates-McKillop Reading Diagnostic Test	2	Individual	6–12	1 hr.	X	X	X	X	X	X		TC
Gilmore Oral Reading Test	2	Individual	6–14	15 min.	X	X	X	X				HBJ
Gray Oral Reading Test	4	Individual	6–18	15 min.	X	X	X	X				B&M
Monroe-Sherman Group Diagnostic Reading Aptitude and Achievement Tests	1	Group	8–14	90 min.	X	X	X	X	X		Arithmetic	NEV

Test		Admin.	Age Range	Time				Comments	Abbr.
Reading Versatility Test	2	Group	11–15 16–Adult	25 min.		X	X		EDL
✳ The Roswell-Chall Diagnostic Reading Test of Word Analysis Skills	2		7–12	5–10 min.		X			EP
Standard Reading Inventory	1	Individual	6–14	40–50 min.	X	X	X		PP
INTELLIGENCE									
✳ California Test of Mental Maturity	1	Group	5–6 6–8 9–13 12–14 14–19 15–21	50 min.				Language and Non-language	CAL
Durrell Listening Series	1	Group	5–7 8–11 12–14	25 min.	X			Part of Durrell Listening-Reading Series	HBJ
Full Range Picture Vocabulary	2	Individual	2–Adult	10–15 min.	X				PTS
✳ Illinois Test of Psycholinguistic Abilities	1	Individual	2–10	1 hr.				Language Development	UIP
✳ Peabody Picture Vocabulary Test	2	Individual	2½–18	15 min.	X				AGS
✳ Slosson Intelligence Test	1	Individual	2–Adult	10–30 min.				General Mental Maturity	SEP

434 ───────────────────────────────── Appendix A

Designed to Assist in Evaluation of:

Name of Test	No. of Forms	Type	Age Range	Approximate Administration Time, Reading Section	Speed	Comprehension	Vocabulary	Word Attack	Spelling	Auding	Other	Publisher's Code
Stanford-Binet Intelligence Scale	1	Individual	2–Adult	1 hr.							General Mental Maturity	HMC
Wechsler Intelligence Scale for Children—Revised	1	Individual	5–15	1 hr.							Verbal Performance, Mental Maturity	PSY
SCREENING TESTS												
Vision: Keystone Visual Survey Telebinocular	1	Individual	5–Adult	15 min.							Far and Near Point, Visual Skills	KEY
Reading Eye Camera	1	Individual	6–20	10 min.							Photograph Eye Motion	EDL
Spache-Binocular Reading Tests	1	Individual	5–Adult	5 min.							Binocular Reading Efficiency	KEY

Auditory: Audiometer	1	Individual 3–Adult or Group		15 min.	Auditory Acuity	MAI
Test of Auditory Discrimination	1	Individual	5–8	20 min.	Auditory Discrimi- nation	AGS
Wepman Auditory Discrimination Test	2	Individual	5–10	10 min.	Auditory Discrimi- nation	JMW
Personality: The California Test of Personality	2	Group	5–8 9–13 13–15 14–21	50 min.	Personal and Social Adjust- ment	CAL
Incomplete Sentences	1	Group and Individual			Personal and Social Adjust- ment	Mch
Dominance: Harris Test of Lateral Dominance	1	Individual 5–Adult		5 min.	Hand, Eye and Foot Dominance	PSY
STUDY SKILLS						
California Study Method Survey	1	Group	12–18	40 min.	Study Habits	CAL
ATTITUDE						
Heathington Attitude Scale	2	Group	6–8 9–11		Attitude	IRA

Name of Test	No. of Forms	Type	Age Range	Approximate Administration Time, Reading Section	Speed	Comprehension	Vocabulary	Word Attack	Spelling	Auding	Other	Publisher's Code
Survey of Study Habits and Attitudes— Brown Holtzman	1	Group	14–21	20 min.							Study Habits	PSY
PERCEPTION												
Frostig Developmental Test of Visual Perception	1	Group and Individual	3–8	30–45 min. (Ind.) 40–60 min. (Gr.)							5 Aspects of Visual Perception	CPP
Purdue Perceptual Motor Survey	1	Individual		1 hr.							Perceptual Motor Abilities	CEM

Designed to Assist in Evaluation of:

Appendix B

Appendix B provides a reference for reading aids based upon the materials that have been cited in this book. Specific information concerning these materials may be found in publishers' catalogues and brochures. The publishers' key may be used by checking with Appendix C.

Many of the cited materials may be used in a variety of ways to help problem readers. The use cited is based upon experience but in no way is intended to suggest that a material be limited to these functions.

The suggested age level must be considered flexible and regarded as the difficult level. The educator will find many of these materials to be used with children of older age and interest levels.

Teacher-made materials are often more suitable to the need of children experiencing severe difficulty with reading. Teachers should take opportunities to update their knowledge concerning materials for instruction continuously. Most journals carry reviews of materials periodically. *Reading Teacher* carries a section on new material each year [e.g., "New Materials On the Market," *Reading Teacher* 32, no. 5 (Feb. 1979): 548–79].

Primarily Designed To Assist in Instruction of:

ALL SKILLS

Name of Material	Reading Level	Interest Level	Format	Publisher
1. Action Reading System	E	S	Kit	SBS
2. Addison-Wesley Reading Program	E	E	Basal	AD
3. Audio Reading Kits	E	E	Kit	EPC
4. Be A Better Reader	S	S	Workbook	PH
5. Breaking The Code	E	E/S	Workbook	OP
6. Breakthrough to Literacy	E	E	Kit	BOW
7. Careers	E/S	E/S	Kit	HBJ
8. Clues to Reading Progress	E	E/S	Kit	EPC
9. Comics Reading Libraries	E	E/S	Kit	KIN
10. Controlled Reader	E/S	E/S	Machine	EDL
11. DISTAR Reading Activity Kit	E	E	Kit	SRA
12. F.A.C.T.	E/S	E	Kit	RAI
13. GO	E/S	E/S	Workbook	SBS
14. The Hilltop Series	E	E	Books	AB
15. Language Master	E/S	E/S	Machine	BHC
16. Leavell Language Development Service	E	E	Machine	CLB
17. Let's Read	E	E	Basal	CLB
18. Merrill Linguistic Readers	E	E	Basal	CEM
19. Merrill Reading Skill Text	E	E	Books	CEM
20. The New Kaleidoscope Readers	E/S	S	Books	AD
21. Newslab	E/S	E/S	Kit	SRA
22. Open Highways	E/S	E/S	Basal	SF
23. Palo Alto Sequential Steps	E	E	Basals	HBJ
24. Peabody Rebus Reading Program	E	E	Kit	AGS
25. Phoenix Reading Series	E	E/S	Workbook & Book	PH
26. Phonetic Keys to Reading	E	E	Basal	EC
27. Plays for Reading Progress	E/S	E/S	Kit	EPC
28. Point 31	E	E/S	Kit	RDS
29. Quick Skills	E	E	Kit	COR
30. RD 2000	E	S	Kit	RDS
31. Read Better Learn More	E/S	E/S	Workbook	GINN
32. Reading Accelerator	E/S	E/S	Machine	SRA
33. Reading Attainment System	E/S	E/S		AAP
34. The Reading Box	E/S	E/S	Act. Cards	EI

35. Reading Laboratory	E/S	E/S	Kit	SRA
36. Reading Response Cards	E	E	Act. Cards	CTP
37. Reading Skill Builders	S	S	Kit	RDS
38. Reading Tactics	S	S	Workbooks	SF
39. Reading Work-A-Text	E	E	Workbook	CAM
40. Scope Skills Book	E	E/S	Workbook	SBS
41. Signals	S	S	Basals	SF
42. Spotlight on Reading	E/S	E/S	Workbook	RH
43. Sprint Reading Skills Program	E	E	Kit	SBS
44. SRA Basic Reading Series	E	E	Basal	SRA
45. Super Kits	E	E/S	Basal	SF
46. Tachistoscope	E/S	E/S	Machine	KEY
47. Teaching Reading Through Creative Movements	E	E	Kit	KIMBO
48. Text Extenders	E	E	Kit	SBS
49. The Thinking Box	E/S	E/S	Act. Cards	BP
50. Top-Pick Readers	E/S	E/S	Books	RDS
51. Webster Reading Centers	E/S	E/S	Kit	WMCH
COMPREHEN-SION 1. Adventures in Reading	E	E	Workbook	SCH
2. Amazing Adventures	E	E	Kit	NY
3. Best in Children's Literature	E	E	Kit	BOW
4. Better Reading Books	E/S	E/S	Books	SRA
5. Bill Martin Instant Readers	E	E	Books	HRW
6. Bookshop	E	E	Kit	DCH
7. Breakthrough	S	S	Kit	AB
8. Camera Patterns	E	E	Books	SAD
9. Comprehension Skills Laboratory	E/S	E/S	Kit	BFA
10. Comprehension We Use	E	E	Workbook	RM
11. Detecting the Sequence	E	E	Workbook	BL
12. Developing Reading Comprehension Skills	E/S	E/S	Workbook	OC
13. Drawing Conclusions	E	E	Workbook	BL
14. Following Directions	E	E	Workbook	BL
15. Getting the Facts	E	E	Workbook	BL
16. Getting the Main Idea	E	E	Workbook	BL
17. Guinness Book of World Records	E/S	E/S	Kit	SIN

Key: E = elementary, S = secondary, E/S = elementary/secondary.

Primarily Designed To Assist in Instruction of:	Name of Material	Reading Level	Interest Level	Format	Publisher
COMPREHEN-SION	18. Incentive Language Program	E/S	E/S	Kit	BOW
	19. Invitations to Personal Reading	E	E	Kit	SF
	20. Listen and Think Series	E	E/S	Kit	EDL
	21. The Literature Sampler	S	S	Kit	LM
	22. Locating the Answer	E	E	Workbook	BL
	23. The Monster Books	E	E	Books	BOW
	24. National Football League Kit	E	E/S	Kit	BOW
	25. New Practice Readers	E	E/S	Workbook	WMCH
	26. Nichols Slides	E/S	E/S	Tachistoscope Materials	KEY
	27. The Owl Books	E	E		HRW
	28. Pilot Library	E/S	E/S	Workbook	SRA
	29. Practicing Reading	E/S	E/S	Workbook	RH
	30. Reader's Workshop	E/S	E/S	Kit	RDS
	31. Reading Comprehension Basic Skills Centers	E	E	Kit	SCH
	32. Reading for Concepts	E	E/S	Workbook	WMCH
	33. Reading For Understanding	E/S	E/S	Kit	SRA
	34. Reading Incentive Program	E/S	E/S	Kit	BOW
	35. Reading Skilltexts	E/S	E/S	Books	CEM
	36. Reading, Thinking and Reasoning	E/S	E/S	Workbook	SV
	37. Scholastic Literature Kits	S	S	Kit	SBS
	38. Scholastic Pleasure Reading Library	E/S	E/S	Kit	SBS
	39. Six-Way Paragraphs	S	S	Workbook	JAM
	40. Spotlight on Reading	E/S	E/S	Workbook	RH
	41. Spotlight on Writing	E/S	E/S	Workbook	RH
	42. Sprint Libraries	E	E	Books	SBS
	43. Standard Test Lessons in Reading	E/S	E/S	Workbook	TC
	44. Star Wars Attack on Reading	E	E	Workbook	RH
	45. The Superstars Series	E/S	S	Workbook	SV
	46. Target Copper—Reading Comprehension Kit	E	E	Kit	AD
	47. Top Flight Readers	E	E/S	Books	AD
	48. Triple Action Unit	E	S	Kit	SBS
	49. Triple Takes	E/S	E/S	Workbook	RD
	50. Understanding Questions	E	E	Workbook	DW

51. Understanding What We Read	E	E	Kit	NY
52. Using the Context	E	E	Workbook	BL
53. Visual-Lingual Reading Program (Tweedy Transparencies)	E	E		TT

FUNCTIONAL READING

1. Following Directions	S	S	Visuals	SBS
2. Getting Applications Right	S	S	Visuals	SBS
3. I Can Make It On My Own	E	E	Resource Book	GO
4. The Job Ahead	E	S	Workbook	SRA
5. Reading Contracts and Forms	S	S	Visuals	SBS
6. Reading for Survival	E	S	Workbook	CAM
7. Reading for the Real World	E/S	S	Workbook	CEM
8. Reading Skills for the Real World	E	S	Kit	BFA
9. Real Life Reading Skills	E	S	Kit	SBS
10. Real Life Reading	E	E/S	Kit	INST
11. Scoring High in Survival Reading	E/S	S	Workbook	RH
12. Survival Guides	E	S	Workbook	JAN
13. What's Cooking	E	E	Kit	BOW

STUDY SKILLS

1. Dictionary Skills	E/S	E/S	Workbook	CA
2. EDL Study Skills Library	E/S	E/S	Kit	EDL
3. Graph and Picture Study Skills Kit	E	E/S	Kit	SRA
4. Map and Globe Skills Kit	E/S	E/S	Kit	SRA
5. Organizational Skills	E	E/S	Workbook	CA
6. Organizing and Reporting Skills Kit	E	E	Kit	SRA
7. Outline Building	E/S	E/S	Kit	CA
8. Reading for Meaning	E/S	E/S	Workbook	JBL
9. Reading, Researching & Reporting in Science	E	E/S	Kit	BFA
10. Reading, Researching & Reporting in Social Studies	E/S	E	Kit	BFA
11. Reading Without Words: How to Interpret Graphic Material	E/S	E/S	Workbook	SBS
12. Research & Study Skills Centers	E/S	E/S	Kit	CA
13. Research Lab	E/S	E	Kit	SRA
14. Skimming & Scanning	S	S	Workbook	JAM
15. Study Skills for Information Retrieval	E/S	E/S	Workbook	AB

Primarily Designed To Assist in Instruction of:	Name of Material	Reading Level	Interest Level	Format	Publisher
STUDY SKILLS	16. Super Syllabo	E/S	E/S	Game	CA
	17. Syllabo	E/S	E/S	Game	CA
	18. Target Purple—Study Skills Kit	E/S	E/S	Kit	AD
	19. Thirty Lessons in Outlining	E	E/S	Workbook	CA
READINESS	1. Adventures in Living	E	E	Books	WP
	2. Alpha Time	E	E	Kit	AR
	3. Auditory Discrimination in Depth	E	E	Kit	TR
	4. Beaded Alphabet Cards	E	E	Cards	ID
	5. Building Pre-reading Skills Kit-A-Language	E	E	Kit	GINN
	6. Concepts for Communication	E	E	Kit	DLM
	7. Developing Pre-reading Skills	E	E	Kit	HRW
	8. Follow the Path	E	E	Act. Cards	TE
	9. Goal	E	E	Kit	MB
	10. Goldman-Lynch Sound & Symbols—Development Program	E	E	Kit	AD
	11. Happily Ever After	E	E	Kit	AD
	12. Invitations to Story Time	E	E	Books	SF
	13. Kindergarten Basic Skills Center	E	E	Kit	SCH
	14. Language Activity Cards	E	E	Kit	SAD
	15. Learning Basic Skills Through Music	E	E	Record	EA
	16. Listening	E	E	Kit	DLM
	17. Listening to the World	E	E	Kit	AR
	18. Peabody Language Development Kit	E	E	Kit	AGS
	19. Peg Board with Designs	E	E	Act. Cards	DLM
	20. Pick Pairs	E	E	Game	GP
	21. Picture Readiness Game	E	E	Game	GP
	22. Read and Tell (Level 3)	E	E	Pictures	MAC
	23. The Reading Bridge	E	E	Kit	BFA
	24. Reading Visuals & Manipulatives	E	E	Kit	CAM
	25. Ready Steps	E	E	Kit	HMC
	26. Sequential Cards	E	E	Cards	INC
	27. Sesame Street Pre-reading Kit	E	E	Kit	AD
	28. Sound, Order, Sense	E	E	Kit	FOL

				Type	Publisher
29.	Sweet Pickles—Early Childhood Program	E	E	Kit	BFA
30.	Sweet Pickles—Readiness Program	E	E	Kit	BFA
31.	Target Red: Auditory-Visual Discrimination Kit	E	E	Kit	AD
32.	Teaching Reading Through Creative Movements	E	E	Record	KIMBO
33.	Visual Discrimination	E	E	Ditto	CPP
34.	Visual Motor	E	E	Ditto	CPP

VOCABULARY

				Type	Publisher
1.	Basic Sight Cards	E	E	Cards	GP
2.	Compound Words	E	E	Game	DLM
3.	Developing Your Vocabulary	S	S	Workbook	SRA
4.	Gold Cup Games	E	E	Game	BOW
5.	Homonyms	E	E	Workbook	DW
6.	Homophone Cards	E	E	Game	DLM
7.	In Other Words	E	E	Book	SF
8.	Lessons for Self-Instruction	E/S	E/S		CAL
9.	Linguistic Block Series	E	E	Blocks	SF
10.	Match	E	E	Game	GP
11.	Non-Oral Reading Series	E	E		PES
12.	Pictocabulary Series	E	E	Workbook	BL
13.	Picture Word Cards	E	E	Cards	GP
14.	Practical Vocabulary	S	S	Workbook	SBS
15.	Practicing Vocabulary in Context	E/S	E/S	Workbook	RH
16.	Sight Phrase Cards	E	E	Game	GP
17.	Spello Word Game	E	E	Game	ID
18.	Target Green—Vocabulary Development Kit 1	E/S	E/S	Kit	AD
19.	Target Orange—Vocabulary Development Kit 2	S	S	Kit	AD
20.	Understanding Word Groups	E	E	Workbook	DW
21.	Vocabulary Builder Series	E	E	Game	CA
22.	Vocabulary Improvement	S	S	Workbook	SBS
23.	Vocabulary Laboratories	E/S	E/S	Kit	BFA
24.	Words to Use	E	E	Book	SAD

WORD ATTACK

				Type	Publisher
1.	All About Reading Box	E	E	Kit	INC
2.	Alpha One	E	E	Kit	AR

Primarily Designed To Assist in Instruction of:	Name of Material	Reading Level	Interest Level	Format	Publisher
WORD ATTACK	3. Basic Phonics Review Workbook	E	E	Workbook	JBL
	4. Consonant Lotto	E	E	Game	GP
	5. Context-Phonetic Clues	E	E	Kit	CA
	6. Durrell-Murphy Phonics Practice Program	E	E	Kit	HBJ
	7. Get Set	E	E	Games	CA
	8. Merrill Phonics Skill Text	E	E	Workbook	CEM
	9. Patterns, Sounds and Meaning	E	E	Workbook	AB
	10. Phonics Basic Skills Center	E	E	Kit	SCTT
	11. Phonics for Fun	E	E	Kit	AR
	12. Phonics Rummy	E	E	Game	KEN
	13. Phonics Skilltexts	E	E	Workbook	CEM
	14. Phonics We Use	E	E	Workbook	MCP
	15. Phonics We Use	E	E	Game Kit	RM
	16. Prescription Games	E	E	Game	INN
	17. Reading Lab 1—Word Games	E	E	Game Kit	SRA
	18. Road Race	E	E	Game	CA
	19. Schoolhouse Kits	E	E	Kits	SRA
	20. Sea of Vowels	E	E	Game	ID
	21. Sound Hunt	E	E	Game	APA
	22. Sounds Floor Games	E	E	Game	SIN
	23. Speech to Print Phonics	E	E	Kit	HBJ
	24. Spelling Learning Games Kits	E	E	Game Kit	RM
	25. Sweet Pickles Phonics Program	E	E	Kit	BFA
	26. Syllabication	E	E	Workbook	DW
	27. The Syllable Game	E	E	Game	GP
	28. Take	E	E	Game	GP
	29. Target Blue: Structural Analysis Kit	E	E/S	Kit	AD
	30. Target Yellow: Phonetic Analysis Kit	E	E	Kit	AD
	31. Vowel Lotto	E	E	Game	GP
	32. What the Letters Say	E	E	Game	GP
	33. Word Analysis Kit	E	E	Kit	CA
	34. Word Game Safari	E	E	Game	BFA
	35. Working with Sounds	E	E	Workbook	BL
	36. Working with Words	E	E	Workbook	GINN
	37. Webster Classroom Reading Clinic	E	E	Kit	WMCH

Appendix C

KEY TO PUBLISHER'S CODE

AAP Ann Arbor Publishers
611 Church Street
Ann Arbor, Michigan
48104

AB Allyn and Bacon
470 Atlantic Avenue
Boston, Massachusetts
02210

AD Addison-Wesley Publishing Company
Sand Hill Road
Menlo Park, California
94025

AGS American Guidance Service
Publishers' Building
Circle Pines, Minnesota
55014

APA American Publishing
Aids
Covina, California
91722

AR Artista Corporation
P.O. Box 6146
Concord, California
94528

AVR   Audio-Visual Research
1509 Eighth Street, S.E.
Waseca, Minnesota
56093

B&M   Bobbs Merrill Company
4300 West 62nd Street
Indianapolis, Indiana
46206

BFA   BFA Educational Media
2211 Michigan Avenue,
Dept. 3064
Santa Monica, California
90406

BHC   Bell & Howell Company
7100 McCormick Road
Chicago, Illinois 60645

BL   Barnell Loft, Ltd.
111 S. Centre Avenue
Rockville Centre, New
York 11571

BOW   Bowmar/Noble Publishers, Inc.
4563 Colorado Boulevard
Los Angeles, California
90039

BP   Benefic Press
10300 W. Roosevelt
Road
Westchester, Illinois
60153

CA   Curriculum Associates
94 Bridge Street
Chapel Bridge Park
Newton, Massachusetts
12158

CAL   California Test Bureau
CTB/McGraw-Hill
Del Monte Research
Park
Monterey, California
93940

CAM   Cambridge Book Company
488 Madison Avenue
New York, New York
10022

CDRT   The Committee on
Diagnostic Reading
Tests
Mountain Home,
North Carolina 28758

CEM   Charles E. Merrill
Publishing Company
1300 Alum Creek Drive
Columbus, Ohio 43216

CLB   Clarence L. Barnhart
Reference Books
Box 359
Bronxville, New York
10708

COR   Coronet Learning Programs
68 East South Water
Street
Chicago, Illinois 60601

CPP   Consulting Psychologists Press
Palo Alto, California
94306

CTP   Creative Teaching Press
514 Hermosa Vistas Avenue
Monterey Park, California 91754

DCH   D.C. Heath & Company
125 Spring Street
Lexington, Massachusetts 02173

DLM   Developmental Learning Materials
7440 Natchey Avenue
Niles, Illinois 60648

DW	Dexter Westbrook, Ltd. 958 Church Street Baldwin, New York 11510	Ginn	Ginn & Company 72 Fifth Avenue New York, New York 10011
EA	Educational Activities P.O. Box 392 Freeport, New York 11520	GO	Goodyear Publishing Company 1640 Fifth Street Santa Monica, California, 90401
EC	The Economy Company 529 N. Capital Avenue Indianapolis, Indiana 46204	GP	The Garrard Press Champaign, Illinois, 61820
EDL	Educational Development Laboratories Huntington, New York 11746	HBJ	Harcourt Brace Jovanovich 757 Third Avenue New York, New York 10017
EL	Educational Insights 211 South Hindly Ave. Inglewood, California 90301	HMC	Houghton Mifflin Company 53 West 43rd Street New York, New York 10036
EnC	Encyclopedia Brittanica Educational Corporation 425 N. Michigan Avenue Chicago, Illinois 60611	HRW	Holt, Rinehart and Winston 383 Madison Avenue New York, New York 10017
EP	Essay Press P.O. Box 5 New York, New York 10024	ID	Ideal Oak Lawn, Illinois 60453
EPC	Educational Progress Corporation P.O. Box 45663 Tulsa, Oklahoma 74145	INC	Incentives for Learning 600 West Van Buren Street Chicago, Illinois 60607
ETB	Educational Test Bureau 720 Washington Avenue, S.E. Minneapolis, Minnesota 55414	INN	Innovations for Individualizing Instruction P.O. Box 4361 Washington, DC 20012
FOL	Follett Publishing Company 1010 W. Washington Boulevard Chicago, Illinois 60607	INST	Instructo Corp. A Division of McGraw-Hill Paoli, Pennsylvania 19301

IOWA The State University of Iowa
Bureau of Audio-Visual Instruction
Iowa City, Iowa 52240

IRA IRA
800 Barksdale Road
Newark, Delaware 19711

JAM Jamestown Publishers
P.O. Box 6743
Providence, Rhode Island 02940

JAN Janus Book Publishers
2501 Industrial Parkway West
Hayward, California 94545

JBL J.B. Lippincott Company
East Washington Square
Philadelphia, Pennsylvania 19103

JMW Joseph M. Wepman, Ph.D.
950 East 59th Street
Chicago, Illinois 60637

KEN Kenworthy Education Service
P.O. Box 3031
Buffalo, New York 14205

KEY Keystone View Company
2212 East 12th Street
Davenport, Iowa 52803

KIM Kimbo Educational Records
Box 55
Deal, New Jersey 07723

KIN King Features
Department 1198
235 East 45th Street
New York, New York 10017

LM Learning Materials
100 East Ohio Street
Chicago, Illinois 60611

MAC The Macmillan Company
Front and Brown Streets
Riverside, New Jersey 08075

MAI MAICO Hearing Instruments, Inc.
7375 Bush Lake Road
Minneapolis, Minnesota 55435

MB Milton Bradley Co.
Springfield, Massachusetts 01101

MCP Modern Curriculum Press
14900 Prospect Road
Cleveland, Ohio 44136

NEV Nevins Publishing Company
810 North Avenue West
Pittsburgh, Pennsylvania 15233

NY Nystrom
3333 Elston Avenue
Chicago, Illinois 60615

OC Oceana Educational Communications
P.O. Box 396
Chappaqua, New York 10514

OP Open Court Publishing Company
LaSalle, Illinois 61301

PAR Programs for Achievement in Reading
Abbott Park Place
Providence, Rhode Island 02903

PE Pro Ed
333 Perry Brooks Building
Austin, Texas 78701

PES	Primary Educational Service 1243 West 79th Street Chicago, Illinois 60649	RM	Rand McNally Box 7600 Chicago, Illinois 60680
PH	Prentice-Hall Englewood Cliffs, New Jersey 07632	SAD	W.H. Sadlier 11 Park Place New York, New York 10007
PP	Pioneer Printing Co. Bellingham, Washington 98225	SBS	Scholastic Book Service Sylvan Avenue Englewood Cliffs, New Jersey 07018
PSP	Popular Science Publishing Co. McGraw-Hill Text Film Dept. 330 W. 32nd Street New York, New York 10036	SCH	Frank Schaffer Publications 26616 Indian Park Road Palos Verdes, California 90274
PSY	Psychological Corporation 757 Third Avenue New York, New York 10017	SEP	Slosson Educational Publications Press 140 Pine Street New York, New York 14052
PTS	Psychological Test Specialist Box 1441 Missoula, Montana 59801	SF	Scott Foresman & Company 433 E. Erie Street Chicago, Illinois 60611
RAI	Raintree Publishers Group 205 W. Highland Avenue Milwaukee, Wisconsin 53203	SIN	Singer Education Division 1345 Diversey Parkway Chicago, Illinois 60614
		SRA	Science Research Associates 259 E. Erie Street Chicago, Illinois 60611
RDS	Reader's Digest Services Pleasantville, New York 10570	SV	Steck-Vaughn Company P.O. Box 2028 Austin, Texas 78768
RE	Reading Education 14506 Perrywood Drive Burtonsville, Maryland 20730	TC	Teachers College Press Teachers College Columbia University 1234 Amsterdam Avenue New York, New York 10027
RH	Random House 457 Madison Avenue New York, New York 10022		

TE	Trend Enterprises P.O. Box 8623 White Bear Lake, Minnesota 55110
TR	Teaching Resources 100 Boylston Street Boston, Massachusetts 02116
TT	Tweedy Transparencies 207 Hollywood Avenue East Orange, New Jersey 17018
UIP	University of Illinois Press Urbana, Illinois 61601
WMcH	Webster Division McGraw-Hill Book Company 1154 Roco Avenue St. Louis, Missouri 63126
WP	Western Publishing Co. 1220 Mound Avenue Racine, Wisconsin 53404
WWS	Weston Woods Studios Weston, Connecticut 06880

Appendix D

IRA CODE OF ETHICS*

INTRODUCTION

The members of the International Reading Association who are concerned with the teaching of reading form a group of professional persons obligated to society and devoted to the service and welfare of individuals through teaching, clinical services, research, and publication. The members of this group are committed to values which are the foundation of a democratic society—freedom to teach, write, and study in an atmosphere conducive to the best interests of the profession. The welfare of the public, the profession, and the individuals concerned should be of primary consideration in recommending candidates for degrees, positions, advancements, the recognition of professional activity, and for certification in those areas where certification exists.

*Code of Ethics, International Reading Association, Newark, Delaware.

Ethical Standards in Professional Relationships

1. It is the obligation of all members of the International Reading Association to observe the Code of Ethics of the organization and to act accordingly so as to advance the status and prestige of the association and of the profession as a whole. Members should assist in establishing the highest professional standards for reading programs and services, and should enlist support for these through dissemination of pertinent information to the public.
2. It is the obligation of all members to maintain relationships with other professional persons, striving for harmony, avoiding personal controversy, encouraging cooperative effort, and making known the obligations and services rendered by the reading specialist.
3. It is the obligation of members to report results of research and other developments in reading.
4. Members should not claim nor advertise affiliation with the International Reading Association as evidence of their competence in reading.

Ethical Standards in Reading Services

1. Reading specialists must possess suitable qualifications . . . for engaging in consulting, clinical, or remedial work. Unqualified persons should not engage in such activities except under the direct supervision of one who is properly qualified. Professional intent and the welfare of the person seeking the services of the reading specialist should govern counseling, all consulting or clinical activities such as administering diagnostic tests, or providing remediation. It is the duty of the reading specialist to keep relationships with clients and interested persons on a professional level.
2. Information derived from consulting and/or clinical services should be regarded as confidential. Expressed consent of persons involved should be secured before releasing information to outside agencies.
3. Reading specialists should recognize the boundaries of their competence and should not offer services which fail to meet professional standards established by other disciplines. They should be free, however, to give assistance in other areas in which they are qualified.

4. Referral should be made to specialists in allied fields as needed. When such referral is made, pertinent information should be made available to consulting specialists.
5. Reading clinics and/or reading specialists offering professional services should refrain from guaranteeing easy solutions or favorable outcomes as a result of their work, and their advertising should be consistent with that of allied professions. They should not accept for remediation any persons who are unlikely to benefit from their instruction, and they should work to accomplish the greatest possible improvement in the shortest time. Fees, if charged, should be agreed on in advance and should be charged in accordance with an established set of rates commensurate with that of other professions.

Name Index

Subject Index

About the Author

Bob Wilson is currently Professor of Education and Director of
the Reading Center at the University of Maryland. He is the
author or coauthor of numerous books and articles. His current research interests center upon the various aspects of
reading comprehension. His writing reflects his public school
teaching experiences as well as his work with students in the
University of Maryland Reading Clinic and in the public schools
of Maryland.

He is a Past President of the College Reading Association
and has been honored by his undergraduate and graduate institutions for his work in the field of reading.